T0333460

Praise for *Chuck Berry*

"RJ Smith's powerful and passionate portrait of Chuck Berry reveals the troubled man behind the iconic swagger and blazing guitar. To know Chuck Berry is to know racial conflicts in America. Smith makes sure you know both."

—KAREEM ABDUL-JABBAR, NBA legend
and *New York Times* bestselling author

"RJ Smith's *Chuck Berry* is a brilliant deep dive into the life of the true king of rock and roll. The irascible Berry shaved with a blow torch and played guitar like a possessed wizard from the Great American Highway. In unexpected ways, Berry was a civil rights revolutionary with songs as his artillery. Smith's fresh anecdotes, musicologist erudition, and page-turning prose are awesome. This is a must-read!"

—DOUGLAS BRINKLEY, author of *Silent Spring Revolution*

"Chuck Berry was one of the first people I knew that was true to life. Just like this book showing the truth to his life. I knew him from the 1950s onward and I can honestly say that RJ truly captured the essence of Chuck Berry as I knew him. You couldn't have a better book on the life and career of my ol' friend."

—BOBBY RUSH, Grammy Award–winning blues artist,
Blues Hall of Famer, and author of *I Ain't Studdin' Ya*

"Chuck Berry is both a national monument and something of an enigma. RJ Smith convincingly connects those two points in his scrupulous account, which is impressively detailed but never dull, and rich in the textures of time, place, personality, and sound. You'll want to read every word."

—LUCY SANTE, author of *Low Life*, *The Other Paris*,
and *Maybe the People Would Be the Times*

"A hungry ear drives Smith's wondrous, brilliant book. Not only does he capture the excitement of Berry's music, he hears the awe of those in its thrall, from his rock 'n' roll heirs to rivals, fans, and mystified bystanders throughout the twentieth century. Smith writes history as though it's a series of tall tales—how else to conjure Berry's brilliance as well as complexities, the unheralded highs and lows, the myth and the man, the man and the strange nation that produced him."

—HUA HSU, staff writer at
the *New Yorker* and author of *Stay True*

"*Chuck Berry* is a necessary book that expands and beautifully complicates our understanding of Berry as a human and as an artist."

—JESSICA HOPPER, author of *The First Collection
of Criticism by a Living Female Rock Critic*

"No one writes about popular music and its icons quite like RJ Smith: his ability to see inside the psyche of the most enigmatic figures, to reveal the soft tissue connecting them to cultural context, to deconstruct how a song actually works, all with prose that borders on poetry. *Chuck Berry* is a masterwork."

—DAN CHARNAS, author of
Dilla Time and *The Big Payback*

An American Life

ALSO BY RJ SMITH

American Witness: The Art and Life of Robert Frank

The One: The Life and Music of James Brown

The Great Black Way:
L.A. in the 1940s and the Lost African-American Renaissance

An American Life

RJ Smith

OMNIBUS PRESS

London / New York / Paris / Sydney / Copenhagen / Berlin / Madrid / Tokyo

Print book interior design by Jeff Williams.

Printed in Poland by Hussar Books.

www.omnibuspress.com

To Margaret, who took me to the library

Father, Father, it's for the kids,
Any and everything I did.
Please, please don't judge me too strong,
Lord knows I meant no wrong.

—GEORGE CLINTON, "Cosmic Slop" (1973)

CONTENTS

Introduction   *xi*

1 The Veiled Prophet   I

2 Life in the Ville   21

3 California on My Mind   34

4 East Boogie   52

5 Oh, Maybellene!   69

6 Chessonomics   85

7 A Harmonious Understanding   106

8 It's *Been* Here   123

9 Everybody Welcome   145

10 "Back in the USA"   166

11 "The Indian Girl"   189

12 Is That You?   199

13 "How Much Do They Owe Chuck?"   213

14 Hercules   225

15 Happy Days   242

16 Chuck Berry's Number-One Hit Record   255

17 "There Are a Lot of Adolescents on the Planet"   266

18 Chuck Berry Wants to Play with You   285

19 Promised Land   302

20 Southern Hospitaboo   316

21 Rock Star   328

22 The Apotheosis of Chuck   341

23 "Make the Arts Safe Again"   360

Afterword and Acknowledgments   366

Notes   371

Index   397

INTRODUCTION

CHUCK BERRY DIDN'T SAY MUCH ABOUT CARS TO WRITERS, WHO didn't much ask about them. Little mattered more. They were a way to present himself to the public as he chose to be seen, and a way to hide from those he did not want looking at him. Cars were a sign of his mastery of success; cars offered a way out. Cars, to Berry, were self-evident in their importance. He loved their surfaces, wrote songs about the freedom they made possible. And once you've written a song about a thing, what else is there to say about it? That was how he viewed the situation.

It was the summer of 2011, and Berry parked his Cadillac behind Blueberry Hill. The St. Louis club was his favorite place to play in the world. Berry entered the back door and took the low stage with his band waiting.

Fans and band alike knew what to expect. On the road he had long played with whatever underpaid local rockers the promoter rounded up, but here at home Berry had his regular band of family members and longtime associates who knew what he wanted. When the Blueberry Hill shows had begun, in 1996, they were barely advertised. Tickets went on sale on Wednesdays, and locals knew to buy early, because by Friday they would be gone for a room that held only 340. Over the years shows these shows became legendary, and by 2011 Berry fans from all over the world were buying airplane tickets to see him. They realized what a big deal this was.

A local fan who had heard him dozens of times remembers. Standing in the middle of the room and counting the number of accents he heard from around the world. "There was definitely an element of 'I'm not gonna be here forever.' And it was interesting to me how many people I know, major music fans, would say, 'Oh yeah, I've got to do that sometime . . .' and had never done it."[1]

It was a late-period Berry show, and the band's work was made as clear to them as if rules were posted on the dressing room wall. Their instructions were to know the material and to not in any way reinvent it, to offer an experience of the music as it had lived onstage now for years and not as it once had existed on a record. The records were pretty irrelevant. To watch when his foot went up at the beginning of the song, and again when he had enough of it. To cast a proper light on the moment, or, really, to keep him centered in that light: a focus that was unfussy, undramatic, neither too revealing nor flattering but that was pitched for a night out in a bar. To clear out of the way for the duckwalk—modified for this stage and this age, customized into something he called the scoot, a bas-relief chicken strut. The performance was a string of bright flashes—the introduction of a song echoing through time, a guitar sound that was dirty and jarring in fresh ways, a solo that cracked open the spaces between the drummer's two and four like an axe in a hickory log. A flow that jumped from one song to the next without messing up, a set of railings that he could comfortably stay between, and then to effortlessly replant the railings in a different place as Berry invariably changed keys, skipped ahead to a different song, forgot lyrics, and shot his bass player a confused look.

And just as the band knew how to handle these moments better than some quartet in Cincinnati or Fresno, so did the hometown crowd wrap him up in their understanding, exchanging glances, a countenance across the floor, *Okay, here we go now* . . . rooting for him. And when, as happened on this summer night, he lost his place in the song, it was the job of the son he called Butch, Charles Berry Jr., to whisper the words into his ear and then, after the moment had passed, laugh at the joke Chuck made of the moment. Fresh white lines painted on the road, keeping the driver moving comfortably down the center of the lane.

Chuck was exploring a plate of the chicken wings he loved, sitting in a small side room, when Blueberry Hill's owner Joe Edwards brought in a guest, a man less than half Berry's age who'd flown in from Washington, DC. They made some small talk about hairstyles and the show. As Berry greeted fans and wrote his name on a few pieces of paper, the visitor, Kevin Strait, a historian from the National Museum of African American History and Culture, handed him a book describing the museum's efforts. In 2011 the museum, a branch of the Smithsonian Institution, was still five years from opening, and its curators were carefully building a collection of artifacts to show Black history to the world. The dress Rosa Parks sewed during the Montgomery bus boycott, Nat Turner's Bible, a shawl belonging to Harriet Tubman, Emmett Till's funeral casket, a Barack Obama campaign button saying YES WE CAN, all of it to the goal of building a cultural narrative of Black life in America. Strait's idea was to have Berry donate his Gibson ES-350T guitar, the one he called "Maybellene."

"Chuck Berry always seemed a long shot," said Strait. "I knew what a private and serious-minded person he was about the business of things."

With Edwards hovering in the background and Berry drawing smiley faces beside his autograph, the historian and the elderly musician shook hands, a noncommittal expression on Berry's face. Then Strait headed back to Washington. "Like all things, it had to happen on his terms," he recalled. "I had to just be patient and wait until he wanted to discuss it."[2]

THE MAN FROM WASHINGTON HAD TIME TO PONDER HIS SHIFTING connection with the musician over the next few months. In the meantime, Berry talked by phone to Lonnie G. Bunch III, director of the museum, about offering the guitar when he floated an unexpected deal: the Smithsonian could get his guitar only if it also took his 1973 lipstick-red Cadillac Eldorado convertible.[3]

It was a surprising, welcome suggestion, quickly followed by threats. Berry sent Bunch a message saying the deal was off; Bunch couldn't be trusted. When Bunch called him to discuss, Berry delivered bad news: "I just found out you work for the federal government." Bunch sent Strait out again.

In November 2011, Strait booked another flight to St. Louis, and upon arrival he got an immediate greeting from the man he had come to see.

"I'm not giving you anything!"

Berry wore his yacht cap and was bouncing along as he said it, on the electric golf cart he drove around his home grounds, Berry Park.

Joe Edwards had picked up Strait at the St. Louis airport, and the two drove out to Wentzville, the small town where Berry had lived for over fifty years. They drove right past the marble sign at the entrance:

WELCOME TO

BERRY PARK

FOUNDED AUGUST 15, 1957

A strip of duct tape covered "WELCOME TO."

The musician and the curator shook hands, and then Strait let the adrenaline ringing in his ears settle to a manageable hum as he pretended that "I'm not giving you anything" could be a door and not a wall. After all, Berry *did* say it with a smile.[4]

Berry Park covered 150 acres and had been intended as a country club for the common man, especially the Black man in segregated Missouri. The grounds encompassed a lake, several residential and office buildings, a massive garage holding an assortment of cars, and a main house. There remained the scorched afterlife of a clubhouse that had burned down in 2003, destroying many rare recordings. Within view was a blue Ford pickup with his dad's name and address painted on the door, the truck Chuck's father had driven for his carpentry business in the 1940s.

Everything that would happen this afternoon would only happen on Berry's terms. He was a quick and thorough negotiator, and he paid attention to contracts.

Around the time Strait went to Berry Park, the Occupy Wall Street movement was building across the country, and Berry was interested, so the two talked about that for a while. He shared a few stories regarding the Jim Crow era, and they discussed how Occupy connected with the civil rights struggle he had lived through. From there, they chatted about baseball—Berry was a huge St. Louis Cardinals fan—and music.

This was negotiating too, part of an uncertain process, and it gave the musician a chance to size up Strait. Meanwhile, the historian was working on a tight schedule. "I had a few hours to convince him." He carried the paperwork for handing over the guitar, and a truck was coming soon for the Cadillac.

Strait plowed ahead.

By the grace of God I remembered about Miles Davis being from St. Louis, and I started talking about jazz and rhythm and blues. And he was talking about what it was like for him in the early days. We were having a conversation that went in several different directions, and I just remembered being captivated—not just because I was there in the kitchen with Chuck Berry, but because he was a knowledgeable guy with a lot of stories to tell.

His guard came down and he kept talking.

They defined the deal before them, says Strait. "Ultimately I said, 'I don't have anything to offer to you except placement in this museum.' I told him I wanted to put him in a room with Duke Ellington, a room where, when it's all said and done, people would understand this lineage of African American music making, the line of great, creative music makers of the twentieth century." Berry listened, and held back a moment before he said, "Alright" in a certain tone. Suddenly Joe Edwards snapped to attention, because *he* knew what that meant.

They talked for several hours, and along the way they worked out the terms of exchange, and Berry felt a need to mark the moment. He went into the kitchen and tossed an ice-cream sandwich in front of Strait. "I ate it willingly," says the scholar. Berry tossed him another one; he ate that too. He fed Strait several more. When Bunch had heard that Strait and Berry were scheduled to have lunch, he had ordered the curator to eat whatever he was served.

They had thought the essence of the man was expressed by a guitar, but Berry knew himself best.

"It was clear how sharp his mind was," says Strait. "I, like everyone else, knew he was a great musical pioneer, and in those moments music had nothing to do with it. Our meeting was all business and he was dictating the terms." They finished signing the paperwork, and Berry took him to another room, a studio, where he worked on music for several hours, thumbing through files on a computer and playing different tracks for the visitor.

When the moving truck arrived, it parked outside the garage that held Berry's cars. The Eldorado hadn't been driven in years, it needed work, the tires were flat. It had rained the day before, so the ground was sodden. Strait and Edwards pushed the car out across a wet field, wheels making deep ruts in the Missouri muck as they slowly shoved five thousand pounds of chrome and steel, eighteen and a half feet long, to where the truck was parked. It took them two hours to roll it through the puddles.

Berry gently excused himself. Strait told him he would take good care of both Maybellene and the Eldorado, and Berry said, "You better, because I plan to live to one hundred, and I'll come get you if you don't!" They shook hands, and Berry spontaneously gave Strait a hug. One hand, however, remained on the car. "It was like he was saying goodbye to it." And then he excused himself before it was loaded onto the truck, says Strait. As if he couldn't stand to see it go.

1

THE VEILED PROPHET

I: WHAT WAS ROCK?

A magazine writer once asked Chuck Berry: *If you had the power to accomplish some new thing, what would it be?* "I'd invent," he responded. "Creating is the next thing to inventing. So I'd want to invent something."[1]

Creating—well, that was an abstraction, it was play, you couldn't hold art in your hands. But inventing involved hard physical work, problem-solving, and these were the highest pursuits Chuck Berry could desire.

He was a lifelong tinkerer, one of the great American makers of the twentieth century. And even in his later years, he longed to build something big.

Which is kind of shocking, not to mention downright nuts, because Chuck Berry *was* one of the great makers of the twentieth century— literally, he was one of the key inventors *of* the era, because he didn't just help make a thing that changed our lives; his conception, rock & roll, created a time. He helped create a hybrid music that had only existed in beta form before, and he made it connect across every conceivable border of American culture. And then it spread. A dominant expression of mobility, the idea that anybody could go anywhere they wanted if their words lined up right, if they saw the staggering openness around them half as clearly as he drew it. Before he came along, *rock and roll* was a verb, a suggestion of sex and body, the blues-based words paired as opposites, gasping and sighing, committing and giving way. Chuck Berry helped turn that verb into a thing unto itself. Within months of the release of his first single, "Maybellene," people were using *rock & roll* in their daily conversation. The words explained what music they liked, then it expressed what in life they liked, and then it was them.

But it's true, you can't put it in your hands or break it apart on your dad's worktable, and to a handyman like Chuck Berry that rendered the accomplishment vaguely suspect. He was not impressed. And for that matter he definitely was not impressed with most of us, either. Conditions emerged that tainted his sense of self and made the weight of his accomplishment difficult to bear, and also, even setting those conditions aside, he still had his own, private doubts about how much he should matter. He struggled, and frequently failed, to feel the love crowds around the world offered him. An interview with him was destined to go off the rails when a journalist asked what it felt like to "invent rock & roll." That hot-wired a feeling which was intolerable, and he took it out on the poor unwitting ones who brought it up. Respect was valuable, but other things, like admiration, love, gratitude, loyalty, they almost *never* delivered on their promise, and what the giver saw in them was a vast field away from what Berry witnessed. In him they created frustration, resentment, made him withdraw into his skin. And with the love for him falling short, the desire to write new songs ebbed too. What didn't ever stop was the desire to stand before an audience and play. He made it impossible to know what he got out of the experience. And that experience, the decades of live shows chased long after the hits had ceased, was itself hard to understand.

It was almost as if he did not want to be understood.

"Would you say, Mr. Berry, that you, single-handedly, invented rock 'n' roll?"

"Single-handedly? Nope. I wouldn't say that I single-handedly invented rock 'n' roll. You see, there's all types of rock 'n' roll. There is rock. And there is rooooooll. See what I'm saying? And then there's rock 'n' roll which is rock 'n' roll, hahahaha. It's just a matter of whatever I've accomplished, which is for others to say, I guess."[2]

He started out by echoing voices and sounds coming to him from far away, from the radio and places outside his neighborhood in segregated St. Louis. He absorbed Ozark Mountain hayrides and hillbilly boogie, put them together with the blues. That was the illegal teenage wedding he brokered at the start of his career. But truly he took in a great deal more, including Cuban boleros, street-corner sweet talk, Mexican songs, Frank Sinatra ballads, and Frankie Laine rawhide melodramas, and more than this he channeled the guitar explorations of outsiders like Sister Rosetta Tharpe, Alvino Rey, Carl Hogan, Charlie Christian. Scraps and rags and things given away for free were pulled together and made into a brand-new flag. He was a great listener, channeling voices of people he had met or read or plucked out of his radio: announcers and gypsies and hoodooers and telephone operators and drunk guys on the barroom floor, poor Black Americans and nobody-everybodies who couldn't believe their luck of landing in this spot with this hamburger dropped down before them, this counter, this song, at this moment in their lives. "'C'est la vie,' say the old folks, it goes to show you never can tell."

There's an early single, "No Money Down," not a celebrated number but one I come back to again and again. At the very beginning of his career the singer is rolling into town full of anticipation, driving his ragged Ford when he spots a Cadillac dealership promising anybody a new car, "no money down." He knows what he wants and dictates the terms to the salesman, who either is too startled to say anything or is unquestionably going to give this unstoppable talker exactly what he wants. Power steering, brakes, jet off-take, whatever that is, a full Murphy bed in the back seat. What we deserve in life presented as a list of demands, the best words flowing, and this dark-skinned newbie sells to the salesman pure talk all the way until our singer drives out of town in a brand-new Cadillac. Chuck Berry imagined himself to be that guy, rolling into any place he wanted to go in America and defining his value. He imagined a culture of access and made things more accessible to folks than they had been the day before he arrived. The music he invented described a place of everyday scenes—hanging in a diner, calling your shots in the market, racing across a white-striped back road so damned fast there's no way the county sheriff is catching you. He made words up, and people moved them into their own conversations. Chuck Berry invented images, and they came alive in the world, and the amazing thing about it was that he would spend the rest of his life thinking about the distance between himself and his invention.

One device from his childhood in particular captured his imagination. It was a perpetual motion machine his dad had made out of wood, wires, chains, and flywheels rummaged from his contracting jobs. By the time Chuck knew what the thing was, it rested in pieces in the basement. But the way the son told it, when he was very young the city of St. Louis displayed Henry Berry's machine in front of city hall, where for six days it operated, the chains keeping its wheels in motion, until the creation eventually ground to a halt.

When Chuck Berry was six or seven, he crept down into that basement and peeked at what was left of his father's efforts: a couple of bushel baskets filled with parts. His father explained what they were meant to do. Perpetual motion has been a fool's dream as old as the pyramids, a yearning to find movement that continues on forever. But for tinkerers like Henry, it was a way to convert the life problem of how to matter into an engineering puzzle. The dad was inspired to rebuild it for the son—it was a six-foot-tall tower of wish with spinning wheels at the top and bottom, weights and counterweights transferring energy up and down, and in between them, balls rolling along a track of Henry's design.

"My dad was in there trying to invent perpetual motion, and I was right there with him trying to get it together," Berry told a BBC interviewer later in life. In his older years he still remembered what the contraption looked like and envisioned each of the balls spinning.[3]

Art gets away from the ones who make it. Everything that rises converges, and people are free to claim the world for their own. There was nothing simple about it, and no simple satisfactions—other than the part about getting paid.

Before it was a commodity and then a kingdom and then a *Jeopardy* question, though, rock & roll was an *invention*, something in a few people's minds that fed others when it was shared. It became political when those who shared it needed to be fed, and it became dangerous when those who nourished from it came to understand that they could live off the power they were holding.

Chuck Berry was born, lived, and died in St. Louis, and he went everywhere.

II: THE AXIS OF INTENSITY

People were crossing borders like never before, moving around the map with impunity. It could be the best thing that ever happened to St. Louis, if it didn't first tear everything apart.

Long before the Gateway Arch parked on the Mississippi River, the St. Louis waterfront was dominated by the graceful Old Courthouse, a masterpiece from its copper-sheathed Italian Renaissance dome down to its grained, golden-oak trim. St. Louis history happened here. Slave auctions were common on the steps of the courthouse in the 1850s, and it was the site of the first two trials of Dred Scott, an enslaved man who argued for and did not win his freedom in court. After the Civil War, the Old Courthouse would be the site of an important legal battle over women's suffrage. Then it became a soapbox for a clamor to move the nation's capitol from Washington, DC, to St. Louis—a movement that captured the support of Walt Whitman, Horace Greeley, and others.

The fact that nineteenth-century influencers could envision St. Louis as the nation's new capital suggests the city's great positioning right as America sought to turn the page on the Civil War. St. Louis bridged the north and south, east and west; it was the fourth-largest city in the country, a vibrant port of entry for European immigrants, and a cosmopolitan river town.

The nineteenth-century explorer and governor William Gilpin believed that St. Louis shared a super-charged east-west meridian with London, Rome, and other great world cities: he called it "the Axis of Intensity." Greatness was in alignment. To secure a glorious future, it seemed St. Louis didn't need much. Just a few deft taps from a master maker's hammer, a set of pressure points along the circumference, and the geode in the maker's hand would split in half for the crystal city itself to fall into view, shining with a light to guide the Republic for the next hundred years.[4]

St. Louis opened strong at the end of the Civil War. Key to future success was putting slavery behind it, no simple matter for a place that had been a leading slave market in a state that had sent over one hundred thousand to the Union army and perhaps thirty thousand to the Confederate army. Missouri had its own star on the Confederate flag, but its legislature had voted to remain in the Union while advancing an official position of wartime neutrality.

In 1865, the Missouri Constitutional Convention met in St. Louis and composed a new document. The Radical Republican party had seized control of the convention and quickly authorized the absolute emancipation of former slaves. The war itself was not yet over, but in St. Louis a celebration roared forth. On Saturday, January 14, 1865, sixty cannons exploded from Clark Street, and at nighttime an "illumination" followed, with fireworks punctuating the evening sky and candles lighting storefronts and kitchen windows around town. Downtown at the Old Courthouse, the *Missouri Republican* described a crowd "of both sexes and all colors" celebrating emancipation. The *Daily Missouri Democrat* reported that "in many parts of the city the colored people had meetings, and their rejoicings were unbounded." Only white males were given the vote by this constitutional convention, but the region was off to what was, if only briefly, a promising start. The city celebrated into the night as "the sonorous voices of the great guns sent their reverberations far and near, telling people from miles around that Missouri was free."[5]

Contemporary historian Colin Gordon describes a principle shaping St. Louis life in the twentieth century as "the conviction that African American occupancy was a blight to be contained, controlled, or eradicated."[6]

The roots of that thinking reach back to the years soon after Missouri's enslaved were freed. The city was growing; by 1880 the overall population was 350,518, and the Black population had jumped to 22,256, or 6.36 percent, from 3,297 in 1860. That increase was enough to make St. Louis's Black community the third-largest in the country, behind Baltimore and Philadelphia. Growth had to be managed, and in the eyes of the city fathers, the brand had to be buffed, because St. Louis's leaders had invested much in an image of respectability and rectitude.

And then in the middle of a national economic depression, in 1877 a series of deep wage cuts for railroad workers led to mass uprisings around the country. In St. Louis railroad workers and many others began marching in the streets. Strikers shut down all local freight traffic, and the protest quickly expanded: deckhands, steamboat roustabouts, coopers, wire workers, and others put their tools down and filled public spaces with banners, music, and shouts. Newsboys stopped selling papers. The city shut down—"even bars and brothels," notes historian David Roediger. The wildcat protest was massive and nonviolent, though there were reports of looters taking food and soap.

But if peaceful, the crowds and the disruption they caused terrified St. Louis's leaders. In response they formed an armed, private militia "invested with powers as a posse comitatus and under orders to shoot to kill resisters." The founders of the militia, the newly created Committee of Public Safety, were a cross section of elite St. Louis, including bank presidents, police commissioners, and leading businessmen.

The local press rendered demonstrators as basically bums and Blacks—a favorite pejorative was *"canaille"* (dogs). The *Missouri Republican* depicted "squads of squalid negroes" who were "whooping" and "dangerous looking," and reported "distressing scenes of terrified women, rudely handled by brutal negroes." The *Post-Dispatch* described the "maniacal yelling" of Black demonstrators. Though out-of-town coverage tended to make less of the Black strikers, the attention paid to their participation is an indication of a kind of racial fear that hadn't existed just a decade before.[7]

City leaders responded forcefully a year later, with a civic demonstration of their own that has repeated annually down to the present: the parade of the Veiled Prophet of Khorassan. Brothers Charles and Alonzo Slayback were Confederate soldiers from New Orleans who relocated to St. Louis after the Civil War and began pitching a secret society to St. Louis elites, one featuring private rites and rituals. The society they had in mind was built on the model of the Mardi Gras krewes of New Orleans, and the origin myth the Slaybacks devised drew on a mystical figure found in a popular work by Irish poet Thomas Moore, his book *Lalla Rookh*. The Slaybacks recast Moore's prophet as a wealthy masked traveler from the East who had chosen St. Louis to be his home.

The founders cooked up an annual parade for the public, with marching bands and floats and trinkets hurled into the streets, culminating with the return of the prophet to his home. The first image of the St. Louis prophet, a woodcut in the *Missouri Republican* from 1878, reveals what the city's leaders had in mind: He wears a white gown, pointed hat, and mask. In one hand he holds a pistol and in the other a shotgun. It sure *looks* like a representative from a notorious American vigilante organization. But since the Ku Klux Klan didn't formally adopt the hood and robes as their costume until several decades later, it's more likely the prophet was inspired by an amalgam of vigilante figures then haunting Missouri and Mardi Gras costumery. Either way it was scary as hell, and as if to underscore an intent to frighten, in introducing him to the public the *Missouri Republican* explained with relish that "it will be readily observed from the accouterments"— meaning the guns—"of the Prophet that the procession is not likely to be stopped by street cars or anything else." This was a show of force, and members of the public better not get in the way.

The Veiled Prophet parade was for the masses and a warning to them too. A year after the general strike had scared the hats off city leaders and revealed a growing fear of Black power in the streets, here were St. Louis's leading lights taking to the streets to reassert who controlled them. The parade was a public celebration meant to foreground civic unity, featuring brass music and fireworks and explosions in the avenues—a reiteration of the spontaneous celebrations of 1865 and 1877, this time, however, rendered as pageantry. The prophet, perched on his float, rolled right past the Old Courthouse. Every year since, the secretive Mystic Order of the Veiled Prophets of the Enchanted Realm anonymously selects a local leader to wear the mask and sit on the throne of the benevolent despot. But though the Veiled Prophet parade (there is also a debutante ball) continues today and remains consistent in many ways, there was one powerful anomaly that first year. At his inaugural appearance, the prophet did not hide behind a mask. He was revealed to be Police Commissioner John G. Priest, the very man who had put down the protest the year before, now in robes, waving, taking a victory lap.[8]

By the time Charles Berry was born, African American St. Louis was wildcatting its own Veiled Prophet festivities, having been shut out of official proceedings. They selected "African Veiled Prophet" queens and courts at parties held in Black theaters and jazz clubs. African American writer Ntozake Shange, who lived in St. Louis in the 1950s, recalled with mixed emotions the mass celebration. "Yes, we traipsed off to the Veiled Prophet parade like the rest of St. Louis, not realizing we were watching a ritual that grew from white supremacy. The Veiled Prophet himself was cloaked in satin and beaded robes. I think he should have been carrying a burning cross, but then I was drawn into the beauty of it all with the rest of St. Louis. There's something about childhood that finds joy and excitement almost everywhere."[9]

WATCHING THE RACIAL COMPLEXITY OF THE CITY GROW FROM HIS home northwest of downtown was Charles M. Elleard. St. Louis was proud of its title "Gateway to the West," but Elleard was all been-there, done-that with the Go West hustle. He had left New York to become a gold miner in California prior to the Civil War, then campaigned as a Whig constable in San Francisco before settling in Missouri during the war. Owner of some two hundred acres outside St. Louis, Elleard sold horses to the Union army, ran a racetrack, and farmed. In the open land surrounding his greenhouses, a trickle of immigrants and African Americans built modest single-story wood-frame dwellings, shotgun structures that flourished in exurbia. As St. Louis proper expanded northward, it made sense that this community, Elleardsville, would join the city, which it did in 1876. In time it became an anchor of Black life in St. Louis, and the home of Chuck Berry.[10]

The story of Black St. Louis in the twentieth century is very much a tale of the struggle for freedom of movement. Elleard himself would have noticed the growing number of Blacks coming to the region, including those dubbed Exodusters in 1879, arriving from Texas and Louisiana after fleeing southern violence. Thousands jumped on steamboats and floated up the Mississippi in hopes of getting to Kansas, and many who were stranded jumped off in St. Louis.[11]

The Exodusters were just the beginning: once the Great Migration was on, a flow of African Americans moved out of the South by the thousands in the early decades of the twentieth century. St. Louis had more than thirty-five thousand African Americans in 1900, enough to make the Black community second-largest in the country behind Baltimore's. It really picked up in the 1910s, when the community grew by 41 percent during World War I.

Just across the Eads Bridge, in East St. Louis, Illinois, the Black population had doubled to almost twelve thousand since the beginning of the war as Black southerners arrived to work in local defense plants. But when striking white workers at an aluminum factory were replaced by Black workers in 1917, racist rage boiled over and Black workers were attacked on the street with guns and pipes, whites burning down their homes and shooting them as they fled.

Between July 1 and July 3, 1917, over a hundred African Americans were murdered in East St. Louis. A *St. Louis Post-Dispatch* eyewitness account described a mass hunt on the streets of the working-class town: "There was a horribly cool deliberateness and a spirit of fun about it," the reporter described. "'Get a n*****' was the slogan, and it was varied by the recurrent cry, 'Get another!'"

Police assisted the violence, blocking off the Eads Bridge and trapping hundreds of Blacks fleeing from the East St. Louis side. Some jumped into the Mississippi River and drowned. Watching from the St. Louis side, Josephine Baker saw it happen. The performer and activist was eleven when the riot occurred. She stood on the west bank of the river as fires lit up the sky.

"We children stood huddled together in bewilderment, not being able to understand the horrible madness of mob violence," she wrote. "Here we were hiding behind the skirts of grownups, frightened to death with the screams of the Negro families running across the bridge with nothing but what they had on their backs as their worldly belongings." The face of a friend of her father's was shot off, and she saw a pregnant woman cut open. "To me for years St. Louis represented a city of fear, humiliation, misery and terror."[12]

Resistance to the growing Black population took various forms. On a December day in 1914, a crowd of five hundred gathered in Forest Park to watch two members of the Sons of the United Confederate Veterans pull the cord on St. Louis's thirty-two-foot-tall monument to Confederate soldiers. The First Regiment Band played "Dixie," and the men in attendance all removed their hats and whooped.

Months after the statue's dedication, a petition was presented to the Board of Election Commissioners calling for a vote "to prevent ill feeling, conflict and collisions between the white and colored races in the city of St. Louis." The initiative would prevent ill feeling by making it illegal for African Americans to live on a city block that was 75 percent or more white. In the spirit of equality, it was pointed out, whites would not be able to live on a Black-dominated block.

Soon afterward, the film *Birth of a Nation*, depicting the founding of the Ku Klux Klan, was shown in St. Louis. Segregationists stood by the door of the theater handing out literature in support of a controversial ballot proposal. Early in 1916, a city ordinance barring integration of white neighborhoods passed with a two-thirds majority. As Roger Baldwin wrote at the time, it was "the first popular vote in the United States on negro segregation."[13]

"Victory" was brief: the United States Supreme Court soon ruled unanimously, in *Buchanan v. Warley*, that such laws violated a property owner's right to sell to whomever they pleased. Property rights trumped racism, but enterprising individuals in St. Louis found other ways to limit Black mobility. A favorite approach was through use of restrictive covenants, which were lists of contractual obligations assumed by the purchaser of a property. Such agreements covered everything from what color you had to paint the house you were buying to what color you had to be to buy a house, and they flourished in America in the 1920s. Deed clauses had stronger backing in court when they were signed by all members of a subdivision or community association, and just these sorts of associations started popping up around St. Louis in the years after World War I.[14]

St. Louis was a pioneer in other approaches as well. Immediately after *Buchanan v. Warley*, zoning became a tool for limiting the free movement of Black citizens. As cities grew, they increasingly seized on the nascent field of zoning law in order to shape the racial makeup of communities. While race-based language could not appear in a zoning requirement, conditions that banned apartment buildings or imposed minimum residential lot sizes had the intended effect of limiting African American movement into new areas.

In 1916 St. Louis hired Harland Bartholomew as a planning engineer. Bartholomew was the Johnny B. Goode of "slum clearance." His mission, as he himself saw it, included helping St. Louis block movement into "finer residential districts . . . by colored people." As Richard Rothstein writes in his book *The Color of Law*, Bartholomew believed that "where values have depreciated, homes are either vacant or occupied by colored people." He began logging every single structure in the city, and as he did so he made note of the race of each building's occupants. In this way he could bird-dog where Blacks were likely to move next. Then the planning commission followed with restrictions making it hard for movement to occur.

Bartholomew was the first full-time planner hired by an American city, and he plotted suburbs and ballparks, dismantling Black neighborhoods in the name of "urban renewal." When he died in 1989, the *New York Times* called him the "Dean of City Planners." He died at the age of one hundred, thus living longer than Chuck Berry (ninety) and Michael Brown (eighteen). He had a huge, though little-understood, influence on everyone who has lived in St. Louis over the last century.[15]

IN HIS 1987 *CHUCK BERRY: THE AUTOBIOGRAPHY*, BERRY TRACES his family tree with a mix of specific details and ambiguity. It's a fascinating full-on opening solo, meandering, fuzzy, featuring Blacks, whites, Indians, European visitors, all crossing state lines, racial lines, and profoundly unequal power lines to follow their hearts and make families.[16]

He traces his father's family as far back as the Wolfolk plantation in Kentucky before the Civil War, then to Ohio and finally to a farm north of St. Louis. His mother's story starts on a Muskogee, Oklahoma, plantation, where a "Chihuahua Indian" cook named Susan and a "fearless African" slave named Isaac Banks met while working on the Banks plantation. They escaped the cultural taboos of their families and eloped to Mississippi; their granddaughter, Martha Bell Banks, was Chuck's mother.

His ancestors don't stay in one place long—even in bondage they change states, work on railroads, or just wander. They aren't defined by racism, and Berry steps lightly on the hardships of slavery or the miseries of Reconstruction that led to the Great Migration. Those existence-shaping historical forces are barely touched on in his account. His is a story of strong-willed individuals who keep some hold on their fate.

One day Martha Bell heard from a Banks uncle in Missouri that she should come up from Mississippi and meet a man the uncle highly approved of. That was Chuck's dad, Henry William Berry. Henry had spent time on a naval ship during World War I and was now in St. Louis, working at a flour mill.

Thus began the courtship of his parents. They were introduced in 1917 at the single biggest social event of the year, held in the area many still called Elleardsville, the annual summer weekend when funds were raised for an African American orphanage. The force behind the event was Annie Malone, a pioneering hair-product inventor and saleswoman. (Malone mentored the better-known Madam C. J. Walker and ran a million-dollar business from her St. Louis neighborhood.)

Malone's yearly event filled both Tandy Park, the center of the community, and the many blocks surrounding it.

Arvell Shaw, a jazz bass player born in St. Louis, carried fond memories of the

> one Sunday a year that they'd have a big benefit for the orphans in St. Louis—it was called Orphans' Home Day.
>
> They used to have a big parade, and it was my first chance to hear all of the bands that were around town—the Shriners, the Knights of Pythias, American Legion.

THE COMMUNITY PARADE SPOTLIGHTED THE PRESTIGIOUS BENevolent, social, and secret societies of Black St. Louis. Thousands took part in the dances and parties that marked the weekend. Everybody was involved: "If you had a little nickel band or nickel drum and bugle corps, you'd get out and put on a uniform and march," recalled a longtime resident decades later.

Berry was born right when the neighborhood was fully coming into its own, growing from 8 percent African American in 1920 to 86 percent a decade later. This steep increase shows the impact of both the Great Migration and the housing restrictions that made it hard to live in areas without a large Black population. The community was a thriving square about a mile across, with a sizable middle-class base and a total population of just over nine thousand in 1930.

"The bulk of the black middle class were a historically new segment that supplied paid services to an expanding African American clientele—schoolteachers, undertakers, lawyers, beauticians, barbers, physicians, nurses, and dentists," writes historian Clarence Lang. He describes a thin wall between these folks and the working class; few could afford to feel too secure. Lang notes that after employment at barber and beauty shops, the most common job for Blacks in St. Louis was going door-to-door selling coal or ice.

The neighborhood Berry was born into featured Black-owned shops and stores and restaurants, Black schools and churches. It had its own flavor and was not the largest African American neighborhood in town. In a place celebrated for its blues and piano players, his neighborhood didn't produce the best music either. It was a little apart and aloof, home to many of the older institutions and hopes of Black St. Louis. Which was a necessity, because just outside the community's boundaries were plenty of places where a Black family would not feel comfortable, plenty of people ready to chase you back across the street. The neighborhood became a world unto itself.

Demosthenes DuBose, an educator born a few years before Berry, recalled life in this corner of St. Louis. The neighborhood, he explained, "was peopled primarily, almost exclusively, by blacks, except for the people who owned the stores. There were restaurants, movies, nightclubs, and schools. There was the Ameytis Theatre in the Poro College Building on Pendleton; the Douglass Theatre on Whittier and Finney, and the crème de la crème, the Comet Theatre on Sarah and Finney. It was the newest, and they got most of the first-run movies, and they would put you out for loud talking. You had to behave yourself there." There were midnight ramble shows at the Comet, where DuBose saw Billy Eckstine sing.

From one angle, it could look like a life forced on those born there. But DuBose, Berry, and others found in this place a self-sufficiency and independence they never forgot. "There was a time when you could have stayed completely in the Black community for almost everything," said DuBose.

Elleard's people had long moved out, and the old wood houses, which wouldn't have been up to city codes, were grandfathered in when the village joined St. Louis. Many were holding up fine, along with many newer brick structures. Covenants marked the perimeter.

By the 1930s a local could go through childhood without knowing there was such a thing as white people. "What first made me aware that there were people whose skin was a different color than mine?" said DuBose. "I have no idea except that the difference was so obvious if you grew up in a self-contained community like I did."

Writer Ntozake Shange felt the community presented her with a jolting duality. "Above all else St. Louis was a colored town: 'a whiskey black space.' That's not to say there were no white people. It's just to say I had to go out of my neighborhood to find some and then they'd wish I hadn't."

By the time Berry was born, those who lived there gave the old neighborhood a new name, one that came with its own cool breeze: the Ville.[17]

CHARLES BERRY CAME INTO THE WORLD ON OCTOBER 18, 1926, making a strong impression from the start. "I was born in the best year of my life. My mother tells me that before I was even dry, I had begun singing my first song; I started crying prior to the customary spank that brings one unto life," he wrote in his autobiography. "For the second show, at an age of five hours, I amazed my mother again by raising my body up with my arms. I tell you, I already wanted to look the world over."

He enjoyed saying that he shared his birthday with Plato and Einstein. This was greatness as birthright, and so what if nobody knows when Plato was born, and that Einstein was born March 14. The point was clear: Chuck Berry occupied himself with greatness and considered his place to be in its company.

His family called him Charles as a boy. Before he was one year old, a freakish event marked the city of St. Louis: the cyclone of 1927. It touched down at one p.m. on September 29, 1927, and in five minutes it had gouged a track twelve miles long and six hundred yards wide through the city, slamming into a high school and killing seventy-eight. "The air seemed to be sheeted with fire, indicating a violent electrical storm," said the *New York Times*. The storm left twenty thousand people homeless.

Four days later, a guitar player in town, Lonnie Johnson, recorded a new tune: "St. Louis Cyclone Blues."

> *The shack where we were living, she reeled and rocked but*
> *   never fell.*
> *The shack where we were living, it reeled and rocked but*
> *   never fell.*
> *How the cyclone spared us, nobody but the Lord can tell.*

The first year of Charles Berry's life, the Veiled Prophet made history, addressing the people of St. Louis for the first time by radio; he spoke about the St. Louis Cardinals and Charles Lindbergh's transatlantic flight, and championed waterfront development. There were forces out there bigger than oneself, forces that buffeted, and there were forces at home to beware of too. Berry acknowledged such problems once in an interview, saying, "My childhood was not so good. My parents were getting divorced."[18]

He referred to affairs his father had. Henry and Martha never went through with the divorce, but there would be undercurrents. Berry's mother wanted to teach school, but Henry wanted her home and made sure her hands were full with six children.

His father grew cucumbers, squash, and tomatoes in the family's garden. There were two washtubs in the kitchen, one for laundry, the other for bathing. Sunday nights were for big dinners when the house was filled ("infested," said Charles) by deacons from their church, praying before passing food around the table.

Central to Charles's own story were two "magic boxes," as he called them: a piano lorded over by sister Lucy, who sang hymns and classical music, and a Victrola record player on which his parents played foxtrots. Charles crawled toward the piano before he could walk, its music pulling him in. And one afternoon a four-year-old Charles tiptoed to the Victrola and put the needle on a 78 recording all by himself. When she heard what he had done, Martha administered "my first whooping," a spanking that he never forgot.

Another sound that filled the house: Martha chanting hymns while she did chores around the cramped space. She wasn't rote reciting, for as she moved through the home, his mom was incorporating her sound into her work, physically massaging the passages into her efforts. She was working music and God into her space, finding a dramatic moment in a line and in her voice displaying the feeling that she was carried away by something more powerful, and as Charles listened from another part of the house, this didn't carry him away so much as make him feel *frightened* that his mother could be weakened by song, and that the feelings bleeding out in daily life could be so powerful that they could make one lose control.

Berry caught pneumonia, bad enough that a nurse came to the house to take care of the child. She was a white woman, and while she worked Charles playfully peeked into her medical bag, pulling out instruments. The nurse spanked him and then his mother spanked him as well, and the discipline excited him. "I became determined to satisfy the nurse's instructions," he remembered. "It wasn't long before the noticeable change in my mischievous nature brought a hug and a kiss from the nurse. The feeling of her lips, the same lips that forgave me after once punishing, has yet to leave my memory. In fact there are things today that I realize are related to the sting that was embedded in my character then."

The feeling was startlingly powerful. Later he would realize that even just *speaking* to a white woman would pull him back to that moment, the instant when desire and punishment came together.

The family bought a radio. Charles would take apart the back of the box, exploring where the sound came from. More spankings followed.

He was curious, undirected. Berry attended kindergarten at Cottage Avenue School, then entered Simmons School, a combination elementary and middle school that filled a formidable structure on St. Louis Avenue. He loved math, hated history, and may have been held back for a year. According to teacher Melba Sweets, Berry was "one of the worst kids I ever knew. . . . He was so bad that he was going to take me on one day by walking out of the room. No kid had ever tried me before. I told him, in the sternest voice I could muster, '*You will be sorry if you walk out of this room.*' It worked, and he turned around and went back to his seat."[19]

Poetry was regularly read and recited at home. Especially the words of Paul Laurence Dunbar, "the most loved poet in our family," said Berry. So central was his writing to the Berrys that when Martha and Henry had another son in 1933, they named him Paul Lawrence Dunbar Berry.

The respect for Dunbar hardly set the Berry family apart. Born in 1872, among the first generation of African American artists to have lived their whole life in freedom, Dunbar was a celebrated poet who also wrote novels, short stories, and lyrics and libretti for the musical theater. He was revered as the first professional Black author, admired by Black and white audiences, and his example—as a shaper of the American tongue—inspired on multiple levels. To Berry's parents he was a symbol of hard work and study. Those who read him were rewarded with a heightened sense of not just what words could do, but what *voices* could achieve. Dunbar had a genius for speaking his thoughts through the shape of other folks' mouths. He was most famous for a group of poems spoken in what has been called Black vernacular, though it is sometimes also referred to as the dialect of minstrelsy. These poems in particular were read around the African American dinner table, recited in school assemblies and at church events from coast to coast.

As the Harlem Renaissance writer Arna Bontemps declared:

The name of Paul Laurence Dunbar was in every sense a
household word in the black communities around Los Angeles
when I was growing up here. It was not, however, a bookish
word. It was a spoken word. And in those days it was associated
with recitations which never failed to delight when we heard or
said them at parties or on programs for the entertainment of the
church-folk and their guests. I was still in grade school when I
first heard a program chairman asking a prospective participant
if he knew a "Dunbar piece" he could recite. A knowledge of
Dunbar's poetry and the pleasure it gave when spoken with a
note of mimicry and a touch of pathos was all it took to melt our
hearts and make us one.

The poems Bontemps heard around the table—"When de Co'n
Pone's Hot," "The Party," "When Malindy Sings," "In the Morning"—
were ones that shaped multiple generations of artists. Novelist Chester
Himes, who attended high school in St. Louis in 1923, said, "Every
black schoolchild knew the poetry of Paul Laurence Dunbar, which
was recited in school." Trumpeter Miles Davis, who grew up in East
St. Louis, celebrated Dunbar's as a singular blues voice, comparing
him to singer Bessie Smith: "She affects me like Leadbelly did, the
way some of Paul Laurence Dunbar's poetry did. I read him once and
almost cried. The Negro Southern speech."

What's fascinating about Dunbar is that he was born in post–Civil
War Dayton, Ohio, not the South, and was the only Black student in
his high school class. The "Negro Southern speech" that moved Davis
and others was both real and an invention. He found voices and strategies for talking to white and Black audiences at a time when they were
hardly talking to each other. Dunbar was a salesman selling his art,
using the way people spoke, as well as the way some people thought
other people spoke, to rope in as many readers as possible. His poetry
could make you feel like he was talking animatedly straight to you, just
that direct, but he was gifted with tricks and contradictions, switching
codes to envision a community of readers greater than existed at the
time of his writing.[20]

Martha Berry tutored her children against speaking what she called "rank Southernism." By which she meant an uncultured tongue, or being so marked by the codes of Black street life that it would limit Charles and his siblings in life. Her son learned something different. From the life of Dunbar it was possible to learn that to speak one way with an audience did not mean that you were part of that audience.

In his autobiographical "The Poet," Dunbar wrote:

> He sang of life, serenely sweet,
> With, now and then, a deeper note.
> From some high peak, nigh yet remote,
> He voiced the world's absorbing beat.
>
> He sang of love when earth was young,
> And love, itself, was in his lays.
> But ah, the world, it turned to praise
> A jingle in a broken tongue.[21]

In the dialect poems that Bontemps, Berry, and many Black families read, Dunbar gleefully offers the equivalent of "I'm just saying" or "Don't take my word for it"—he used the conversational tone to win your confidence. His work was performed constantly in his lifetime, it was pop culture, and he was in demand on the lecture circuit. All of this would have inspired the young Charles Berry, who was building a spotty scholastic record but an exemplary one for curiosity about the world.

Later, in a conversation between Robbie Robertson and Berry, Robertson would ask Berry of his young self, "Where did this guy ever hear of Beethoven and Tchaikovsky?" Where did his songwriting come from?

"It came from *poetry*," Berry answered. "Poetry portrays a scene or a story and that's where my lyrics would originate from."[22]

Robertson asks if poetry wasn't seen as highfalutin back then.

"I don't know," Berry answers placidly. "Beatniks were into poetry."

Chuck Berry always cared about poetry. It began for him in the Ville, where his family traced the words of Paul Laurence Dunbar with their own voices.

THE DEPRESSION WAS AT ITS WORST, AND THE BERRY FAMILY WAS holding on uncertainly. By 1933, 70 percent of Black St. Louis was unemployed, and another 20 percent had found only part-time work. Henry worked three days a week at a flour mill until 1935, when he got a job doing carpentry for a realty company owned by a local German family. He was paid seventy-five cents an hour and denied raises, the employer explained, because Henry was barred from the white-only union, and therefore the boss was free to pay him whatever he wanted.

To make ends meet, Henry bought a used GM truck for thirty bucks and sold vegetables in the Ville. At six in the morning he drove to a produce market, filled the truck, and then Henry and the children circled the blocks around their church and Tandy Park, hawking the day's harvest.

Charles would stick his head out the window, calling in rhythm to the motion of the truck, looking to catch strangers' attention, to find the right words, the right note to turn a head and make a sale. "The huckster business," he called it. "Shouting the familiar cry of the street merchant. I loved to open my mouth wide, pitch my head into the air, and sing out 'Apples, tomatoes, potatoes . . .' Whatever came to mind, we sang it."[23] Free-market improvisation, it would have fed Charles's sense of invention, his desire to create something in the moment that rewarded him with welcome attention. It would have fed the family.

Late in life, he was asked a question about the influence of gospel music. Given that so many early rockers who grew up close to the faith carried church sounds into their own, how come Berry did not? To answer, he left church and God behind, returning to the Ville's streets and the days going door to door with fresh produce.

"My dad had a business of his own, selling groceries," he explained. Father and son carried baskets of vegetables to strangers' porches, showing the goods, the youth handling money when he was ten or twelve.

"I sold a lot because I was young, and they kind of bought from my ingenuity trying to sell."[24] You put something across on the porch, and you watched if they liked it or not. He paid close attention.

These are the sounds filling ten-year-old Charles Berry's life: the multiple voices of Paul Laurence Dunbar and the sound of his own voice, greeting strangers and friends from the street.

2

LIFE IN THE VILLE

A PORTRAIT OF A TEN-YEAR-OLD: CHARLES IS DRESSED IN JACKET and tie on the roof of a house, adjusting the angle of a backyard telescope. It is probably June 8, 1937, the day of a rare solar eclipse; the telescope is pointed up at the sun.

It's hard not to read a lot into this image. The youth with his eye on his surroundings. The man who favored facts, reason, over emotion. Berry got his money's worth with that telescope. When that kid in two-tone shoes surveying the neighborhood grew up, he would focus tightly on small things meant to stand in for his whole world.

Charles Berry the writer was purposeful about what he put before us. While a student at Simmons School, he hung out at a sandwich shop across the street. During lunch, seventh and eighth graders would eat fast and then dance. In his autobiography he describes being a regular at the shop, peering through the glass of the jukebox. There were big band records like Count Basie's "One o'Clock Jump," Tommy Dorsey's "Boogie Woogie," Glenn Miller's "In the Mood," boogie-woogie piano-pumping tunes and blues records.

For the rest of his life, when he was asked what music influenced his own, the answer was typically a list of names presented with a boredom he wanted the interviewer to feel. But there was a time when that kid with the telescope wanted you to understand there was this room he stood inside and it buzzed with the energy of eight beats to the bar, with a smell of onions on the grill and bodies in motion on a humid St. Louis afternoon, and it had an abundance of sounds, laughter and a cash register ringing. Most of all, the sensory overload was organized, and made sensible, by the low-end hum of a piano player's left hand. This was the peak moment of boogie-woogie swing music, a sound that sorted out youth and age, those who knew from those who did not, life at home from the world out there.

Chuck Berry's music brought that vision—diverse bodies filling a floor in sync with a beat—to the world. He didn't do it alone and he didn't do it on purpose, not at first; he just remembered how he felt in this place and put all of that and more into the music he made. And when people heard, it was understood not as Berry's glory but as the audience's, a multiethnic audience that would increasingly tilt white as he conquered America. The music conjured a place. But it's useful to note that before the image of the candy store, the soda fountain, the grill, the diner with little jukeboxes on each table, Pop's Chock'lit Shoppe, Arnold's Drive-In, Bob's Big Boy, the after-school spot where the kids all met, before that grease pit became an all-American cradle of teen culture, the adolescent American melting pot, one place was a refuge for Berry and his friends. They were not welcome elsewhere.

When they ventured downtown to shop, the parents of those middle school students knew they would not be welcome at lunch counters and cafés. Theirs was not the legal segregation of the Deep South, with signs posted and law enforcement eager to back it up. But hate was real, and Black families knew it. In St. Louis there was the ambiguous institution of the standing counter—some department store dining rooms and other places would not serve you at all, and some would do so grudgingly, without letting you sit at the counter or in a booth. A Black patron would have to stand at the counter, in an aisle, in an out-of-commission freight elevator, or even in a restroom. "You had to say, 'Well, yes, I want a hamburger,'" recalled Pearl Shanks. "Then people would hand it back to you and you stand right there and you eat, and you block that aisle full of people trying to go to the counter you couldn't go to."

From the mid-forties through the end of the decade, African American women in St. Louis helped form the interracial Civil Rights Committee and then the Congress of Racial Equality (CORE), which organized sit-ins to protest their treatment at high-profile lunch counters and soda fountains. The most visible protests, well ahead of the more celebrated ones that took place elsewhere a decade later, used nonviolent direct action while Black shoppers attempted to be served at the Scruggs, Vandevoort & Barney; Famous-Barr; and Stix, Baer & Fuller department store lunch counters. Organizers of weekly protests sat, ordered coffee and food, and, when denied, spent hours knitting, reading the Bible, or doing college work. According to one historian, "These quiet hobbies and pursuits, much like the crisp, elegant clothes they wore, were part of a carefully orchestrated pageantry that asserted the demonstrators' middle-class 'respectability' and cleverly aimed to shame white patrons."[1]

The parents were asserting their respectability and demanding the right to public access. The children, the kids putting nickels in the café jukeboxes, were using money to define themselves as individuals. As the US entered World War II and the Great Depression ended, employment was easier to come by in St. Louis, and they had money in their pockets. A Black consumer class was taking shape as young men and women declared themselves equal by their growing spending power.

Charles was alert to the brand names in his home, and now that the Great Depression was ebbing, the family was able to buy things they'd held off on. He noted how they got a "four-legged Quaker gas stove," a Philco console radio, Whirlpool washing machine, and a pedal Singer sewing machine. Spending power to one generation was a way of asserting your rights. To their kids, it turned into a way of asserting one's pleasure. "Fun and money were coming more and more close to home week by week, and everyone was buying many things they'd always wanted," Berry could see. Both sounded good to a teenager.

CENTRAL TO FAMILY LIFE WAS ANTIOCH BAPTIST CHURCH, WHERE Martha sang in and directed one of the choirs and Henry oversaw the deacons. The six children attended Sunday school and assorted church events. Antioch Baptist was established in 1894 and was an anchor of the Ville. During Charles's youth James E. Cook was its pastor; he was trained at a Lutheran seminary and was also a doctor at Homer Phillips Hospital, a block from where he preached. "It was a silk stocking church," says Reverend Doctor F. Delano R. Benson Jr. "We didn't do all the shouting stuff. If the people got happy, they might wave their fans."[2]

Antioch had a fine musical director in Kenneth Brown Billups, a force in the Ville and beyond for decades. Billups would direct the nationally broadcast gospel group Wings Over Jordan in the late 1940s. Martha did everything she could to get her husband to become a pastor, but it was not to be. Henry sang too. "Oh, those Baptist hymns!" Berry enthused. "Mom brought Dad into the church choir. He had a beautiful voice, very low, and he led the bass section, and Mother sang all day long."

When he heard boogie-woogie, Berry said, he literally lost all interest in music without a beat.

"Are you religious?" he was asked.

"I believe anything that's true is what's going to carry you through. Truth will shine. Truth—"

"Sets you free?"

"Yeah. And I've been unfree, too."[3]

Interviews and his autobiography make clear that as far as Charles was concerned, the spirit of Antioch Baptist failed to move him, even in his youth. He was a child full of questions, wondering if heaven would be segregated and why his prayers were not answered. The music sung in Antioch concerned a Paradise somewhere a long way off, but Berry's concerns were rooted in the Ville. An interest in girls came early. Desire weighed him down, and by the age of twelve, he said, he felt a decision was approaching, when he had to choose whether to carry the weight of his transgressions or to glory in his adolescent hungers. "I sinned again and then again. Still I prayed forgiveness each time without realizing whether forgiveness was or wasn't granted."

Guilt—he consciously decided in his early teenage years to live free of the judgment of the church and his parents. Honesty was essential. He didn't want to lie about it; honesty required him to decide on which side of the line he wanted to live. And so for the rest of his life the church would be a symbol of stability and judgment and guilt—abstractions he aimed to throw off.

Henry was working for a property management company, a financial boon to the family. Charles was helping him install showers in a country club in Glen Crest one afternoon, and as he wandered off over the rolling grounds he drifted happily, observing white couples in various stages of lovemaking.

He pulled up by a creek, where a white man and woman lay on a picnic blanket. The man's hand, he remembered, was beneath her dress. That's when they heard him, and the man made a sound, inviting Charles to join them. The man asked for his name and what he was doing at the club; Berry felt powerless to lie and trapped. His watching implicated him, and the white couple could easily implicate him in something further. The woman whispered to her partner and then spoke to the boy.

"She told me I was off limits and had violated the law, that if I wanted to avoid being arrested, I was to do as I was told or go to jail for trespassing," Berry remembered. She told him to bend over and rub her feet, which he saw both as a gift and as a threat. He couldn't believe they were letting him do this, but he knew how dangerous it was—St. Louis wasn't the heart of Dixie, but a Black boy could disappear from anywhere for the claim of touching a white woman. The couple whispered some more, and Berry heard her say he was "a good one."

"I was shaking like a leaf on a tree when she insisted sternly that I kiss her feet before she let me go. They were smiling, seemingly satisfied, when they ran me off with a further threat of arrest if I told my father where I'd been."[4] It was the first encounter with racism he ever described having, presented as a tale of erotic discovery.

THE VILLE COULD SHELTER ONE FROM RACISM, BUT LIFE THERE came with its own pressures. Free Blacks had lived in the area since before the Civil War, and the Ville had a long-standing sense of itself as distinct from the two other Black enclaves of St. Louis. Ville citizens felt they knew how to negotiate a solid life parallel to white St. Louis and strongly felt that the South did not define them. Meanwhile, the

Great Migration continued to bear Black southerners to their city, most settling into the Jefferson-Market and Mill Creek Valley areas.

Folks in the Ville had a name for the places where recent arrivals settled: Little Memphis. The newcomers had felt the full brunt of Jim Crow and poverty, and in the eyes of others, both continued to mark them. Edna Mckinney, a city employee, recalled, "It was almost like they were foreigners, because, well—they talked—their language was so different and the favorite term that they used all the time would just make me fall out laughing, 'I reckon.' I know a girl, she's been here two years, but she still says, 'I reckon' or 'you reckon?' . . . They just had that southern twang."[5]

Later on, Berry would vent about journalists who didn't quote him correctly and had him saying stuff like *lawdy* in interviews. "My mother never imagined we were white . . . because we were black, that was plain as day," he explained. "But it was her plan that I be able to mix with whatever people I wished and do it in a correct way so as not to stereotype myself." Attentive to the dialect of Paul Laurence Dunbar and with ears attuned to an array of white and Black voices, Berry was presenting who he was to others by how *he* spoke. If words defined your place in society, as *reckon* or *lawdy* might, what words did he want to choose? What place in society did he want to occupy?

In other ways too, Berry was aware of distinctions made within the Ville. He entered Sumner High School in or around 1940. Sumner was the first Black high school erected west of the Mississippi River, and it was proudly viewed as a factory for progress. The school was named for the Massachusetts Republican senator Charles H. Sumner, an abolitionist who argued a pioneering case against public school segregation in Boston. When Black community leaders organized at the turn of the century to move Sumner from the Mill Creek Valley neighborhood, where it abutted train yards, factories, and pool halls, to the Ville, they were saying how much both the school and its new home embodied their aspirations.

St. Louis built at the new site a first-rate three-story Georgian brick school, in which generations of college-educated Black teachers, many with PhDs from elite institutions, taught high school students. Their standards were exacting, and among just the musicians who attended Sumner were such folks as Oliver Lake, Tina Turner, Lester Bowie,

Robert McFerrin, Baikida Carroll, Grace Bumbry, Billy Davis Jr., and Oliver Nelson.

Skin shade mattered at school. "What all this color ratio really meant was nothing, but we kids seemed to harp on it," Berry said. "I was beginning to think of people in the form of poetry: 'If you're white, you're all right. If you're yellow, you're fair fellow. If you're red, you're low bred. If you're brown, don't come 'round, and if you're black, just stay back.'"

To onetime student Salimah Jones, "Everything at Sumner had to be extra. If you were dark, you had to be extra smart. If you were dark, you were on the back line of the dance group and you didn't get starring roles unless your parents were someone important," she recalled in an oral history. ("I don't know why they always put me in the top row," Berry would say of his own class pictures.)

"If you didn't have really sharp clothes, you were not considered 'in,'" said Jones. "I knew all of this, and I was afraid to go to Sumner."

For about a year in the 1920s, the family of African American writer Chester Himes lived in St. Louis and enrolled him at Sumner. "He 'hated' Sumner, finding his fellow black students 'cheap-smart,' 'city-dirty,' 'preoccupied with themselves,' and 'quick to ostracize and condescend,'" wrote Himes biographer Lawrence P. Jackson. Himes loved sports but hated the school athletes, preferring instead the roughhousing of the boys in Tandy Park.[6]

Berry craved motion, and soon he craved a way out of Sumner and the Ville. It took him three weeks to build a bicycle from scavenged parts, and once he put it together he would ride bikes far from home with friends Lawrence "Skip" Hutchinson and James Williamson. "I began to wiggle from under what few remaining restrictions Mother and Daddy had at our home," he said.

There was a teacher he responded to, Julia Davis, whom he had first encountered at Simmons and then again at Sumner. "She's a Baptist, but she was like a Catholic nun in the classroom," Berry said. Davis had his respect. "She taught in the avenue of perfection. We tried to come close."[7]

Davis grew up in the Ville, and was the kind of teacher who asked how your day was going and if you'd had breakfast that morning. *Did you read that book I lent you, and how is your mother feeling?* She drew kids out and had a passion for words.

She was committed to bringing African American history into Sumner classrooms, not simply incorporating it into history classes but making sure it filtered into all lesson plans. "She singlehandedly made the St. Louis Public Library stock books on black history, and she conducted a radio program in black history as early as 1942," wrote American studies professor George Lipsitz. "Miss Davis told her students about John Berry Meachum, who secretly conducted a school on a riverboat when the state of Missouri outlawed education for Blacks in the 1820s, and about Homer G. Phillips, who badgered white city officials until getting them to allow the establishment of the hospital for Blacks that later bore his name."[8]

Davis's drive made her a great fit for Sumner, where the high school paper was named *The Collegiate*. This place was demanding. Berry was on another track, one he was working out for himself. His intellect was voracious and asymmetrical; it didn't fit the grid of a defend-your-point institution. Sociologists don't have a precise category for the kind of young man Berry was. He couldn't buy the clothes the top-ranking guys sported. He cultivated a sense of humor to win over skeptics, and that helped, but even Dick Gregory, another kid from St. Louis, got his head handed to him at Sumner. The girls there laughed *at* Berry as much as with him and gave him a name: "Ol' Crazy Chaws Berry."

Along with his Frankenstein bike, he eventually managed a broke-down 1934 Ford costing thirty-five dollars (he didn't have the money and his dad refused to cosign, but sister Thelma came through). The key broke off in the ignition, a fact that did not escape others' notice, who took advantage to go out on joyrides in Charles's car. He told himself that because the football players "borrowed" it and fucked their girlfriends in the back seat, he was reaping respect on campus. There is a rubric for the kind of person Chuck Berry was in high school: he was a *nerd*. And he strove to find a way to shake that distinction.

Music was balm to his wounds. "My *first* inspiration was Nat Cole, in high school," he explained. "By nature I'm a lover, you see, but I never could get a chance to *love*. No girlfriend, because I always had a gift of gab and I always did like comedy you know and poetry. [But] comedy is too silly for love, and poetry too serious. So you see, I was always left out."[9]

You can't find him in Sumner yearbooks, and he missed classes. But one part of Sumner held his interest: the music room. He spent a lot of time in there, learning saxophone, piano, and drums. Davis recognized Berry's interest and encouraged him to explore it. Soon he would be using music to define himself to others.

The way he framed it, he made them forget all about Crazy Chaws Berry at a 1941 Sumner all-male musical revue, when he performed a pop hit riding high in Black America, "Confessin' the Blues," by Walter Brown and the Jay McShann Orchestra. The show was the kind of high-minded event that would have featured standards and light classics, where the pitter-patter of polite applause was expected. Berry had something different in mind.

The blues weren't being taught in the music room, and they would have been contraband at home; a song like "Confessin' the Blues" was learned from the jukebox at the joint near school. School reminded him daily how little he knew, while "Confessin'" was a roar of experience, a grown-ass man testifying to the power of a woman who does not feel the same way. Berry sang it to the student body with a friend, Tommy Stevens, playing guitar, and when he was done he remembered the applause. "It wasn't a raunchy song, but it wasn't 'I Dream of Jeanie' either," he said. "I sang my heart out. I just felt so good. Where did I get the courage?"[10]

The applause made him realize he wanted more than half the attention coming his way. He decided to learn the guitar and get it all. "It's all mathematics," Berry believed. "If I could play and sing, well you know, then he wouldn't have to play and I could do it all by myself at home. So I started picking and plunking. He [Tommy Stevens] was nice enough to show me some stuff. After you play one thing, you really like an instrument, it just snowballs and I kept adding to it."

He got a four-string tenor guitar from a school friend and started working out the chords to St. Louis Jimmy Oden's "Going Down Slow" and Big Maceo's "Worried Life Blues." He wasn't focusing on the singing but trying to get the sound of the guitar right. And Julia Davis planted the idea that he could make a living as a musician playing the guitar.

"My determination to play guitar and accompany myself while singing became an amendment to my religion," Charles said. The response to his "Confessin' the Blues" brought him a "personal blessing": the attention of female students. There was a time when tension between Charles and his father led him to leave home and live with his sister Thelma. That helped with his ongoing study of girls. So did the darkroom of his cousin Harry Davis.

Every week after Sunday school Charles would drop in on cousin Harry, who was a few years older and deftly took the teenager under his wing. Harry "was highly endowed with a talent for science along with a sincere love of photography." He had books on chemistry, rocketry, astronomy, hypnotism, and other stuff—Davis provided a conduit of science and rational thought to Chuck, plus also plenty of dirty pictures. "Harry fused the rocket that launched my journey on the road to a love of science and photography," enthused his younger cousin.

Davis was interested in Charles's beautiful older sister Lucy, begging to let him photograph her. He gave Charles access to his collection of pictures as well as use of his darkroom, and he taught him how to develop, print, and enlarge photographs of his own. Over time, Harry would refine his pitch for taking revealing shots of women in St. Louis, and Charles was entranced by the work product. There in the red glow of Sunday at cousin Harry's, with pictures of scantily clad women on the darkroom wall and books of scientific learning pulled down from the shelf, Berry gained an extensive understanding, as he saw it, of essential mysteries of the universe.

His education continued. The teenager jumped on a city bus and rode downtown to a dodgy block with a burlesque joint he favored. He was fixing to look at women, but when he got there, heading down an alley to peep through the stage door, Berry saw something which fascinated him even more. He spotted a well-dressed drunk on the ground pressed against a wall, and a character stealthily standing over him with his hand reaching into the drunk's pocket. The prone man watched passively as the thief boosted his wallet, too inebriated to do anything about it. The whole thing transfixed Berry.

He told the story as an example of why he never liked alcohol and mistrusted those who did. But something else was going on in the scene that interested him. This is a parable of peeping. Berry goes to look at bodies and finds the most fascinating one by accident. There was power in standing back and viewing someone else in a vulnerable moment, and more power still if the one being watched couldn't do anything about it.

The impact of Harry on young Charles's life can be seen in assorted ways. Photography appealed to Berry, so much that years later, even in the wake of the smash success of "Maybellene," he would introduce himself with a business card slapped into a stranger's hands. It said, "Charles Berry, photographer."[11]

And over the years Berry would amass a vast collection of cameras, video monitors, darkroom technology, and recording devices, all of which he said began with Harry's inspiration.

School did not interest him, music hadn't snared him yet. Berry got a job in a radio repair shop and for a long moment found a subject that absorbed him. He began pulling the guts out of a tube radio and trying to figure out how it all operated. For a while, he says, the work was so appealing he stopped visiting Harry. On assorted levels, he was looking at the world practically, seeking mechanical answers to questions outside the scientific realm. This much was clear: taking things apart explained the way the world worked far better than a sermon.

He went with his dad on jobs where Henry was sent into white homes. It interested Charles, not least because the situation was fraught with danger and possibility while the man of the house was away. He watched from behind his dad once when a woman wearing only her undergarments answered the door. Henry instructed his son again and again never to speak to white women who answered the door. "I would be helping Dad to fix a lock, and the women would bring some oranges or something. Not all women, but some women were forward. Firstly, Daddy would ignore them. I would wonder why Dad wouldn't laugh if she would laugh." They would flirt with Henry and point out what a cute son he had. Henry's way was to speak as politely and tersely as possible.

"He taught us not to say anything and not to smile. If you did, you'd get your neck broke. He wanted to keep us alive."

Conversations with white workers were complicated too. There was plenty of racism in the all-white unions, which chose to view Charles's dad as undercutting their ability to make a living. Union carpenters would step to Henry, who would attempt to defuse the situation in ways that, to the young Chuck, couldn't help but seem timid. "Once they talked to him and found he was a religious man and, what's more, humble while being questioned, there was never any trouble. Dad had a way of showing he was 'in his place' and not a trouble-maker."

Henry shared homely aphorisms with his children—life lessons like "What a man believes; thus is it so," "A dollar saved is a dollar made," "Young men dream dreams while old men see visions," "Take what you have and make what you want." And at home, the music often came courtesy of sister Lucy, who played the piano and sang in her fine contralto a repertoire of classical numbers and parlor hymns. Lucy was winning awards for her singing, and the local Black press covered her success. Charles felt she hogged the piano.

In the summer of 1944 a civic organization sought to whip up unity across racial lines for the war by putting on a patriotic show in St. Louis. Lucy was invited to appear as a local luminary, singing beside W. C. Handy, composer of "St. Louis Blues," poet Langston Hughes, bandleader Noble Sissle, and actor Don Ameche. At the end of the evening, which was attended by some thirteen thousand in a local park, a massed choir of a thousand voices sang "Onward Christian Soldiers" and "God Bless America."

There were values you were supposed to hold dear, just as there was music you were supposed to care about. Lucy's music filled the house, but Charles and some of his siblings were infiltrating the family unit with records like "C.C. Rider" from Big Bill Broonzy and "Romance in the Dark" by Lil Green. He was playing the pioneering guitarists Lonnie Johnson and Rosetta Tharpe, Tampa Red and Arthur Crudup. "But Lucy stuck with stuff like 'Ave Maria' and 'God Bless America,'" said Berry.

One Sunday in 1941, after the weekly meeting of the Baptist Young People's Union, Berry rendezvoused with a girl named Doris Wilder. He was fifteen, she was seventeen. The story of how he lost his virginity is unexceptional: Doris guided him from the meeting to her home two blocks away and then showed him what to do. Somebody else was watching: "The people next door were looking right at us. I never thought about that because I was so excited!" he explained. Wilder's neighbor spilled the beans to her dad. At the church deacon's meeting two days later, Deacon Wilder broke the news to Henry, who summoned his son for a conference with a leather razor strop in his hand.

It's interesting. Rock & roll would be built in no small part on the back of a driving beat and gritty vocal propulsion that the sanctified Black church gave to the world, sometimes willingly. But the music of Chuck Berry would be notably free of a direct influence of the church. And yet, though he turned away from the Baptist spiritual life, one aspect of church, as filtered through his family, influenced him greatly. The judgment and shame that came from messing up. The punishment that arrived with sex.

His father gave Charles an extended beating, which he described almost like a boxing match. Not on a physical level, because one man fought and the boy absorbed it, but on an endurance level. And by the time it was done, Berry said he felt like a different person—definitely beaten up in one sense but eventually also freed and left to figure out manhood on his own. It sounds like the kind of beating you have to bear, and when you do, you learn you can. After that, Henry could never discipline him again. His father's beliefs—his father—would no longer guide him, and home would no longer be the shelter it had been.

When he faced hardships or questions about life or morality, when he wondered if he was looking at the world the right way, home was no longer where the answer was found.

"Music is science. Everything is science. Because science is truth," he learned from life. Charles Berry was looking for truth.[12]

3

CALIFORNIA ON MY MIND

He tested community consensus. His buddies called him Slick.

Charles and two pals would ride around on bikes at night and siphon gas from trucks parked in a coal yard. That meant hopping a nine-foot padlocked fence while lugging five-gallon gas cans. The final time they pulled the stunt, a can tipped over inside the fence, and one pal wandered off while another stood around smoking. His pants caught on fire, the fire hit two other cans that exploded, and the three boys felt the flames as they topped the fence and fled on foot. Cars drove past, and Berry worried there were witnesses. After that, he said, they stuck to breaking into cars, shoplifting, snatching hubcaps, and peeping through windows.

By summer's end of 1944, Berry and his buddies "Skip" Hutchinson and James Williamson hatched a plan. They had all dropped out of Sumner, and in November they loaded into Berry's 1937 Oldsmobile, having decided to drive to Los Angeles.

Nothing happened as planned. They wanted to go far from home and find out what you'd never learn on a block in the Ville. In a car lot Berry had spotted a burned, chamberless .22-caliber pistol. He threw it in the car, and they were off.

They headed for Hollywood. About an hour out of St. Louis in the rural town of Wentzville, they tried to eat at the Southern Air, a roadside family restaurant. The trio was denied a table and told to order around the back, where an employee served them on paper plates. Four decades later, Berry would own the Southern Air.

By the time they got to Columbia, Missouri, 120 miles away, they'd stopped to patch their tires four times. They slept in the car parked by the highway. As they approached Independence, they had another blowout, driving into town on rims and sleeping in a public park that night. No more spares, little money: the Ville was looking better than it had in a while.

Skip said, *Stop the car, pick me up in fifteen minutes, I'll get us some money.* The others wondered what the hell he had in mind. When he told them he planned on robbing one of the shops they'd just passed, the other two said they were in. So they circled the block as Skip entered a bakery with a fish knife, coming out with sixty-two dollars. They split the cash in a YMCA room that night.

It was clear how this whole trip might work out. The next day they drove into Kansas City and settled on a barbershop. Charles grabbed the broken pistol, Skip behind him, and when Charles went through the door he shouted it was a stickup and demanded the cash. The barber's hand slowly reached toward his pocket, and Skip yelled, "Watch him, Slick!" Charles snapped to attention, barking, "I'll kill you!" and the barber's hands raised into the air.

"Get the bills, Slick!" Skip shouted. They made thirty-two bucks that night.

On the fifth day Skip clutched his knife, and they hit a small clothing store for fifty-one dollars, snatching some shirts on the way out the door.

They were ready to declare victory and get back to St. Louis. But when they got as far as Columbia at three thirty in the morning, Charles's Oldsmobile threw a rod and ground to a stop at the side of the road. They tried to wave down the occasional passing motorist for a push but received shouts of "Go home, n*****s." Finally, "a kind, middle-aged gentleman" slowed down in a 1941 Chevy coupe and asked if they needed help. Charles grabbed his pistol, leaned into the driver's window, and told him to slide over. Which he did—all the way over and through the passenger door, running down the road to a pay phone. Skip and Charles both jumped in; James was sitting in the back seat of the Oldsmobile and not appraised of Berry's improvisation. They were yelling for him to steer as they suddenly lined up behind him and started pushing, not giving James time to move to the front seat.

Bumper to bumper they were moving fast, coming into Kingdom City at forty-five miles per hour as James did his best. Berry saw state troopers watching as they rolled past a truck weigh station, and he tossed the gun fragment out the window.

But it was over, sirens blaring in the early morning. The stolen car glided to a stop, and James slowed to a halt a ways up the road. The troopers were on the lookout for two Black car thieves, but James hadn't figured that and trotted back to discover that his buddies were in handcuffs. He helpfully explained he was with them. They cuffed him too and took the three to the Boone County jail.

Five days went by before the teenagers were allowed to call home. Charles spoke to his old man, who in his decades on Earth had successfully managed to avoid all encounters with the justice system. A lawyer in Columbia told Henry he would represent his son for $125, and he took on the other two for free when their parents cut them loose. Twenty-two days of nothing later the lawyer showed up, met the three, and told them they should plead guilty and request the mercy of the court. Charles said okay.

Full confessions followed as Berry took the cops to where he had tossed what was left of the gun. The court appearance lasted twenty-one minutes. They all pled guilty, and each was given a brutal sentence of ten years in jail. Years later, when a lawyer asked him if he had ever been convicted of armed robbery, Berry replied, "Sir, that trial happened so fast I don't know what it was. It was robbery, I am sure."

The charge was a felony, first-degree robbery, issued just after he had turned eighteen. He would call it a "youthful spree" and describe himself "a downbound trainee in bandidoism." The reckless seriousness of their intentions, and the recklessness of their actions, likely had a significant impact on his life.[1]

Missouri sent him to the Algoa Intermediate Reformatory for Young Men, eight miles east of Jefferson City. The facility housed twenty stone-and-brick buildings on a hill overlooking the southern banks of the Missouri River. Algoa was created in the early 1930s in a reform-minded effort to convert incarceration into an educational experience. Operating on an honor system, it had no high walls, armed guards, or corporal punishment. There was vocational training that skewed toward agriculture (131 Holstein cows and two hundred acres were set aside for farming) and courses in auto mechanics and woodworking, a band, an orchestra, and a chorus.

A Missouri report from 1942 lists 572 white and 125 African American inmates. Offenses span from seven rapes and six manslaughter convictions down to thirty-eight charged with "stealing chickens at night." World War II had drained Algoa of resources, and there were only two high school classes available by the time Berry arrived. Racial tensions were rife at Algoa, where Black inmates were required to say, "Yes, sir" to white supervisors. The reformatory had a troubling practice of sticking newcomers in a stifling cell for thirty days upon arrival, on the professed claim that solitary confinement would deter them from running away. Once he cleared his thirty days, Berry moved to the Black dormitory.[2]

The prisoners gave him a nickname: Wild Man. While he did his time, Berry formed an alliance with a musician named Sam Alexander. "Po' Sam," as he was called, was a guitarist and tenor saxophone player from Kansas City with a reputation for showmanship: he would swing down from the rafters of a venue holding on to a rope while playing his horn. He and Berry formed a gospel quartet and a seven-member band that played upbeat blues for prisoners.

The singing was fun and, better still, it became a ticket out of the reformatory. A white missionary named Mother Robinson who worked there took an interest in the quartet, driving them to Jefferson City to be baptized and then booking them singing gigs. The quartet performed in Kansas City and St. Louis, where Chuck got to have dinner at home with his family.

The mentorship with Alexander, who was about nine years older, seems like a crucial alliance. Alexander was a versatile musician connected to the vibrant Kansas City scene; in 1942 he played guitar on an independently released 78 with boogie-woogie pianist Everett Johnson. Berry and Alexander had what Berry called a "boogie band" in Algoa, and they'd sing and play for the prisoners in the evening.

Boogie: the word was power, and the power first flowed from the keyboard. The city surrounding Berry as a boy was full up with stomping piano players, ragtimers, bluesmen and -women, and most of all boogie-woogie pounders, players who had taken the sound that flourished in remote turpentine and lumber camps in the Midwest and the South and brought it into twentieth-century big cities. They succeeded with anchor-punch left hands on the bass keys, beating eighth-note patterns (eight to the bar!) that fit into the twelve-bar structure of the blues, their music gutting the blues of its self-knowledge in favor of communal festivities. A great left hand could make the men and women of a work camp in the tall pines do things they wouldn't recall doing the next morning—it controlled movement, and body parts, and morals.

It set listeners bobbing their heads, for boogie-woogie was up-and-down music, and its gathered force sent messages down the spine to that same muscle set that projected it out again and down, stomp, to the dance floor.

Texas pianist Robert "Fud" Shaw claimed that his playing gave him magical powers: "When you listen to what I'm saying, you got to see in your mind all them gals out there swinging their butts and getting the mens excited. Otherwise you ain't got the music rightly understood. I could sit there and throw my hands down and make them gals do anything. I told them when to shake it, and when to hold it back. That's what this music is for."[3]

During the Great Migration, when boogie-woogie moved into Indianapolis, Chicago, St. Louis, then East to New York and Pittsburgh, it got flashier and more tuneful. In St. Louis, its fusion with the blues took on a strong local flavor. But everywhere it went, boogie-woogie signified a disreputable sophistication.

Chuck Berry was taught by St. Louis, and St. Louis was full up with boogie-woogie players during his musical education. Among them: Charles Thompson, who was proclaimed the best alive at Tom Turpin's Booker T. Washington Theatre when he beat sixty-eight players in a two-week-long ragtime competition in 1916. At the time of his death in 1964, Thompson was said to be the last piano player alive to have known Scott Joplin.

Walter Davis, who, with a spectral few notes hanging overhead, delivered the futility of a four a.m. walk. He was a desk clerk at the Calumet Hotel. Roosevelt Sykes, built like a button mushroom, a button mushroom wearing a Stetson hat. Twin brothers Aaron "Pinetop"

Sparks and Marion "Lindberg" Sparks, whose criminal records got cited the few times they got written about at all.

"A solid rumbling tone is endemic to the music," underscored a leading scholar of the form, and by the 1940s that rumble was shaking structures beyond the musical kind. Boogie-woogie had just become *boogie*, a sound that got at things, carnal things but also philosophical things that helped folks live through times. It had a moment of glory among big bands and motion pictures of the 1940s, and the music that the Hollywood tunesmiths and the gin joint professors alike purveyed could communicate rhythmic adorability, pinkie-ring sophistication, or freight-train inhibition breakdown—for something so elemental, boogie-woogie was good at a lot of different stuff.

But it was a piano sound, and Wild Man and Po' Sam were . . . guitar players. A rhythmic broadening was taking place, and though they were socially marginalized, the Algoans were in the thick of an important musical moment. Not for nothing did they call what they had made a *boogie band*: the sound of eighth notes fitting into larger patterns was infecting other instruments, and the patterns became more insistent as they traveled around the band. At this same moment, John Lee Hooker, a bluesman in Detroit, was in the studio working on how to drop that piano push into *his* guitar playing, and he began singing, "I feel so good—I want to boogie" on a song called "Hastings Street Boogie." What Hooker was getting at and the reform school boogie band was doing was also happening in New Orleans and other places. A good feeling, a low rumble, moving like a rhizome beneath the soil. Disconnected individuals would start to come into alignment with one another.

There was a new assistant superintendent at Algoa, Mr. Cockrell. His wife was friendly and wandered around the grounds alone at night. Berry's good conduct record earned him a new assignment: houseboy at the assistant superintendent's quarters. "Miz Cockrell" requested that Charles deliver her laundry to the house, and she stroked his face with her fingers once while telling him to "stay as nice as you are."

She had expressed an interest in his music. One afternoon the superintendent's wife invited the boogie band to play for her invited guests at a white dormitory. But when the musicians arrived, she and a nineteen-year-old friend were the only ones there. It was late

afternoon, and midway through the performance she waved Berry over
to come dance with her.

While the interracial couple danced, a group of about thirty white
prisoners had finished work assignments and were returning to the
dorm. They surveyed the scene and became enraged, Berry remembered, blocking the exit from the building. The white group made
threats, and Cockrell commanded them to move away from the exit
and let the band leave, but they weren't about to take orders, so she
and the trapped band moved farther into the building. Berry said that
with her knowledge he slipped away to her living quarters, evading
the mob.

After order had been established and Berry had safely made it back
to the Black dormitory, things cooled down with the assistant superintendent's wife. The dangers of an interracial affair in the South were
hard to make any more visceral than within the state's penal system,
surrounded by white criminals and officials of the state. If Berry connected the moment to one years before on the country club grounds,
he never said so. What he did say was that "the lure and temptation
were driving me mad."

Sam had left Algoa, and Berry applied for an early parole. On October 18, 1947, his twenty-first birthday, Berry was handed a train ticket
from Jefferson City to St. Louis.

HE HAD BEEN A TEENAGER OBSESSED WITH SEX AND CARRYING A
weight of shame about it. Then came his bungled crime spree, and he
lost three years of his life to Missouri, time spent with boys and men,
rapists, car thieves, and chicken snatchers. How this period affected
him he did not explore in public. He came back to the Ville a man,
hoping to catch up on all that he'd missed.

The city he returned to in the late 1940s was itself changing.
St. Louis was reaching its population peak of 856,796 in 1950, and its
Black population had grown to about 154,000.[4]

Approximately one in five living in the city were African American. They were pushing into areas previously barred to them, particularly in the wake of a 1948 Supreme Court ruling, based on
a St. Louis family's attempt to buy a home just outside the Ville.
In *Shelley v. Kraemer*, the court ruled that restrictive covenants

were legally unenforceable, and the immediate impact was that more neighborhoods were opening up to Black homeownership. White flight ramped up; over the next two decades, more than half the white population moved out of the city. In other ways too, tensions were on the rise. When city officials tried to change Buder Park's designation from a white to an African American playground in 1946, the Klan erected a ten-foot-tall flaming cross in the park and left a white hood with "KKK" written across it.

In the summer of 1949, three Black teenagers were confronted by a mob of 150 whites when they tried to swim in the Fairground Park public pool. Police called approximately one hundred reserve officers to the melee, while white mobs combed the neighborhood looking for Black people to attack. According to historian Joseph Heathcott, "A subsequent investigation turned up numerous incidents of violence, including attacks on black youth by whites armed with knives, baseball bats, and lead pipes."[5]

In the Ville there were acts of what the press had taken to calling "juvenile delinquency," including a four-day crime wave in 1945, when two Sumner athletes were shot and police arrested members of the Termites gang. Fear of an explosion of juvenile delinquency fed public sentiment that police were needed to monitor Black citizens throughout the city.

The Ville remained very much a self-contained community in the late 1940s. Efforts were ongoing to revive traditions that had taken a hit during World War II. There were big plans for the fifty-ninth annual May Day celebration, to raise money for the Annie Malone Orphan's Home, in Tandy Park, the green space at the heart of the Ville. For the first May Day since wartime rationing of meat had been declared, barbecue was back on the menu. The *Argus* enthused, "The grounds this year will be gaily decorated with the many novelty, hot dog, ice cream and soda booths. And hundreds of Volunteer workers will be on hand to serve the great throng of citizens expected."

On May Day 1948, Charles was still trying to make up for lost time. He was walking around with a buddy, his Buick parked nearby in case he met someone and an opportunity for making out presented itself. "Two angels" appeared before them, he later remembered.

"Hello, what's your name?" he asked.

"Themetta," one said while licking an ice-cream cone.

"Themetta Themetta?" he asked cutely.

"No. Themetta Suggs."

"I had gone to church, and my niece wanted to go to the parade that was over at Tandy Park," Themetta remembered in a 2019 documentary. "And there was this guy standing under a tree. And as I passed him I thought, hmm, he's kinda cute!" The sun was shining in his eyes—she could tell he had brown eyes. And he said, "Hello."[6]

Suggs was a calm beauty with dramatic cheekbones and a delicate, pointed chin. She loved the blues. Her people were from the cotton country of Marshall County, Mississippi, a region decimated by the boll weevil in the 1920s. Suggs lived with her mom and was walking with her niece when she met Berry.

The guys asked if they could walk together, Berry pairing off with Themetta, and when the ladies didn't say anything in response, the men joined them.

There was a carnival near where the Suggs lived, and they drove over there, sharing cotton candy as the sun went down. They rode rides and played games, and then, after dropping off the niece, Berry and Suggs went for a drive, parking at O'Fallon Park. It was there that he came up with a nickname for her, one he used for the rest of his life: Toddy.

The attraction was mutual and strong, and within a few months they were planning a life together. On October 21, 1948, they went downtown to the municipal courthouse on a cold Monday morning to get their marriage license. "Tiresome—Legalities," Berry wrote on a page of a photo album, but the accompanying pictures show the couple beaming like a pair of matinee idols. First, though, Berry had to introduce Suggs to his parole officer, whose permission was required for any license bearing his name.

Berry worked at the General Motors Fisher Body plant on Union Boulevard in North St. Louis, making $93.77 a week after taxes, sweeping the shop floor. He also continued his education on guitar. Ira Harris, a pal from the Ville, had given him lessons in high school, and now Charles sought him out for more. Harris introduced him to guitar chord books published by Nick Manoloff, and Berry scrutinized them in a very individual way. Not able to read music, and not accepting the idea that notes had been assigned letter names, Berry gave them numbers and created his own notation system. "That's the way I learned to do music," he said. "Through mathematics."

If you had a friend who was listening to guitarist Charlie Christian in 1950, you knew a pathfinder. Christian was a pioneer who turned the electric guitar into a solo instrument and then was gone before most folks knew he was here. Ira Harris shared his interests with Berry during their lessons. "He was into jazz," Berry said, "and the way he could manipulate the sound, I knew I had to do that. He played a bit like [Charlie] Christian, and a lot of what he showed me is a part of what I do."

Around June 1952, Berry got a call from his old high school sidekick Tommy Stevens, with whom he'd performed "Confessin' the Blues" to the Sumner student body. Stevens was now leading a nightclub trio in a joint across the Mississippi called Huff's Garden, and his other guitar player was unavailable; was Charles interested in filling in? Indeed he was, and from there, the story goes, Berry made his first appearance as a professional musician. It's the story he told writers, and it has become the accepted version.

However in 2019 a collector in St. Louis purchased the program for an August 27, 1949, show that took place at the Castle Ballroom. The evening, promoted as "Harlem in St. Louis," was an old-fashioned vaudeville-style revue, featuring among others Iola Nelson, billed as "Our Famous Torch Singer," the Young Sisters and their electric batons, tap dancing by Shirley and LaVern Young, and Teddy Riddlespringer, listed as "King of Boogie Woogie." Also on the bill was "Charles E. Berry," doing a "BLUES, ON HIS ELECTRICAL GUITAR (and his famous recitation)," and his sister Lucy, singing "My Hero" and "Vilia."[7]

While the nature of the event can't precisely be determined, several clues guide us to one fascinating aspect of the show. The title "Harlem in St. Louis" certainly foregrounds Blackness, and the program further bills itself as "an all colored Revue," even though some of the performers were not African American. The show's producer and emcee, Mort S. Silver, was a Jewish entertainer from Duluth, Minnesota, who had a long career on the RKO and Pantages circuits and performed in blackface; the program lists him singing "Mammy" (which Al Jolson famously sang in blackface in *The Jazz Singer*). It's surprising, at least by the light of the twenty-first century, to consider that Chuck Berry's first public performance was as part of a blackface minstrel revue.

Minstrelsy was a form of show business born of the wish by whites to denigrate African Americans, and its life force was a procession of racial stereotypes asserted in performances that regularly included comedy, songs, and dance. Whites would cover their faces in burnt cork and perform for curious, typically northern, audiences. Minstrelsy was most popular in the decades before the Civil War, though by the time of Berry's youth, aspects of it still survived on the periphery of show business.

It is impossible to render the minstrel show with nuance on a page or two. Many books have explored its implications. One aspect of blackface performance that is especially hard to comprehend today is that many Black entertainers also took the stage in blackface after Emancipation. Well into the twentieth century, traveling shows featured great Black actors, singers, dancers, and comics performing as African Americans. It was demeaning, yet it offered opportunity and income, and artists as different as Sammy Davis Jr., Bessie Smith, and Louis Jordan participated early in their careers.

White performers as varied as Bob Hope, Shirley Temple, Fred Astaire, and Judy Garland all performed in blackface. It was transatlantic entertainment, but it was local too, if you lived in St. Louis. In 1999 a photograph of Missouri's fifty-first governor, Mel Carnahan, hit the newsstands; it showed him in blackface in 1960, singing a tune as part of a Kiwanis Club minstrel show. Blackface was everywhere, and it lived a very long life, long enough to possibly have launched the career of Chuck Berry when he debuted in "Harlem in St. Louis."

St. Louis never got to be the United States capital. It did, however, get to be the home of a great band with a clumsy name: the Jeter-Pillars Orchestra. In these matters, perhaps the city was blessed twice over.

Jeter-Pillars was founded by James L. Jeter, an alto saxophonist, and Hayes Pillars, a tenor man, who had played together in Alphonso Trent's Dallas-based jazz ensemble until it broke up in 1933. They formed a group of their own and were hired in St. Louis at the Club Plantation the following year. The Plantation was owned by mobster

Tony Scarpelli and catered, as it said on their promotional material, to "white patronage only." Black musicians working the Plantation entered through the back door.

The Jeter-Pillars Orchestra was several crucial things. It was a leading "sweet band," meaning it favored lavish harmonies and arrangements that did not give huge play to soloists. Jeter-Pillars was also a so-called territory band that lived on the road and through its connections to a region, and like many territory groups it did not record a lot. They went on the air in St. Louis in 1934, playing live six nights a week on WIL, then moving to KMOX. (The Berry family listened to KMOX at home.) They also played on a nationally broadcast program, *The Fitch Bandwagon*. It was never an all-out jam band like Count Basie's, but Jeter-Pillars easily could have been, given the amount of great musicianship passing through the ranks. Drummers Jo Jones, Kenny Clarke, and Big Sid Catlett all signed on, saxophonist Jimmy Forrest and trumpeter Clark Terry. With the sweet stuff they built a gingerbread house, and then, on the third set of a Saturday night, they would blow its roof off, letting soloists cut loose. When Duke Ellington heard them in 1939 while in town, he extracted their young bass player, Jimmy Blanton, who then all but established the bass as a solo jazz instrument.

Jeter-Pillars played picnics in Tandy Park and at the Y Circus, a big annual event at the Pine Street YMCA in Mill Creek, where local musicians played the first half of a bill and national acts like Ellington played the second. They were a landmark in St. Louis.

"The Big Band Era is my era," Berry enthused. "People say, 'Where did you get your style from?' I did the Big Band Era on guitar. That's the best way I could explain it." Jeter-Pillars would have been on his mind because they were already doing the big band sound—with prominent guitar players.[8]

The orchestra featured a procession of innovators who were exploring amplification in the 1930s, this just a few years after the electric guitar was introduced on the mass market. Key to the orchestra was Floyd Smith, born in St. Louis in 1917, who started playing ukulele in the early 1930s and joined Jeter-Pillars in 1936. He performed what some argue is the first electric guitar solo on record, 1937's "Lazy Rhythm."

Two years later Smith was in Andy Kirk's Twelve Clouds of Joy, with whom he recorded "Floyd's Guitar Blues," probably the first hit instrumental to feature an electric guitar. Smith had taught himself Hawaiian guitar while with Jeter-Pillars, and he played this lap steel instrument on "Floyd's Guitar Blues," which gave the song a distinctive weeping, lanky feel.

It's a rich moment, when journeymen were the history makers and novelty numbers were altering the music's direction. While some touted examples of electric guitar's first appearances sound merely like amplified acoustic performances, "Floyd's Guitar Blues" is an invention that couldn't exist without an alternating current. Chuck Berry heard it. Chuck Berry played it: retitled "Blues for Hawaiians," his version of the song was released under his name in 1959 on the album *Chuck Berry Is on Top*.

When Smith left, Jeter-Pillars rolled on. There's anecdotal evidence that for some period of time, Smith was followed by Charlie Christian, the most important early figure on electric guitar. When he joined the Benny Goodman Band in 1939, Christian suddenly became a jazz phenomenon. His revelatory solos were clear and precise, unadorned and glorious, like a Shaker glider. That was clear after 1939, but his moves in the years just before are frustratingly vague. Christian came from Oklahoma, and ultimately he helped make the guitar an integral melodic part of the jazz band. He was a blurry young man who didn't seem to have a lot to say when not playing. When he drank, standing in the street outside the club, he would dance.

Christian lived frantically, as if he were desperate to communicate his knowledge before his imminent demise. And however Christian touched Berry, a transfer was made.

Berry was inspired by another who had likewise learned from Christian. Carl Hogan, a St. Louis–grown guitar star, had a major influence on Berry, who saw his own playing as a hybrid of both their styles.

"Charlie Christian was the best guitar player, and he never looked up from his guitar," Berry said. "The greatest guitar player that ever was, Charlie Christian. And Carl Hogan, he never looked up from his guitar. Most of my licks came from Carl Hogan and Charlie Christian." In interviews Berry preferred to describe himself as a synthesizer of diverse sounds; here he implies he added some showmanship to the mix. "But because I've put a little dance with it, I guess they [meaning the audience] appreciate hearin' somethin' along with seein' something."

In the early 1940s Hogan played in Jeter-Pillars, and he then appeared in George Hudson's orchestra when they replaced Jeter-Pillars at the Plantation. From 1946 to the end of the decade, Hogan played in Louis Jordan's Tympany Five; at the same moment Berry was in Algoa working out his band approach to the boogie-woogie sound, Louis Jordan was getting marquee branding as "The King of the Juke Box" for definitively doing exactly this, playing tricks with the scale of things—turning big band dynamics into a cocktail-shaker-sized domestic entertainment.

Jordan's band lifted boogie-woogie's eight-to-the-bar off the piano player's back and spread it across the bass, guitar, and drums. He overlaid that weight-bearing repetition with a shuffle beat, a misleadingly simple rhythmic pattern on which swing drummers thrived. A onetime musical cohort of Po' Sam's had a pithy description of how the shuffle sounded: the drummer "brushing the perimeter of the drum so it sounded like someone whispering 'shoot the cow, shoot the cow.'" These innovations, endemic not only to Jordan but popping up on the West Coast and at King Records in Cincinnati, created a new group dynamic that briefly flourished in the 1940s and early 1950s.

Such groups were dubbed "jump bands" and their sound "jump boogie." Berry loved the style, and he studied the cultural figure that Louis Jordan cut: Jordan was a commanding stage presence whose songs offered pointed commentary in a humorous way. Jordan wasn't a crooner *or* a bluesman; he was an observer on the street, coping with situations through wit and jargon, a sketch artist whose words were carefully chosen to fall precisely into the bounce beat, which felt as casual as one palm crossing over another.

Both the band and the easygoing word-hurler captured Berry's attention. But as he learned his instrument, it was Jordan's guitarist, Carl Hogan, who so riveted him that Berry memorized Hogan's cocky solos. When he recorded "Johnny B. Goode," he repurposed Hogan's lead into Jordan's 1946 "Ain't That Just Like a Woman (They'll Do It Every Time)" and made it the intro to his 1958 hit.

Nobody knows much about Hogan, who never seems to have been asked for an interview. But one thing people do know about this important figure was that he also loved to tinker. "He was full of weird musical ideas," said Aaron Izenhall, trumpeter with Jordan. "He was always working on inventions, including one that involved only using one central peg to tune all six strings on a guitar. God knows how that would work, but he continued experimenting."

Chris Columbus, the drummer in Jordan's band, recalled, "He was not only inventive musically, he was inventive mechanically; he was always devising new material to make guitar strings from, and at one time he played an Hawaiian guitar, using the steel on the strings."[9]

There isn't a lot of Hogan on record. Berry heard him live, however, and perhaps frequently in St. Louis. Hogan was a rhythm player—he joined Jordan's group as a bassist before sliding over to his real calling. He played on the top of the beat, which was fresh, and he put his weight on the second and fourth beat in the measure, and these two things rendered him sly, together, casually commanding. Never playing too much, Hogan neatly jibed with Jordan's wit, because they both were a bit about the wink. He left Jordan in 1948 and died in St. Louis in 1977.

NOTE THE BILLING AT THE CASTLE BALLROOM IN 1949: TWENTY-three-year-old "Charles E. Berry," playing a "BLUES, ON HIS ELECTRICAL GUITAR." Chuck Berry learned from the start on an instrument that had hit the market not even twenty years before. The people he listened to, stole from, and cultivated as teachers—they learned first on an acoustic guitar and then struggled to make sense of that knowledge in a changing era. Berry didn't need to adjust his approach. His approach was shaped from the start by the nature of the electric guitar.

Around town, countless newcomers were also learning. There was no single way in, no body of musical examples to guide you into the fold. There was no fold. Musicianship couldn't hurt, but an ability to take apart a radio might also prove crucial. You found your own way. Berry could go to Ludwig Music House and buy himself a guitar. But around him in St. Louis were folks up from sharecropper plantations in Mississippi who first learned from a diddley bow—a single string nailed to the wall of a shack and plucked. They followed that line and ended up, some, trying to sound like Floyd Smith and his Hawaiian guitar. There were people with soldering guns trying to amplify their own stringed instrument and tyros making instruments out of vegetable crates and gasoline cans. In St. Louis there were all kinds of people on guitars, and they were all, at the same time, inventing a new noise. You could pay a teacher to tell you you were doing it wrong, or you could find somebody making it the way you liked and start talking to them nicely. There was no wrong way to do it.

Did he *want* to do it?

The music had first occurred to him, Berry told himself, as a way to make a little cash. That was an explanation his father would understand. In 1948 he and Toddy lived in a boardinghouse on Delmar Boulevard owned by his uncle, where he focused on making money. There were brief stints at the Fisher auto body plant and at the St. Louis Ordnance Plant on Goodfellow, making howitzer artillery shells. With his brother Hank, Charles assisted his dad on home renovations in the morning, while Toddy worked at a dry cleaner. It was the life a lot of young families were living in the postwar years; the middle class was opening up, and there was growing reason for Black families to think that, with hard work, a better life was available.

Charles and Toddy lived rent-free in a basement on Delmar, with Charles doing repairs and caretaking for the building. A tenant, "a single, unbiased Canadian woman," struck up a conversation, and he was intrigued. She invited him to her place and closed the door behind him. She was white and kind, and the mutual attraction excited and frightened him. Sensing his anxiety she soothed that he need not be afraid, he had a right to be with her. She invited him back another night when things weren't so stressful. They had sex when he returned.

Somebody—Berry assumed an ex-boyfriend—called the police. The next day a patrol car took him to the police station for a conversation with three white officers. A sergeant sidled up to him, a baseball bat balanced on his shoulder. The patrolman who picked up Berry was there, and so was a captain, the three settling in to interrogate the Black caretaker.

They said the bat would be applied for every lie they heard. Berry seized on a falseness in the whole scene—he didn't feel like they were really going to hit him so much as they were playing a part in a larger act—and believed that he could guide their behavior with a performance of his own. So he mugged the way he knew they wanted, acting scared, cringing, indicating he understood who was in charge.

One of them adjusted Berry's head, putting it in line with the bat, and barked, "Did you fugger?"

"No, sir. A white woman? No, sir!"

The batter acted out a swing.

Berry laid into his denial, with a mix of cowering and clowning, and when he sneaked a glimpse of one of the men, he saw a laugh being suppressed. It was a relief. Then the other two laughed out loud, and the moment ended. They let him go, warning that he would be watched.

Berry lost the apartment, and the couple moved briefly to his parents' house. But he could have lost more. Reflecting on the sex later, Berry realized that it was as close as he had been to a white woman since he had been eighteen at Algoa. He was vividly reminded that even behind closed doors, when consent was clear and he was assured of his right to be there, even then his safety was uncertain. But he also learned that he had the skill to manage situations that were intriguing, and one thing that made them intriguing was danger.

Daughter Darlin Ingrid was born in October 1950. By then Berry had a janitorial job at WEW, a radio station offering community programming that included guitarist Joe Sherman. An "outstanding" rhythm and blues man in St. Louis, according to Berry, Sherman sold him a used Kay electric guitar for thirty bucks. Within a few months, he bought a secondhand magnetic wire recorder, and on it began storing both his readings of poetry and his electric guitar playing.

Lucy Berry by now had put aside singing and, along with sister Thelma, learned hairdressing via the Poro System, a method franchised by Annie Turnbo Malone. The millionaire businesswoman had left St. Louis in 1930, but her name still rang in the Ville as a powerful expression of Black capitalism. Her annual May Day celebration was where Berry's parents had been introduced and where Charles met Themetta Suggs. Soon Charles, too, would study the Poro System.

As a stab at respectability or at pleasing his parents, getting a Poro diploma, followed by working in his sisters' hairdressing business, made sense. Charles and Themetta meanwhile bought a three-room brick house on Whittier Street and set about filling it with symbols of success: a Muntz television set to watch Milton Berle and Jack Paar on, a Zenith hi-fi console.

One day his old high school sidekick Tommy Stevens approached with a pitch. It was early 1952. Stevens had a combo to his name and needed a second guitar player to fill in for a few nights. Berry said sure, and soon he was playing regularly with Stevens.

Now he was a professional musician, and he joined the local chapter of the American Federation of Musicians. The name on his union card, however, appeared a little screwy: Charles Berryn. It looked like a typo, but it was no accident. Maybe he liked how the pseudonym he had concocted sounded like *Baron*; he certainly liked how it hid his identity, at least a bit, from his father—the deacon, the disciplinarian. "I didn't want him to know I was playing, that's for sure," Berry said.

It appeared that way on billing with Tommy Stevens. "That was to protect his father so the church would not cast him out or thought, 'This child is in the devil's music' or whatnot," Themetta said. Ultimately, of course, the church found out and confronted Henry Berry. A meeting was held. "The church decided it's okay to have Berry as your son and playing rock and roll music," said Themetta.

Had he been a better criminal, would he have ever gotten to this place?

There was the disruptive power of boogie-woogie and the jump blues, and then there was the pull of home, of the Muntz TV and the Zenith hi-fi.

There was Charles Berry the father and family man, and there was the guy with his electric guitar. Already in his mind two distinct figures, separated by a single letter.

4

EAST BOOGIE

He was a pale ghost blowing past stop signs with a speed that irked local cops. A skinny cipher, photographed in a shiny suit with a scuzzball tie around his neck after he'd wrapped his car around a telephone pole on an oily St. Louis street.

The local media took offense at his routine. From the late 1940s until the early 1960s, they called him "Hot Rod" Moore and accurately dubbed him a "notorious traffic offender." Robert H. Moore's existence was monotonously simple. It seems likely even *he* didn't know why he kept doing the stuff he did, which when you boil it down was just getting in one or another expensively customized Ford his wealthy doctor dad had bankrolled, then flooring it in one end of town and out some other. Hot Rod Moore drove fast and evaded police. It was the right amount of initiative to electrify teens all around eastern Missouri.[1]

In 1948 he turned sixteen and earned his first speeding ticket; a year later he was barred from driving within city limits. He did eighty miles per down Lindbergh Boulevard, and Dad wanted him to do jail time, but then, legend has it, the Automobile Club of America posted bail and he drove again. Dad took his car away, but Mom took pity and bought him a new one. By the early 1950s St. Louis politicians campaigned on how they would contain his contagion. In 1954, he earned an eight-month jail sentence for leaving the scene of an accident in Mexico, Missouri, laconically telling a deputy sheriff, "I guess I got what I had coming." They let him out after four months when he agreed to hand over his Missouri license. But then he got one from Illinois, and still he persisted.

He didn't have a single point to make or one object he was rebelling against. What he had were fans, young fans, swooning over speed, reporting sightings around the map. Local radio broadcast the rumors from Wildwood or Rolla or Jefferson City, and that was enough for the sheriff to set up roadblocks on the highway. He was a resistance leader way out ahead of his people, showing up in several spots at once, hiding out in sleepy country towns. People believed he had safe havens set up outside St. Louis, "special hiding places along the way, such as barns, garages, woods, and even under bridges in dried up creek beds; resting places where he stashed food and fuel."

In 1956, US senator from Kentucky Estes Kefauver chaired federal hearings on the rise of so-called juvenile delinquency in the hotbed of St. Louis. Richard Amberg, publisher of the *St. Louis Globe-Democrat*, must have been thinking about Hot Rod Moore when he testified: "It is significant . . . that the crimes which have most aroused the community in recent months [include] the abandoned and reckless drag races on our public highways."[2]

All over St. Louis, and all over the country, leaders expressed concern about drag racing, knife packing, incendiary youth.

Charles Berry himself was obsessed with cars. Because of speed, and also because they were good for having sex in, he had decided. The hot-sheet motel rooms some guys used cost two bucks, he had noticed, and your own car did not. He also observed the very real freedom of movement cars provided, and how a Black man driving through St. Louis in a fine vehicle was a statement beyond words. Not for nothing would he one day brag that he was the first in his family to own a Cadillac.

Route 66 passed right in front of the Automobile Club of America's office on swanky Lindell Boulevard. One day around 1950, on a lark, Berry tried to join the club—they were quietly excluding Black members, and he got it in mind to commit stealth integration. "But it was too heavy for that time," he said. Several years running he was told they were still considering his application, come back later.

Meanwhile, as he waited for his AAA membership to come through, Berry worked on his twang. It started while he was playing with Tommy Stevens, a regular Saturday gig at Huff's Garden in Belleville, Illinois, in June 1952. Huff's Garden was a nineteenth-century public garden with entertainment. Stevens's trio had an unusual lineup: leader and Berry on guitars, and an alto saxophonist. Their set featured blues and ballads. Stevens was happy to let Berry try something new if it got a good response from the audience. The country songs Berry introduced in Belleville brightened the shows, and the Saturday crowds were picking up.

One regular was a recent transplant from West Virginia, a piano player named Johnnie Johnson. Years later Johnson remembered what most impressed him at Huff's Garden: "The reason I liked watchin' Tommy's band was 'cause they had this fella playin' guitar and singin' that could make me laugh more than anybody I ever saw."

The country tinge shocked audiences, and to Johnson and others it registered initially as something to laugh *at*. "They would be playin' a regular blues set when all the sudden this man would break into a country song—what I called hillbilly music—which was a music I knew and liked 'cause I'd grown up around it in West Virginia."[3] It wasn't even Berry's playing that interested Johnson, so much as his inherent skills as a comic performer. Berry made him laugh.

"The funny thing about it was that this man was black and his audience was black and they wanted Muddy Waters—the blues. And I was surprised 'cause the people seemed to really get a kick out of it when Tommy would have him do his little songs."

It was a disruption and a challenge to the audience, and way beneath that, something was coming into focus too. And since Berry almost certainly sold it with a theatrical twang not just in his guitar but in his voice, it came across as performance, play—a Black man in the role of a hillbilly. There was something to the hillbilly act, Berry must have thought, worth further exploration. Those in the audience were interested in exploring it themselves.

"They would perform, a little circle of people in the club would form a circle and they'd start a square dance," said Johnson.[4]

"They'd be hollerin' and dancin', havin' a good ol' time," he remembered. Looking at them through his hooded eyes, Johnson made estimations.

He was the kind of club piano player that used to stock saloons and cafés off the highway, the guy who took it in and kept it there with a poker face to the world. If the stuffed head of a feral pig fell off the wall during the Wild Boar Lodge mixer for the Amalgamated Meat Cutters convention in East St. Louis and knocked the fez off a celebrant, Johnson *might have* done so much as clock the pig's descent with one eye, grunted, and kept playing "I Apologize." If a lady cut in on another lady's man and the second woman pulled a pistol from her handbag and pointed it at a third lady who was pulling a brick out from under a stool in order to come to the aid of the first lady while her man ducked behind the jukebox, Johnson's left hand would never have lost the beat. He drew the drama around him into his bulky frame and he kept on playing, because that was what you were paid to do, and that was how you stayed alive. Johnnie Johnson maintained a steady disposition.

"Johnnie was laid-back and laid down the law at the same time, if that makes sense," said jazz bassist Mark Peterson, who played with Johnson later on. "He was very diplomatic in his approach; he was a jolly man. And if he saw you had talent, he wanted to help bring it out, but he didn't want to dictate. 'Whatever you have, I want you to use that to make it happen'—that was his way."[5]

After Johnson's old lady in Chicago split on him, he dropped down to East St. Louis in 1950. He came to visit his brother, but the brother accidentally shot himself and died. Johnson was feeling low his first few years in East St. Louis, and that must have factored into his decision to find a steady gig where he could let his music do the talking and a little money—twenty-six dollars a night and tips divided among three people—could be made.

Settling into an ongoing stand at the Club Cosmopolitan, he had put a cocktail combo together, playing jazz, standards, and the blues. And then his saxophonist, Alvin Bennett, had an aneurysm before the biggest working night of the year, New Year's Eve 1953, and Johnson rushed to find a backup. "We didn't know how sick he was at the time," he told writer Travis Fitzpatrick in 1999; nobody knew that Bennett would never walk, let alone play the saxophone, again. "There was a lot of folks, including me, who was sorry to see that man put down his horn. . . . Alvin was a good man, fun to be around and he could play, boy. I guess if he had made the show, I wouldn't have gotten together with Chuck, and I guess that was pretty important. But I tell you what, if Alvin could still play, he'd be first on my list anytime. People forget how good a saxman he really was."[6]

Suddenly in need, Johnson called the guitarist he'd watched at Huff's Garden.

"What's the matter, you couldn't get nobody else?" Berry responded.[7] He did the gig that night, and so began his ongoing role in the Sir Charles Trio.

That New Year's Eve, drummer Ebbie Hardy, Johnson, and Berry were meshing together nicely, so Berry decided to unpack a country and western shuffle called "Mary Jo," which he had played with Tommy Stevens. He was entertaining himself, first of all, mugging and gesturing and really selling the song, and why not, it was New Year's Eve and the house was loaded. "Well let me tell you, the people loved him. They just ate it up," Johnson recalled. "And I felt really happy for Chuck, because like I said, that was real brave of him."[8] Brave because this was a crowd looking to hear the blues and a wailing sax on a party night. "I guess I should have known. The public was always lookin' for somethin' new, and a group of black men playing hillbilly songs was definitely new." Soon the proprietor of the Club Cosmopolitan suggested that Johnson make Berry a full member of the trio.

The Cosmo, as it was called, occupied a former neighborhood supermarket on Bond Avenue on the south side of town. Behind it they grilled meat and sold plates of food. Across the street was a city park where frolics were known to occur. In the 1950s the club was run by Joe Lewis, an African American police officer. It was founded in the 1940s by Joe and his brother Tom, both of whom were precinct committeemen in East St. Louis.[9]

They were charged, and acquitted by a jury, of killing a man trying to break into a home near the club in 1945. Challenging the white Democratic machine of East St. Louis, the Lewis brothers worked to get Black candidates elected, and their efforts repeatedly got them into trouble. Their liquor license was revoked in March of 1946 (Joe was charged with physically attacking the state inspector who cited him). After which gunshots were fired into the Cosmo and a bomb was dropped on the club in April, blowing a ten-foot hole in the roof and damaging a fancy glass bar. The brothers blamed the attacks on the mayor and in response wrote a letter to President Truman, saying they had been denied police protection due to their political activities.

East St. Louis was a focal point. The poet Eugene Redmond grew up there in the 1950s and called it "East Boogie," while the poet Henry Dumas, also living there in the 1950s, preferred "East St. Hell." Either way, life there could be rugged and contentious, and all kinds of stuff went down out of sight of folks across the river in St. Louis.[10]

A mile and a half south of the club was the vast Monsanto factory, producing PCBs and venting a cloud of funk that hung over the region. A short drive north was a string of small Illinois towns in which the blues was turning into rhythm and blues, and where electric blues musicians like Little Milton, Earl Hooker, and Freddie King lived in the 1950s. Towns and settlements, including Madison, Brooklyn (aka Lovejoy), Eagle Park, Fireworks Station, all had places for Black musicians to play. Little Milton remembered Fireworks Station fondly: "Everybody used to play there because at that time the area was completely wide open, stayed open 24 hours if they wanted to, and most of them wanted to. Boyd Gilmore and his group would come in, and several others: Elmore James, Muddy Waters, and whoever."[11] This region across the river, a patchwork of unincorporated and overlooked areas, became a musical hotbed from the late 1940s through the following decade.

The Cosmo had a reputation for attracting higher-end clientele. There was a mural on the wall, painted by Berry, of snowy mountains. Even white fans came to hear the Sir John Trio, taking up almost half the filled room. The hillbilly tunes were on the increase, and Berry was loving it.

The Cosmo gave them a regular Friday slot in which they played pop standards, boogie-woogie, blues, and country numbers. Berry was also writing and performing poems, like one called "Beer Drinkin' Woman," which featured him talking over casual music from Johnson and Hardy. And he worked up pantomimed bits, like "the Buggy Ride": Berry driving a buggy while his woman, a gal he very much wants to seduce, rides beside him. As he steers and woos, his actions get more and more suspect, until Johnson lightheartedly flips on a police siren perched on top of his piano.

For the next year and a half, Berry, Johnson, and Hardy would play together on a regular basis at the Cosmo. Lewis's club was just a shade out of the way—a good place to experiment while you watched your audience grow.

HE SHOOK THINGS UP BY ADDING COUNTRY SONGS "JAMBALAYA" and "Mountain Dew" to the repertoire. "I heard a lot of country music stuff and copied a lot," he explained. "I guess I couldn't have said I was playing country. But I was stabbing at it."[12] Johnson, and most in the audience, might have understood what Berry offhandedly called the "hillbilly act" as a gimmick, and on one level that's what it was. But Berry didn't dream it up and didn't look far to find it, because it was there in the home where he lived, outside in the Ville and all around St. Louis.

"I grew up on it. That's all we heard for a period," he told one interviewer.

"There was a station in my hometown played country music—Louvin Brothers, Hank Williams, Kitty Wells."

Interviewer: "Do you think that went into your music?"

Berry: "Oh, of course it did."[13]

Country music, in its various modes, had been a part of Black life in St. Louis for decades. Trumpeter Clark Terry, who was born there a few years before Berry, recalled that although jazz was what he liked, his father preferred country sounds, much to his regret. Ike Turner called country his favorite kind of music. The idea that it is an inherently white form is disproved both by country's origins and its audience.

When blues guitarist Moody Jones came to Missouri from Arkansas around 1927, he lived in East St. Louis, forming a band to put food on the table. It wasn't blues that paid the bills: "We were playing hillbilly all out there, Western songs, hillbilly and Western. We were out there at that time. No blues," he said. The band he formed, the All Stars, featured Jones playing a gas can fitted with a banjo neck, a washtub customized to hit bass notes, and a mandolin. "We played a few blues, but we was out there to make a buck and we couldn't get nothing much for the blues at that time, so we learned to play everything," explained Jones.[14]

Berry's interest in country began with the family radio. "Actually, it all started back when I was listening to station KMOX in

St. Louis which is theoretically an Okie station and I got turned on by the sounds."[15] Besides playing records by country and western stars, KMOX for many years featured live broadcasts from its studios. Country and western programs on St. Louis radio in the 1940s and early 1950s featured a mix of studio musicians paid to play country, pop, jazz, or whatever; traditional musicians hoping to get a foothold in the growing country hierarchy; and show business journeymen who followed work from station to station. Singer and guitarist Roy Queen, for instance, had a program on KMOX in the late 1920s, then went to Oklahoma to join up with western swing bandleader Bob Wills before returning to St. Louis radio and planting Wills's sound in Missouri. In the late 1940s, Queen teamed with Pappy Cheshire to present *Uncle Dick Slack's Barn Dance*, a nationally syndicated program.

Cheshire was a song and dance man from Emporia, Kansas, who traveled the country during the 1930s running a stock theater troupe. Then he played hillbilly characters for low-budget Hollywood studios, appearing in Ma and Pa Kettle comedies. But in St. Louis, Cheshire was known to radio audiences as the "maestro of the mountains." He didn't play an Ozark character; he *was* one as far as they were concerned. Working with Queen, he wasn't more or less "real" or "authentic" than his rootsy costar. Neither the actor nor the guitar player was more important to creating country and western culture.

Country music in St. Louis, as well as everywhere else, was a blend of show biz, folk, and artisanal skills gathering in the marketplace. Pappy Cheshire didn't invent the character he played; the hayseed was a longtime staple of vaudeville. (On Berry's first stage appearance, in 1949 at the Castle Ballroom, Edith Maxville was listed in the program, performing as a "Hill-Billy from Arkansas.") He, and Chuck Berry after him, just took something patrons enjoyed as a put-on and, over time, gave it new meaning

IN 1954 BERRY ENTERED A LOCAL STUDIO AND MADE HIS FIRST record, playing guitar in a group recording under the name Joe Alexander and the Cubans. Information logged at the session, which has been examined by collector and writer Duane Marburger, lists "Charles Berryn" on guitar, Oscar Washington (recording under the

name of his daughter, Faith Douglass) also on guitar, Freddie Golden
playing bongos, and Alexander—who was billed around town as
"Calypso Joe"—singing. In his lifetime Berry never acknowledged the
record's existence.[16]

The Cubans recorded four songs on August 13, 1954, at Premier
Recording Studio. Two, "Oh Maria" and "I Hope These Words Will
Find You Well," were released on 78 and 45 rpm records for the tiny
Ballad label. There is nothing on this single that sounds like the music
Berry would make over the next few years, and neither song is especially interesting. "Oh Maria" is a tale sung by a Trinidadian man who
sails to the US only to get kicked out of his apartment for not having
a job. "I Hope These Words" and "Oh Maria" are Latin-inflected ballads; while the latter features a deft solo by one of the guitar players, it
bears no obvious marks of Berry's soon-to-emerge sound.

Oscar Washington, who booked the session, played on it, and
owned the Ballad label, was an underfunded entrepreneur with many
talents. He had an interest in music, poetry, and writing, and he wrote
the lyrics that accompanied St. Louis tenor saxophonist Jimmy Forrest's 1952 song "Night Train," which was a hit for James Brown.
Washington composed songs for saxophonist Earl Bostic, who like him
was born in Tulsa, Oklahoma.

The single barely made it out of St. Louis and was only discovered by a local collector in the late 1970s. Marburger had been asking
around about recordings Berry might have made early on in St. Louis
and was introduced to Washington, who was happy to tell his tale.
Washington explained that Berry asked him for help making a record
under his own name. That may even be why he was on this record at
all—to crack the door open to recording a session with Johnnie Johnson. "Chuck wanted me to record him, and I didn't want to do it. That
was the biggest mistake of my life," the founder of Ballad said. Though
studio documents indicate two other songs were recorded that day,
there's no evidence they were ever released.

Berry denied he was a member of the Cubans, but "Charles
Berryn" appears on paperwork filed with the American Federation
of Musicians. At a performance at Six Flags in St. Louis long after
Berry had become a star, Marburger asked him about the Cubans.
Berry gave no response. "He acted like he didn't hear my question

or he didn't want to answer," said Marburger. "That was just something he did one day a long time ago."

In the early 1950s, Berry was a student of recording technology as well as of the electric guitar. He had bought a secondhand wire reel-to-reel recorder from Joe Sherman early in 1951, a crucial purchase: "I think I would have stolen it if he hadn't sold it as I was completely fascinated by its reproduction qualities," he said. "It was that inspiration that started me to recording the first of my original improvisations, both poetical and melodical."[17] Taking the recorder over to his friend and teacher Ira Harris's house, Berry recorded Harris playing guitar licks in a Charlie Christian style, learning Christian's style in this way.

Furthermore, it helped clarify for him that making recordings was what an electric guitar was *for*. And if he was among the first generation to learn music on the instrument, he was also among the first generation with access to affordable and easy-to-use recording technology.

The breakthroughs that made it possible happened somewhat accidentally. And like so many breakthroughs, this one was uncovered in a German castle filled with Nazis.

The castle in question, in Bad Nauheim, had become a Nazi communications center by the spring of 1945. After the German surrender in May, an American soldier was shown a pair of secret machines, high-fidelity Magnetophons, advanced recorders that used magnetic tape to produce a sound quality that was nearly indistinguishable from the sound of a live performance. Jack Mullin, the American, was an audiophile. He shipped a pair of Magnetophons and fifty reels of German tape to his home in San Francisco.

Eventually Mullin made adjustments to the German product and struck a deal with the Ampex Electric and Manufacturing Company allowing them to market the new technology to the world. Mullin had friends in high places; pop singer Bing Crosby was just then looking to find a new sponsor for his radio show. And he was looking for a way to avoid doing all his radio shows live. The Ampex technology provided him with a promising new tool. By using a high-quality recorder Crosby could make multiple versions of a performance and then piece together from different takes the best version of a "live" show. It freed up his schedule, and listeners didn't mind in the least.

It was a risky move that only a superstar could have attempted. The assumption had been that radio audiences craved realness, a truth in sound that could only come via live broadcast with a live audience hearing the work of live performers. But Crosby's listenership didn't drop off when the network broadcast recordings of his voice. Stations, not to mention artists, took notice.

Radio opened up to recordings at a time when national broadcasting networks were facing steep competition from independently owned stations, whose numbers grew from 45 in 1945 to 916 in 1950, enough to control 44 percent of the national market. After World War II the FCC was licensing new stations by the hundreds, and the innovative recording technology meant they didn't have to hire a house band and live musicians to succeed. The emergence in 1949 of the seven-inch 45 rpm record, a sturdy new music format, further fed the postwar radio explosion.

Change was affecting record labels too. The three major national labels were poorly set up to connect with modern, hyperlocal listeners. They existed to sell music coast to coast. Having a record that was a hit only among people who liked hillbilly music, or blues from Chicago, or polkas, people who lived in Texas or Terre Haute, didn't generate the kind of profits they demanded. So along with independent regional stations and markets there emerged a wave of independent labels thriving on the new and the niche, the more modest profits deriving from a zydeco or gospel or rhythm and blues hit. A single station would have to pay the network to get access to Crosby's voice, but the record labels popping up around the country were supplying their product to stations for free. Heck, some were paying *them* to give their records a shot. That was a good business strategy for anybody who owned a new station.

These labels contracted with a growing wave of regional distributors and hired go-getters who drove from town to town with trunks full of discs. They were pitching to radio stations and wielding books full of the names of DJs and their tastes: this one liked jump boogie tunes, that one like honky-tonk music. This one liked whiskey, and that one, with a top-rated show in Indianapolis, liked redheads. The DJs were giving their listeners what they wanted, and the distributors and small labels tried to give the DJs what *they* wanted.

The people responsible for the boom in independent labels in the years after World War II were unlike the stable pros who ran broadcast networks and the big three labels. They reconfigured the market, with new notions of how to sell things and how to get the public's attention. In the words of musicologist Albin Zak, they were "opportunists, idealists, scoundrels, pirates, dreamers, tough guys, free spirits, swindlers, and quasi- and not-so-quasi-gangsters, all pursuing the next hit. Some were ethical, some were not. As they hung onto a tenuous existence, they clawed for every nickel, and of the hundreds that set out on a wing, a prayer, and a song, few survived for long." They were individualists looking over their shoulder for the coming ice pick. But, as a collective force, Zak wrote, "their energies reoriented the pop music economy," and before the decade was over they would assert control of that economy.[18]

In the case of Oscar Washington, who gathered Joe Alexander and the Cubans into his studio, terms like *dreamer* and *idealist* seem closest to the mark. Around the same time he was writing songs for Charles Berryn to play, he was also running the science department at Vashon High. But records like "Oh Maria"—dream tickets printed by people wishing to be something they weren't, be it Cubans or Trinidadians or hitmakers—were the coin of the moment, and anybody who was making them, or listening to them, might imagine themselves capable of striking it rich.

The pop music supply chain transformed itself almost monthly from the late 1940s on. You could read about it in the trades or hear it happen in your hometown. Jesse Burks, "Spider" as he was known professionally, was a graduate of Sumner High who was a few years older than Berry. He proceeded to an engineering degree at the Hampton Institute in Virginia, only to find once he graduated that he couldn't get a job as an African American engineer. Burks returned to St. Louis and offered his services to the new independent radio station KXLW upon its launch in 1947, promising station managers that he could bring them Black listeners with a daily program of jazz and rhythm and blues. The first Black disc jockey in St. Louis, Spider Burks was a motor-mouth and a master of catchphraseology, saying, "Let's nail the ceiling to the roof" when a hot one hit, signing off shows with a pointed "And remember, it takes the black keys as well as the white to play 'The Star Spangled Banner.'"

Burks did so well he had *two* shows on the station, and he earned enough before the decade was over to be driving a pink Cadillac across town. All over the map broadcast antennas were rising, indie record label reps were beating a path to the source of the signal, and a guy with a colorful way of talking was standing there to greet them all. Spider Burks started with a young Black listenership and expanded rapidly from there. The fan letters from white listeners and hate mail from racists, he said, both made clear what was going on: he was bringing in more listeners and different listeners than he or KXLW had expected. Soon white kids wanted to join the crowd at the shows that Burks promoted on air.

He presented events at Club Riviera, bills popular with the Black audience the Riviera skewed to, though not exclusively. Unusually for St. Louis in the 1940s, the club did not restrict by race and in fact included the significant words "everybody welcome" in advertisements. In November of 1947, Burks announced a free show for teenagers at Club Riviera, featuring Cab Calloway, trumpeter Cootie Williams (capitalizing on his hit "Cowpox Boogie"), Italian American shouter Frankie Laine, and singer Dinah Washington. The club could hold fifteen hundred, but when three thousand Black teenage fans showed up hours early, traffic was blocked and a kerfuffle erupted. "They broke down the doors, windows, tables and chairs and left the place a wreck," reported the *Globe-Democrat*. Forty-year-old bandleader Calloway sat in a parked cab for half an hour before he dared push his way inside. Burks was greeted like a visiting dignitary, all but mobbed by thousands of fans, said the newspaper.[19]

The show specifically celebrated, and hoped to mobilize, the growing teenage audience, young fans not allowed in most St. Louis nightclubs. In the *Globe-Democrat* archives a photo shows an all-Black crowd packed tight and smiling for the camera under the Riviera marquee, a group portrait of a gathering power. They may have scared poor Cab Calloway, but there's nothing but calm joy on their faces.

Chuck Berry surely knew some who were there that afternoon, and he would have understood the new social force represented by such a crowd. Sooner than he knew, the white kids far outside the picture frame would take the center, and when *that* picture was developed it would show a mass of white faces. But Berry remembered how it was when integrated audiences were the exception, and the musicians and their audience alike were Black.

"Black people were buying records. Black people were always buying records a lot," he once lectured a white interviewer.

"The first records that were out were black, they were made of black material. The only thing that wasn't black was the label."[20] As his voice rose, he expanded on his theme. Labels, *they* could be white, red, yellow, he averred, but the music was none of those things. "The grooves, they are black and the black people were buying them. Don't you be fooled by that! They were buying everything, they were doing everything." He reached a sermon pitch. The only reason Blacks didn't control the market was because even with so many Black artists, there were so many more white consumers.

But he remembered an earlier time. "Don't think that just the whites bought records and listened to music."

AROUND THE TIME BERRY AND JOHNNIE JOHNSON WERE establishing themselves in East St. Louis, a young man was hustling his rhythm and blues band into a Clarksdale, Mississippi, studio. Ike Turner was recording for the LA-based Modern label, and this was a big-enough deal that Modern's cofounder, Joe Bihari, had come to Clarksdale to watch.

It was Bihari who had lined up the room for the session, but the Hungarian Jewish entrepreneur hadn't realized the implications of booking a band of roughneck African Americans in a studio in the white part of this Mississippi town. The way Turner put it later, "There weren't no n*****s supposed to be across that side of the railroad track."

A mob descended on the building. "The white folks came into the studio there and tore all the wires out of the walls and ripped them up. They told Joe Bihari, 'Don't you know that us white folks don't associate with these n*****s? What the hell do you think we fought the Civil War for?'" To which Bihari responded, "I don't know what you fought it for, but you lost."[21]

Briskly after that, Bihari left town, and Turner and his band, the Kings of Rhythm, were driving up Highway 61 to St. Louis. Ike had a sister there, and now seemed like a good time for visiting. Upon arrival, the Kings of Rhythm took a liking to the region.

To Turner, St. Louis was a jazz town, and he was a thrasher. The place was an opportunity nobody had yet figured—it wasn't Chicago, the musical mecca farther up the same highway, but it wasn't Clarksdale either. He was going to become big in this new place or die trying, and the first prospect soon happened while the second, through no fault of his own, somehow did not.

Turner's ears were tuned in Clarksdale, where he had become a talent scout for small labels, steering B. B. King, Howlin' Wolf, and others to record deals. He was also a DJ, playing blues and country music side by side. He had vision. In East St. Louis he focused on being a keyboardist, guitarist, and bandleader, and he used his band to construct a hard-edged sound that cut blues guitar and boogie-woogie to the frame of a pop song.

Turner's hearing was oddly binaural: he was listening way up close, able to tell when somebody was flubbing a note or playing out of tune, micromanaging musicians to a tyrannical degree. Yet simultaneously he was listening as if from a distance, ready to throw it all away and start over, ready to pick up a new gimmick or toss out a key member with a shrug. Often while his band played a show in East St. Louis, Turner was in the back room throwing dice. But listening. With Turner everything mattered, and nothing was so important that it couldn't be trashed and scrapped for parts.

One place they called home was the Fireworks Station, a blues stage that welcomed the Kings of Rhythm with open arms. According to Jimmy "Popeye" Thomas, a singer with the group, the place smelled good. "Oh, shit, man, funky. Hot. Fun. Total fun," he recalled. "Fish, hamburgers and fish be smellin', funk be flying. Dance floor in the middle, music be loud and hot."

The band drank a lot. The way Thomas told it (to writers Bill Greensmith and Celia Huggins), "Them cats could put away alcohol, man. Vodka. They used to love vodka. That was their drink. You couldn't smell it, because Ike would fine them if he knew they were drinking. Although he knew they were drinking they would still hide it."[22]

Jesse Knight was a young bassist in the group; Ike called him Junior. Junior tried to run with the older guys, but he was struggling, falling asleep on the bandstand. Once they had a gig outside East St. Louis, at a place with trash piled by the bar next to the bandstand. "Garbage cans, where they dump the lemon peels and soda tops and shit," said Thomas.

"We was up there playing, Junior on the end, drunk, noddin', playin'. He'd wake up and Ike would be giving him a dirty look." Junior tried, he tried joking about it and messing with somebody in the crowd, do a little dance, hoping that would bring him to life. "Anyway, he knew he was gonna get fined, because he knew Ike had pinned him, but he was still trying to put on a brave face and he couldn't, and he fell asleep again."

If you could have seen him, laughed Thomas. "It was funny because we was in the middle of this number and everybody was cookin'." Ike *could* see him. "And Ike kept looking at him, standing there, dirty look. 'Just watch this motherfucker, watch this crazy motherfucker—don't, don't touch him.'" Singer and pianist Fred Sample tried to wake Junior up, but he was unconscious—still playing, but unconscious. "Wasn't missing no notes. Then crash!" Turner had lifted him and dropped him upside down in the garbage can. "Legs in the air, bass over behind the bar, shit feeding back, everybody falling out laughing. Now, we got to help him up out of the garbage can, put him back onstage. Crazy. He just couldn't handle it."

These guys were skinny hungry, and Turner worked the group until they were concise. Little Willie John, a rhythm and blues singer, wanted to take them on the road, but Turner felt he was making too much money in East St. Louis to head out anytime soon.

Having been a talent scout in Mississippi, and knowing many of the key independent-label players, Turner was always thinking about the next deal. Blues singer Little Milton observed him lining up money, arranging stuff, things nobody in the band quite had a handle on. "He was like the brain thing."

Many of the band members lived together in a dwelling on Virginia Place that they called the House of Many Thrills. After playing at a club, and then somewhere after that, they invited all the women to come over. Turner: "Guys used to come by and they'd know their women or wives were in there. They'd be mad, and take a shotgun and—boom!—shoot at the side of the house."[23] Once they drove on, the dudes' only problem was that they had to turn at a corner in order to drive back the way they had come. By which time Turner and the band would have run out their back door, hopped a fence, and lined the next street to form a shotgun firing line. First they'd shoot out the tires of the guy's car, then they'd drag him out of the vehicle.

In the middle years of the 1950s, Berry and Turner competed with one another for regional primacy. Sure, Little Milton and Albert King were living and playing in the area, "but they was, excuse me, little shit compared to Ike and I," Berry explained. "We was the biggest shit around."[24]

They were an interesting set of contrasts. Turner's dad was kidnapped and lynched by a white Mississippi mob when Ike was eight; he was a product of Jim Crow society and viewed success within the Black community as his surest route to survival. Berry had seen plenty of racism, but he was a product of a far more fluid, and urban, culture. He was drawing whites into the Cosmo and pondering where that might lead. Turner was focused on the blues, testing its essence with blasts of speed and electricity; Berry was listening to the radio, drawing from diverse influences.

The big money was in St. Louis. But when the blue laws shut down the bars there at two a.m. on weekend nights, East St. Louis burned on and on. And so these bands, chased by their young Black and white fans, would play in St. Louis—sometimes as many as three paying gigs in one night. Battles of the bands, battles for the St. Louis women. The race to hit those three bookings was deranged: "We go to one gig, man, unload, everybody grab a piece of shit, stick it on the wall, PA things. In fifteen minutes we'd have the whole thing set up and cook, I mean be ready to burn," Jimmy Thomas remembered. Then on to the next one, and the next, and then they would head across the river.

You might imagine after that much sweat that folks would be ready to call it a night. Instead, a caravan squared up: Blacks and whites, musicians getting into their Cadillacs, and frat boys and cooks and hillbillies and whatnot all honking behind.

"We used to line up, man, like maybe fifty cars of kids," recalled Turner. "As far as you could see was cars. . . . It would cost 15 cents to cross the toll bridge to East St. Louis, man, we would get up to fifty, maybe sixty miles per hour, and all of us would just go straight through the toll. Nobody paid."[25]

It was glorious, said Thomas. "It's a wonder we didn't kill ourselves, we used to drive like maniacs through St. Louis, man, across them bridges and things at night. Fuck, it was like madness."

5

OH, MAYBELLENE!

THE VEILED PROPHET WAS AGELESS: HIS FACE HIDDEN BEHIND A beaded mask, he seemed ancient and unknowable. The Veiled Prophet *parade*, however, was exactly seventy-six years old in 1954. And as St. Louis geared up for the annual spectacle, civic leaders were planning a few big changes to the celebration.

On each of the twenty parade floats would be mounted a generator, freeing the parade from having to tap into streetcar lines for electricity. Planners also announced they were seeking a fresh theme in hopes of increasing interest among young people, settling on one emphasizing music heard in the city. So that fall, when approximately 550,000 lined the seven-mile route, parade-goers were called on to applaud the theme "The Veiled Prophet Salutes the Municipal Opera."[1]

A longtime underground tradition ran parallel to the parade, popular among kids from the 1930s onward. Robert Tooley, den superintendent of the Veiled Prophet organization, recalled it later for a historian. "Every confectionery in the city I think stocked peashooters before the parade," Tooley remembered. "That way you'd get these peashooters and these dried peas and you could shoot them at the floats and, hell, when we tore those old trailers apart I'll bet you we found, gee-whiz, hundreds of thousands of dried peas between the boards of the trailers."[2]

In 1954, the Veiled Prophet parade offered the youth of St. Louis floats honoring *The Mikado* and *Naughty Marietta*.

Across the Mississippi River in East St. Louis, a ten-minute drive and a world away from the Prophet, Chuck Berry's audience was growing. He was surprised to find white folks composing as much as 40 percent of the Club Cosmopolitan crowd.

As he refined his act, Berry relied on what he'd learned about the local community. Along with swing, hillbilly music was the sound he heard most often around St. Louis. But swing, he could tell, was on the way out, while country was creating identity for people who were just beginning to think of themselves as needing an identity.

The Delmore Brothers string band all but wrote the anthem with 1946's "Hillbilly Boogie," its lyrics celebrating a new type of neighbor: "a fella from Alabama way / he plays the blues in a different sort of way / he's got no piano going eight to the bar / but he picks out the boogie on his old guitar / he plays the hillbilly boogie in a lowdown way." Black music—the blues, the eight-to-the-bar left hand—was crossing over into country, and with the advent of electric guitars it would ramp up even more.

A tune from 1950 came out of nowhere to make the point. Arkie Shibley was a country singer from Arkansas playing in the shipyard town of Bremerton, Washington, in a honky-tonk called the Peedle Weezer. Shibley sang a new song called "Hot Rod Race," about an epic car chase across Southern California, and when it got a great response he put it out as a single himself. "Hot Rod Race" is a Dust Bowl talking blues told by a guy who pulls out of San Pedro in his Ford one night, "ripping along like white folks might," when he's challenged to a race. It was raw and wrong and went to number five on the *Billboard* country chart.

Hillbilly boogie was a sound and increasingly a culture just like jump boogie was on its side of the racial divide. And by the mid-1950s, it expressed itself in numerous ways. Around St. Louis and just north of East St. Louis, "hillbilly parks" were on the rise, recreation areas where families could grill hamburgers, sit in their cars and watch a movie, and hear country stars playing outdoors. Johnny Rion, a local country radio celebrity, had a chain of hillbilly parks in Illinois and Missouri in the 1950s, where Lefty Frizzell, the Wilburn Brothers, Hank Snow, and others performed.

Berry—a student of the radio, always listening—started to think about it in an almost mechanical way: *to play music for more people, find out what they want to hear.* But of course there were already places for Blacks to play, other places for whites; there were radio shows for country music, other shows for rhythm and blues. Berry's radical act was to have a laugh by pretending distinctions didn't matter. "If you ever want to see something that is far out," he said, "watch a crowd of colored folk, half-high, wholeheartedly doing the hoedown barefooted."[3] Berry saw this as just the beginning.

He inserted what he termed "fictitious impressions" of white folks into his delivery. Bearing down on certain words, he got a country feel across: "I stressed my diction so that it was harder and whiter," he said. In fact he seems to have had strategies behind all the music he was performing at the Cosmo. The balladry of Nat King Cole enticed him, but he used the same word again, *diction*, to describe how he made his presentation of a ballad feel authentic—interestingly not a musical term, but a word related to talking or being understood. He was aiming to create a rhetoric of sentimentality. He loved the blues too, but knew he had to find a process for communicating them, code-switching, choosing consciously to "deliver the down-home blues in the language they came from, Negro dialect." Key to getting a song over was positioning himself in various cultural traditions, and it started, he said, with his voice, the sound of words and the weight he put on them and where they fell around the beat. "It was my intention to hold both the black and the white clientele by voicing the different kinds of songs in their customary tongues," he wrote. Paul Laurence Dunbar could not have put the point any more clearly.

Meanwhile, his guitar playing turned more adventurous and was itself becoming increasingly rhetorical. In 1954 he was playing full choruses without repeating things. He and Johnnie Johnson were conversing in their solos, seizing on a pause in the other's play to jump in with an aside, or to pounce on what the other had just said and flip it in a different direction, in a back-and-forth that itself became a set piece in the show. And sitting in the middle of the stage, looking out at the audience while sharing his disbelief at the antics, was drummer Ebbie Hardy. When he laughed, he flashed an outsized crooked tooth; Hardy was a stand-in for the audience, grounding their uncertainty. He didn't necessarily know what was coming next either, and if it was okay with him, it was probably okay for everybody else too.

THE PIANO PLAYER WAS NO EFFUSIVE FRONT MAN, AND HIS default setting was to get along. He didn't want to lead; he wanted to survive and play the music he liked. That was it.

The guitar player, though, he had things in mind. He wanted to make records, as the unsatisfying experience in the Cubans had shown. He wanted to squeeze feelings out of the audience and have their eyes on him. He wanted to take over the act and couldn't think of a good reason not to. And neither could Johnson.

"Chuck was a hustler. He had a car; he was more of a talker than I was. He could get jobs. If he could get jobs, why not name the band after him?" was the way Johnson framed it.[4]

Almost like he was trying to talk himself into it.

"I could see Chuck taking over," said Johnson with a palpable shrug, "but that's his personality type."

The crowds were good and the waters were still, and Berry was inclined to do something about that. The trio was still making that twenty-six dollars plus tips and splitting it all three ways, which could amount to a whole lot more than twenty-six dollars divided by three on a good night. And on one particular good night, it was Berry who went through the room and collected the tips. When he was done, he didn't say anything more about it.

Berry gave the others a ride home. Hardy was dropped off first, the quiet, beaten-down drummer—he got out without a word. Then on to Johnson's place, with Berry looking straight ahead, mouth shut. Johnson was staring at the driver in profile.

"Don't you have some money for me?" he asked.

"I don't know what you're talking about."

"I know you got that tip money."

Berry got a dead walleye look on his face, one that many others would observe in the years ahead.

In his adolescence Johnson had been a brawler, fighting not for kicks but from a rage that he took out on others—he beat one fellow almost to death with a railroad spike, and another time split a stranger's nose with a horseshoe, blood spilling everywhere. Johnson scared himself and at the age of fourteen had turned to the piano as a way to keep out of trouble.

Berry was looking at him now, saying, "They came to see me, not you. Nobody cares about you."

Johnson didn't raise his voice. He just said, "I know you're new to this scene, but we are a trio and we're gonna split the tips three ways."

A period of staring followed these words. Then Berry pounced out of his car, announcing, "You want the money, come and take it!"

Perhaps he had mistaken Johnson's quiet manner as an admission of defeat. Johnson climbed out of the car and leaned into the guitarist. Berry threw a punch that didn't connect, and Johnson pushed him into a fence, pinning him by the throat. Now Berry looked startled: "We fighting!" he shouted.

"Damn right we fighting. Give me my money," said Johnson. Berry quickly handed over two-thirds of his take, for Hardy and the pianist. Johnson said they didn't have that kind of trouble again.

Tommy Stevens made a play for Berry again in 1954, offering him four nights a week at the Crank Club, a spot just a short walk from where Chuck's parents lived. He played there billed as "Chuck Berryn," with a band of his selection, before Johnson and Joe Lewis lured him back to the Cosmo.

The trio was now playing around the wider area, and Berry had a comfort level onstage that let him try things out on a trusting audience. The country dance songs, for sure. But that just flung the gates open, and in his generous spirit he then presented everything, as someone who was exhaling the world he absorbed from the radio and records.

A music journalist asked him how audiences responded to his shows in the 1950s, and he said,

> There's a great span in music, and variety I cherish. When you go to hear jazz, very often that's all you hear. Same thing with other types. But if you like all music, then variety adds to the performance.
>
> We'd do "Day-O," by Harry Belafonte, "Jamaica Farewell," then jump back with some Muddy, then some sweet Nat.

BELAFONTE, WATERS, AND COLE, COMMANDING BLACK VOICES bringing all of America into their house of music.

Tellingly, there was only one song he wouldn't play in the clubs. "No spirituals, though. I always say, when you sin, go ahead and sin. When you ask forgiveness, you know—keep it separate!"[5] In that explanation of what he liked to play—hillbilly and blues, Caribbean picaresque and a lover's ballad—is the world he wanted you to hear *him* into: a generous place for feeding your hungers, a place where there was no shame in nourishment.

There were lounges featuring blues shouters in one part of town, and honky-tonks to hear pedal steel guitars elsewhere. They were for adults, and effortlessly were they divided, formally or by custom, along racial lines. But there was a place where you could hear all kinds of music, and it was the room of the house where the radio was playing. The radio stoked Berry's sense of what was possible in America.

Toddy had a major role in shaping his thinking about performance. He didn't bring her to the Cosmo, but at other places in that moment she watched and gave him her thoughts. Being from Mississippi, he explained, she was able to turn his focus toward "theories regarding racial tactics, that some whites seem to still favor."[6] He says this in his elegant, indirect way, but the words are easy to unpack: she taught him how to speak to white people.

There was value in keeping the audience growing and diverse—financial reward, for starters. And Berry clearly noted how white teenage audiences were becoming a social force capable of carrying the music to a broader audience. He credited his southern-born wife for helping him strategize a connection with white listeners and helping him see the symbolic value of youth culture. She was, he declared, "the greatest cause of my being able to reach the level of success that had and has come to me so far."

In May 1955 Berry drove to Chicago. Later, he sometimes made it sound like it was his first visit, other times that he'd hitchhiked or "hoboed" there before. Either way, it was a natural destination. St. Louis was a great blues town, but Chicago was bigger, and Chicago had Muddy Waters. The first time he heard the singer and guitarist, Berry said, "he cracked open my soul to everything he said in his songs. I felt like I knew him."[7]

Now Berry wanted to meet him.

He wanted to meet Waters in the hope that the recording star could give him advice about following in his footsteps. So he drove to Chicago with his high school friend Ralph Burris in his red Ford Country Squire station wagon. The friends caught a few performers that weekend, but Waters was the one that mattered, and after watching him Berry went up and told him he was a musician too. He asked the totemic Waters if he would help him get a recording contract. Waters thought a minute, perhaps wondering if he was making a mistake recommending this stranger to his own label.

Waters said the visit happened at the Dew Drop Lounge, where he had a regular Sunday matinee gig. He gave Berry the address to Chess Records and told him that the office opened at nine, so get there at ten, when Leonard Chess would arrive. "Tell Leonard Chess I sent him there!" Waters said.

Chess Records had only recently rented space in a one-floor brick building at 4750 South Cottage Grove Avenue. Berry waited from a store across the street, and when the guy in a suit he figured to be the boss approached, Berry made his move before the gruff label head made it through the front door. Chess listened right there, never sitting down for a full-on meeting. He suggested that Berry come back with a recording that showed what he was about. That was all the encouragement the man from St. Louis needed, and he promised he would soon return.

Berry, Johnson, and Hardy hastily recorded a four-song tape that included a rattling, fast hillbilly number they featured in their Cosmo sets, "Ida Mae," based on a traditional fiddle tune called "Ida Red." Johnson was skeptical about making a record and was doing it as much to humor Berry as because he thought something might come of it. He had gotten this far thinking that life at any time was as good as it was likely to get. "If he wanted to make a record, I wouldn't stand in his way," the pianist said.[8]

But Berry was intent on getting back to Chicago, and within days he drove up again. The name on the tape he handed over: CHUCK BERRYN. Leonard Chess and his brother, Phil, thought that was his real name.

Interestingly, rumors circulated for years that Berry also approached other labels in Chicago. Johnson said he visited Vee-Jay Records, a Black-owned independent a few steps from Chess, where Jimmy Reed, the Spaniels, and the Staple Singers had recorded. Phil Chess also said there was a time when Berry was exploring other options. "We thought he'd never come back. And he came back. He was at Mercury and they turned him down. And then he went across the street to Vee-Jay at that time. They turned him down. And he came to us."[9]

The first time Berry met him, Leonard Chess had remained standing, going through his mail, politely hearing the guy out. When Berry returned with his demo tape, Chess was sitting down. He focused on what he called the "hillbilly tune," something different that might make a connection. Chess set up a recording session for Berry's group: May 21, 1955.

WHEN BERRY, JOHNSON, AND HARDY STEPPED INTO UNIVERSAL Recording Studios, they were in the most technologically advanced studio any of them had yet set foot in. Maybe that impressed them. Perhaps they were impressed by who else had recorded there. Just days before, Duke Ellington had come by, and a few months before that Bo Diddley had cut his debut, "Bo Diddley" and "I'm a Man," at Universal for Chess, that single now climbing the R&B charts. Muddy Waters himself had made his most famous records right there, and in a few weeks another of Berry's idols, Nat King Cole, was scheduled to come by.

But what should have impressed them more than any of this was that Universal was where Jerry Murad and the Harmonicats had recorded "Peg o' My Heart." Some recording sessions change the direction of the music business. Others create hit records that top the charts for weeks. And then there are sessions that are looked back on with a shocked expression, if they are remembered at all, with a face that says, "How did they ever cut that?" "Peg o' My Heart" was all of this and more.

The Harmonicats were a trio of mouth organ virtuosi, two-thirds of which had broken off from Borrah Minnevitch's Harmonica Rascals in the 1940s to pursue their fortune on the Chicago nightclub circuit. They sought to record a sentimental Irish number they had played to great success at Helsing's Vodvil Lounge in Chicago but were having a hard time lining up the cash to pay for studio time. Finally, Universal's founder, Bill Putnam, cut them a break, taking a percentage of whatever might come from the session. "Peg o' My Heart" was recorded early in 1947; the Harmonicats had gone to the studio on the forty-second floor of the Civic Opera Building late at night, after playing a show.

Putnam had a notion. He walked down the hallway to the men's washroom, surfaced in marble tile. Placing a speaker in the space, and then a microphone before it, Putnam recorded the chord, bass, and chromatic lead harmonicas and guitar from down the hall as they played "Peg." The chord harmonica, up close to its own microphone, sounded dry, while the echo from the bathroom, miked and played back in the studio, added a thick layer of emotional distance. When the song was released in April, it instantly turned heads. "Peg" provided no fixed sense of place, for the Harmonicats one moment sounded like they were right in your lap and then suddenly were jamming from a distant, misty lake.

The inventor of the recording machine, Thomas Edison, was fixated on making high-quality likenesses of original sounds. And for decades that compulsion was the underpinning of the record industry. Until the Harmonicats met Bill Putnam, more or less, records were expected to be a literal rendering of the sounds made in a room. But the very room evoked by "Peg" was a funhouse, and the sounds were a joyfully shifting experience. When it was released, the press was full of early reports of flying saucers. Putnam hired an airplane to fly over Chicago and drop cardboard discs that looked like his record on the heads of unsuspecting citizens.

"Peg o' My Heart" was the first commercial recording to use echo creatively and commercially—a major step forward in the idea that a record could utilize sounds that nobody had heard before. It was bound to happen for somebody; Jerry Murad and friends were just the right harmonicas at the right time. It was an accident. The song was number one on the charts for weeks. Putnam and the Harmonicats showed how much a record could be its own manifest thing—call it art, call it novelty, but either way they were getting out of Helsing's Vodvil Lounge, and the checks did not bounce once they started raining down.

Soon Chess would build its own proper studio and gain a deserved reputation for sonic excellence. But they hadn't earned it as of May 1955, and so the Chess brothers beat a path to Putnam's place.[10]

Whatever else Chess and Putnam had in common, both recognized the trending power of artifice. Muddy Waters, Chess's moneymaker, is celebrated as a voice of unimpeachable authenticity. But it does no disrespect to his music to point out that he also first registered to many listeners as a novelty—his electric guitar sound arrived with little context, so jump in and ride. Not fake, but concocted. "Bo Diddley" and "I'm a Man" featured a reverb effect on the guitar and an echo on

Diddley's voice that supersized his bluster. Both shouted that this cartoon had taken over your radio.

Now entering Putnam's space were three guys from St. Louis. Berry arrived with a blond Gibson ES-350T arch-top hollow body. He huddled with Leonard Chess, and Chess turned his entire focus to the hillbilly song that Berry had included on his demo. It was built on the outline of a fiddle number that western swing star Bob Wills had recorded, "Ida Red." Berry had reworked it and was singing the name "Ida Mae" in order to distinguish his song from its origins.

Chess brother Phil was at the session, helping the band set up, buzzing around. Musicians on the label could go years without knowing which Chess brother was in charge, but Berry, an astute judge of where the power was in a room, kept his focus on Phil's older brother. "Leonard Chess was the whole of Chess Records," Berry declared. "Phil was an associate, he was an aide, and he was on salary. Leonard was the big kingpin. And it was Leonard's from the beginning and until he died."[11]

Also in the room was Willie Dixon, a centerpiece of the Chicago blues scene whom the brothers relied on to manage a session from the floor. Dixon was a kangaroo-sized man who played a stand-up bass, and his embrace of the instrument was a scene unto itself, Berry recalled. Dixon brought a booming, material sound to the session, but the other three didn't know him, and his presence slowed things down as they tried to get a definitive take.

Leonard Chess was in a small side room looking through a glass window at the musicians as he controlled an Ampex monaural quarter-inch tape recorder. He had no musical background but good ears and vivid communication skills. Chess noted that "Ida Mae" was a problematic title, first because it sounded too rural for the label's big-city market. Also problematic, it did little to obscure the connection to the popular Wills song. Chess wanted a new number, not a cover whose royalties they would have to share with others. So everybody in the studio started kicking names around for what they were about to record.

They needed a name with the same amount of syllables to fit the beat. Berry says he instantly came up with "Maybellene," thinking back to a children's book he knew about a cow. An account accepted by others in the room came from Johnson, who recalled Leonard spotting a bottle of Maybelline brand mascara in the studio, asking, "Why don't we call the damn thing Maybelline?" and then altering the spelling to avoid a trademark violation lawsuit.

With a fresh name and a day ahead of them, they faced a song that no one knew quite how to recast. The biggest problem was outside the room: how to arrange a number that blurred the lines between country and rhythm and blues, that was neither Black like an Ike Turner record nor white like a Hank Williams one. Was it a goof, a parody? Was it for Muddy Waters's grown-up fans or for teenagers or . . . who? Here was a song with numerous possible distinct audiences, and that right there made it unlike most songs. A category fallacy could kill it, and Leonard wasn't going to spend unlimited time in the studio to plumb its depths. Phil Chess himself admitted they were flying blind. "You have to remember, we didn't have anything to compare it to. This was an entirely different kind of music."

Leonard fussed and called for retakes as he tried alterations that didn't bring it into any better focus. One thing Berry instantly understood from observing him was his innate ability to explain himself across cultural borders. Leonard and his brother had been born in Motol, Poland, and spoke Yiddish in the household. Only after they arrived in Chicago in 1928 did the boys learn English. One word more than any other, Leonard found, helped him get his point across in the studio: *motherfucker*.

Motherfucker was Leonard's placeholder and punctuation mark. It was what he said when he was displeased or wanted to keep things moving or when he was excited or didn't know what else to say. *Motherfucker*s filled the room as Ida Mae became Maybellene. They did thirty-six takes of the song, with Berry standing and sitting, with Berry altering the twang of his voice, with Berry down the hallway singing from the bathroom. One time Leonard came into the studio himself, waved Ebbie Hardy aside, and beat his drumsticks on a phone book to see if *that* was what the song was missing. It was not. Motherfucker!

The group took short breaks, during which Johnson occupied himself with a slow piano blues that contrasted with the blazing beat they were wrestling. But after three dozen takes, when Leonard decided whatever they were going to get they had gotten already, Chess noted the obvious: Were they ready to cut the other song, the B side, of the record they were trying to make?

The band hadn't planned that far ahead. Suddenly the jam John-son had served up during a previous break, which may have been a song they had played at the Cosmo, was sounding pretty good—a morning-moaner that put a listener in a room where the molecules of smoke and dust had seized up, a grainy photo of eternity. How about *that* thing? somebody asked.

Berry was adept at turning out rhymes over a blues roll, improvising a new tune on top. And that's how the blues song they played, "Wee Wee Hours," came into focus, inspired by Joe Turner's "Wee Baby Blues" and finished in fifteen minutes. It has some of the burnish of a Nat King Cole ballad, and a lot of the nothing-to-lose slog of Charles Brown's piano blues. Johnson called it "the first song we did, Chuck and I, that was all our own."

They celebrated with an order of burgers and a flurry of hand-shakes, and then came paperwork for Berry to sign in Chess's office. The Missourians piled into his red station wagon with the mattress in back and headed home.

Berry, Johnson, and Hardy fell back into their regular gig at the Cosmo. On July 5, a song titled "Maybelline," listing Berry as composer, was registered with the US Copyright Office of the Library of Congress.

Leonard Chess, meanwhile, went out on the road, making agree-ments with distributors, bartering with DJs to get the music on the air. He took "Maybellene" with him on a trip to New York, playing it for influential DJ Alan Freed, whose *Rock & Roll Party* was heard in mar-kets around the country. Freed's show was listened to closely by record people because it routinely introduced Black music to white ears.

Freed didn't just play the record Chess gave him; he was bumper to bumper, side to side with it, spinning "Maybellene" for two hours straight one night and giving it an emphatic send-off. "Maybellene," released in July and buoyed by airplay Freed and then others gave it, elevated fast.

Phil Chess was visiting his daughter at summer camp in Wiscon-sin. He heard the song on the radio and rushed to call his brother. Leonard cut him off. "You better get your butt back here," he barked. "We got so much order—we don't have any records."

Chuck and friends, late 1940s.

Harry Davis/Bill Greensmith collection

Young Charles, late 1930s.

Harry Davis/Bill Greensmith collection

Henry Berry's van. *Harry Davis/Bill Greensmith collection*

Martha Berry, Chuck's sister.

*Harry Davis/
Bill Greensmith collection*

Chuck's sister Lucy Berry.

Harry Davis/Bill Greensmith collection

**Chuck Berry in
St. Louis, late 1940s.**

*Harry Davis/
Bill Greensmith collection*

Portrait, 1948.

Harry Davis/Bill Greensmith collection

CASTLE BALL-ROOM

AUGUST 27th, 1949

SYLVIA BOONSHAFT FOUNDATION
OF ST. LOUIS

Presents

"HARLEM IN ST. LOUIS"

Produced and directed by Mort S. Silver

- - PROGRAM - -

— Part 1 —

Number 1 — OVERTURE.."RAJAHS OF SWING"
Number 2 — MORT S. SILVER...CURTAIN INTRODUCTION
Number 3 — SHIRLEY AND LaVERN YOUNG...TAP SPECIALTY
Number 4 — BETTY DOUGLAS.............................PRIMA DONNA, "ONE KISS"
Number 5 — CHARLES E. BERRY...........................BLUES, ON HIS ELECTRIC GUITAR
(and his famous recitation)
Number 6 — IOLA NELSON, Our Famous Torch Singer..........."BABY WON'T YOU PLEASE COME HOME"
Number 7 — JANET ROSSEN, Child Star.........................." 'A' YOU'RE ADORABLE", SONG AND DANCE
Number 8 — FRED BLOCK...IN HIS OWN COMICS AND
SONG AND DANCE INTERPERTATION
Number 9 — LUCY ANN BERRY — Mezzo Soprano, (Prima Donna)......................."MY HERO"
Number 10 — DON SHAEFFER.."LITTLE WHITE LIES"
Number 11 — EDITH MAXVILLE — Hill-Billy from Arkansas...."I'M GOING BACK TO WHERE I COME FROM"
Number 12 — MORT SILVER..EMSEE — COMMUNITY SING

— INTERMISSION —

— Part 2 —

Number 1 — RAJAHS OF SWING — OVERTURE
Number 2 — IOLA NELSON............................"CAN'T HELP LOVIN' THAT MAN OF MINE"
Number 3 — CHARLES E. BERRY...ELECTRIC GUITAR
Number 4 — BETTY DOUGLAS.............................JEALOUSIE, (PRIMA DONNA)
Number 5 — DON SHAEFFER...SO HELP ME
Number 6 — LUCY ANN BERRY.............................."VILIA", (Mezzo Soprano)
Number 7 — JANET ROSSEN.............................SPECIALTY TAP DANCE
Number 8 — MORT SILVER.."MAMMY" (EMSEE)
Number 9 — EDITH MAXVILLE, Our Hillbilly............."CAN'T MAKE A LADY OUT OF ME"
Number 10 — TEDDY RIDDLESPRINGER, King of Boogie Woogie.................THE CHILD WONDER
Number 11 — FRED BLOCK.................................COMEDIAN, SONG AND DANCE
Number 12 — THE YOUNG SISTERS..................................ELECTRIC BATONS

— FINALE —

MUSICAL DIRECTION...PROF CLIFFORD LAIRD

Thanks to Harry Weisman, Sylvia Boonshaft, Cecil Scott for their most sincere
and untiring efforts to make this a success, also those who have placed ads
in this program as well as Seidel Coal and Coke Co. for the ticket ad.

Charles Berry's
1949 debut program
for "Harlem in
St. Louis" revue.

*Harry Davis/Bill
Greensmith collection*

September 1952 publicity photo.

Harry Davis/Bill Greensmith collection

Themetta Berry.
Harry Davis/Bill Greensmith collection

In Harry Davis's
darkroom, early 1950s.
Harry Davis/
Bill Greensmith collection

September 1952.

Harry Davis/Bill Greensmith collection

Berry was walking past a tailor shop in the Ville when he heard the song playing from a storefront. Not wanting people to notice him listening, he kept walking back and forth on the sidewalk until the song was finished. Then he ran home and told his family.

And when the man known in the Ville as "Charles" and at the Crank Club as "Berryn" held his record in his hands, the name on it was "Chuck Berry." He tried to establish a distance between "Charles" and "Chuck Berry": "Chuck Berry, that means it's all music, because Chuck Berry is music. But Charles Berry is a man who has certain things that he wants to keep to himself," he explained later.[12]

"Maybellene" was the first of what he called "the car songs." It was "a yearning which I had since I was aged seven to drive about in a car. I first started driving at 17—one year earlier than I should have. It was my fascination for the roads, for driving, motoring, which prompted me to write those songs."[13]

Chuck Berry wasn't a hot-rodder, but he *was* a total gearhead, a rebel who saw technological expertise as the great leveler. You may have money, you may be white, but if you were up against somebody who knew how to make the most of their tools, you had a fight on your hands. And if you were up against Berry, you were going to lose. That's what "Maybellene" is about.[14]

The story is elemental. A poor man in a Ford with a V-8 engine racing a wealthy man in a Cadillac for the right to be with the woman who goes to the victor. Maybellene is the storyteller's girlfriend, but she loves the race.

The singer is jousting, but he's behind when his V-8 overheats, and he slows down to let a sudden cloudburst cool it off. There's something magical about this moment, the singer controlling nature and his materials. When this crafty wheelman spots the Cadillac struggling up the next hill, he makes his move. He catches her, end of song, Berry's guitar cooing in the fade-out as he's rolling in his sweet baby's arms.

It's a drive-in movie for all of America. Later, after everybody knew what Berry looked like, thoughtful writers would examine how, besides being a song about class pride, it was a song about racial equality. An ambitious, fast-thinking Black kid with gifts challenges assumptions of what could happen in America.

But at the time few knew who he was, and the song itself had a special rapport with the southern white consciousness. Weeks after it was released, a twenty-year-old white singer from Tupelo, Mississippi, put "Maybellene" in his show, Elvis Presley performing it live on the *Louisiana Hayride* radio broadcast August 20, 1955. "We only learnt it a couple of days ago," he told the Shreveport Municipal Auditorium crowd. "It's a song about . . . ," and he pauses, trying to explain it. "A song about . . . ," the audience is wondering now. "It goes something like this." And when he shouts, "Maybellene!" they start screaming because they had just learned Berry's song too, and they all knew what it was about.

Radio was voracious, playing more records than ever, and records stoked the ongoing transformation of an audience: young people were tuning in, eager to hear music from distant places, from people unlike themselves, when presented the opportunity.

There was a new fluidity, shaped by strangers. "Maybellene," a song about blurring white lines, marked this upheaval.

Simultaneous with its release in July 1955, the Sydney, Australia, *Morning Herald* reported a fireball falling from the sky and landing in Chicago. Six young children playing in their yard were nearly hit, said their father, Jim Gutillo. He described to a reporter "a blue thing with a yellow tail" landing at his feet,

> right in the middle of my kids. The children thought it was a message container from a flying saucer.
> I told them they had been reading too many comic books.

The meteor was accompanied by a noteworthy odor.[15]

Gutillo said he feared the impact would obliterate his family. However, all escaped injury, according to the newspaper. The kids were alright.

In his September 3, 1955, Rhythm–Blues Notes column, *Billboard*'s Paul Ackerman wrote, "The 'Maybellene' Sweepstakes shifted into high gear the past week." As labels raced to get competing versions out, Ackerman underscored a key sign of the record's importance: that an original song by a Black artist was doing better on the pop charts (number twelve that week) than the covers of it that were rushed out by white singers (Jim Lowe on Dot, Johnny Long on Coral). Berry's song had just topped the rhythm and blues chart. Ackerman also noted that jump boogie singer and saxophonist Big John Greer had an answer record out, "Come Back Maybellene."

At the same moment, *Cash Box*, a music-business trade journal, published a startling special editorial titled "What Is Pop?"[16] America's compartmentalized sense of itself was breaking open, and white Americans were forced to take at least fleeting glances at how others outside their immediate experience lived. "What is happening more and more in our national life is also happening in our music," *Cash Box*'s editorial voice declared.

The writer might have had in mind how 1954's Supreme Court ruling in *Brown v. Board of Education of Topeka* was, by the summer of 1955, reshaping American institutions large and small. Interstate travel was becoming a way for those interested in advancing racial equality to hold out for equal treatment under the law—why did people have to move to the back of the bus when they crossed a geographic line on a cross-country trip?

Cash Box acknowledged that the world was theirs too. In the world of record buyers, "An integration is taking place so that we are developing a taste which is a combination of all the regions of the United States rather than have different tastes kept exclusively for one area, one group of people."

The established practice of whites covering rhythm and blues songs and landing them in the pop charts disempowered Black labels and artists. Black creativity was used to move money into white pockets. New Orleans musician Dave Bartholomew put it as well as anyone could: "There was no way I could overcome that," he said. "That was actually a segregation move. It was actually the whites covering the black music."[17]

Cash Box: "Since the war there have been two distinct factors affecting our pop music." The first was country songs crossing into the pop fields. (That would have included the likes of Tennessee Ernie Ford's cover of Merle Travis's "Sixteen Tons" and Mitch Miller's smash "The Yellow Rose of Texas.") The other factor, noted the writer, "was the still continuing impact of Rock 'n Roll on the pop field." Black regional sounds were being embraced by the pop charts. And those sounds were here identified by a term unfamiliar to most Americans, even to many musicians who made the music in question: *rock & roll*.

Cover songs from marginalized fields were now taking the main stage, and after a period when folks like the Fontane Sisters and Pat Boone could make money with inferior versions of Black songs, the music was being embraced in its original form. By asking "What is pop?" the *Cash Box* writer was getting as close to asking "What is America?" as the magazine's readers would let it get in 1955, but the question remains a good one. If pop was formerly whatever white artists and labels took and repackaged and said it was, a new definition was now needed. *Cash Box* offered one: pop is America without borders.

> With no more physical frontiers left to conquer, it almost seems as though we have set out to conquer our regional frontiers, make the advantages of each part of our country available to all the others.
>
> This can only mean a greater appreciation of music and songs on the part of all our people and wider, expanding horizons for the music business as a whole.

Meanwhile, in August 1955, Emmett Till, a fourteen-year-old from Chicago, was murdered in Money, Mississippi, after a white woman fabricated the story that he had flirted with her.

In September, rising country music star Marty Robbins released his cover of "Maybellene."

What was pop? The sounds that had been shunted from the mainstream. The music finding a home in places where the folks who made it would still not be invited. "Maybellene" was in the top five on the pop charts by the fall of 1955, and none of the white acts who tried to ride his song could touch his success. Black acts were crossing over, and Chuck Berry was doing it in the boldest manner of all. Not with vocal group politeness and good manners; not with strings and impeccable musicianship, refinement and superb engineering. Not by representing himself as anything other than human, not a cartoon, not a clown. He wasn't trying to court you, please you, or reason with you, he was exactly like the singer in "Maybellene"—fixing to blow you away. There was no appeal, except for this: Follow me!

6

CHESSONOMICS

CHESS'S BUSINESS WAS BUILT ON HITS, AND BY FOLLOWING A HIT with fresh product while listeners still remembered the singer's name. The Chess brothers impressed on Berry their interest in recording a follow-up to "Maybellene." And so, in September 1955, Berry headed back to Chicago.

To be under the sign of Chess Records in the mid-1950s was to be touched by the Maxwell Street Market. It was a West Side gathering place, a nine-block open-air bazaar buttressed by retail shops. Maxwell Street ran east–west, and at the intersection of Maxwell and Halsted, the spindle of its havoc, much was for sale.

Starting in the 1880s the neighborhood around Maxwell Street was settled by eastern European Jews fleeing the pogroms. Peddlers sold from wooden carts, and the street turned into a gathering spot where deals were made. It became a congested thrum, especially on Sunday, after the Jewish Sabbath had ended. On Sunday the market was best navigated on foot, a loud, brash exchange place where diverse tongues were spoken.

By the 1920s the businesses around Maxwell Street were still largely Jewish-owned, but the people living there were increasingly

Black and Mexican. In the 1940s upwards of seventy thousand bargain hunters would visit on a given Sunday. Throughout much of the
twentieth century, Maxwell Street was a sensory overload, a smell that
hung in your nostrils, a soundbath, an emulsion stuck to the bottom
of your shoes. It rewired the creativity of the writers, musicians, and
artists who were drawn to the scene.

Art critic Jerry Saltz went there a lot growing up in Chicago in the
1960s. "It was a door to another world that was living parallel to ours
and—what's the word? *Adjoined*. There are adjoined rooms to life, and
the gates between them seemed to be lifted once every week. Sunday."[1]

> A tableful of mix-and-match brown shoes
> Cheese graters and egg beaters
> Girdles, neck braces, zippers
> Old bottles
> 78 rpm records
> Turtles
> Rusting carburetor parts

Things had been sold at one point, and then moved around and
sold again, and again. Years might go by but the stuff remained, and
here it finally landed on Maxwell Street, sold one final time.

Here's a job you can't do anymore. They had pullers on Maxwell
Street. Meaty figures who blocked foot traffic while picking off strays
from the human stream, shoving them in the direction of a rack of
suits or the entry to a jewelry shop. Hey, this was Chicago; pulling was
a union job (Retail Clerks Association). Pullers were just more proof
that on Maxwell Street, capitalism was a full contact sport.

The unofficial motto of the market was "We Cheat You Fair." And
though there were plenty who did not adhere to even that vague principle, what comes across in many accounts was an understanding that
the hustle and the deal were put into a great many words, and words
flowed in both directions between buyer and seller, and when it was
done nobody should claim too loudly they did not know what they
were getting.

In her short story "Dirt," Sandra Cisneros, who grew up in Chicago, described a family's Sunday trip to the market.[2] The narrator's

dad takes the family up a flight of stairs to a shoe store and engages in a long and brutal haggle between races. They go down the stairs, they eat, he comes back hurling insults and is insulted back, and at the end comes out with a pair of shoes. Bargaining was a form of culture; it was where rough edges were smoothed over and boundaries were abraded.

There are people who claim that Maxwell Street was the most integrated place in the segregated metropolis, full of Blacks, Mexicans, Jews, Greeks, Roma, all on the hunt for a discount. From difference came community, barriers and egos broken apart by the buck. Community building through combat. Everything was available for a price, and prices were always other than indicated.

Along the way, the street had become a testing zone for local blues musicians by the 1930s. A juke souk. Players were hired to stand outside a shop and let their music do the pulling. More often, they would park in any spot not covered by a cart, table, or stand and play for change. Big Charlie Jackson, Daddy Stovepipe, Robert Nighthawk, Jimmy Rogers, Little Walter, Honeyboy Edwards, Bo Diddley, and many more performed there on their way up or down.

And one Sunday in the early 1950s, before he was a household name, Muddy Waters looked across the waves of people all marketing their goods and spotted one head bobbing above the others, a guy he didn't know yet but could tell was somebody to know. It was Leonard Chess, selling records on Maxwell Street.

It made total sense. Before an artist arrived at Chess Records, they might very well have played on Maxwell. And once you recorded for Chess, they might find themselves metaphorically right back on Maxwell Street, bought and sold for the going rate of the moment.

Chess Records was molded around Maxwell Street's free-market brutal humanism. It informed how the brothers did business, and it informed how they made sound too. Leonard's dad, Yasef Czyz, had arrived from Motol, Poland, in December 1922. He Americanized his name to Joe Chess and, with a brother-in-law, went into the scrap trade, renting a cart and horse (three dollars a day) and beating Chicago's alleys, calling for junk they could resell to the glass and metal dealers. By 1935 Joe and his son Leonard had a business of their own, Wabash Junk Shop, at 2971 S. State Street. Eventually, when Leonard's younger brother, Phil, got involved in 1942, the name changed to Chess & Sons.

They created a market for tossed-off, disrespected things. They were not alone on Maxwell, where dead things were brought to life. Everything up for grabs; everything falling apart.

"It was free! Everybody was giving it away," remembers Jerry Saltz. "We were building a city and then selling it off as the scrap merchants. Each of us putting our part in it, together building this pre-cyberpunk *Blade Runner* existence, but it wasn't cold that way or dark that way— for one day a week it was like church for losers, outsiders who now were equal. Just for a day I could see my privilege for the first, maybe only time, when I was there. Like, whoa this is big. This is really big."

WHEN CHUCK BERRY RETURNED TO CHICAGO, TO PLAN HIS second single and make several important business decisions, he drove straight into the world of Maxwell Street.

His name was filed with the Library of Congress, documenting that he was the sole composer of a song spelled "Maybelline" on July 5, 1955. A revision was made on August 2, fixing the spelling and adding Russ Fratto and Alan Freed as composers. When Berry received his first royalty statement and saw their names as cowriters, he had questions.

Freed, well, he would have heard of Freed, who had helped make the song a hit. Whatever else there was to say about giving him a third of the songwriting royalties in exchange for introducing listeners to the song, there was pure business logic to paying someone to help you make more money.

Few, however, knew Russ Fratto. He was a card-playing pal of Leonard's and the landlord of Chess Records' building. He owned Victory Stationery, a print shop one door down on South Cottage Grove Ave. Unlike Freed, Fratto couldn't advance Berry's career.

A record business insider named Teddy Reig said that Fratto was connected to the Chicago underworld. "This guy was doing all the printing for the Chicago numbers racket," Reig said. "He was lending Leonard money, which led to the syndicate having a beef with Leonard." In order to square this disagreement, Reig said Chess extended Fratto a third of the writing credit for "Maybellene."[3]

Berry was working the math. Tim Gale, one of the few talent agents signing Black performers and putting them on the road, told Berry, "You can ride on this three years," meaning he had that long to sing "Maybellene" before he was history. Meanwhile, guys he'd never even met were taking two-thirds of the songwriting royalties for his song. There was a lot to learn in not a lot of time.

Freed became one of his teachers. His notoriety started in Cleveland in 1951, where on WJW Freed played music he had heard others call rock & roll, Black music that most listeners flagged as rhythm and blues. Soon he would blend white teenage sounds into his *Moondog House* radio shows and get a good reaction from his growing, racially mixed audience. He booked Paul Williams, Tiny Grimes, and the Dominoes in a concert he called the Moondog Coronation Ball, drawing at least six thousand mostly African Americans to a packed Cleveland Arena in 1952. Not long after the first act began, the Cleveland cops shut the ball down, and the first rock & roll concert in history also became the first rock & roll riot.

All around the country, old business networks were being lifehacked. Early in his career, Freed worked as a classical music DJ when he was approached by Leo Mintz, owner of the Record Rendezvous record shop, who offered Freed money to host a late-night radio program—one targeting the Black adults who filled Mintz's store. Small-business connections were crucial to getting ahead for DJs, independent labels, and musicians alike.[4]

In 1954 Freed moved his massively successful show to WINS in New York, where the Black and white music he was now fully playing side by side was heard by Black and white fans in growing numbers. He picked up an influential mentor: Morris Levy, a jazz club owner and label head with connections to the Genovese crime family. Levy was a businessman with contacts who could increase sales and get records played. His importance to the early growth of rock & roll was undeniable.

Freed wore gold-buttoned, penny-candy-colored plaid jackets; don't blame Levy for that. But in other ways, the older man guided the newcomer. Freed lived recklessly in the moment, making deals left and right and burning money at both ends, and Levy helped him hang on a little longer. Soon after the DJ first came to town, Levy told journalist Fredric Dannen, "The manager of WINS says, 'Moishe, we have a problem. Alan Freed's been in town a week now, and he's already given away a hundred and twenty percent of himself!' He had a lot of talent, but he was also a little *nuts*." Soon, Levy was managing Freed and taking 50 percent of what he earned beyond WINS.[5]

Levy found Freed a venue to present his first rock & roll show in Manhattan, an ice rink at Columbus Ave. and Sixty-Sixth St. They partnered in music publishing (a field Levy learned could be amazingly profitable). They even talked about starting a label together, which made sense: a DJ who "writes" songs, releases them on his own label, and then plays them on the air surely cuts out the need for a lot of middlemen. That one never came to pass.

They were among the first to recognize the economic possibilities of the music, and they were on the hunt for ways big and small to get paid. Freed's radio show was now called *Moondog's Rock & Roll Party*, until the blind, avant-garde street musician named Moondog sued for copyright infringement. Appearing in court with ragged floor-length robes, long hair, and a Viking helmet, the musician was able to show that he'd performed as Moondog since 1947, winning an injunction against Freed. WINS pressured their star DJ to come up with a new name.

Soon, Levy and Freed were spitballing what to retitle the franchise. "Alan was having a few drinks and bemoaning the fact that he had to come up with a new name," Levy recalled. "To be honest with you, I couldn't say if Alan said it or somebody else said it. But somebody said 'rock and roll.' Everybody just went, Yeah, *Rock and roll*." The phrase had been around the edges of pop music for a long time and was now moving to the center. Somebody was going to take credit. Say what you will about Levy and Freed, but they weren't newbies. So they incorporated in order to trademark the term *rock and roll*. Freed had heard the phrase years before in Mintz's record store in Cleveland, and it was shouted on the lyrics of blues and R&B discs Mintz sold, where it was used as a euphemism for fucking. It was preposterous: the blunt mobster and the loud-suited pitchman plotting over drinks to own rock and roll.

The plan went nowhere. The company they formed, Seig Music, filed a copyright notice, but it was instantly obvious that policing any claims on the term *rock and roll* in 1955 would be impossible, as the phrase was increasingly in common use.

In Cleveland, Freed had been visited by the owner of the small jazz label Royal Roost, a fellow named Jack Hooke. He wanted Freed to play Royal Roost's records. They hit it off, so much so that the DJ invited Hooke to manage his career. A few years later when Freed came to New York, Hooke handed the management of Freed over to Levy while continuing to work as a talent buyer for shows Freed promoted.

Hooke grew up in Brooklyn knowing the man who was now his partner in Royal Roost, Teddy Reig. The latter was a character who self-identified as a "jazz hustler." Reig was rotund, a great mambo dancer whose twin delights in life were good music and accumulating airspace between individuals and their currency. Lucky for him, the music business presented numerous ways to combine his passions.

In a small, remarkable autobiography, Reig sketched himself: "I'm sixty-five years old and never did a day's work," he boasted. "This business is still supporting me. I've been a hustler all my life, up to the point of death, at which time I split."[6] He was a product of the swing era; he put recording sessions together and loved bringing a new jazz record into the world. He didn't think much of the rock & roll crowd and didn't respect most of the guys who were catering to it.

One day an up-and-coming record producer named Bob Weinstock came out of a Manhattan jazz club when he noticed a black Cadillac drawing up to him, window down, and a voice saying, "Get in, kid." A football player and military police officer in the National Guard, Weinstock wasn't too worried, so he climbed into the back seat next to Reig.

"You're fucking up the jazz business," Reig began.

"What do you mean?" His complaint was that Weinstock was paying musicians union scale for recording sessions rather than screwing them and forcing them to record an extra song on the house. "Why should I fuck them?"

"Yeah but you're ruining the business."

"What business? Your business? Fuck you. Open the door and let me out."[7]

"Don't talk to me like that. You see the two guys sitting up front?" Reig asked. They were big and wore suits.

Weinstock screamed a few threats of his own, saying you can beat me now but you'll be dead tomorrow, and got out of the car.

They were immersed in jazz and show business connections and soon became good friends. Such folks would make the coming world of rock & roll possible.

In July of 1955, just as "Maybellene" was taking off, Leonard Chess called Berry in St. Louis. He said Jack Hooke was flying in to introduce himself and was bringing a management contract from the Gale Agency for Berry to sign. The paperwork promised $40,000 a year for three years, a bold deal in that era. Hooke and Reig would work on Gale's behalf to oversee his career, it was explained, and Reig would accompany Berry on the road, making sure the contract with the venue was observed correctly and ensuring that Berry was paid the proper amount.

In about a month of "Maybellene" taking off, Berry had been shot into a higher orbit. It was like he had gone to sleep counting dollar bills in the tip jar at the Cosmo and woke up having lost as much money (to Fratto and Freed) as he'd ever made. Then this stranger was flying in to greet him with a check for $40,000. The marginally paying music work he'd done for years suddenly was assigned a vastly different value. There were people and more people in the background, and sums moving around.

He needed to get comfortable playing shows for strangers. Hooke and Reig booked some quick tune-up gigs, including a week in Gleason's Musical Bar in Cleveland and three nights at the Copa Club in Youngstown. Color photos from Cleveland show Berry with a brand-new haircut and without the mustache he'd soon grow and never shave, playing a Kay Thin Twin guitar. His trousers are baggy and clash with the shoes. Behind him is a local band of white musicians who look fresh out of high school. It's August 1955: the bow-tie era of rock and roll. Berry had been making $20 a night in St. Louis and was getting $800 for the week at Gleason's club in Cleveland's "Little Harlem."[8]

There was a quick detour to Chicago to record, and then the band drove to New York City to play the Brooklyn Paramount Theatre.

Billed as "Alan Freed's First Anniversary Rock 'n' Roll Party," it was a weeklong celebration of his first year in New York. The Paramount was a four-thousand-plus-seat rococo movie palace in a busy intersection of downtown Brooklyn. The nightly lineup included vocal group the Cardinals, who had formed in the 1940s, and Nappy Brown, a singer with "Pitter Patter" on the rhythm and blues charts. There were new doo-wop acts the Harptones and Nutmegs, four scoops of vanilla from

Tennessee named the Four Voices, and a trombone-playing nightclub singer from Allentown, Lillian Briggs. Headlining was Tony Bennett, purveyor of the Great American Songbook and seeming quite adult, even then, in the context of Chuck Berry.

Putting a bunch of acts together on a bill wasn't itself new. Black promoters had sponsored "Jazz Cavalcades" on the West Coast since the mid-1940s. The Gale and Shaw agencies had billed all-day R&B events in the early 1950s. Morris Levy had put jazz bands on the road in package tours. Now he was sharing his experience with Freed, who was sharing his income with Levy. What was different was the racial and generational split of both the talent and the crowd. And the number of burgundy seats they needed to fill.

On September 8, opening the week of shows, a line of teens four deep reached around the block. Broadcasting his WINS program live from the Paramount, Freed stood on a fire escape and pled with listeners to *stop* coming to Brooklyn, because Flatbush was immobilized.

Teddy Reig viewed it from the street. "The kids came in and they tore the hall up like you never seen a hall torn up before in your life," he recalled. "They broke about 12 store windows, stole the suits." They cleaned out all the fancy furniture from the lobby and the Paramount's deluxe chrome water fountains.

Reig had lined up police.

> Didn't mean nothing. I had to go and get Italian hoodlums to break jaws. At one point, I'm sitting there minding my own business, and somebody yells, "Fight! Fight, Teddy, hurry!" I fly through there and I see a kid and a man, and I tried to break 'em up. The man started swinging at me, I threw three punches and broke his nose, closed his eye, he was bleeding like a pig. You know who it was? The treasurer for the Paramount chain.
>
> Everybody was doing *everything* up there: fucking, sucking, smoking, drinking.

REIG SAID, "WHEN WE PLAYED THE PARAMOUNT, I TOLD THE MANAGER, 'I don't want no money, all I want is the concession to fix the seats.'"[9]

The show was a tightly scripted affair, stage-managed by pros able to get ten acts on and off after a song or two each. Berry bought brown shoes and twenty-two-dollar rayon suits for his trio, and then realized that when playing five shows a day, it was good to have a change of clothes ready. East St. Louis had not prepared him for Brooklyn.

Tony Bennett was supposed to anchor the bill, but the kids surging through the lobby were not impressed by his suave artistry, attacking cardboard cutouts of Bennett as they crashed through. He would plead that he'd "burst a blood vessel in his throat" and bail out. The crowd appreciated Nappy Brown, but not the crew-cut Four Voices—they wanted to stomp, not swoon. When Freed called out Berry's name from the stage, *Billboard* reported, "the Chess artist tore down the house with his knock down drag out version of 'Maybellene.' He went off to a sensational hand."

By packaging diverse acts performing pop, jazz, and R&B, playing seven or eight shows a day, and appealing to a rowdy young crowd of Black, brown, and white faces, Freed had dropped a frame around a new experience and sold it. Rock & roll was pandemonium on a schedule; they ran a movie to clear the house and bring the next crowd in. *Cash Box* reported the shows grossed $178,000 for one very long week in Brooklyn. Freed shattered the Paramount's old attendance record, set by Dean Martin and Jerry Lewis years before.

Hooke and Reig put Berry on the road, a string of shows over seven weeks, one-nighters and longer theater runs, on a package tour with Buddy Johnson and Black doo-wop groups the Four Fellows, the Spaniels, and the Nutmegs.

The week in Brooklyn was a vision of a future maybe, if kids were still listening to the music in a few months. Unlike the Paramount Theatre lineup, the performers Berry was traveling with were all African American, and the tour was headed into the Jim Crow South. They would experience weeks of driving Dixie roads policed by southern officers enforcing separation of the races in the venues and the places musicians stopped between venues, be it Austin, Atlanta, Chattanooga, or Norfolk.

The tour was headlined by Buddy Johnson, a swing band leader from South Carolina who had moved into the jump blues field. He had been traveling the backroads, the Chitlin' Circuit of Black clubs and halls, since the 1930s, and the kind of show Berry was a part of Johnson had seen for many years. The audiences were Black working people; the shows included comics and dancers doing things not right for kids to see. Suddenly whites were coming out as well.

When Henry Berry talked about the South to his son, he tried to warn Chuck of the kind of violence his own family had experienced. Chuck heard weakness in his father's fear and was eager to prove him wrong.

Setting up in the Duval Armory in Jacksonville, Florida, the musicians heard white voices saying, "You boys" in a certain tone. Then an old white stagehand flashed the N-word to a horn player. That night maintenance workers took a rope and strung it down the center aisle, marking one side Black, the other Caucasians, for a show that turned out to be standing room only and two-thirds white. New problems.

By law, the races had to be kept physically apart. By the end of the show, Berry and the band couldn't help but notice the wave of white listeners jumping up onto the stage to greet them. After grousing earlier about the hostility they'd encountered, now "we overwelcomed" the visitors, he said, "extending hugs and some kisses."[10] Always alert to who was looking from the periphery, Berry noted the white cops and stagehands, sensed their reluctance to break up what was happening spontaneously onstage while the show was going on—"they could only stand there and watch young public opinion exercise its reaction to the boundaries they were up against," said Berry. "Almost as if it was rehearsed they hugged, kissed, greeted, or shook a hand and filed off to the exits untouched by the helpless, amazed security."

What he saw told Berry his father was wrong. The fact that a Black star could literally touch white people showed racial progress was happening. The look on the white faces offstage suggested he was getting away with something. Both feelings interested him.

In his autobiography, Berry writes that they were in Mobile, Alabama, the next night. Jacksonville had left him emboldened. "We were determined, at least I was, to bring those southerners to accept us for what we thought we were: northern artistic performers and not Yankee black lord-knows-what." There's a lot left to unpack in that sentence— Berry's desire to be viewed differently from the older, southern musicians, maybe a desire to be judged in terms not of his race but of his art.

Mobile practiced the same rope diplomacy as Jacksonville: the room was separated, and Berry started feeling the divide in a profound way. He was doing "Maybellene" and really playing the bumpkin, doing his chicken-peck dance thinking the African American side was going to be particularly amused, only to find the whites enjoying it while Blacks were standoffish. He was offering commentary, but it was being heard as pandering. So now he had his "mind on getting next to my brethren and sistren."

Back at Chess, in Berry's first session, Leonard Chess had told him that a blues like "Wee Wee Hours" was only going to reach Black folks, while there was something about "Maybellene" that registered beyond. Something about the song made it "Anglopinionated," in Berry's loaded word: white folks liked it. On the one hand, that's where the money was, and the largest-possible audience. On the other hand, Mobile presented him with a visual representation of how an African American audience might feel about it.

So: the blues. Berry shortchanged the white folks in Mobile, bowed to the other side, and made clear this was for them. He worked his blues tune in a sensual way, he ad-libbed words and moved with a physicality that drew groans and sighs from the audience. "How beautifully the black side began to moan," he declared. "It was just like we were all then boarding da' ol' ribba-boat, about to float into a land of flawless freedom."[11] There is a lot to unpack in that sentence too.

When they finished the show, their bus was surrounded by police, who formed a gauntlet the performers passed through. Musicians and fans alike were unhappy with the effort to keep them apart, and voices were raised from the crowd, mocking the law. It got worrisome, though nothing bad happened.

Berry could see the opportunity for racial progress and the opportunity for sticking it to the racists, all in the same context. In the smaller and more adult venues, fans were free to come backstage, "visiting the artists, and whatnot," Berry said. "Whatnots were real nice then."

One other difference between the traveling show and the Paramount Theatre bill was that this one featured "the Queen of the Quiver and Shake," dancer Queenie Owens.

The night typically began with a performance from Owens, in her mid-twenties though looking like a teenager. "These audiences were full of men all fired up, and her job was to go and get them ready for the show," said Sharon Stokes Williamson, a family historian and grand-niece to the late Queenie Owens. "Buddy Johnson would call her out, but she was pretty shy."[12]

Queen Esther Owens was born in Allendale, South Carolina, in the Depression. But not long after her birth, her brother and father beat up a white man, and the family packed in the middle of the night and fled to Savannah, Georgia. Her family was deeply Baptist, and Owens ran away at sixteen. Her cleverness and beauty frequently worked in her favor, as they did when, not long before the 1955 tour, Owens won a "Fine Brown Frame" beauty contest.

"Fine Brown Frame" was a hit song by Johnson in 1944, and he was holding beauty contests by that name in every town he played, offering the ultimate winner a loving cup, one hundred dollars, and three weeks on the road with the band. They kept doing it year after year, long after the hit fell off the chart. In 1955, when Owens won, her prize was a slot shake dancing while Buddy's band riffed away.

Her shyness became a part of her act. The hotshot who currently had a hit on the pop charts made it part of *his* act as well, says Williamson. Berry would play his guitar, coaxing her from the side of the room to the front of the stage. "He called her Queenie, though her name was *Queen*," said Williamson. "Chuck would call out, until the whole room was calling too: 'Go, Queenie, go! Go, Queenie, go!'"

She was one of two women on the bill, the other being Johnson's sister Ella, the singer in the band. But of the two, Owens was the only one who would "be taking stuff off and sometimes, well, she'd get down to just these little things over her breasts and a few other parts," Williamson explains.

The men got worked up. "And so she needed protection, and guys in the band were very protective of her—because some of the men in the crowd, they would hide out after the show and try to rape her—they wanted her to finish the show."

Berry looked out for her, and Williamson believes the two dated, but her great-aunt never told her that. The musicians would drive off in a caravan of station wagons, making sure everybody left together.

Decades later, when Berry was playing Baltimore and members of Owens's family asked her if she was going to see him, they got a brisk dismissal.

"Well, my grand-aunt could speak colorfully," says Williamson. "I think something must have happened between them. Because she would call him a sucker. She'd say, 'I don't want to see that N-word.'"

Queen Esther Owens died penniless in 2012. She was wearing stiletto heels and dating men three decades younger until breast cancer took her down. Even after she died, however, a song Berry wrote, which the family is convinced was inspired by her, became a hit and has been played ever since by the Rolling Stones and bar bands in Uzbekistan. Go, Little Queenie.

WHILE HE TRAVELED WITH BUDDY JOHNSON, BERRY'S NEW SINgle, "Thirty Days," came out in October of 1955. Musically it continued his hillbilly boogie, and lyrically he made a string of appeals to a lover to come back, which he frames as if they were appeals for another kind of fair play. First he employs a "gypsy" woman's magic, then confers *in camera* with a judge, then gets a warrant from the sheriff. If the warrant doesn't work, he vows he'll go to the FBI and then the United Nations. It's a committed push for justice, and a faith that justice is out there to those who don't fold.

Country music icon Ernest Tubb dug "Thirty Days," recording a more reserved version. The African American newspaper the *Pittsburgh Courier* reported that in Philadelphia, "Chuck Berry seems to be the favorite artist on the jukebox at South Broad's Lincoln Luncheonette. Perhaps the 'men in blue' who stop there for coffee find the singer's waxing of '30 Days' groovy."[13]

White cops in Philly enjoyed Berry's music, and so did whitehatted Texans like Tubb. His records were getting play all around the country—folks knew what he sounded like, but they didn't yet know what he *looked* like. He had a sound that defied categories and was on the country, pop, and R&B charts. But when a DJ introduced him on a Florida stage or when a New York officer pulled him over, they were both profiling him. There were plenty of artistic reasons to want to elude definition.

Reig went on the road with Berry, making sure he got money after the show. He was heavy yet fast on his feet, sported a tight little jazz moustache and a pile of Victor Mature curls. He relished a chance to get in the face of a Youngstown club owner and make a compelling case for following through on an agreement. A worldly fellow who knew the mechanics of taking care of an artist on tour, Reig must have looked like a good Berry-whisperer to Chess and the Gale Agency.

Berry was not impressed. He hadn't spent much extended time with white folks, let alone white folks who were presented as his savior. Leonard Chess was fine. He just wanted to make a deal, and a record, and then do it again. But this guy was nonstop.

You couldn't trust him, that was Reig's charm. Record producer Bob Porter explained, "Teddy always used to say, 'Look, when I go to dinner, everybody eats!' What he neglected to add was that he had a very big appetite, and he always ate first." He was skimming, reflexively, night after night, and Berry was one to notice. When setting up a show, Reig would demand $5,000 from the club and then tell Berry they had agreed on $3,000, pocketing the difference. Contract language called for an extra payment if the house was full, a percentage of the gate if a certain head count had been reached. Noticing a good crowd, Berry would say surely they triggered the bonus, and Reig, sadly shaking his head, would explain they had come close but just missed it. It was clear what was going on.

Hooke knew it and was outraged. Not because of what Reig was doing to Berry, but because he wasn't cutting Hooke in on the take. Berry searched for a way out. He got his hands on a check made out to Berry but endorsed and cashed by his manager. He followed him to an airport runway, stomped onto the plane Reig was taking, and showed him the check. And like that, Reig—or as Berry called him, "Teddy Roag"—and Hooke were expelled.

It was a small defining moment. When Chess listed Freed as cowriter of "Maybellene," it helped a great record become a hit, no certain thing. Freed had incentive to play it, and others in the field followed his lead. Berry saw what Chess was building, a blues and rock & roll hit factory. He saw less clearly what Freed was building—Freed didn't precisely know either—but indisputably Freed was where the excitement and money were.

Now Berry had kicked out some of the structure holding him up. He knew what he had, and he saw it was worth protecting. Not for him his own Colonel Tom Parker. He started running his own show on the road, getting paid what he had been promised. That meant carrying a gun. It was the first step in building a business benefiting Chuck Berry.

ALL THOSE RECORDS BEING MADE TO FILL RADIO TIME AND jukebox space led to a wave of independent labels built by former junkmen, wrestling promoters, gangsters, and corner-store merchants. At the moment, they were giving the industry a run for its money. But their knowledge was varied and spotty. They needed a dependable source of profit to invest in their enterprise. One by one, those that survived learned the ins and outs of royalties.

The Chess brothers found their way to the music business in a way that had logic, but only because their specific gifts made it pay off. From scrap collection they moved into running a liquor store, and then a bar and after-hours spot called the Macomba Lounge in the 1940s, where Leonard booked jump and jazz acts.

He and his wife, Revetta, played bridge with another couple, and their friends invited Chess in on a small label in 1947. The label, named Aristocrat, grew into Chess in 1950. Chess was using an attorney for label business who had an office in their building. In lieu of paying him, they let the attorney set up a publishing company to handle their royalties.

Fobbing off royalties on a guy who offered to administrate them for free seemed like a good way to avoid paperwork when you weren't scoring hits, but as Chess started having major success ("Rocket 88" by Jackie Brenston and His Delta Cats, and Howlin' Wolf's "How Many More Years," both from 1951), Leonard and Phil turned their attention to the collection and payment of royalties.

The Chesses contracted with a start-up company founded by Gene and Harry Goodman, brothers of jazz star Benny Goodman, Chicagoans whose family had come from Russia and Romania around the same time the Czyzes arrived from Poland. Gene and Harry Goodman launched ARC Music, which stood for Aristocrat Record Company. They would publish music recorded on Chess. At the time of a recording session the Chesses gathered musicians' signatures on songwriters' and artists' contracts. The documents went to ARC, which filed the copyright with the Library of Congress and handled administration of the paperwork. In the 1950s artists very often did not know the value of their work and flat-out sold their rights to labels like Chess that offered them a sum up front in exchange for a chance to record.

Journalist John Broven interviewed Gene Goodman for his history of independent labels, *Record Makers and Breakers*. Goodman was candid. "We had an understanding," Goodman quietly explained, with Chess.

"Anything that Leonard had a record on, he paid the artist direct or the writer direct: Chuck Berry, Bo Diddley, 'Book of Love,' or anything else. He would combine the artist royalty and writer royalty as one. I would only pay those writers when I got a cover record or foreign royalties would come in."[14]

What Goodman is saying is that ARC arranged with Leonard Chess to avoid making royalty payments to Berry and others. It wasn't huge money at the time; publishers got two cents on a record, Goodman says, so a million-seller would have netted $20,000, half of which was supposed to be shared with the songwriter.

Goodman was dismissive of artists who complained about not getting royalties on music they had composed or recorded. They still had the opportunity to earn it back on the road. "A lot of these artists shouldn't have any compunction about what they lost in royalties," Goodman explained. "I don't know whether or not or how much, if anything, they were cheated by these record companies, because these [record] people worked hard to get a record played." That became a common justification for doing wrong by recording artists: owners of the label worked hard and deserved whatever they could get.

Dick Alen, who would manage Berry on the road, said that in this era artists typically had a handful of years to make their money, and it was understood they did that in performance. "There was always another act ready to take their place," explained Alen.[15] Berry sought to control getting paid on the road, the part of his operation he could most easily oversee.

Leonard Chess didn't present himself as a creative force. He was a businessman who didn't cave when he thought he was right. "Chuck and Leonard had a very good relationship," said Chess songwriter Billy Davis. "But I must preface it by saying Leonard had a very good relationship with just about everyone that you witnessed him with, whether it was a Chuck Berry, a Bo Diddley, a Muddy Waters, or an Etta James, or the program director from some big pop station. He had the personality; he had a way about him that he came off—in those days you would say 'straight.' Whether he was or not, he gave you the feeling that he was being straight with you and leveling with you. He didn't say a lot of things, and he was one of the people where his word was his bond, to a great extent."[16]

If anything the Chess brothers were above average in their treatment of musicians, being both attentive and paternalistic. Red Holloway played tenor saxophone on many Chess sessions in the 1950s, and he had an expansive view of the brothers. With the Chesses, a good player could find work, but "you would never get too much money." The brothers, he explained, meted it out in lump sums when you made an emergency appeal, rather than when it was due. A musician might get emphatic about money they were owed, and the brothers would send him to a Chevrolet dealer they knew. "'So you need a car? Go down and tell him I . . . ,'" Holloway recalled.

> The average brother, he'd say, "Yeah, man, look here, that dude's alright. Look here what he's got me, a new Cadillac."
>
> Well, basically, there's two ways of looking at it. They were alright. I wouldn't say they were crooks or nothing like that.[17]

HOLLOWAY ADDED THAT IF A MUSICIAN CAME IN ASKING FOR A loan, they'd often get it and might never pay it back. If there was a ledger, it was imprecise and elusive.

This was a dose of the Maxwell Street We Cheat You Fair credo. In a 1983 conversation between Phil Chess and Charles Walton, a drummer on the scene who had known the brothers since their days of the Macomba Lounge, Walton laid it bare: "You almost treated them like they were your children," he said of the musicians.

"Well, they wanted to be," Chess responded.

Phil Chess floated the concept of the "advance royalty," citing the example of a musician whose wife was having a baby in one hospital, while his "old lady" was having a baby in another. He asked Phil to pay the latter bill so his wife wouldn't find out.

Phil cited such payments—the cars, the bail, the money to get out of a jam in the Deep South—as things musicians conveniently forgot about. Things given in the "family" manner, and he bemoaned the modern age when people started to complain about their rights.

"You know 'this wasn't right,' 'that wasn't right,' which I'm not gonna dispute," Phil acknowledged. "I'm not gonna defend. I know in my mind what it was and that's it."[18]

OVER THE YEARS BERRY WOULD BE ASKED WHAT HE THOUGHT OF Chess giving two ringers songwriting credit for "Maybellene." He was someone who never acknowledged anybody getting the better of him. What good was getting mad now? But in a 1979 interview, he took a different turn.

He was asked if he got everything that was due to him from Chess.

He turned it back. "Did I?" *Hmm* . . . "Does anybody really know? How can you tell what is 'due' someone who creates?" he asked. "Oh, you can sit down with pencil and paper and do marvelous things with figures—and I have no doubt some of these things were done. Did I get money from my records? Yes I did and I do, but I don't say I was ripped off. I was basically unknowledgeable about this business and when the time came to sign certain papers . . . well, I signed!"

No way is he going to confess disappointment. He's more willing to suggest he had it coming. He wasn't going to let it happen a second time. "You write songs and you sing; you are in business for yourself. You struggle and you learn and you pay to learn just as if you went to a school. I'm still learning and I'm still paying."

What about Alan Freed? "How did I feel about Freed's name on my record? How COULD I feel? He was an important man in the business and if this was the way it was done, it was DONE, and as I said, no one can say what is due someone who creates. All things have their price. I paid and I WAS paid and I'm still paying and being paid."[19]

A process began for him, and it never stopped. You get hit and then you get up and don't get hit the same way again.

At the end of 1955, having just turned twenty-nine, Berry visited Chicago with the trio and recorded "No Money Down," a stop-and-go blues about having the money to buy your dream ride, cash making all men equal.

The B side cut that day would be one of the oddest records of his career.

"Downbound Train" is a wordy tale of a stranger passed out on the barroom floor. Berry dreams he is riding a train with a blood-soaked engine, an imp stoking bones into a motor running on lager beer, and Satan himself jerking the throttle. The hallucination is unlike anything else Berry ever recorded.

He took a songwriting credit, but the text comes from a piece of American rhetoric familiar to many in his parents' generation, "The Hellbound Train." In rhyming couplets "The Hellbound Train" presents a deranged vision of the path to perdition. It had been around for a long time, and by the 1930s it had many variations. It was one of the most famous cowboy poems, anthologized by John A. Lomax in *Cowboy Songs and Other Frontier Ballads*. In the version from a collection of Ozark Mountain songs, Satan mocks the cries of those onboard: "You robbed the weak an' done wrong to the pore." Newspapers published it all the time early in the twentieth century.[20]

His father, Berry said, gave him the idea to set the ballad to music—a dad who brought hellfire home and recited poetry at the table. "The Hellbound Train" was delivered in sermon form in Black and white churches. The traveling African American evangelists James and Eloyce Gist, makers of street films shot in Depression-era neighborhoods, filmed an indelible visual sermon called *The Hell-Bound Train* in 1930.

There's a striking set of couplets common to most versions:

> *The passengers made such a motley crew,*
> *Church member, atheist, gentile and Jew, . . .*
> *Yellow and black men, red, brown and white,*
> *And all chained together—a horrible sight.*

A prophecy that all become equal under the laws of heaven and hell.

You can almost hear Leonard Chess cursing in the studio, warning his star away from bringing God and racial politics into a pop song. Those lines get cut, but those who knew the source material knew the message.

"No Money Down" backed with "Downbound Train": Two road songs, two paths to American community. A pairing that together asks the question "For what shall it profit a man, if he shall gain the whole world, and lose his own soul?"

The single was released in January 1956. That same month, Berry performed for a week in Buffalo, at a long-forgotten spot called Mandy's. Named after owner Irving Mandelcorn, Mandy's was a jazz club in the early 1950s that expanded into rock & roll.

Berry loved his time there: he celebrated it as

a new experience in meeting people in a different atmosphere. An intoxicating one. I had never, even in the city of New York, been so warmly accepted in such a close-knit working and social environment as I was here.

About twenty of the three hundred nightly patrons were black people, but I only learned that most of them were black because they acknowledged it.[21]

At Mandy's "there were some who appeared white to me but declared and enjoyed being black, although they looked whiter than most whites. The white people there mixed with the blacks who were black as well as those who appeared white, leaving no black blacks or white whites feeling uncomfortable." It's a puzzling passage, fine wordplay that achieves an incantatory tone, as if repeating certain categories of identity loosened their hold on us all. It's clear he relished his experience playing at the club and saw it as a place where identities were more flexible than in other parts of his life.

Mandy's, and the Black hotel he stayed at, the Vendome, were both well known in Buffalo as queer spaces. Mandy's is remembered fondly in oral histories of Buffalo lesbians as not per se a gay bar, but a place where gay people, especially lesbians, knew they could go and not be harassed. Interracial couples were common at Mandy's, and it was a place where Jacki Jordan, a Black butch woman, performed and emceed regularly in the 1950s.

Berry says Mandy's got him thinking about his experiences playing for segregated audiences in the South just months before. No ropes down the middle, and by his eyes no harassment of performers or patrons. It offered a hopeful, elusive way forward, a vision of line crossing, and harmony, that he yearned for.

7

A HARMONIOUS UNDERSTANDING

THE ORIGINATORS, THEY WERE DIFFERENT. FROM-ANOTHER-PLANET different. To us they seem more fun, weirder than the folks we have today. They had to be. In order to make something out of nothing, pull together a new culture out of whole patches of skin and canvas and landscape while in the shadow of the Cold War and racism, they had to be strange. They had to go big.

My friend, Jim, who lives in New York, met Bo Diddley several times over the years and always came away with a great story. Once Jim was backstage at an oldies show at Madison Square Garden when Diddley moved toward the catering table. "They gave him an enormous piece of apple pie, and Bo sat down to eat it," said Jim. But first, Bo dug into a bucket of butter on the table, "and on the top and bottom he spread a half-inch layer of butter. Then he picked it up and ate it in two bites."

The originators were different, their appetites larger than life.

Bo and Chuck came up at almost exactly the same time, and they got along great. "Chuck Berry and Bo Diddley were the first two people out here to be called rock 'n' roll," Bo boasted. They had many similarities, Bo being a tinkerer like Chuck, making his first electric guitar with pieces of his mom's Victrola record player and playing it through the family radio. "I didn't *buy* me no electric guitar; shit, man, I had to figure out a way to *make* me one!"[1]

Bo had come to Chess before Chuck in 1955 and got hazed by Leonard Chess in much the same way. In March of 1956 he went to Universal Studios and laid down "Who Do You Love?" which would be one of his biggest songs. One memorable lyric goes:

> *Night was dark but the sky was blue*
> *Down the alley, ice-wagon flew*
> *Hit a bump and somebody screamed*
> *You should have heard just what I've seen*

Gothic, cartoony, and it doesn't quite make sense. One time when Bo was playing City Gardens in Trenton, my friend Jim went backstage and chatted him up. He had a burning question: What did those lines about the ice wagon even mean? Bo was wearing a black shirt, black slacks, black cowboy hat. He explained that he had written a different set of words, but in the studio Leonard Chess made him rewrite them while he waited. Here's what Bo intended to sing:

> *The night was black, the sky was blue*
> *Around the corner the shit-wagon flew*
> *A bump was hit and a scream was heard*
> *Someone got hit with a flying turd*

In the early 1980s Jim was working in midtown Manhattan, and since he was near Times Square he decided to stop by Show World, an anchor of the neighborhood. The place was sometimes called the McDonalds of sex, and Jim popped into the Triple Treat Theatre to see if any of his friends were working. In the bookstore was a large man in a cowboy hat and long leather coat. Hey, Bo Diddley.

"What are you buying, Bo?" Jim asked.

Bo held up *Maximum Perversion Volume Three*, with a dwarf, a snake, and a woman on the VHS cover. Bo flashed a wide grin.

The originators were different. In singer Etta James's autobiography *Rage to Survive*, she talks about Diddley's fascination with cameras, describing a hotel party involving Little Willie John, Little Richard, and the Shirelles, while Diddley wandered around with a camera. "Bo's been making movies—private movies—for over thirty years. Child, Bo's got him some movies you wouldn't believe," wrote James.

It's a story as American as apple pie and *Maximum Perversion Volume Three*. Pushed to the margins, they made the margins seem like an incredible place to be.

They were mad. "These early fifties rock & roll guys—they were all insane!" explains musician and writer Deke Dickerson. "They were all out of their minds."

And "Chuck Berry is sort of famous for being a complete nut."[2]

OVER THE NEXT FEW YEARS, EVENTS PLAYED OUT IN WAYS BEYOND anyone's control. Nobody ran the store. It helps to understand what was changing by noting how the words used to describe the music changed. Jerry Wexler was the *Billboard* writer who coined the term *rhythm and blues* in 1949, as a replacement for the problematic "race" charts. Although he wasn't running the store either, Wexler saw the big picture better than most. Rhythm and blues was Black music made by Black people for Black adults. But around the time Diddley was turning domestic appliances into electric guitars, Wexler noticed how white kids were getting interested in R&B, and he knew what that could mean—on a business and cultural level.

For the music to succeed with a broader audience, certain things would have to happen—starting with a new name. Wexler stanned for "cat music" for a few years and then capitulated to what the Black underground had churned up and Freed had seized upon: *rock & roll*. Wexler's *rhythm and blues* nomenclature masked a racial grouping. The one folks like him were eager to introduce defined a consumer group. "What determines a particular demographic or a particular market is not who plays the music now or who sells the music, it's *who buys the music*," he declared. "So-called rhythm and blues was bought by black people. It's an unfortunate truth of merchandising in a free enterprise society that you need to target your audiences."[3] If the tumblers all lined up in a new way, though, the prize was going to get a whole lot bigger.

New listeners wanted new personalities they could attach to, ones they had a part in creating and that they weren't inheriting from their parents. They weren't going to riot for Cab Calloway anymore. They didn't have to. In 1956 fans were rioting for Fats Domino, *four times*— in Roanoke, Virginia; San Diego, California; Newport, Rhode Island; and Fayetteville, North Carolina. This was new.

As "Maybellene" broke loose in the fall of 1955, a wildman was tracking its progress from New Orleans. Little Richard had been trying to make a hit record for years with little to show. Now he was holed up in J&M Recording Studio on North Rampart Street, working with a group of musicians itching to break out themselves. The Black man producing the session, Bumps Blackwell, had written to the white guy in California he was working for, Art Rupe, owner of Specialty Records, about the power of "Maybellene." Like the rest of the country, Blackwell had heard it. Better than most, he understood what it could mean. He was writing Rupe in the middle of a recording session in hopes the Los Angeles–based label owner would get behind Little Richard and the record they were making at that moment: "Tutti Frutti." Blackwell wanted Rupe to understand that it existed outside rhythm and blues. "Tutti Frutti," like "Maybellene," had the power to change stuff.[4]

"Tutti Frutti" took hold of the moment upon its release in late 1955. Berry heard Little Richard, of course, and he understood what "A-wop-bop-a-loo-bop-a-lop-bam-boom!" meant.

Berry and the combo set up in East St. Louis to formulate a response to "Tutti Frutti." "I have stood on the stage at the Cosmopolitan, thinking of how I could produce something like Little Richard's 'Tutti Frutti,' which was really sizzling at the time," he said.

A vocal clarity needed to be achieved. Richard had managed it one way; Berry also looked back to a singer who captivated him. "When I went into writing 'Maybellene,' I had a desire or *intention* to say the words real clear. Nat Cole taught me that. Nat Cole had a diction that was just superb."[5] The challenge for him was achieving clarity while being more ambitious in his songwriting: how to get across new stories and language in an emerging rhythmic storm.

IN 2002, BERRY WOULD BE A PARTY IN A LEGAL DISPUTE IN WHICH he was required to talk under oath about his songwriting process. It was a rare lucky moment when he had incentive to open up. Answers rolled out, and what becomes clear is how much a group process gave birth to many of his songs, and how much it came not from sitting down with paper and pen but from musicians comfortable with each other fumbling through an older song in order to obliterate it.

"I didn't know you got paid for writing music or I would have jumped in foot first," he said. "I knew you got paid for *playing* music."[6]

For him, writing could not be separated from playing music. He viewed himself in the mid to late 1950s as a performer, and his songs flowed out of his performances.

How did "Wee Wee Hours" come about? a lawyer asks Berry. The source of the song, Berry explained, was "inspiration, feeling, the feeling of the blues, yeah." Sitting before a camera and a group of attorneys, trying to get at what musicians in the combo brought to a record, he talks about a player's personal style, and how it defines their contribution, and how their style can be a good thing or a bad thing, varying from one night to the next.

"These are songs that you won't hear," he says calmly.[7]

"Wee Wee Hours" came together over many nights in the Cosmopolitan, and everybody in the group had to settle on what it was about. "We were playing for four dollars a night, it didn't matter what we played, we weren't getting paid peanuts. Now, when we went to record, all of this is in our souls now."

They were playing a ballad from Big Joe Turner called "Wee Baby Blues," and over time they were unplaying it, messing with it, absorbing Turner and making his number their own, and the reason they could do this was because nobody in the crowd knew them yet and nobody had any expectations, so a trio could pass it around and around, change the words and bring themselves into Joe Turner's world.

They didn't read music; they were working off verbal cues and feel. To Berry the song didn't have an end until it came out on a record, which to him froze it in place. Maybe even killed it, in a sense, or anyway stopped its growth. The process out of which the song flows Berry likens to a jam session, and every time they played it, their blues was different—"It might have been another song entirely with the same music, blues are like that." The song didn't become what we know, he explains, until Leonard Chess selected one version from a group of recorded options made in a studio on a given day. But Berry makes clear he doesn't think that one is necessarily better than versions that were played in the studio before or after.

A question from an attorney: Do you recall ever bringing to Johnnie Johnson or Ebby [*sic*] Hardy a completed song, ready for recording?

Berry: There is no such thing.

It's not just the blues, or "Wee Wee Hours" he is talking about as being unfinishable. Berry explains how they were kicking around a "simple" rock & roll style at the club that fit different songs, a consistency that one might liken to a groove. After they had established a way of working with each other, and then working to make songs together, the process wasn't about bringing in a finished tune and pruning it like topiary. It was about *playing* with everybody throwing ideas in, seeing what each player's style did to change what was thrown in.

Berry strongly suggests that songs like "Roll Over Beethoven" and "Johnny B. Goode" came out of this collective process.

Did he dictate the details of these songs? he is asked. "Frankly, actually, I didn't have to," Berry answers. "There was a harmonious understanding after a few recordings, that when I stop singing, Johnnie played this riff, or that riff, or that riff." Johnson would play, Berry would "implicate the rhythm," and Johnson "would remember the thing that I liked so much, and the same thing would happen, turned around, when I would play the riff, that I'd ask him to play a certain thing, seemed like to me, he would just fall in."

Everybody surrendered to this harmonious understanding. "And today, that same harmony exists, you know, if we play somebody else's song."

As they gathered to play in the wake of "Maybellene," he and Johnson naturally fell into this mutual way.

Berry led these sessions, verbalizing ideas and putting them into an order, a new experience for him. "Johnny would say, 'When I met Chuck, he only knew 12 songs,'" said a musician who had played with both. The process was more familiar to Johnson, who had been in groups in West Virginia, then the Marines, Chicago, Detroit, and East St. Louis, steeped in the African American tradition of listening and revising in real time. Take strangers with diverse backgrounds, levels of education, accents, repertoire, and styles, put them together. Make something new.

It's easy to imagine that Johnson was doing much to gently steer the younger, less experienced, and more ambitious guitar player through the shoals of the jam session. He had been there before.

Now, in the early part of 1956, that process was changing. The group could no longer workshop raw material live; they were expected to deliver finished songs. They played around town, and in mid-April Berry, Johnson, and probably drummer Melvin Billups drove to Chicago and recorded a batch of new songs. They were informed by having played on the road to white and Black audiences.

Among the numbers he took with him to Chicago was a full-on celebration of the new music taking shape. The new tune starts as another of his "complaint" songs, the way "Maybellene" called his girl to task or how "Thirty Days" petitioned the government to bring his gal back. Here the singer promises to let the local DJ know that classical music isn't cutting it anymore.

As he worked on the new tune, Nat Cole was on his mind. Berry admired the singer's diction, in which "you could hear every word—his esses, tees, gees and pees." Clarity was crucial, because the new song had a lot of words flying by fast. "When you are singing 'Roll Over Beethoven' you've got to be distinct in order to get your message out," he explained, which meant finding a way to make it sound legible.

Because there was a message here. By the end of the song, "Roll Over Beethoven" was not some guy complaining; it was some guy jumping into a crowd and calling a meeting to order. To make his point he had better say things right.

Early in 1956 Cole would have been on Berry's mind for another reason. On April 10, Cole had just begun playing "Little Girl" for an all-white audience at the Birmingham, Alabama, Municipal Auditorium. A voice from the back shouted, "Let's go get that coon!" and three thugs raced down the aisle, climbed over the footlights, and charged him.

One swung on Cole, and as the singer was knocked off the piano bench a microphone hit his face. Rumors of possible trouble had led law enforcement to plant plainclothes officers in the house; when those cops charged the goons, the uniformed officers began battling them, believing more attackers had arrived.

The curtain dropped; the dance band with Cole was British, and in the chaos they performed "God Save the Queen." Cole shakily reemerged. "I just came here to entertain you. That was what I thought you wanted. I was born here. Those folks hurt my back. I can't continue because I have to go to a doctor."

The attackers were members of the North Alabama Citizens Council, part of a racist mass movement that had sprung up in the wake of the Supreme Court's *Brown v. Board of Education* decision in 1954, which abolished segregation in public schools. The Alabama group was founded by Asa Carter, a secret leader of the state's Ku Klux Klan chapter. Carter presented himself as a responsible alternative to the Klan, calling on jukebox programmers to boycott the new music and protesting with signs declaring "Bebop Promotes Communism." The Citizens Council attacked rock & roll in Carter's newspaper *The Southerner*, calling it "animalistic," "congo rhythms," and "jungle music." Rock & roll, Carter said, "got its start in Negro night clubs and Negro radio broadcasts and its influence was spread by the NAACP."[8]

The Citizens Council understood that Cole was no rocker, but he was a Black man with cultural clout and admired by white Americans, and to them that made him a threat to the cause of segregation.

The Birmingham attack was a national news story, focusing attention on threats of violence issued by southern racists. The singer suffered mild physical injuries and was certainly traumatized. Standing on the tarmac of an Arlington, Virginia, airport three days after the assault, Cole told a network newsman if they were looking to attack a rock & roll musician, "then I'm the wrong guy." Scoffing at the reporter, he said, "You don't know what rock n' roll is!"[9]

When Berry went into the Chess studio on April 16, newspapers across the country were still reporting on the attack.

> *Well, if you feel and like it*
> *Go get your lover, then reel it and rock it*
> *Roll it over then move on up just*
> *A trifle further and reel and rock with*
> *One another*

A week later, Cole appeared in St. Louis's Kiel Auditorium. Perhaps Berry was there to see his hero. A lot had happened in the week since the assault on a Birmingham stage.

Black voices attacked the violence, but some criticized Cole, as well. The *Chicago Defender* editorialized that he was "dead wrong" to sing for white-only audiences and labeled him "an insult to his race [who] should have known better." Cole had asked why the racists had attacked him when he had never protested segregation. This brought him criticism from the NAACP.

In St. Louis, he sat down with a columnist from the *Argus*, who was clearly offering a chance to reset the narrative. Cole remained indignant.

"I've always tried to help my race—what did I do this time?" he asked. "I'm a performer. I don't know why all Negro performers have to be such outstanding diplomats and so thorough in his field that he must dictate where he will or won't play. You'd be surprised how much effective good we do with the support of the white and colored fans."[10]

Roy Wilkins, the executive secretary of the NAACP, had sent him a telegram, declaring, "This is a fight which none of us can escape. We invite you to join us in a crusade against racism." Cole resented the public shaming and claimed an entertainer's right to detachment from current events.

Cole had been born in Montgomery, Alabama, where, four months before the concert in Birmingham, activists had begun a year-long boycott of a public bus system that forced them to give up seats to white riders. The effort involved perhaps forty thousand African American protesters and was the largest act of public defiance of the law by Black Americans up to then. Because it was a national story, strangers would ask the celebrity from Montgomery about it.

"I've said many times it's a wonderful, wonderful thing," Cole warily told the *Argus*, "and I have never known anything to make me so proud of my race." But he asked people to remember he couldn't just wave a magic wand and make "all that nonsense down there" disappear.

"Some people must be taking the King in my name seriously," he said.

That was once a viable role for a Black star: no politics, keep a wall between yourself and the white audience, and stress that you were just an entertainer putting a smile on people's faces. Besides its other merits, it was calibrated to keep an artist physically safe, but that was no longer working so well.

Along came Cole's greatest disciple, who looked at the news and knew that the old role was no longer possible. So Berry put a new one together on the fly and, using the voice of a stranger in a crowd, tried it out on his exploding audience. Berry didn't know if it would keep him any safer. But he acted utterly impervious.

Mark Stewart, aka Stew, is a performer and playwright who teaches songwriting for the musical theater at Sarah Lawrence College. Stew challenges his students to find another line in the history of songwriting as concise and powerful as three words by Chuck Berry: "roll over Beethoven." "How did he sum up this historical shift he and others had just set in motion?"[11]

A devoted Beatles lover, Stew describes a 1963 interview in which the Beatles are asked what they will do if their careers have already peaked. George Harrison says he might start "a business of my own by the time we do, um, flop. I mean, we don't know. It may be next week, it may be two or three years."[12] Ringo jokes, sort of, about establishing a chain of hair salons.

"She Loves You" has just been released in England. "Please Please Me" was out in the US. But they don't seem too sure. Chuck Berry seemed *certain*.

"He knows this is going to last," Stew said. "Even before he got control of the dial. Maybe he was just faking it until he made it, but you really feel it." He's calling a meeting to order, kicking over dead white guys. He's talking about a cultural shift, and not just one in music. "This Black guy with that hair says, 'No, that's all about to go away,'" Stew noted. He knows everything is about to change, knows his music's success is tied to his ability to convince skeptics, and so he sells his world like a prosperity gospel preacher, like a used car salesman, like the most confident man in the kingdom.

"You are not on top anymore," Stew hears in "Roll Over Beethoven." "And come on—it's more than something momentary; he knows it's a historical shift. He condensed into three words this hugely disruptive power."

In the wake of his assault, Cole lamented, "I could have been singing 'Nearer, My God, to Thee' as far as those guy were concerned." Berry was shrewder than the Citizens Council when it came to understanding symbolism. He focused his attention on a bust decorating music rooms everywhere, a symbol of elitism, grown-ups, and whiteness. He gave the old fellow a shove.

"Roll Over Beethoven" was released in June and climbed to number two on the R&B charts and twenty-nine on the pop. Soon, Berry was on another package tour, "Top Disc Stars of 1956," featuring Carl Perkins, the Spaniels, Illinois Jacquet, and Shirley and Lee.

Before their early July show in Columbia, South Carolina, Perkins heard a knock on his dressing room door. A man poked his head in, asking, "Who Carl?"

Perkins jumped up to greet him.

"You know, I thought you was one of us," Berry told the twenty-five-year-old composer of "Blue Suede Shoes."

The Tennessee-born Perkins, a white son of a sharecropper, said that below skin level he felt they were pretty much the same: "pink meat and red blood."

"I like your attitude, brother," Berry said. "Love your attitude."[13]

That evening during the show, fans stormed the stage, and some were pinned against the front when Perkins played. Cops came, and in the chaos rioters vandalized Perkins's Cadillac. Shaken, the singer left the tour for a while, and when he returned he and Berry continued their friendship.

Berry would catch a ride from one town to the next with Perkins. They talked about country music, and the rockabilly star was surprised by how knowledgeable Berry was. Perkins broke out into one of Jimmie Rodgers's "Blue Yodel"s, and Berry interrupted: "That second verse belongs in 'Blue Yodel No. 4,'" he pointed out. Perkins said Berry knew many Bill Monroe songs as well. They drove to the next segregated show, singing "Knoxville Girl" in a Cadillac.

Transit itself could be life-threatening if one was pulled over in the middle of the night. Talking to white fans after a show: risky. Black musicians couldn't stay in the hotels where white performers stayed and often had to sleep on the bus.

Carl Sally was an eighteen-year-old college sophomore from Ohio, a saxophone player and bandleader who signed on to a tour with Berry in Chicago in 1956. He loved the work and was having the time of his life.

"Chuck was a good guy. But you didn't get real close to him; he was always on the go," said Sally.[14]

He knew his value—and his value as a drawing card was just fabulous.

He'd do "Roll Over Beethoven" and people were screaming, like ready to have a riot.

THEY PLAYED A STRING OF SHOWS TOGETHER, AND SALLY CREDITS Berry with giving him a career preparation that he was still applying in 2020.

What he remembers most about the weeks on the road with Berry was feeling the guitar on the stage. The whole platform moved with the vibrations of the speakers, a sound entering your body. "There were no words for it. It just did something to you down there, and the feeling stayed with you," said Sally.

To be creating that feeling, and controlling it, was its own physical sensation. Berry discovered this and turned it to his advantage, walking around the stage as the guitar and floor hummed, moving his guitar in different ways as he played in order to alter the room's vibrations. He discovered that playing the guitar had a physical component: moving around with the instrument changed the sound, changed the feeling, and changed the mood of the room. "If you have it set up just right, and it starts to vibrate on your body, then you know that you've got that sweet spot!" said Charles Berry Jr. "My dad used to say, 'It makes your insides feel good just playing the thing!'"[15]

"A guitar just didn't sound like that on record, and once you felt it, you wanted to feel it some more," said Sally. Yet he jumped off the tour when it took a bend to the Deep South.

> An agent said to me, "Carl, now I want you to realize, it's gonna be a little different and some restaurants and restrooms won't be available. You can't stay in hotels with the Caucasian boys." I had a mixed band back then . . . and he said, "I want you to ride in separate cars."
>
> I told that agent you can take that job and stick it.

Sally was a teenager and Berry a thirty-year-old man; the response to Jim Crow was in part generational, the older musicians considering it a hazard of a job they felt lucky to have, while younger folks weren't settling for a rope line down the middle of the room.

How was life on the road in the early days? a writer asked Berry many years later.

"It wasn't so hard."[16]

Really?

"You could make it hard, but it wasn't that hard most of the time. You eat out on the road, there's a restaurant. You can go in the front door but you can't sit down. They won't serve you." You could go to the back door and get something to eat. The alternatives were all bad. You can scrounge from the closest vending machine, "baloney and cracker dust. It'll kill you."

Huh?

"Twinkies and that kind of shit. It'll rot out your stomach forever, ruin you for good. You've got to keep up your strength on the road or you can get sick and never be the same. If your stomach's bad, forget it, it's over."

Road food could kill you, but Berry was also speaking metaphorically. A diet of rage could likewise do you in. Not bending to the system, until you felt yourself doubled over.

"But if you went around to the side window they'd give you a hot plate and what you wanted. You had to eat it standing up or in the car but you got to eat it. Some guys wouldn't do it, they'd rather eat baloney and cracker dust. Not me. I wanted to stay healthy and do my thing."

On the tour with Perkins, he also befriended a white songwriter named Bobby Charles. The nineteen-year-old Cajun was likewise signed to Chess, and there was a good tale to that, because Charles was signed before anybody at the label had laid eyes on him. Back home in Abbeville, Louisiana, at thirteen, Bobby Charles Guidry was singing rhythm and blues with a band. A hot song he wrote led a local record store owner in early 1956 to call his friend Leonard Chess in Chicago and pass the phone to Charles, and after the kid sang his tune, "See Ya Later, Alligator," Chess offered him a contract sight unseen. Charles recorded it for Chess in New Orleans, but it was too late. By the time he was summoned to Chicago for a meeting with his label head, "when Leonard saw that I wasn't Black, he almost had a frog," Charles remembered. The song was quickly covered by Bill Haley & His Comets, who had the far bigger hit, and the new kid was put on the road with Berry.[17]

Charles stayed in Black hotels and got cursed out when restaurant owners saw him walking off the tour bus to place an order for a bunch of Black folks. "I thought I was going to get hung trying to buy fifty hamburgers," he said.

"Chuck Berry and I got along real good together," Charles recalled. "Chuck got me a little guitar and tried to teach me the guitar, but I could just never learn to play the guitar and piano." When the bus pulled up at a roadside restaurant, Berry once explained, "We had a swinging thing goin'—he would go in the front door and I would go in the back door." Charles liked sandwiches and Berry liked hot meals. So after Berry ordered at the back door and Charles walked through the front, they met outside and traded.

"We even got stopped for riding together, two males," said Berry. "It was outrageous."

THAT SEPTEMBER, BERRY RELEASED A SINGLE WITH "TOO MUCH Monkey Business" on the A side. The beat was faster than that of "Roll Over Beethoven" (by now Chess was speeding up the tapes so that Berry's voice sounded higher, younger). The song is a snapshot gallery of people from daily life: someone working in the mill while bills pile up at home; a customer resisting a seller's "buy now, pay later" pitch; a guy getting pressured to marry someone he doesn't want to; the caller who just lost a dime in the pay phone. You or he could have been many of these folks, and that was a central point.

In a song about wrestling with the world's demands, work and money are the problems, but so are school and partnering up and anything else that is what you are supposed to do rather than what you want. For all the talk that would eventually come about Berry being the poet of teenage American life—an interpretation he was happily willing to summon in order to dispatch questions of "What does it mean?"—in "Too Much Monkey Business" he offered quick sketches of diverse people, only a couple of whom were plausibly in their teens. Everybody's story marks them as different, but their discontent spills across the distinctions and blurs them together. He was singing a mural, depicting what people secretly wanted and what they endured.

It's a chain of people brought together in a commonwealth of dissatisfaction. And also brought together in the playfulness Berry conveys, in an internal rhyme scheme and a choppy rhythm that wrap up everybody's wants in a shared push and pull. "I don't want your botheration, go away, leave me be," he finishes—that *botheration* really is one of the best words he ever came up with. He's so good at capping the chain of laments that you don't even notice the first word in the line—I. He's all the people in the song. An artful way of saying, "Hey, I see you; do you see me too?"

He completes every one of his character sketches by singing there is "too much monkey business for me to be involved in." Berry wants off the normal path, wants to look into folks' faces outside the bus, poke around with Carl Perkins and Bobby Charles, two guys who wanted off too. Everybody in the song just strugglers and shruggers making do until their Cadillac comes in.

Plenty has been made of how his fast-talking delivery was a rap road map. It surely matches the empathy and voraciousness of the Beats. Bob Dylan took "Too Much Monkey Business" and ran with it in another direction: erasing this word and that over and over and writing enough new ones in the blanks that his "Subterranean Homesick Blues" became a picture of America as a jangling Mad Lib on wheels.

Nobody on the pop charts was this open to American life in 1956. Walter Winchell said, "'Too Much Monkey Business,' a new tune, will probably appeal to those who like noise."

The other side of the record was written in Carl Perkins's Cadillac. "Brown Eyed Handsome Man" is about all those places it was dangerous for a man like Berry to go, and then goes there, over and over.

"Brown Eyed Handsome Man" fundamentally depicts what people will do for love. But once you know that Berry is using "brown eyed" as a euphemism for "brown skinned," the lyrics get more interesting. The first verse describes a man who's been arrested for vagrancy, a common charge used to lock up Black people in the North and South. He's on trial when the judge's wife calls the district attorney—and in 1956 you could safely assume the judge, his spouse, and the DA were all white—and demands this handsome man be freed.

Next, Berry's in a plane over the desert, and out the window he spots a woman walking the dunes to hook up with another brown-eyed fellow. It's been like this "ever since the world began" he sings. It's Hiding in plain sight: a song of interracial attraction. The lyrics describe how the Venus de Milo (a symbol of whiteness to match a bust of Beethoven) lost her arms "wrestling" with the brown-eyed man.

Berry was a lifelong baseball fan, and "Brown Eyed" was written during the final year that Jackie Robinson, the man who broke baseball's color line, played ball. The song finishes with the brown-eyed man up to bat, the game on the line, and he hits a home run to win it all. In the song he starts out as a victim and ends as a hero: an Everyman winning cheers as he breaks taboos left and right.

"It's easy to forget just how radical those founding artists were when they supplanted what came before," says guitarist and founder of the Black Rock Coalition Vernon Reid.[18] "Though the context has been lost in the haze of nostalgia, these were dangerous, dangerous, dangerous people making dangerous music in a time when it was risky. He recorded 'Brown Eyed Handsome Man' at a time when there were laws against miscegenation. In a time of out-and-out segregation, Chuck Berry was a sex symbol!"

Reid points out that the song came out less than a year after Emmett Till was murdered. "Chuck Berry really walked right up to the line with tunes like that. And there were people that were, like, they were none too happy, because there was a growing culture very attuned to the double entendre. And these people were sexually explosive."

The music is expansive, everybody riding the lilt of Willie Dixon's repeating habanera bass pattern. Buddy Holly, Waylon Jennings, and Robert Cray all made memorable covers, and Taj Mahal took it all the way into reggae. Just after "Brown Eyed Handsome Man" came out in September 1956, Elvis Presley, Jerry Lee Lewis, Johnny Cash, and Carl Perkins sat around a piano and played it while the tape recorder rolled; as Perkins guides them through the tune, the delight of the so-called Million Dollar Quartet is palpable. Walter Winchell, no doubt, would have hated it.

THE PEOPLE WHO MOST VISCERALLY DISPLAYED THEIR HATRED OF rock & roll were not all robe-wearing southern clichés. Some were fringe characters, others were religious and community leaders. They lived everywhere.

John Wilson Hamilton lived in St. Louis. He might have been described as a blue-eyed balding man, a little stocky. Hamilton, an intense newspaper publisher, was known around city hall. He hated jazz, rock & roll, and integration.

A St. Louis Argus writer who was profiling Hamilton for the Pittsburgh Courier noted his thin-lipped smile that registered as a smirk.

Hamilton was the thirty-seven-year-old editor and publisher of the *White Sentinel*, a monthly publication dedicated to white supremacy, anti-Communism, and anti-Semitism. Its motto was "Racial Integrity—Not Amalgamation." Hamilton's writing and activities had given him stature in far corners of the country and, in midwestern polite society, an invisibility that was useful.[19]

He had moved from Boston to St. Louis in 1947 at the direction of his mentor, Gerald L. K. Smith, a minister, white supremacist, and founder of the isolationist America First Party. Until they met, Hamilton was in Boston, dabbling in Republican politics and claiming to have been a leader of the Young Communist League. Smith had formed his Christian Nationalist Crusade, an anti-Semitic hate group, in St. Louis in 1942. After Hamilton heard Smith speak, he became a follower and member of the demagogue's inner circle, joining the Christian Nationalist Crusade and making connections with the toxic mix of haters that Smith tried to unite in the 1950s. That very much included Asa Carter, the ringleader of the Alabama Citizens Council and the chief racist behind the attack of Nat Cole.

The organization Hamilton formed in St. Louis, the Citizens Protective Association, showed up in the middle of racial violence in St. Louis, Chicago, Boston, and Detroit. Hamilton was active at least until 1958.

Popular culture was a regular focus of his work. In the pages of the *White Sentinel* and elsewhere, Hamilton viewed jazz, Hollywood, *The Ed Sullivan Show*, calypso singer Harry Belafonte, and Chuck Berry as harbingers of the race mixing that would destroy America.

It didn't all happen in the Deep South. Hamilton, Carter, and those like them were fringe dwellers in the pre-internet age, and we will never know the precise shape of their efforts. They were productive, their hate petals strewn all around.

The music was not guaranteed to prevail. Racial equality has yet to prevail.

The originators were different from us. Operating in chaos, they acted like they had already won.

8

IT'S *BEEN* HERE

In his Greenwich Village apartment, a would-be screen-writer put the finishing touches on his dream project, a musical that would feature pop acts of the moment. As he revised, Milton Subotsky heard the music of Chuck Berry played on the radio. Subotsky admired the songwriter and believed that "Too Much Monkey Business" was "what life is all about."

He grew up in Brooklyn and was an active member of the Fortean Society, which investigated paranormal phenomena around the world. He was a lover of science fiction and pop songs; the high point of his life might have arrived in 1962 when Gene Vincent recorded his composition "Spaceship to Mars."

In the fall of 1956, however, Subotsky was completing the movie that would launch him as a filmmaker, a project for which he would be listed as a producer, screenwriter, and composer. *Rock, Rock, Rock!* featured Tuesday Weld, Chuck Berry, Valerie Harper, and Cirino and the Bowties. The plot involved a high school senior in need of money to buy a prom gown. Subotsky envisioned a picture packed with his songs, and when he took his concept to DJ Alan Freed for financial backing, it turned out Freed had his own ideas about which songs and singers to use. In the end, *Rock, Rock, Rock!* featured musical acts

LaVern Baker, the Moonglows, Frankie Lymon and the Teenagers, and the Johnny Burnette Trio. Freed got top billing and ended up cast as a DJ with numerous music-business connections.

"Well, the story's nothing to shout about," Subotsky told a writer, just as the film opened to the public. "But I think the kids'll really dig that music."[1]

Milton Subotsky had his head screwed on differently: he was interested in a quick buck and a giggle. *Rock, Rock, Rock!* was the third and final picture Will Price would direct. The film was shot on an $80,000 budget over a tight nine days in a Bronx studio. Released on December 7, 1956, it opened in more than four hundred theaters.

Berry performs in one scene. Never mind Alan Freed, the singer seems far more engaged before the camera than does the thirteen-year-old Tuesday Weld. He earned an outsized share of praise for his pantomiming to his new single "You Can't Catch Me." Berry's comic performance was enough to make him, in the eyes of a *Billboard* reviewer, "the most impressive act in the picture. He mimes the lyrics of the tune with hands, feet, face and body movements, all but making a humorous ballet of it."

The film had an innovative side hustle: selling a soundtrack record and profiting off music used in the picture. Once Freed got involved, gangster Morris Levy and his associate Phil Kahl signed on. Freed's publishing company, Snapper, published the songs used in the film and then licensed them to Patricia-Kahl Music Publishing in a deal brokered by Kahl and Levy.

Freed produced a soundtrack album that included three Chess artists: Berry and vocal groups the Moonglows and the Flamingos. The album wasn't sold commercially, merely distributed to DJs on a national level as a means to promote the film. Besides starring in the film, Freed owned 10 percent of it as a producer, and he made money from Snapper by publishing fifteen of the twenty-one songs. The DJ-only release would lead to the payment of performance royalties to Freed and others.

In a few months Chess commercially released an album that recycled the songs by those three acts and random others, getting one more bite of the apple from music used in the film. *Rock, Rock, Rock!* was an unambitious piece of filmmaking, but its business plan deserved to be taught at Stanford.

BERRY'S NEXT PROJECT WAS A MORE INTERESTING "FILM." Released in March 1957, "School Days" was built over his own complicated feelings about high school.

"I used to look at that song as a throwaway, but that song is *cinema*," says the songwriter Stew. He notes a story synched to the music from the beginning: the guitar chords jangling like the first bell of the day.[2]

Then comes the singer's voice, cutting through whatever daydream you were in. Waking you up in the director's world. "A lot of people can write cool poems, but to also deliver it in such a seductive way that you don't even *realize* it's poetry," said Stew. Then he made the chef's kiss gesture.

Stew sings:

"Workin' your fingers right down to the bone / and the guy behind you won't leave you alone"? Oh my God, how did he do that? I could write songs for the next two hundred years and never think to mention the guy who wouldn't leave me alone—*which every single person alive has experienced.*

It continues with an establishing shot open through the front doors, camera floats down the hallway into the classroom, it does close-ups there and you see the teacher who doesn't see how mean she looks, it goes into the cafeteria and the woman serving food, you see how she looks.

Is this even three minutes long? It's like Scorsese.

The movie is delirious, unrelenting: it calls itself "School Days" and meticulously sketches school's nature, yet it is 100 percent about what comes after. "Close up your books, get out of your seat, down the halls and into the street." At the end of the school day, at the end of the song and somewhere outside of it, is where life is: on a record playing on the jukebox where the kids are going. "Hail! Hail! Rock and roll, deliver me from the days of old."

At a July 1956 US Senate hearing on juvenile delinquency in St. Louis, the city's superintendent of public schools, Philip J. Hickey, described a central cause of the explosion of youth crime: "Our young people of today have far too much leisure time." St. Louis's top prosecutor, Edward L. Dowd, a former FBI agent, chimed in at the hearing to say, "I would suggest, the unsupervised use of the automobile" was the source of the problem.[3]

Too much free time and too much access to the road. And here came Chuck Berry saying what's wrong with the world was too little of both. Who were you going to believe? Berry had just written the first protest song of rock & roll: a protest against boredom. No wonder the song has been called a harbinger of the Free Speech Movement.[4]

Blind faith in books and leaders would only provide more of the life you at fourteen had already learned to dread. "School Days" builds to a moment it does not land on. Berry doesn't show us deliverance. The doors just fly open and there you are, out on the street.

Maybe this is why, as the songwriter Todd Snider has said, Berry as much as tells the listener, "'Hang on through the tough time 'cause the good time is coming' . . . without ever having to say something as trite as that. Which for me is the best non-use of something as phony and deceptive as an alphabet. Chuck Berry uses words against themselves and they deserve it."[5]

Words lie: Chuck Berry spoke the truth.

"School Days," Stew tells his students, is the rare kind of song that is so good you might not feel like writing one yourself afterward. How can you compare? "What he's doing is pretty complicated. How does he tell all these stories, utilize these images—what was his precedent? Nothing against Robert Johnson or Gershwin, but what was *he* listening to or reading that allowed him to create with such detail and economy and then deliver in this voice? Those lyrics seem like he picked them up off the ground, like they've been around forever."

"On February 15, 'The Greatest Show of 1957' shoves off," *Billboard*'s R&B columnist cheered in January. "Has Butte, Mont., ever had a chance before to dig the likes of Lavern Baker, Clyde McPhatter and Chuck Berry?"

Thus began a massive year of travel. "The Greatest Show of 1957" was assembled by Irvin Feld, who had started out owning a pharmacy and would end up owning Ringling Brothers and Barnum & Bailey Circus in the 1960s. But in the 1950s, Feld was probably the greatest packager of rock & roll. Fats Domino was his featured act, and that ensured him both a good turnout and controversy, given the series of disturbances at Domino shows in the year before the Greatest Show.[6]

Feld's tour also featured Bill Doggett and vocal groups including the Five Satins, the Five Keys, and the Moonglows. Meanwhile, the crowds were growing, and they were getting whiter, younger. There were no adult comics, no shake dancers as part of the entertainment.

Paul "Hucklebuck" Williams and his band backed the acts, and accompanying the show were valets, wives, girlfriends, seamstresses, and publicists among the one hundred people filling two buses while playing eighty straight days and nights. They would be motoring through the segregated South during the first half of the tour, a South stirred and heating up as the Montgomery bus boycott continued.

In January 1957, four Black churches in Montgomery that had supported the boycott were bombed. Reverend Martin Luther King Jr. and others formed the Southern Christian Leadership Conference that same month, a civil rights group that began planning nonviolent direct action in protest of segregation. The Greatest Show of 1957 was passing through an increasingly fraught southern landscape.

Berry had been impressed by the way fans and performers found a way to mingle after shows on his previous cross-country tour. Now he was eager to push the boundaries of allowable contact in ways that made the older performers on the bill nervous for their own safety.

Soon, he would express interest in being the headliner on such shows, when the top slot holder was paid more. But Berry had learned one advantage of playing early in the day: it left him with maximum time to scout the house for women. In Houston he got off the stage and made his way to the whites-only balcony. After watching Berry, a policeman was about to make an arrest when the tour manager stepped in, apologizing profusely and extracting his star.

After a March 27 show in Little Rock, Arkansas, bandleader Paul Williams observed Berry kissing a white girl while the venue cleared out. That was enough for Williams, who didn't wait for the bus but grabbed a cab back to the hotel, fearing what might happen to any Black man caught in the vicinity of Berry at that moment.

Three nights later, they were on a late drive into Mobile, Alabama. Guitarist Bobby Parker recalled the countryside decades later: "There were signs all over the place, 'Welcome to the Home of the Ku Klux Klan' and all that." It was late, and the bus had just broken down.[7]

As they came to a stop in the dark, smoke pouring from under the hood, the musicians wondered what they were going to do. The sheriff showed up, banged on the bus door, and brought his dogs in. The white driver explained that they were on their way into town when the engine seized up.

"What you got in here?" the driver was asked.

"Well, we got a busload of Negroes in here."

It was starting to feel like they might not make it in time to their show.

The sheriff demanded the bus lights be turned on.

"Who are these people in here?"

"Well, sir, you have Fats Domino, you got Chuck Berry, you got . . ."

Now the sheriff was getting mad, and he told the driver to stop lying. But somebody backed him up, and then he looked excited. He told them to wake Berry up and bring a guitar. "I want to see if he's telling a lie."

And when they rousted Berry and handed him an instrument, the officer demanded he play some songs. For the next few minutes the sheriff was personally entertained by Chuck Berry.

The mood lightened as it became clear the lawman was a fan. Delighted, he helped them get their bus repaired, and by midmorning they were on the way to the stage.

Such encounters didn't make Berry any more hesitant to cross the line. Those around him noticed his remarkable behavior. "I saved Chuck from near death many, many times," explained Allen Bloom, an employee of Irvin Feld traveling with the Greatest Show. "In those days it wasn't exactly 'Southern hospitality.' Chuck had a perverted sense of whatever. The closest call was in the Carolinas."[8]

This was probably several days after Mobile, on April 4 or 5, when the show played Charlotte and then Winston-Salem.

"He was caught in the back seat of his car with a young white girl. I was able to talk the police out of putting him in jail forever or lynching him and got him out of town."

The shows themselves were endlessly exciting. Few had been to performances like this before; they wouldn't last long. But for now, nobody knew how to act when the music started, and spontaneity flowed.

When the tour came to St. Louis, the jazz-loving writer for the *Argus* declined to name any of the acts he saw, not even the hometown star.

But columnist Buddy Lonesome could not let pass the amazing scene he had witnessed. "The close harmony between teen-agers of both races at the rock and roll show, Saturday night, it can best be described as a complete 'togetherness'—was reassuring to see. Their adulation of the stars of the hit show, which at times bordered on hysteria, was not confined to squeals and groans from any particular segment of the audience, they all hollered."[9]

He reiterated that he wished it was music he liked, but then added, "I must concede that the harmony that exists between the races at such tumultuous shows bodes well for racial integration in this country, racial bigots notwithstanding."

A regular feature was Bill Doggett, the R&B bandleader, offering a sultry "Honky Tonk (Part 1)," his hip-grinding, inhibition-loosening pleasure. In one southern town, saxophonist Clifford Scott drew the Black and white kids out of their seats, and they began dancing in the aisles, Scott presiding over a long moment of spontaneous integration. The cops moved in, ordering the song to end. Then, according to writer Rick Coleman, the band moved into the record's B side, "Honky Tonk (Part 2)," and dancing continued.

Honky-tonk part three transpired later, in the parking lot. Gerald Early: "Those were the years, then, in which America recognized, and cringed before, the social reality that would not hide itself anymore, before the reality of a miscegenated culture in which, beneath the mask of inhuman racial etiquette where everyone supposedly was as separated as the twin beds in the bedroom of nearly every 1950s TV sitcom, there lurked an unquenchable thirst for mixing. And the 'new' popular music helped to expose the false separation of America from itself, by revealing the culture's essential fusion all the more inescapably."[10]

Chuck Berry was an African American astronaut on an extended solo flight to violate established practices in business, culture, social mores, and laws. He was putting everything on the line. It was confusing to those around him, and he doesn't seem to have tried to explain it, maybe not even to himself. But he was just getting comfortable.

In the spring of 1957, at the Exhibition Forum in Vancouver, BC, on March 6, Berry was interviewed by DJ Red Robinson.[11] Pulling Berry to the mic ten minutes after he'd been onstage, Robinson said, "I think the kids are enjoying it, from the applause that's leaking through the wall here."

Berry: "I'm hoping so."

Robinson: "Tell me Chuck, where do you hail from?"

Berry: "I hail from San Jose."

Robinson: "San Jose. Pardon my geographical . . ."

Berry: "California. 150 south of Frisco."

Robinson: "Of course. It's sunny down there, doesn't rain like it does—"

Berry: "Thank you."

"Nice country."

"Yeah."

San Jose became his fictional hometown around the beginning of 1957. It was his declared birthplace in press material. It was an exotic-sounding map point a long way off that didn't sound Black or white, and maybe that's why it became his shadow home. When he tells Robinson, he even says it with a Spanish accent. This was a game Berry liked to play over and over, until fame made it impossible: to uproot assumptions about who he was. When he died, the Root, a thoughtful and culturally savvy website written by and for Black people, declared, "Charles Edward Anderson Berry Sr., was born on Oct. 18, 1926, in San Jose, California."

San Jose had many purposes. When you are smuggling contraband music across the Mason-Dixon line, it's better if people don't know too much about you. He left a crooked trail. The photographs Chess and Berry sent to venues he visited were frequently doctored to lighten the skin tone.

IN MAY 1957, CHESS RELEASED BERRY'S FIRST ALBUM, *After School Session*. It includes a few hits and a lot of B sides, a typical 1950s jumble at a time when indie labels saw albums as afterthoughts. And yet *After School Session* makes a strong case for a figure Berry never became. Take out "School Days," "Too Much Monkey Business," and "Brown Eyed Handsome Man," and this becomes a cohesive album, the sounds of a guy who wants to let his guitar talk for him, searching for a way to sew a wide variety of American music into a suit that fits. There's a cha-cha ballad, a blues played on a steel guitar, a Mexican-tinged instrumental, and the expansive curiosity "Havana Moon," a lovely unmailed postcard from an island somewhere, a sideways attempt at calypso that surely paved the way to ska. And there is "Together (We'll Always Be)," a vocal group exercise like Berry never did again, opening with perhaps the richest, most environmental guitar chords he ever played. *After School Special* isn't the public face of the man—that's the singles—but it shows the many guys Chuck Berry was, and it suggests the American hybridizer he might have become if he had continued pulling these threads together. Asked once if it was possible to draw lines between rock and boogie-woogie, country and blues, he reached deep. "No, you can't draw *any* lines like that. You can't draw a line between science and religion, man! Even the edge of a razor blade is round if you get up close to it. It's like a shadow on the wall—no sharp edges."[12]

He wanted to blur lines as well as step over them. On the album cover is a photo of Berry. And how does Chess describe him on the back of *After School Special*? "Our Rock-A-Billy Troubadour." There was money to be made when bookers didn't know that the troubadour they were paying for was darkly complected, and once listeners bought your records and paid to hear you live, maybe it didn't matter as much.

Johnnie Johnson told a story about this era, how he and Ebbie Hardy would be on the stage playing for a while, and the announcer would finally introduce Chuck Berry. "And there would be a lot of 'ooh, ahh,' you know, like this ain't supposed to be a black man, it supposed to be a white man singing this kind of song, you know. And while he was getting his self together and you could hear through the crowd—'I thought he was white.' 'I thought he was white.' And then he would strike out on his song, you know. So it was really a novelty on that deal 'cause a lot of places we played until he got there, they thought he was white on account of the songs he was singing."[13]

Chuck Berry loved messing with people and keeping others from defining him. For a while he encouraged people to think he had Pacific Island bloodlines. Marshall Chess, Leonard's son, picked up a strong Polynesian vibe from Berry. An early promotional shot features him shirtless, coiled around a guitar on the floor beside a potted fern, a rock & roll Gauguin moment. Berry told folks he was partly Hawaiian (and named a daughter Aloha). "I think that something with his being Hawaiian was knowing that he could be more successful if maybe he wasn't black," speculated Chess. As he once said to writer Mark Jacobson, in the right light, "people say I even look white."[14]

Johnson and the trio drove into Manhattan and were pulled over by a New York cop. When the singer handed him his driver's license, Johnson peeked at it and was startled to see Berry identified as "Indian." He had a sound that defied categories and was on the country, pop, and rhythm and blues charts. But when a promoter introduced him on a Florida stage or when a New York officer pulled him over, they were both profiling him. There were plenty of reasons, artistic and otherwise, to want to elude detection.

The imaginary San Jose would not last forever. Muddy Waters, thirteen years older than Berry, grew up on the Mississippi Delta with the certainty that his music would only succeed on the "race" charts. That generation harbored mixed feelings about the success of those who followed in their footsteps. "Till the Rolling Stones came along, your daddy and mommy didn't want no race records in their house," Waters once lectured a white interviewer. "Now Chuck Berry, he could come into the home 'cause they didn't know if he was black or white. Hell, if the mothers knew he was as black as me, they'd say—'no man, don't bring in that n***** music. Not in my home—not that n***** shit.'"[15]

But for a time they didn't know, and Berry did what he could to sow confusion, and thus have his music get in the house first.

In the dressing room at the Vancouver arena, DJ Red Robinson asked Berry about the band he used on the road. Berry explained that the trio playing on the Chess records was not with him this trip. "I'm not taking them on the road because of the, uh, tax problem." That's a reference to the IRS hitting him hard in 1956. "And also the, uh, *character problem* I'm having with my outfit." That was a reference to the drinking of Johnson and Hardy.

Berry did not like alcohol or being around people who were impaired. The members of the group had abruptly been fired.

According to a longtime watcher of the music scene in St. Louis, Tony Cabanellas, "People who have known Johnnie will say he had alcohol addiction issues and that they might have been his way of compensating for his resentment."[16]

Johnson's drinking even made the pages of the *Argus*. On May 3, 1957, it ran a short article headlined "Johnnie Johnson Drinks Alcohol": the pianist had been hospitalized in serious condition at Homer G. Phillips Hospital, the African American hospital in St. Louis, after drinking a half pint of rubbing alcohol.

"He was found doubled over and grimacing from terrific pains in his stomach. He was taken to the hospital where he was pronounced suffering ingestion of methyl alcohol, condition serious."

With Johnson in the hospital, Berry drove alone to a Chicago session that produced "Rock and Roll Music."

Unlike "School Days," which is really about rock & roll music, "Rock and Roll Music" comes fully as advertised. Then again, even here, he is sliding all manner of subjects in through trapdoors built into his words.

At the top chorus he offers plain-speak, the understanding that the backbeat—the two and four beats punched like they usually weren't on pop records—was crucial to how rock & roll worked. He's selling something big and amorphous to newcomers by focusing on his beat: you can't lose it. Crucially, he's making the case for this new thing by presenting himself as an anointed fan, a convert to the cause. He's selling music as something more than music, more like a mission, and once you get it you, too, are going to want to share it with others.

The verses seek to contrast rock & roll with other music. Modern jazz is okay, he says in the first. These lines feel like a kick against bebop (too fast and hard to dance to) and also against pompous big bands like Stan Kenton's thirty-nine-piece Modern Music Orchestra. In the summer of 1957 bop trumpeter Dizzy Gillespie lamented in the Black press the firing of a St. Louis DJ for playing jazz instead of rock & roll. Or, as Gillespie called it, "that tom-tom rock and roll." The nightlife columnist for the *Argus* noted that such comments were "only the beginning: the 'Sports' are really going to fight the suffocating tide of rock and roll—Selah!" There is an underlying tension to Chuck's line about "modern jazz" that was timely and now lost to time.

The recording loads up echo on the guitar and drums, a rarity for Berry; writer and editor Joe Levy hears in this a reference to Elvis and Sun Records' popular slapback sound.[17] There's another reference to Elvis when Berry refers to dancers who get "all shook up." You can hear "Rock and Roll Music" as Berry turning the radio dial, looking for his place on the spectrum. He shrugs off tangos and mambos—as Levy puts it, the song "is an act of self-definition" in the face of fads and competitors. He's gesturing at all these crazes, as they were commonly configured in the press, and declaring that *his* work is different. It will stand.

The song starts in the here and now, but we move "across the tracks" so we can hear the real stuff. No reference to country music anywhere, not across these tracks, just the sound of "my man" on a wailing sax, which Berry compares to a hurricane. Heading into a storm.

We transit again. We're "way down south" in search of a party, and the words Berry uses to describe the fun are a pair of old words with African roots, *jubilee* and *jamboree*.

Berry describes this backwoods frolic as so country the revelers drink homebrew from a wooden cup. Whether that cup is a dipper or a gourd or something from mama's cupboard, whatever potion we are swallowing, it's clear we are out in the woods, so far out that when everybody feels the need to dance, they enter an altered state and get "all shook up." Nothing could be newer, or older, than that.

He's an advance man for a product (a tune, a fad, a new old jamboree), he's selling his stuff from a simple platform. In the summer of 1957, when he was recording "Rock and Roll Music," folks still hadn't settled on what to call the sound. A popular alternative was Alan Freed's new phrase, "The big beat."

DJ Red Robinson again: "This music called the big beat, do you think it's here for a few more months or a few more years?"

Berry: "It's been here. It's *been* here. No, it's been here for a long while. As long as music will be here. It's rhythm and soul put together, that's this big beat that you speak of. No, it isn't new—it's new to a lot of people, believe me. But it's not new. Been around a long time, just being introduced under a new name."

A funny thing happens in the last verse of "Rock and Roll Music." Berry sings, "It's way too early for the congo, so keep a rockin' that piano." What's that about? He probably means to say too early for the *conga*. That dance step fits with the mambo and tango he's mentioned, and it's too early to go dancing because it's not night yet. But Chuck Berry doesn't make many mistakes with his words, and if he chose to say congo instead of conga, it has meaning.

"It's *been* here," he exclaimed in Vancouver. It passed through the place called Congo Square, which Berry might even have seen when he traveled through New Orleans the year before and again about a month before he recorded "Rock and Roll Music." The conga drum was played there, in the one space in New Orleans where enslaved people could play drums on Sunday. The conga that comes from the Congo. A oneness, then, among the sound and place. All of which underscores how "Rock and Roll Music" steers the music forward *and* backward in time. This will be something you will want to be a part of, he begins by cheering. Then he says: this backbeat is ancient, and lived long before Elvis Presley.

The truth is, as Levy says, "like all instruction songs about dancing, this is actually a song about sex." That made it rock & roll.

WHEN BERRY SINGS THAT THE TIME'S NOT RIGHT FOR THE CONGO, he finishes his rhyme with the tune's last words: "so keep on rocking the piano." It wasn't Johnnie Johnson rocking on that song; he was possibly still in a St. Louis hospital at the time of the May 1957 session. Elevating the song was a mysterious Chicago bluesman named Lafayette Leake. He doesn't play a solo on the number, exactly, but he plays all over it, raining goofer dust down from the sky for two and a half radiant minutes.

Born in Winona, Mississippi, in 1919, Leake learned blues and boogie-woogie from a musician named Big Rabbit. With that knowledge he traveled north. "The reason I moved to Chicago was really to try to better my financial condition," he wrote in a biographical note. "There are not many opportunities in a small town to develop yourself and I always wanted to get a chance to accomplish something." Leake came to Chicago and learned from a piano player named Chank Hester, and then hooked up with Willie Dixon, who was crucial in getting session work for him with Otis Rush, Bo Diddley, Little Walter, Howlin' Wolf, and the Dixie Hummingbirds.

By way of a reminiscence, a writer observed that Leake "seldom if ever appeared in the clubs, either as musician or listener, and aside from quiet friendships with a few people like Billy Boy Arnold and the late Little Brother Montgomery, he seems to have remained almost entirely isolated from the social circle of Chicago bluesmen."

Brother Montgomery's wife, in fact, found Leake so internal and silent that when she first met him she thought his mind was not right. Leake was discovered unconscious in his apartment in 1990, having died some length of time before. An acquaintance wrote, "After Leake died, rumors flew that he'd been found dead or unconscious in the street, that he hadn't even had a home during the last months of his life, or that he'd moved away and had died somewhere outside of Chicago. All of them were false, but they serve to illustrate the anonymity in which this seminal blues artist lived much of his life." His playing was the loud part. He read music, and though he said little, he once told a writer, "I can play Chopin."

"Rock and Roll Music" was the first song he ever recorded.[18]

ABOUT THAT BACKBEAT, AND ABOUT CONGO SQUARE: BERRY called New Orleans "the gateway from freedom." He learned that was where most Africans were "sorted through and sold."[19]

In mid-1950s New Orleans, Little Richard was ensconced in J&M Studios recording "Tutti Frutti." His band was led by drummer Earl Palmer. Predisposed to jazz, Palmer employed the shuffle beat—a repeated pattern of dotted quarter notes paired with eighth notes—in his playing. The shuffle was the basic pulse of jazz, blues, and swing. But when Palmer was with Little Richard, who was screaming his head off and pounding steady eighth notes on piano that burned finesse away, suddenly that shuffle felt embarrassing. Right there in the studio Palmer was struck by lightning: he needed to match what Richard was doing on his own instrument. So he put down the flyswatter and picked up a hammer.

The studio was two blocks from Congo Square, and it was the birthplace of rock & roll drumming. Palmer pinpointed a problem—essentially, how to keep up with Little Richard—and solved it in desperation, and those who would follow thrived by his example.

It came in a flash. "What I remember about those sessions is how physical they were," he told writer Tony Scherman. "You got to remember how Richard played—can you imagine matching that? I'll tell you, the only reason I started playing what they come to call a rock-and-roll beat came from trying to match Richard's right hand. *Ding-ding-ding-ding!*"[20]

When he looked back on it later and described the introduction of the eighth-note assault on pop music, he saw Chuck Berry's guitar and Richard's piano as neck and neck writing the first draft of history.

"I don't know who played that way first, Richard or Chuck Berry. . . . But with Richard pounding the piano with all 10 fingers, you couldn't go against that."

If I may: The backbeat is the brakes on a bike; it checks your speed while it keeps you tied to the musical bars, to the structure that is grouped in twelve-bar units, and forms the shape of the song. Straight eighth notes—not to mention the savage sixteenth notes Richard kicked out—tend to break apart structure; they were a bike customized without brakes, jumping past bar lines and throwing you into the arms of God. Richard and Chuck both had a lot of that feeling, but there were key differences too. As far as how they envisioned their whole band sound, Little Richard was Shiva the Destroyer, exploding the universe in order to create a new one, while Chuck was a truly great community organizer. He was building something measuredly, making sure a foundation was in place that would last.

Berry created a feeling of reckless abandon *and* a way to hold on to your lunch. How did he manage that? As Earl Palmer, that bomb thrower, explained with the disdain that a prophet feels for someone who turns his own religion into their self-maintenance program, "Berry was playing that rhythm on guitar already. But his dumb-as-shit drummer stuck to that two-four."[21]

Okay, that's one way to say it.

Another would be to say that in Chuck's band, the drummer went one way and Johnnie and Chuck veered another. The drummers Berry used—Ebbie Hardy, Jasper Thomas, and occasionally Fred Below—mostly didn't try to match Johnnie and Chuck, and they weren't supposed to. They hit that backbeat sparely—often they were the only spare thing in the sound. Meanwhile, Johnnie or Chuck is hitting all kinds of eighth and sixteenth notes, and the other one of them is pushing a shuffle into the sound, which meant the beats were locking some of the time and flying apart at other moments. They knew each other so well one knew when to be hitting a shuffle and the other to hit the straight eights. Parts of a song change it up, and the overwhelming feeling is of two systems never quite in sync and never all the way out of it. Instability in motion. The experience is overwhelming, confusing, neither this nor that. Little Richard was religion, or if you want, oblivion. Chuck was pure fun.

Key to everything they did was the faith they had in drummer Ebbie Hardy. He played with Johnson before Berry joined, and he set the template going forward. Far from being anybody's "dumb-as-shit drummer," he found an understated, assertive way to hold together all the rhythm pouring from piano and guitar.

"He's like the mystery guy!" said Tom Maloney, a guitar player who has worked with Johnson. "Johnnie didn't talk a lot about him. Drummers always try to play the way Chuck did the beat on guitar—and that's a big mistake. He had a way of doing things. . . . A perfect example is 'Maybellene.' He did what I call a two-beat"—and here Maloney goes boom pop, boom pop—"and then there's that swing"—one-n-two-three-n-four. "Ebbie could shift in between those two in such a great way while keeping the snare drum popping on two and four."[22]

Maloney emphasizes how important it was that Johnson and Hardy were older guys creating teenage dance music but not using the jazz and blues that had shaped them:

> Ebbie had an unusual style but, again, who are these guys copying? They had to pull it out of the air, basically. But if you listen to "Maybellene," it had a country two-beat boom pop boom pop, but *then* when Chuck takes his solo they are off to the races and they are swinging like crazy. And then back to that boom pop boom popping. That's an incredible thing to be shifting back and forth to.
>
> But these guys were *men* who had played serious music. And it had this wonderful swing and Johnnie plays these jazz chords behind it in a way no teenager could quite get to—they hadn't lived long enough to play that yet. And so Ebbie was right there with them at the birth.

Hardy grew up in East St. Louis and learned the drums at Lincoln High School. Miles Davis went to Lincoln a few years before Hardy, and both musicians studied under band director Elwood C. Buchanan, formerly in Andy Kirk's orchestra. (Buchanan famously rapped Davis's knuckles with a ruler until he stopped playing his horn with vibrato.) Hardy played with Albert King and with Ben Thigpen's jazz band. According to his son-in-law, Abraham W. Bolden Sr., Hardy had an offer to join Ike Turner's band. But he stayed close to home and raised a family.

"He was on the quiet side when he was sober, but once he got a little alcohol in him he was a jokester," recalled Bolden.[23]

His influence on Berry's sound outlasted his seat in the band. Frantic, logical, playfully aggressive, it became a template for bands playing bluegrass, country, R&B, and newer things. Jim Dickinson, a keyboardist, Sun Records recording artist, band leader, and philosopher, said he heard what Berry's band was doing in *all* the music coming up around him in the South of the late 1950s, flowing through Sun and Memphis and beyond. Dickinson gave the totality of it a single name: Chuckabilly.[24]

AFTER A SUMMER BREAK, IRVIN FELD RESUMED THE "GREATEST Show of 1957" that fall. It became a markedly different tour for several reasons. White teenage balladeers were a thing the promoter had resisted up to now, but he caved, adding the hot sixteen-year-old Lebanese Canadian sensation, Paul Anka. Also on the bus were the Crickets and the Everly Brothers. The rest of the lineup included Berry, Fats Domino, Frankie Lymon, the Drifters, LaVern Baker, Clyde McPhatter, Johnnie & Joe, the Bobbettes, and the Spaniels. They traveled in two buses with "GREATEST SHOW" splashed across the side.

As they met in New York City and prepared to leave, the newcomers had a chance to get to know one another. Don Everly took one look at Buddy Holly and the Crickets and decided their Texas accountant couture wouldn't cut it with young audiences, directing them to a show business tailor he knew. He also urged Holly to get hipper eyeglasses. Berry, meanwhile, took the Everlys and the Crickets to Broadway, introducing them to Lindy's New York cheesecake.

From the start, the white and Black artists got along well; they were rolling dice in the back, and Holly became an avid gambler. On late-night rides, the Drifters serenaded with a cappella gospel hymns, while Berry snatched the bus driver's intercom, dropped it inside an acoustic guitar, and made up songs for the rolling party.

The white stars admired Berry. He loved the Everly Brothers' music; "Wake Up Little Susie" had only come out that September, and for the rest of his life it would be one of the songs he most wished he had written. Buddy Holly and the Crickets studied Berry's songs and played them at sound checks. "There was a real camaraderie there at the beginning of rock and roll," Don Everly noted.[25]

Still, having whites and Blacks together complicated things. When they traveled the South, they encountered the hostility. Once when the bus parked beside a café, a man called out from behind the counter, "We don't serve n*****s." Berry, ready with his smile, responded, *"That's alright, I don't eat 'em."*

Holly then declared, "If you can't feed these fellas, we're not gonna eat here either!" All left together.[26]

Starting in late September, shows were booked for five cities in a row—Columbus, Georgia; Chattanooga, Tennessee; Birmingham, Alabama; New Orleans, Louisiana; and Memphis, Tennessee—where it was illegal for white and Black performers to appear together on a stage. Indeed, it was illegal even for the white bus driver to hang out backstage. The white acts took those dates off, and everybody reconnected in Oklahoma City, where they headed to the West Coast.

At some point in the fall, Berry got a fat check, and he bought a Cadillac.

The biggest difference in this part of the tour was newcomer Anka, the teenage crooner. In the spring when the tour played Ottawa, a stranger gee-whizzed his way backstage to Berry's dressing room, where he sang to the startled star a ballad he had written. The tune was named "Diana," and Berry called it "the worst song I ever heard," Anka remembered.[27] Berry told his visitor "not to quit my day job." Fats Domino was more polite when Anka visited him, but no more interested. Security removed him from the backstage area.

Undeterred, that summer Anka went to New York to record his number. And by the fall "Diana," a wholesome teen swoon song, was number one on the R&B charts and two on the pop. Months after getting tossed he was performing with Berry and Domino, singing his song to appreciative crowds.

"Diana" was one of the original examples of a trend much of the industry cheered on. It was a milk-fed ballad, expressing heartfelt concerns. It had a backbeat worth losing. Many believed this was where the music was headed.

Nobody seems to have had any problems with Anka on the tour, though it was noted when he accidentally pulled the plug on Holly one night, and his propensity for backstage pranks and wisecracks directed at guys twice his age was remembered. "I was an irritant, just by being who I was," he admitted.[28]

A strange ritual happened in Moscow, Iowa, on the night of October 28. The stars of the show forcefully steered Anka to the hall's basement, where LaVern Baker announced she was formally initiating him into show business. Anka's clothes were torn away, and after he was stripped to his underwear Baker slathered him in "blackened cold cream." Cutting open a pillowcase, she doused the teenager in feathers. It was a jokey reenactment of a tar and feathering, and whatever feelings Anka had about it he kept out of his autobiography.[29]

The incident might have signified an induction into show business, but truthfully Anka had already been jumped into the inner circle: he had appeared on *American Bandstand*. In August, a hit Philadelphia-based TV show went national, and two days later Anka appeared before its studio audience, introducing himself to the nation with his song. *American Bandstand* featured recording artists pantomiming as their latest record played, and at a time when Black faces with hits might otherwise have flooded into homes coast to coast, the rising tide of the serene teen stars and the hit show worked together to check that progress.

Anyway you looked at it, Dick Clark was a smart cookie. The show's host had previously been a big band DJ who, until he took over *Bandstand*, "didn't know Chuck Berry from a huckleberry," as a peer put it. But he was a quick learner, an Alan Freed hijacked from Morris Levy and shipped off to charm school. His clothes did not scream, "Let's boogie"; his manner was polite. *American Bandstand* was an immediate hit and Clark an ascendant gatekeeper.[30]

The show began in 1952, with a format featuring Philadelphia high school kids dancing on local TV. It practiced a bureaucratic form of discrimination, with teenagers writing in to request to dance on the show and screeners seizing on white-sounding names to invite. When Blacks arrived with a ticket on the day of the filming, they were told their clothes didn't fit the vaguely worded dress code and sent packing.

By the time *Bandstand* went national in 1957, there were demonstrations against rock & roll in major northern cities and radio stations refusing to play the music all over the country. Washington, DC, had banned Fats Domino from playing there, claiming it would take the entire police department to protect the city from rioters.

Rock & roll put Black and white teenagers together in a shared physical space and was thus viewed as a social problem, because a great many people viewed integration as a social problem. Give Dick Clark some credit, then, for putting many African American performers on the air to play their current hits. Clark built a program that confirmed growing evidence that teenagers were a huge demographic with spending power and an ability to shape social trends. And he put his studio audience, dancing and watching the performers, before his American camera, a picture of rock & roll fandom that was as white as a tablecloth.

Black teenagers in Philadelphia knew the score and tried to subvert the ban—there were brawls in the *Bandstand* parking lot—and they contacted the Black *Philadelphia Tribune* to present their case. Black fans had heard rock & roll longer than most white ones; heck, they had even made "Diana" the top "R&B" song in the country.

After *Bandstand* became a national hit, showing in after-school time slots, others of course noticed the complexion of the teens dancing to the music. They also noticed how Clark treated his white and Black performers differently. After playing, white acts joined the fans dancing to records, while Black performers were steered to a table, where they signed autographs.

The *St. Louis Argus* observed the double standard and launched a letter-writing campaign at the beginning of 1958. The paper sent a telegram to Clark and urged readers to write him. In a front-page article, editor Howard B. Woods wrote, "Now that *American Bandstand* is making a serious bid for wider national audience, the market differences in the handling of Negroes, both as artists and as teenager participants, lands as a major problem to the production."[31]

Clark didn't seem to think it was any serious problem; he continued on as before.

Three decades later, when Berry, Little Richard, and Bo Diddley were talking informally to one another while a camera recorded them, it was clear how much this still mattered to them.

They were reminiscing about Freed, and Diddley remarked how he had defied the system to bring races together. He might have had in mind the TV show Freed briefly had on ABC in 1957; in a notorious moment, Black singer Frankie Lymon danced with a white woman on national TV, and Freed's program was quickly canceled. "Community traditions," Berry says lightly.

Then, says Diddley, "Our good friend Dick Clark came up with the television thing and started putting us on *American Bandstand*." But Berry is not having it.

"I got something to say—but we couldn't dance! We couldn't participate in the audience," he says animatedly.[32]

Diddley tries to give Clark a pass.

"*Why was it done?*" Berry says, raising his voice. "If he didn't want it to be done. He was the master of ceremonies."

Diddley: "I couldn't answer you."

"Anybody who allows the traditions to stand and maintain . . . ," Berry says.

Berry himself debuted on *American Bandstand* in November 1957, pantomiming to "Rock and Roll Music." But he made his biggest contribution to the show with a song that was recorded in December. He said it was inspired by a scene he'd viewed while playing Ottawa in April. He watched a young blond girl holding an autograph book high, pushing her way backstage to musicians one after another as they came offstage. She made an impression on him, and the song Berry wrote, "Sweet Little Sixteen," is a tribute. "Sweet Little Sixteen" was the first of a string of songs Berry wrote about young women moving through life with agency.

The songs that girls would dance to were the ones that got played on the radio; the boys knew it, even if they didn't comprehend. Chuck Berry knew it too, and he celebrated the girls. The songs that got played were the ones that became hits. Girls, more emotionally developed than boys, were the tastemakers, the teenage consumers who mattered most. On that level too, Berry was impressed.

Female fans were characterized by journalists and commentators of the time typically as either victimized angels or creatures of chaos, up to no good. The magazine *Seventeen* was alert to their market force earlier than most (first publishing in 1944), followed by *Dig* and *'Teen* in the year of "Maybellene," and then the deluge: *16*, *Teen World*, *Teen Time*, *Teen Screen*, *Teen Parade*, *Modern Teen*, *Teenville*, publications targeting teenage girls.

Berry saw outsiders forcefully making choices, expressing bits of who they were through the marketplace. He was complex enough to champion their independence and talented enough to make it the subject of a handful of terrific songs "abounding in nuance and genuine respect," in the words of Ann Powers.[33]

Dick Clark also grasped where the market power rested. Girls, in the words of a scholar who studied the early history of the show, "were the target audience of *American Bandstand*."[34] Clark understood that if you had the girls, the boys would follow, and that's why there were more girls than boys on his dance floor. The very fact that *Bandstand* aired on living room TVs between school and dinner in most markets underscored the domestic nature of Clark's rock & roll.

In "Sweet Little Sixteen" Berry cannily points out places where girls like his subject are screaming for the music. Texas, Frisco Bay, his own St. Louis, and New Orleans. Sweet Little Sixteen the girl is in and at a time when kids on the move were projected as scary beings—hot-rodders and juvenile delinquents—Berry gave them his respect and made them the subject of his music.

"'Cause they be rockin' on *Bandstand* in Philadelphia P-A," he sings. The moment Dick Clark heard "Sweet Little Sixteen" early in 1958, he had a good feeling about it. "Sometimes we heard a hit the first time we played the record," he said. "Chuck Berry's 'Sweet Little Sixteen' was like that."[35]

Clark played the heck out of the song, and the girls and boys responded.

Muddy Waters had called it: at first Berry "could come into the home 'cause they didn't know if he was black or white." Now they knew, and Berry was a regular on national TV. Thanks to the back pat to *American Bandstand* that Berry dropped into his new tune—and thanks to teenage girl power—he had the biggest hit so far in his career.

9

EVERYBODY WELCOME

THE SONGWRITER BEN VAUGHN AND HIS BAND WERE MAKING their way through St. Louis's Lambert International Airport in 1987 when he and accordion player Gus Cordovox spotted Chuck Berry walking toward them. Carrying his guitar with great purpose. This was heavy.

Vaughn froze in his tracks, but Cordovox went forth and shook Berry's hand. Then he came back and whispered, in awe, "My hand smells like aftershave."

"So we all stood there, smelling his hand. That's as close as I ever got to Chuck Berry," said Vaughn.[1]

Berry was going through the same gate they were; the rock band from New Jersey followed from a safe distance, watching with intensity when Berry's Gibson ES-355 went through the X-ray machine. "I wanted to see what the guitar looked like on the screen," Vaughn said. "I wanted to see if there was anything special inside." He was looking for something secret that could explain the unexplainable. "There was nothing stashed in there, no guns, no special electronics. It looked kind of normal," he says with a shrug.

The mystery of a guy who worked miracles on his guitar survived security inspection that day. But the mystery only exists because of a song Berry wrote. Chuck Berry was rock & roll's first guitar god, and "Johnny B. Goode" sings the praise of the god he created. The Johnny in the song comes out of nowhere and, through hard work and genius, makes a place in the world.

"Johnny" would all but define Berry as one of the most influential instrumentalists ever to live. And yet for anybody seeking to master the song itself, being able to play a guitar was secondary. What mattered most was fitting the words to the beat, something not unlike dancing with a jackhammer.

"You know," Berry once explained, "maybe it is true what they say, that playing these Chuck Berry songs is easy. But try singing them. The words come out hard, like bullets."[2]

Back in the 1970s, Tomato was a high school band of no special reputation from Philadelphia, getting nowhere slowly while playing in the manner of Grand Funk Railroad and Blue Cheer. To get a foothold in the club scene then, a band needed to be able to make people dance. So Tomato decided, in a last act before giving up, to rename themselves the Derelicks and start playing Chuck Berry songs. They played "Johnny B. Goode" and "Rock and Roll Music." People *did* dance, and they found nominal success.

But first, the singer and guitarist for the Derelicks, Ben Vaughn, had to come to terms with Chuck Berry's bullet-like precision on "Johnny B. Goode."

> What I had to learn was you had to do it pretty much exactly the way he did it. Because if you drop one word or put a "but" or "'cause" or "well" in like singers do, you lose a word. It's compact writing, and every word is important.
>
> I remember stumbling over "the people passing by they would . . ." I dropped the "they" and I fell short at the end of the line. I was a beat short and I was lost. I had to go back and figure out "What am I doing wrong?"

You would likely never notice the complexity of the song because it moves in such a relentlessly straight line, with the streamlined simplicity of an arrow shot out of the ground. The first verse setting up the tale is a long single sentence, and the rest of the song runs on after it.

"Johnny B. Goode" isn't Berry's story, not in any literal sense. Johnny is a country boy, born in the Louisiana woods, illiterate and poor, and the singer was none of those things. Originally that country boy was a "colored boy," but Berry realized that such lyric clarity would keep Johnny off the radio. The change does something interesting to the song, turning the story of a fictitious performer, a Black man who becomes successful by working hard, into a true story about a real Black performer named Chuck Berry. His lesson is that to be a success in America, you have to play along—it's best to hide defining parts of yourself from common view. Fitting in means cutting out.

But Berry, it seems clear, wanted listeners to understand that the essence of Johnny's story was *his* essence. He picked "Deep down in Louisiana close to New Orleans" as its starting line, he said, because New Orleans was a slave port. And he picked the "Goode" of the title because Goode was the street he grew up on.[3] Was he saying this was a story for all African Americans? He had written a song about a hardworking man whose labor would win him the love and respect of the masses. And he was performing it—the song, and also the plot of the song—every night in sportatoriums, nightclubs, and on movie theater stages.

And if, in the years immediately predating Johnny's appearance in March 1958, a figure *was* rising above all other rock & rollers, a performer whose name would be in lights and just for that would draw strangers out of themselves, and if Elvis really was a poor country boy, well, wasn't that something? Some folks thought he'd written a song about Elvis. Chuck didn't ever say much about Elvis, but he did quietly say this about his signature number: "I imagine most black people naturally realize but I feel safe in stating that NO white person can conceive the feeling of obtaining Caucasian respect in the wake of a world of dark denial."

IN EARLY FEBRUARY 1958, AS THE WORLD WAS ABOUT TO MEET Johnny, Alan Freed announced the lineup for his "Big Beat" tour. It included Berry, Buddy Holly and the Crickets, Frankie Lymon, Danny & the Juniors, Screamin' Jay Hawkins, and the Chantels. A new act who had recently broken through, Jerry Lee Lewis, would also be featured prominently in the show. The forty-four-day tour would launch late that March.

Freed in 1958 was at the peak of his influence, with a series of popular low-budget films, his *Big Beat* TV show airing in New York City, and his radio program. Though he is sometimes depicted as greedy and shallow, interviews from this era show Freed taking principled, risky stands in favor of the music and its fans. He placed the blame for juvenile delinquency at the feet of parents, not teens, and he stuck up for Black acts. Asked about Elvis Presley, Freed gave him his due as a singer ("the only white man who can really sing the blues"), noted his white privilege, and suggested that Presley might have a brighter future in film.[4]

Up close one saw hypocrisies. But from the theater seats Freed was a blunt racial egalitarian. "He talked about Chuck Berry all the time, and would give long lectures on the importance of the Black artist in America," said Kim Fowley, a fan who knew Freed in his final years. "He explained how white acts covered and exploited the Black artists and how the public and consumers didn't know."[5]

He was a vulnerable hack. Money and booze flowed through his enterprise; he was transactional, and yet he booked and played the music that he liked, and he liked the good stuff. Freed enjoyed calling the shots in the middle of the storm, and quite often he was adept at it. But being adept was different from mastering the storm.

His motives baffled folks. "Freed, to me—and I talked to Chuck Berry about this," Screamin' Jay Hawkins once said with confusion. "We all tried to figure out Freed."[6]

Onstage at Cincinnati Gardens, Wichita Forum, and the other stops of the Big Beat tour, Freed stomped onto the stage in his "pop's a pimp" suit, thumping a telephone book like it was the Good Book and exhorting the masses, copying popular preachers of the era. As musician Lucky Millinder noted, Freed radiated "the fire and excitement of a Reverend Billy Graham."[7]

The tour came to the Industrial Mutual Association Auditorium in Flint, Michigan. The I.M.A. was a redbrick building with a flagpole in front and the names of World War II veterans on the wall. There were two shows on a Sunday in April, one in the afternoon for the white kids, and a second with a floor show at eight for Black adults. A young white fan named John Sinclair was there for both.

"It was a weird show, the first rock & roll they had for white people at the I.M.A. The Big Beat show acknowledged that there was a big white audience for the music," said Sinclair. "We were all fanatics—we liked to dance and it was a thrill to be around people who made the music. To go there twice in one day was like going to heaven," he said with a laugh. "That was the shit, man. Only cost $2.50."[8]

He doesn't remember Freed there, but Sinclair remembers Berry vividly. "It was Chuck Berry, man, the greatest of all time. There was nobody greater. It was like seeing Bird [saxophonist Charlie Parker]: he invented this shit. And then he did his duckwalk, and you saw the monster. He was Chuck Berry! Your heart would be doing it hard."

He notes how Berry and Jerry Lee Lewis fought over who would get to close a show. Freed's solution was to let them alternate. For the white kids' show in Flint, Lewis held the top slot. For the performance that night, Berry was the finisher. "He was the greatest—he blew Jerry Lee Lewis away," said Sinclair. "Jerry Lee Lewis is a bad motherfucker, and Chuck mopped the floor with him. Chuck came out and fucking murdered, I will never forget that."

Sinclair said he could sense the tension between the two. By some accounts, the friction began on the tour's opening night at the Paramount Theatre in Brooklyn. The white rocker from Ferriday, Louisiana, was hotter than anybody and coming off two number-one records in the previous year; now his "Breathless" was near the top. But on their late-March opening night, Freed made Berry the closer.

A seething Lewis put everything into a set that culminated with "Great Balls of Fire," during which he reached into his piano, pulled out a Coke bottle filled with gasoline, poured it across his keyboard, lit it on fire, and then played a combustible finale.

He made note of Berry's reaction: "First time I ever saw a colored guy turn white," Lewis said.

As he stomped off the stage he stared Berry down, daring him to "follow that" and then calling him the N-word. That's how Nick Tosches describes it in his 1982 biography *Hellfire*. The overtones—southern shame, rage, and racism in a bonfire—have floated above the story ever since. The truth is elusive. Lewis sometimes denies using the term, or denies the whole thing. Sometimes he just smirks. He has recast it as something that happened *to* him: he can play the victim of hearsay or the bad boy tweaking racial sensitivities, depending on his mood.[9]

Berry didn't tell any version of the story. Asked in 2003 if he liked Lewis, his response came from a remote place. "He's an artist that I played with a number of times," he said, employing words that might as well have been extracted from the Coolerator. "I don't know what you mean by like."[10]

They came to the Boston Arena on May 3. Freed hated Boston. After a 1956 show where kids tore up some seats, the Boston police invited him to the station for a chat. Emerging afterward, he called them "a bunch of rednecked old men."[11] He next drew fire after a 1957 show for a disturbance in the subway that the city tried to pin on him.

The Boston Arena appearance was nothing out of the ordinary off-stage. Several bottles were thrown, and the arena manager was angry that kids were standing on seats. A fight broke out.

Lewis had just finished playing, and Berry was doing his set. One report suggested that a woman jumped onstage and tried to grab Berry's genitals; Buddy Holly's biographer says a woman leaped onto the stage, "grabbing the crotch of one of the singers."[12]

The house lights went on, and Boston police officers declared that the show was over. Somebody came to the microphone and announced, "It looks like the police in Boston don't want you kids to have any fun." Most accounts report that was Freed. He denied saying it. One witness claimed it was Jerry Lee Lewis. In any case the event ended. Bottles really began flying then from all directions, and a group of fans tied colored bandannas signifying gang affiliations around their heads. A frightened Berry charged onto the drum riser and looked for a safe place to avoid getting hit.

Forced onto the streets around the arena, teenagers jostled, robberies happened, there was brawling along racial lines, and a nineteen-year-old sailor from Stoughton was stabbed. The police department quickly blamed Freed. On the street, witnesses alleged police violence. Meanwhile, how much criminality actually occurred was never clear, because the Boston police admitted they made no arrests of any robbers, brawlers, or stabbers. The only person arrested was Freed, who was charged with inciting a riot.

By the time the streets were cleared, maximum damage had been achieved. Not in the eyes of the sailor who got knifed. "It was a really good show," Albert Raggiani said. "What a crowd!" But using reports of the crime spree, the mayor banned rock shows in the city. A spokesman for the Archdiocese of Boston charged, "Rock n' roll influences and excites youth like jungle toms readying warriors for battle. Inject a wrong word or misunderstanding and the whole place blows up. The suggestive lyrics on r&b records, of course, are a matter of law enforcement."[13]

Freed denied criticizing Boston police, but the fallout was intense. Tour dates were canceled. A bill banning rock & roll from all Massachusetts government buildings was entered by a state legislator. Freed was charged under a state "anti-anarchy" law, one used to prosecute communists who advocated government overthrow.

His trial on the anarchy charge dragged on through late 1959, when the state tabled his prosecution. But by then Freed had quit WINS in New York, complaining the station didn't give him support, and then he lost his slot at WABC. Soon a "payola" scandal involving DJs taking money and gifts to play records would target him.

A sweeping generality rose from the streets of Boston and from hundreds of other such battlegrounds turned into tourist traps. It went like this: thanks to the music of Chuck Berry, Jerry Lee Lewis, Buddy Holly, Elvis, and the rest, youth culture prevailed. The power of teenagers together won. America won. But what Boston shows in miniature is that as late as 1958, there *was* no single youth culture. There were many youth cultures that did not line up and even ended in bloody disagreement with one another. Ready to tie their colors around their heads and stick a knife in somebody. They broke over racial and class lines, ethnic background and questions of faith and the color of your bandanna. They came together in motorcycle and fan clubs, sororities, gangs, social organizations, after-school dance parties, and hotrodders. Groups that got together on a street corner to sing, and groups that got together to plunder the community. Like Alan Freed, this disorder would not last much longer.

Freed had a simple, and perhaps dangerous, faith: "Rock 'n' roll is kids. It's not me or Elvis Presley or anyone else. The music belongs to them—they had a need for it and they discovered it. I don't set the pace—these kids do."[14]

But by 1958 a more unified, rational structure emerged. An audience defined by marketplace choices. *Bandstand* became *American Bandstand* when the show went national in August 1957. The show's audience for years going forward left out much of what was on view in

Boston as Chuck Berry played: interracial dancing, African Americans, juvenile delinquency. A slice of the rock & roll audience now stood in for the whole before a national TV audience.

PAST JOLIET, ILLINOIS, FRESH SKID MARKS ON ROUTE 66. IKE Turner was heading home from a show in Chicago when somebody in the car noticed the burnt rubber running from the road to a Cadillac askew. "Hey, that's Chuck Berry's car," Ike said. "Pull over, man."

Berry was asleep when Turner's singer Jimmy Thomas tapped on the window and offered to drive him home. Berry was testy. "Hey, man, you a good driver? You motherfucker, you look—you young-assed punk-assed n*****s, you all tear my car up, man." Thomas was startled how old-man Berry was being about his transportation. "He'd made 'Maybellene' and all that stuff about cars, and you'd have thought he was a real speed freak, but he was just the opposite, he was so paranoid about speed."[15]

"Okay," said Berry, "drive, but don't go over fifty." It pissed Thomas off, because Route 66 at three a.m. was owned by fast-hauling truckers and other speeders.

"So I nursed Chuck and them back to sleep."

He drove—his way—and made it to St. Louis in an hour. "We here!" said Thomas.

"What? Say, man . . . you been driving my car at 100 miles an hour."

Thomas said, "Yeah, man, but you here, ain't ya?"

Chuck Berry's guitar was a tool, a contraption. His Cadillac *was* Chuck Berry. He showed off his first car registration to a visitor once, preserved in a scrapbook, as if it explained everything. "All you had to have was a car and a guitar and you could make it in the world," he said while beaming.[16]

Growing up American in the middle of the twentieth century meant being steeped in the mythology of the open road. Driving gave access to the shared goals of self-direction and autonomy. Putting your car on everybody's road became an essential expression of democratic participation, a driver joining other figures in motion. Anonymous, you were as valuable as the person in the next vehicle, white or Black. As Chester Himes put it, "They don't discriminate against cars, just people."[17]

In the era of the Great Migration, the Black press encouraged car ownership and published advice about where Black families should vacation. Automobility was framed as a way of evading, or creating private space outside of, Jim Crow realities. African American writer George Schuyler suggested in 1930 that the main reason Blacks owned cars was to circumvent segregated transportation.

"All Negroes who can do so purchase an automobile as soon as possible," he urged, "in order to be free of discomfort, discrimination, segregation and insult."[18]

Buying a house in a nice part of town might not be possible—it often was not in St. Louis—but buying a nice car and driving through town was. Historian Paul Gilroy has noted that Black Americans' "distinctive history of propertylessness and material deprivation" drew them toward a kind of property that conveyed status and could be taken with them.[19]

In this regard, the Cadillac became iconic. From the time of slavery, whites viewed Black bodies as existing for work; here was an opportunity to move leisurely down wide streets and be viewed in repose. The very joy and self-possession cars made possible created rage in some white observers, a reaction easily exploited, for instance, by politicians employing the stereotype of the "Welfare Queen," driving a Cadillac, wearing fur, manipulating a system meant to exclude her.[20]

Isabel Wilkerson, in her book *The Warmth of Other Suns*, tells the story of an African American doctor in 1955 who wanted to buy a Cadillac but was steered to used cars by a dealer who judged him unlikely to make the payments. Such consumer profiling, enacted in countless settings, might have been one inspiration for Berry's "No Money Down," where the Black buyer storms into the dealership and makes sure his wishes are respected.

Owning a nice ride and displaying it on the avenue, notes Gilroy, granted a degree of social status and citizenship "that were blocked by formal politics and violently inhibited by informal codes." In the early years of the twentieth century, one powerful African American was pressing for full citizenship in the court of public opinion. Jack Johnson was a great boxer who had won the world heavyweight title in 1908 and then found no white boxers willing to fight him. In St. Louis in 1912, Johnson made a weeklong theatrical appearance. The fighter invited a local writer for breakfast, a platter of ham and eggs and a wad of money as big as a shoebox resting before him on the table.

Johnson wanted to respond to white criticism of his lifestyle.

"I live well, yes; and I have automobiles, four of them, but what of it? My living doesn't cost me a great deal," he said. "Automobiles are my only real dissipation. I love them as I would a stable of horses."[21]

He laughed off the criticism that he was frivolously wasting his money. "When I am not busy making money I am driving one of my machines." It doesn't cost him much, he underscored with a smile. "Perhaps a fine now and then for going too fast."

Just his appearance rolling down the street drove police mad. He joked he could get a speeding ticket for backing out of a driveway; his citations became national news stories.

A wire report appearing in numerous papers described his visit to train in San Francisco in 1910. Johnson, who "seems to have a genius for making himself offensive in public, gave good exhibition of this faculty today when he came down Market street in [boxing promoter Tex] Rickard's big auto seated in the tonneau between his white wife and Mrs. Little, wife of his manager."[22]

Johnson was dressed in "glad rags, silk hat and sparkling diamonds." The car stopped at saloons and booze parlors as Johnson made the rounds. "Every day finds him in his motor speeding around the city in full view of the passing throng, a part of his training system that he seems to enjoy more than sparring or punching the bag," bemoaned another newspaper account from San Francisco. The promenade was an affront to all those who would insist that Black bodies were meant to sweat for others.

ASSISTANT NIGHT CAPTAIN ANDREW PALLARDY OF THE ST. CHARLES, Missouri, police department was observing traffic on Highway 74 early in the morning of June 2, 1958. He watched as a car drove less than a thousand yards on a flat tire, coming to a stop on the highway shoulder. What got Pallardy's attention was the car itself: "He was driving a 1958 pink Cadillac."

Pallardy made a U-turn across the divided highway and pulled up directly behind the vehicle. St. Charles County was about forty miles northwest of downtown St. Louis. The Cadillac came to a stop a few yards outside the county line.

Pallardy said he approached because he thought the driver might need assistance. But then he observed the man, who was fixing his flat, struggle to get the spare tire out of his trunk.

It "led me to believe that he knew nothing about removing it, that that was possibly a stolen vehicle," said Pallardy.

"Being a police officer, I was very suspicious."

Ordinarily, a driver fumbling with their spare tire might be a good definition of someone in need of help. But by now the officer had seen that the driver was a Black man and that in his passenger seat sat a white woman. She was seventeen-year-old Joan Mathis, a girlfriend of Berry's who lived in St. Louis. They were returning from shows Berry had played in Topeka, Kansas, and Omaha, Nebraska.

Pallardy ordered her out of the car and tried to ask a question. Berry told her to keep quiet. Because the officer had decided Berry was suspicious, and because the Cadillac had come to a stop a few feet outside St. Charles County, Pallardy called the state highway patrol.

Some twenty minutes later Trooper Paul Neumann arrived. Noting Berry's driver's license had expired, Neumann put him under arrest. Trooper Neumann told Pallardy to watch Berry and Mathis as they stood by the back of the Cadillac while he searched the car. Beneath the driver's seat he found a .25-caliber French MAB pistol, fully loaded, one in the chamber.

Berry was taken to St. Charles police headquarters, where he was questioned by the chief of police and FBI agent Thomas Dempsey. It's unclear from available court records why an FBI agent would have been called in so quickly on a run-of-the-mill arrest. Neumann would later say that it was routine for St. Charles police officers to not make an arrest on a lapsed driver's license, not even with a gun in the car.[23]

The *Argus* reported, "St. Louis's homegrown rock and roll king has a new record out called 'Johnny B. Goode.' But police in St. Charles think the title is a misnomer. They think 'Johnny' has been far from good." Berry was fined thirty dollars for driving without Missouri plates and having an expired driver's license.

The bigger problem was the French pistol. Berry explained that he needed it when club owners withheld payment after a show, but Missouri law barred ex-felons from owning a gun.

Bail was set for Berry and Mathis, who was listed as a material witness. According to the *Argus*, "The bail was no problem, however, for

Chuck Berry peeled off $1,250 in cash from a roll that would choke a mule, and put it on the line, so he and Joan Mathis could go on their way."

On June 10, Berry and Mathis were trailed for two miles as he drove along Natural Bridge Road just after midnight. The police car pulled him over—weaving dangerously, the officer said. Berry was ticketed for the expired license again, arrested, and released on bond for "careless and imprudent driving."

A day later, Berry was due in court for a hearing on his firearm violation. His new lawyer, Merle Silverstein, was flabbergasted by the scene. Silverstein didn't follow rock & roll and had no idea who his client was. Waiting outside the courthouse in St. Charles, the attorney saw "two hundred screaming girls around the building just fighting to touch him," he said. "One girl said, 'Sign my sleeve!' And another girl who didn't have any paper said, 'Sign my hand!' I heard her say, 'I'm never going to wash this hand again.'"[24]

The judge held off on making a ruling on the felony gun charge. The next day, Berry was in Chicago, recording "Carol" at Chess.

JACK JOHNSON ONCE ENTERED THE BOXING RING IN PINK PAJAMAS, and the Los Angeles Pavilion about tore itself apart. A "screaming, caterwauling, belligerent pink," wrote a sports reporter. "Any fellow who could gaze one rapt, fascinated glance at those pinkies and not go down to defeat, paralyzed, must be a better fighter than Brother Jack." It was 1902, and he was fighting Jack Jeffries. Jeffries was knocked out in the fifth round, "a jounce of dead flesh" that Johnson picked up off the ring floor.[25]

Something about pink and black drove some folks crazy. The welterweight champion Sugar Ray Robinson got himself a pink Cadillac in 1950—flamingo pink, Robinson stipulated—drove it through the heart of Harlem, and parked in front of the bar that bore his name. "That car was the Hope Diamond of Harlem," Robinson declared.[26]

"When people think they recognize a celebrity, they hesitate a moment," he wrote. *Is that who I think it is?* "But when they saw me in that car, they didn't have to hesitate. They knew. There was only one like it—Sugar Ray's pink Cadillac."[27]

In the summer of 1958, Chuck Berry made a controversial appearance at the Newport Jazz Festival. George Wein was festival organizer, in recent years bringing jazz to the leisuring upper crust of Rhode Island. John Hammond sat on Newport's board of directors and was pushing Wein to inject Berry and Ray Charles, inject rock & roll, into the 1958 festival. Wein admitted he worried that Berry would be an embarrassment.[28]

Berry drove to Newport in his pink Cadillac, customized with a rack of air horns peeking over the fender, Venetian blinds obscuring the view into the back seat, and a racoon tail dangling from the tailpipe. It was like the Sex Pistols pulling into a megachurch.

Jack Johnson: Sugar Ray Robinson: Chuck Berry. African American grandeur. This was not the collective assertion of craftsmanship and group standards that the jazz musicians who reigned at Newport represented; this was stick-your-neck-out star power. It was style and fire, condensed like the Hope Diamond.

The vintage jazz band backing Berry at Newport featured masters of the 1920s and '30s who maintained rigid backbones and exuberant smiles, the kind they had been showing white audiences for decades. In the documentary *Jazz on a Summer's Day*, they can be seen holding back their support for the newcomer.

Emcee Willis Conover introduces Berry to the audience by saying he was "from St. Louis, with three records which to date have sold more than a million copies apiece, even by record company report— Chuck Berry!"

Berry corrects Conover's math, noting he has a dozen records out, and says it is an honor to be "among such great musicians and such fine people." Those proud jazz veterans proceed to haze Berry, doodling across "School Days" in a way that makes clear they didn't care enough to offer robust mockery. Drummer Jo Jones is not about to stoop to a backbeat, and between songs he, trombonist Jack Teagarden, and trumpeter Buck Clayton exchange remarks to one another. They don't provide much backing, save a maniacal squalling clarinet solo from Rudy Rutherford on "Sweet Little Sixteen." As the headline in *Variety* put it a week later, "Jazz Purists Razz Berry at Newport." Berry visibly would not be offended. He holds his ground, performs for the large audience that drove in to see him, and plays a guitar that sounds rawer, more defiant, with each song.[29]

This is an incredibly dense passage of Chuck Berry's life. He was creating a body of work that would build a musical, rhythmic, and lyrical vocabulary for rock & roll. He would help generate the imagery and subject matter that would fill the charts in the next few years.

There was a business to build, and a family that was growing.

See him holding the Newport stage. To his back is a Black past that offered him scrutiny and shade. In front of him young white Americans, moving to his guitar.

There were currents that he had started, while others he gladly rode forward. There were watchers just now bringing him into focus. A lot was going on. Perhaps a roomy luxury vehicle with a wide windshield provided a clear view of the way ahead.

SHORTLY AFTER RETURNING FROM NEWPORT, BERRY WAS INVITED to meet with US Attorney Frederick Mayer in downtown St. Louis. Mayer was conferring with the FBI about Berry. The meeting was a social call to tell the star that federal officials were aware of potentially prosecutable actions, and to let him know that while they wouldn't file new charges at the moment, they could later, should Berry break the law.

The gun charge was a worry: driving across state lines with it made it a federal violation. But the larger charge they were measuring him for involved his travels with Joan Mathis. The FBI now knew he had been with the teenage St. Louis woman just before he was arrested in St. Charles and on a separate trip weeks before, when she accompanied him on the Freed tour through the Midwest.

The Mann Act was the name of a federal law criminalizing travel across state lines with a woman "for the purpose of prostitution or debauchery, or for any other immoral purpose." The felony (named for Illinois congressman James Robert Mann) was passed in 1910 and signed into law by President William Howard Taft. It was a quirky antique that had helped establish the FBI early on.

The act emerged during an age of social upheaval, as waves of Americans were moving from rural regions into cities and women were entering, and remaking, the male-dominated workforce. Simultaneously the dawn of the twentieth century saw a wave of immigration to the United States, triggering social anxiety which itself helped shape a stereotype: the dark-skinned newcomer exploiting naive young white women who left home and entered the big city. There were widespread rumors of national prostitution rings, run by immigrants and preying on unschooled, trusting women.

The Mann Act was also known as the White-Slave Traffic Act, underscoring both the race of the women it was meant to protect and the purity it claimed was being besmirched. The law was passed when the FBI was still called the Department of Justice's Bureau of Investigation, and the bureau's growth was significantly rooted in its prosecution in court and the media of thousands of cases under this popular law in the 1920s and '30s.[30]

The vagueness of its wording—what exactly was an act of debauchery?—gave the bureau a moral crusade that helped its budget and mandate grow in its earliest years, and provided a strong tool for criminalizing consensual sex acts the bureau decided were out-of-bounds. The mere wording of the charge in the press could turn a man's rendezvous with a mistress into a tabloid sensation.

The most famous application of the Mann Act displayed its racist undertones. Jack Johnson in 1908 had become the first African American to be the world boxing champion, making him a hero in the eyes of many and a force to be stopped to many others. Bureau agents had amassed a file on Johnson's private life and tried and failed a first time to prosecute him. Then they enlisted a white woman who had traveled with Johnson in 1909 and 1910 who was willing to testify. An all-white jury found the champion guilty in June 1913.

The stereotype of nonwhite men as sexual predators had made the ruling possible and now surged through American culture. Black men working in barbershops and as porters were fired by white employers out of spite and fear in the wake of Johnson's prosecution; white theater owners stopped booking Black entertainers, while white-owned newspapers across the country directly threatened his life and encouraged vigilantes to take him out.[31]

The champion skipped bail and fled the country, traveling the world for the next seven years. He had lost his fortune defending himself in court; few challengers would fight him, and he was unable to find work. A global outlaw, Johnson in 1920 turned himself in and served time at the federal penitentiary in Leavenworth, Kansas.

That was the law and the history that the US attorney wielded when Berry came for a visit in late summer 1958. Berry knew he was being watched.

A few weeks later, a jarring incident.

Berry arrived early for a show at Lakeside Amusement Park, in Salem, Virginia, where he was headlining a bill also featuring Lloyd Price. Before performing, he walked the park grounds. A Black man strolling an amusement park in Jim Crow Virginia already was likely to draw a degree of attention. Then the performer, wearing a suit and shiny gold tie, came to rest at the door to the women's bathroom. A partition blocked viewing through the door, and Berry was seen acting giddy, clowning, jumping up to peer over the partition.

An off-duty white police officer watched Berry as he bounced up and down and arrested him. He explained to the cop, "I'm Chuck Berry."

"I don't care if you're Elvis Presley, you're going to jail," he was told.

The performer quickly posted bail and made it back in time for his show that night. He left Salem afterward. The *Roanoke Times* reported that a local judge found him guilty in absentia of a Peeping Tom charge. His $156.25 cash bond was forfeited, and Berry was sentenced to sixty days in jail. "Should he return to Roanoke County, he could be required to serve a jail term," the news story declared.[32]

"As far as we know, he never did set foot again in the county," said journalist Tad Dickens in 2021. Witnesses have suggested that Berry seemed drunk (though he was not a drinker), and that he was merely goofing for the park patrons. Whatever else it was—dangerous, thrilling, exhausting—rule breaking was also getting flat-out harder to do when everybody was watching.

THREE YEARS OF PERFORMING HAD CHANGED HIM. THE ROAD HAD made Chuck wealthy, and he'd encountered all kinds of people outside the orbit of the Ville. His songs were rich with the farawayness of the country. Berry liked touring for reasons beyond the living it afforded him. And yet for all of that he remained deeply tied to St. Louis and was setting down more roots.

In April 1957 he paid $8,000 to purchase thirty acres in Wentzville, a quiet country town in St. Charles County. The property was just wheat fields when he bought it, but Berry intended to build a community there.

The next summer, his family moved into an eleven-room home at 13 Windermere Place in St. Louis. According to one neighbor present at the time, Berry paid for the turn-of-the-century three-story mansion with $30,000 cash. Daughters eight-year-old Ingrid and six-year-old Melody played in the ballroom on the third floor.

Windermere Place was a block-long private street in a once firmly white neighborhood. In the 1950s, several well-off Black families moved in, including that of poet and playwright Ntozake Shange; in her novel *Betsey Brown*, Shange described life on Windermere, Betsey fighting with siblings over watching *American Bandstand* or *Howdy Doody*. Blacks were relocating to the area and white flight was underway, but on Windermere enough whites stayed to give the street a feeling of ease distinct from tensions elsewhere in the city.[33]

In the Berry household, a Silvertone Console High Fidelity record player that was able to spin Themetta's 78 blues discs as well as long-play albums was a center of attention. There was a reel-to-reel tape deck, an FM radio, and a full-sized television.

Chuck was on the road for weeks at a time, and when he came home he wanted the whole block to know it. "I remember him coming home and he loved opening up his attaché and he'd show us the cash," recalled his daughter Melody. Berry would buy bags full of White Castle burgers and give them out to the children in the neighborhood. "Everybody would say, 'Your dad's so cool!'" remembered Charles Berry Jr. Hamburgers for all, an integrated street; Windermere Place was an idyllic image of success.[34]

With a growing interest in investments, Berry set up a business office. An important new figure in his life, Francine Gillium, was helping him out. Berry said they met when he was playing a weeklong stint at a club in Pittsburgh. It was 1956, and the blond-haired, white twenty-year-old asked for two autographs.

The next show, she came back with her mother. In the course of a week Francine Gillium had become devoted to Chuck Berry.

A year later she moved to St. Louis. Berry put her up in a local hotel, but the hotel didn't allow him to visit with her. So he moved her to an African American hotel, and ultimately into his and Themetta's old house on Whittier Street. Gillium—Fran, he called her—became his business manager and aide for the rest of his life. "There had never been another woman, including my wife, who had shown such interest in my career and public image," he said. "This young, rapid-but-distinctly-speaking girl was taking me by storm, pouring out the possibilities that could snowball my destination into a long, sunny career. I thought that her acquaintance was good to have, better to develop, and best to keep."[35]

Early in 1958 Berry appeared on *Dick Clark's Saturday Night Beechnut Show*, casually mentioned he was starting a fan club, and invited Clark's viewership to join. The announcement came as a shock to his assistant, who found herself opening over three thousand pieces of mail the following week.

Gillium and Berry created a corporation for the real estate he was buying and set up an office for his various projects in a building he owned on West Easton Drive. They formed Chuck Berry Music Incorporated, his own music-publishing company. Meanwhile, bags of mail for the Chuck Berry Fan Club continued piling up.

He hectored her on how to answer the office phone, ringing Fran randomly to hear how she greeted strangers, then gave her notes on improvement. The fan club was heading toward seven thousand members, and Berry had her alphabetize all members by state and city and required phone numbers whenever possible. Demanding in a voice both kind and coaxing, he displayed a need to assert order, to dominate.

"He has taught me control—control of myself and others, especially in situations that involve me," Gillium said. "He has taught me to be a pathfinder; I knew he was one when I first met him."[36]

On occasion she accompanied Berry on the road, operating, he would explain, as his manager and helping make sure he got paid the right amount. He sometimes introduced her as his wife.

The situation could lead to amusement when they traveled in the South, where a white woman accompanying a Black man became the subject of unwanted attention. Berry was meeting her at a New Orleans airport, having befriended a pair of lawmen while he waited. When Gillium walked off the plane, his friends charged up and pretended to arrest her, while Chuck hid behind a cigarette machine, cracking up.

Having formed the fan club, together they opened Chuck Berry's Club Bandstand in a basement space at North Grand and Delmar Boulevard. Club Bandstand was an all-ages space where fans could gather and dance, and Berry and other musicians would play for them. Members showed their membership card to get in for free.

By mid-December of 1958 Fran and Chuck had obtained a liquor license, and the place became a nightclub. She ran the room from behind the bar: pouring drinks, watching the door, fielding calls regarding bookings and business deals and beer suppliers. Berry had a social ambition as well: he wanted to create a space like the Buffalo bar, Mandy's, that had made such an impression on him. An integrated nightclub just down the street from the St. Louis landmark movie palace the Fox Theatre, where Berry had been denied admission as a Black youth.

"My aim had been to draw a biracial clientele like that I had seen around New England," he explained.[37] He advertised his intentions in the *Argus*: "EVERYBODY WELCOME."

In the next year, the Club Bandstand would be joined by the Holy Barbarian, an integrated St. Louis Beat hangout where the guitarist Grant Green played a legendary stand in an integrated band. The Holy Barbarian was run by Ollie Matheus. "He had this long white hair, and he was this kind of white guy that when you heard him talk you *knew* he was down in the trenches. He had your back," said historian, writer, and documentary maker Sharony Andrews Green. "He was a radical. When he put Grant Green on his tiny stage, he was basically telling the police 'Come after me.'"[38]

Berry was a different kind of entrepreneur, but both were on uncharted ground in St. Louis. City officials took note. According to a story in the Black press, in 1957 Berry was arrested for the stickup of a St. Louis insurance agent. The police showed the agent a picture of the star, and the victim identified Berry as the robber. Berry produced a contract showing he was playing Baltimore at the time of the robbery, and he was released. But why would they show his picture in the first place?

Sometimes he told Fran to grab a pad of paper, they were driving out to Wentzville. Chuck said he was building a grand place he was going to call Berry Park. What she saw was somewhat plainer: yellow mud that her high heels sank into while she followed him around the grounds.

He parked his car by the stranded bus—one he'd bought for a West Coast tour he'd arranged in 1956. In a playful, insistent voice he tossed her ideas to write down: what could go where, how big a building should be, where a road could be built and a lake dug. Berry himself made the illustrations that would guide the architect he picked for Berry Park. "Mr. B proved to be a true engineer, complete with slide rule, drawing board, and colored pencils," said Gillium.[39]

Berry Park called out for a manifesto. Building it was important to him, and he wanted it to be something slightly parallel to the world: a place where he could relax and where the public could come and let their guard down. A studio to record, a venue to hear music played by others. A grounds where swimmers did not face segregation. Prince built his Paisley Park; it was a symbol of who he was and the world he wanted to superimpose on this one, an estate and an arts center, a private utopia where creativity might flourish among those who were invited. Thirty years before, Berry Park was a home turned inside out, a vision open to the public. Somewhere to be free.

"It goes a long way back. When I was a child I lived opposite a park but my father forbade me to go there. We moved somewhere else, and the same thing happened. You see, it's a psychological thing," Chuck said. "When I bought the land to develop it was just wheat land." To build there, and then to let the world in, would be to heal.[40]

He wanted a big green space, a lake stocked with fish, trees to block the view, and the public wandering through—Black and white explicitly on even footing. He had country clubs in mind, for sure, but a club for everybody who could respect everybody else. Something like a public park, really, and like an amusement park—he was shooting for that kind of fun.

On a tabletop at his St. Louis mansion, Berry imagined the place he wanted. There were model trees on the table and buildings marked out on a map of the grounds. "He designed it up on the third floor of Windermere," daughter Ingrid said. "It's a dream that came true. It was his dream."[41]

With the help of Chuck's dad and brother, the core of Berry Park was built. They cleared the land and put buildings up. They faced opposition from white citizens of St. Charles County, noted Charles Berry Jr. "My dad just took it as a challenge. . . . He caught hell back in the '50s before Berry Park opened up—St. Charles county would come out, constantly come out and bust him for absolutely no particular reason. Just because, hey it's Tuesday."[42]

There must have been some Disneyland in his imagining—a landscape that opened almost at exactly the moment that "Maybellene" was released—and an influence from the hillbilly parks, the working-class recreation areas scattered around St. Louis. Maybe he thought about it in terms of the white country club where his dad had taken him to work when he was a kid. Berry Park would be a place to start something that should have happened naturally. A place to undo damage previously done.

That was the promise of "Johnny B. Goode": that a Black man, even if masked as a country boy, knew he could win and would make others know it too. A Jack Johnson who could be understood and move from villain to hero. Nat King Cole—they wanted to kill him. Berry paid him tribute every time someone asked who he got his music from.

That's where he was at the end of 1958. His name was in lights.

10

"BACK IN THE USA"

NORTH CAROLINA WAS GETTING FARTHER AWAY BY THE MINUTE, the skinny country boy thought. He was parked in coach on a Qantas flight to Australia when he heard unexpected sounds drifting from the first-class compartment: intricate country harmonies, a mandolin.

George Hamilton IV was a teen pop star with a gold record to his name ("A Rose and a Baby Ruth"). Above the sounds of the jet, somewhere over the Pacific, he heard the country duo Louvin Brothers singing.

Following the sound, Hamilton flagged down a stewardess and poked his head into the front of the plane, where he saw Chuck Berry reclining, his feet perched on the headrest in front of him, a battery-powered record player on his chest.

The younger man poured out his surprise to find that the guy he was going to share a stage with on a tour of Australia was into the Louvin Brothers' *Tragic Songs of Life*. "I'm a child of the south and I just did not expect to find a Black man listening to country," he said later.[1]

Berry tossed it back in Hamilton's face. "White boy, didn't you ever listen to 'Johnny B. Goode'?" he said pointedly before quoting his own lyrics: "Just a country boy . . ."

Looking Hamilton over, Berry added that he also liked the Grand Ole Opry, though unlike Hamilton *he* had to listen from the street out front, because Black fans were barred from "Whites Only" shows at Ryman Auditorium.

"Chuck had a huge chip on his shoulder about the race issue," said Hamilton. "And with very good reason." However, they quickly became buddies; in Honolulu they roomed together at the Surfrider Hotel, then hit the beach the next morning, Berry dapper in orchid-print trunks and shirt and Hamilton whiter than his new friend had even guessed. They posed for a photograph with their arms around one another, an image that shocked Hamilton's mother-in-law in South Carolina.

The "Shower of Stars" tour Chuck headlined also featured Bobby Darin, Hamilton, Jo Ann Campbell, and Australian rocker Johnny O'Keefe, playing twenty-one shows in eight days. It was Berry's first time traveling beyond North America.

"George and Chuck, they were good friends," remembered guitarist Lou Casch. "They had one thing in common—photography." The friends walked the streets of Sydney, photographing fruit carts and sidewalk scenes.[2]

Berry was aware of the stares he got from Australians. Hamilton felt that the attention came from locals who were shocked to see a fashionably dressed Black man. "I think people must think I'm one of those Aborigines," Berry declared.

All the acts were backed by the Dee Jays, a sharp group of Australian jazz players. Lou Casch was the Dee Jays' guitarist and leader, and he recalled the casual way Berry first met the band that would support him for the Australian shows.

Chuck's limo rolled up to the venue when the Dee Jays were eating lunch. "You guys play blues?" the American in suit and sunglasses asked, sizing them up. "Yeah," somebody answered. "Any key you mention." Berry called out Charlie Christian's "Seven Come Eleven," and as the guys played Berry pointed to different instruments, telling one after another to take a twelve-bar solo, until ultimately the headliner was satisfied. He watched them play his songs, but Berry didn't join in. "Guys, all you have to do is watch my right foot," he declared. When he brought it down, it meant the song was done. With that, so was Berry: "See you in Mel-born," he said, getting back in the limo.

The brusque disregard for basic interaction with musicians he'd be depending on was an emerging characteristic. You could be offended by it, if you wanted. There were other concerns he needed to address. Berry had heard that the electrical current in Australia was different, so thinking his instrument wouldn't work, he left it at home. That forced Casch to scramble to find an electric guitar, no easy thing in Australia in 1959.

Between shows, Casch, Hamilton, and Berry would play records and talk in Berry's hotel room. "I was the only colored guy in the Dee Jays," said Casch. "Chuck and I kind of gravitated together." Casch had grown up in West Sumatra, Indonesia, where he attended medical school when World War II broke out. He joined the Indonesian underground and fought the Japanese occupation; after the war, he fought the Dutch occupation. He resettled in Australia in the late 1940s and hitched a ride with Johnny O'Keefe, more or less the Elvis of Australia. The only dark-skinned musician in O'Keefe's band, Casch was dubbed "the Witch Doctor."

They were three thoughtful people far from their respective homes. Casch broke down the status of Indigenous people in the Australian society of the 1950s. By then the First Nations people (a modern term that acknowledges Aboriginal and Torres Strait Islander people) had lost claim to most of their land and were denied many basic rights and government services other Australians enjoyed.

The Americans were curious about Australian racial dynamics; Berry asked how come he hadn't seen any Aboriginal people anywhere in these major cities. Hamilton compared the plight of the First Nations people to that of Black people under the Jim Crow segregation he'd grown up taking for granted. Berry, though choosing his words carefully, was listening to everything and filing it away.

"George said we couldn't do this in some parts of the States, meaning Blacks and whites couldn't stay in the same hotel," Casch remembered. "Chuck changed the subject. He said, 'Let's cool it. Let's have another scotch.' It wasn't that he was uncomfortable talking about those things—more like he didn't want to be impolite when he was a visitor in the country."

A radio host in Melbourne remembered a conversation with Berry where he brought up First Nations people, adding, "I hate being here, Stan. I can't wait to get back home."[3]

The second half of the tour featured several days of shows at the Sydney Stadium, a solid old building with wood floors that resonated when fans stomped their feet. If Berry knew of the venue's history, *it* would have resonated with *him*, for the stadium was built in a hurry in 1908 in order to facilitate a title fight between Jack Johnson and the white world heavyweight champion, Tommy Burns.[4]

Johnson had been stalking the Canadian fighter for two years, trailing from Europe to Australia, challenging him for a shot at the heavyweight title. White boxers had refused to fight him, but in Sydney, Burns relented. They fought on Boxing Day, and by the eighth round many fans were shouting for the police to intervene, so badly was Burns's face swollen. By the fourteenth round, the police inspector finally relented, making Johnson the first Black heavyweight champion of the world. Writer Jack London was in attendance, and he wrote thereafter of the need for "a great white hope" to avenge this Caucasian humiliation.

Berry and the others dressed in smelly rooms that had been used by generations of boxers and wrestlers, the scent of sweat and liniment thick in the air. You entered the open-air arena through a long barbed-wire tunnel, mobbed by shouting fans, "teenage hands trying to grab your hair, your tie, your plectrum, your everything," recalled Casch. It was a long walk from the dressing room to the stage, set up in the middle of the boxing ring. The stage itself revolved, and the overall feel was that the performer was the gladiator confronting a seething force.

It was a complicated trip, one that had Berry thinking about race and power on a global level and talking about it with several friends who jogged his thinking. How they stirred him up, he didn't directly say.

But the tour focused his attention on the treatment of the First Nations people, which he heard all about. And it didn't escape him that Australians thought he was one, which troubled him. The colonialists who governed Australia from 1788 until 1901 had a pejorative term for Aboriginal people: Blacks. Although, unlike many American states, Australia never endorsed slavery on a governmental level, it had an undeniable history of slavery, racism, and forced labor. Chuck came back to a Missouri where he was able to buy a house and start a business he advertised as open to all. He had Berry Park to develop and more hits to write for an exploding audience. He believed in America.

When he got home, he didn't seem to say anything about the conversations he'd had or to particularly talk about the trip (though he does say in his autobiography that, walking past singer Jo Ann Campbell's room, he got a peek at her naked).

Quickly after the tour, Berry wrote a song that celebrates home. The joy he felt saturated his performance as he giddily offered a full-throated whoop upon his return to American soil.

In "Back in the USA" Chuck doesn't detail what he loves about America. It turns out being home means being in motion—he mentions the skyscrapers, the freeways, notes the bigness of the country, and name-checks certain big cities. It's a song about reconnecting, alright, but reconnecting with driving around and looking out the car window. And you never really *see* any city. Being in America means moving from one place to the next.

Instead, he's out "looking for a drive-in," for some place to get a burger and hear a jukebox play. Berry knew he couldn't order a bite in just any old place in his hometown, let alone south of St. Louis. But he saw it changing and felt he was helping make progress.

"What's that saying, the best way to eat an elephant is one bite at a time? Well that's what he did," said Charles Berry Jr. "He took that whole thing about segregation and not being able to walk into the front doors of places he was going to play and took it as a challenge: I could sit around and brood and go on the blame game trip and not make any progress *or* take this as the challenge it is."[5]

There are no people in "Back in the USA," just "I." Coming from a place where he'd gotten several quick lessons in history, there's no history, no past in this "USA," just now. Home means access to anything you want. It's a calculating song, brined in hope.

When Greil Marcus asked him in front of students in Berkeley in 1969 about writing "Back in the USA," Berry sidestepped the heart of the question, how he felt about America.

"That was strictly my experience in Australia, which was a drag, I mean really a drag. I never found even a hot dog," he responded.[6]

"I mean, the food is way out, and at that time 'down under' was still down under, and it was really just a drag trip. I was down there two weeks, and I didn't enjoy myself, so I was just glad to get back into the USA." A group of Berkeley students would not be the audience he chose to share his patriotism with.

Chuck, as Lou Casch had understood, possessed a "social conscience," though he was not "a social commentator." Australia gave him a certain new perspective, and he applied it precisely when he returned. He rarely spoke about it again.

Etta James, who sang backup on "Back in the USA," said she didn't like working with Chuck in the studio. You definitely couldn't get anything you wanted when you backed Berry; he only fed the singers cheese crackers and peanut butter from a vending machine. The songcraft, however, she admired. "His songs were smart because, unlike most of us, he was aiming straight at white teenagers, the saddle shoe crowd. He had a marketing mind; he sang and wrote to sell."[7]

James takes a reasonable position that Berry was just giving the white kids what they wanted. But *he* wanted it too. Berry believed in America. He pushed through barriers, and when they gave way, the lesson was that actions worked, certainly more than words.

A long time later, a white reporter asked him about the racism he'd encountered over the years. Berry flared.

"This is the greatest country on earth. I was in Australia, and I found out they wouldn't even let a Black man become a citizen there. That's why I wrote that song. You know 'Back in the USA,' don't you?"[8]

HE PERFORMED IN THE 1957 FILM *MISTER ROCK AND ROLL*. THE third film he appeared in, and the first in which he acted, came out in the summer of 1959. *Go, Johnny, Go!* was another attempt by Alan Freed to wring money from the big screen: he produced, his business manager Jack Hooke was an associate producer, and Gary Alexander wrote his one and only screenplay, a tale of a young rocker named Johnny Melody who, through the patronage of Freed and the support of loyal friends like Berry, was about to make it very big.

Go, Johnny, Go! begins with Berry singing a version of "Johnny B. Goode" featuring a horn section, just because. The film amounts to a visualization of Berry's rock & roll founding myth. The Johnny in question now has a face—a white one. Johnny Melody is a sweet-voiced orphan who, with the support of Black peers like Berry, is destined to eclipse them on the world stage.

Made fast in a Culver City, California, studio, the film was directed by Paul Landres, a journeyman of good notice who was busy in 1959, having shot three episodes of *Bonanza*, four *Man Without a Guns*, six *Man with a Cameras*, three *Sky Kings*, two *Riflemans*, and almost certainly more TV work besides, while also making two other feature films.

Berry has a lively screen presence, and if he had been groomed the way Elvis was, and given the time to rehearse his lines, he might have made more and better films. On the set, he felt nervous and out of his element. "They gave me a ticket, sent me to Culver City with my guitar, they threw a script in front of me and we started shooting the next day," he said. "The next day I came and I think I had read the script, but after I'd read it, you know it's like a book, it doesn't say anything. You're not interested in it and I didn't remember any of it."[9]

He had to be talked out of leaving before shooting was finished, and those on the set experienced his hostility. "He had a dressing room—he'd walk right by you to get to his room and have no idea you were even there. He cared about nobody else," said the film's star, singer and teen idol Jimmy Clanton. "He was an asshole. I'm a Christian, and that guy was the opposite of any God-fearing person I have ever met."[10]

The finished film was a number of firsts and lasts. It was the last one Freed would make: by the end of the year he had refused to testify before the grand jury investigating payola, and he'd lost his TV show on WNEW-TV and his radio slot on WABC.

Go, Johnny, Go! features the only movie footage of Ritchie Valens—the singer shows up at a jam session and plays "Ooh! My Head" for Freed, who bolts before the song's over so he can find Johnny Melody. Clanton, who played Johnny, had grit and rhythm, but still, it's weird to see Freed bail on Ritchie Valens. And it must have felt curious for Berry, seeing his Johnny character brought to life by a white boy from "deep down in Louisiana, close to New Orleans." (Clanton was from Raceland, Louisiana.)

Berry had invested in America. His dad taught him about hard work, and now Chuck was wealthy, with a life neither his parents nor the students he went to high school with could have dared hope for. America rewarded the risk-takers, and Berry was feeling bold.

He put together a fall tour of small venues and private shows, including a late-August date in Meridian, Mississippi. The South had a network of college fraternities that booked performers. But in the 1950s, southern high school fraternities also hired major talent.

In Meridian, Theta Kappa Omega, or TKO, sponsored dances at the Officer's Club at the local airport, Key Field. Past shows included Jimmy Reed, George Jones, Huey Smith, Hank Snow. That summer, after an assessment of fraternity finances indicated they were not so good, three members of TKO nonetheless felt so strongly about inviting Chuck Berry to town that they voted to raise money themselves for an August dance.

Berry flew in weeks before, to pick up advance payment. Fred A. Ross was a rising politician in Mississippi, the sheriff and tax collector for Lauderdale County, which held Meridian; his son Fred Ross Jr. was a member of TKO. "I suppose Fred was a classic juvenile delinquent, perpetually in trouble and sometimes dragging us with him," TKO member Charles Broome wrote in an unpublished account of the show.[11] Fred's dad had sent him to military school, and when that didn't straighten him out he banished him to Jackson, Mississippi, where he lived in a mobile home park beside Highway 80.

Fred and cohorts greeted Berry at Jackson's airport and guided him to the mobile home, where payment was received. Dressed in a dapper gray silk suit and a tweed driving cap, Berry looked to be a private-school tutor, visiting hopeless high school kids to provide a remedial lesson. He rolled with the idea that a bunch of Mississippi teenagers were booking him. He turned down a beer, sipped on a Coke, pocketed a roll of bills, and in twenty he headed out, agreeing to play the Officer's Club later that fall.

When he touched down on the day of the show, Berry was in a good mood, exclaiming, "I felt like the stately son of Stonewall Jackson." His mood changed slowly. The venue was an ex–army barracks. The show was by all accounts a success, Berry playing several sets for a southern crowd that knew how to move. "It was strictly a dance, not a concert in the modern sense," Broome recalled. A hot night with Berry and local musicians wailing in short sleeves, sans jackets.

Ross had been driving Chuck around town, and during intermission he scooped up the star for a visit to the Northwood Country Club. Northwood was one of the older clubs in the South, and proudly noted that its clubhouse was a replica of Mount Vernon, George Washington's home.

But if Ross had figured he could show off Berry to fellow members, he had miscalculated. It was explained at the door that his guest, being a Negro, would not be allowed entrance. Ross floated the idea that this wasn't a Black guest he was bringing, but an employee, more or less, being paid to play a few songs on the club's piano for the members during a break at the dance.

Upon his return to the Officer's Club, Berry played another set. The sweat was flowing, and, reading his audience, Berry filled the air with lurid versions of his material.

"Reelin' and Rockin'" went blue in Meridian, Berry describing a wild night of rockin':

> We did it in the kitchen,
> We did it in the hall,
> I got some on my finger and I . . .

Berry's fingers were very long and thin, and as he waggled his index it became a fine means of illustrating the point:

WIPED IT ON THE WALL!

He pantomimed the act and then dropped into a low duckwalk.

It was wonderfully filthy; fraternity brothers whooped, but some of the teenage girls seemed offended and walked off the dance floor, while others flickered smiles.

The room murmured and Ross sidled over and told Broome, "Chuck wants us to get him a date after the dance." The Black female backup singer was suggested as a possibility, but that was not what Chuck had discussed with Ross. He was expecting a white woman, and it was up to Ross to come through.

An investigation of subsequent events at the Officer's Club, conducted by Lauderdale county attorney Paul Busby, supported the contention that Ross had struck up some sort of a deal with Berry. But if that was the case, not all parties had signed off. During a break in the show, Berry went to his dressing room, and Ross managed to steer a twenty-year-old woman backstage to get, he said, "an autograph." A few moments later she was seen bolting out of the room, her face registering unhappiness as she raced up to the young man she'd arrived with. He seemed unhappy too, and a new mood passed over the room.

Chuck boogied on until a little past midnight, when a club staffer abruptly grabbed the microphone as a mob formed. The employee quickly said the show was over and that everybody had to leave at once.

A side door flew open, and it looked to Broome like Berry and the band bolted out of there in a single liquid motion. Outside, an angry crowd merged and went hunting for Berry, who by some accounts was hiding under a nearby barracks building. Three cars full of Meridian police officers arrived and escorted him and Ross, the would-be procurer, to the local police station for their safety.

The singer arrived at the police station as the crowd was raging, shouting things at the two who had schemed to degrade Meridian's womanhood.

Berry spent fourteen hours in a jail cell with a shirtless man. Later in the day, he posted $750 in bail and was escorted to the airport by the same three police vehicles that had extracted him from the crowd. They stayed with him right up the runway, practically onto the plane, knocking on the door until a stewardess opened it and expressed befuddlement that a Negro with a briefcase was the one holding up their takeoff. He told her he was a French diplomat on a mission—no way did he want to be identified as the guy all the papers were already saying had tried to "date" a southern belle.[12]

To the *Baltimore Afro-American*, Berry spun it as a case of him wanting to play on but the venue expressing otherwise. They killed the electricity, and the crowd flipped, he said.

This boy came across the room and called me a smart n***** for something I said about continuing to play, and that was it.

That's something you learn about kids, they can turn on you quick, if they don't have proper discipline and leaders and balance.

"I have wondered what might have happened if the mob had caught up with Chuck Berry. Probably a beating, maybe worse," said Broome. "There were certainly people in Meridian capable of much worse." Alton Wayne Roberts, the Klansman who reportedly shot civil rights workers Michael Schwerner and Andrew Goodman in the summer of 1964, was from Meridian. His brother, Raymond, was a member of TKO. "It was a violent town and a violent time," said Broome.

Black coverage was sympathetic, but Berry was criticized too. A. S. "Doc" Young, entertainment columnist in the *Los Angeles Sentinel*, wrote, "This corner will present an album of Chuck Berry songs to the person who sends in the adjective which best describes his recent action: he tried to date a Caucasian girl in Mississippi yet!"

New York's *Amsterdam News* ran the headline "Don't Even Ask for Date in Dixie"; its story claimed Berry "will not sing one of his hit tunes, 'Back in the USA,' in Dixie again."

Except, of course, he *would*. He had coolly come to town alone, befriended the son of a local pol (and future segregation champion), and crashed the Northwood Country Club. If the way they treated him bothered Berry, he gave them zero evidence. He had shot a look to Meridian, the face of nonchalance. Driving alone into town, playing piano for the country club crowd, pfft, then insisting on your contractual right to fuck a white twenty-year-old woman a little later, and shrugging off all that ensued is a performance as incredible as anything he did on the stage at the Officer's Club.

He moved through Mississippi in a silk suit and his English driving cap, with full attention and no great surprise. That is the sum of the words behind "Back in the USA" too, for all the emphasis he gave them. *I go here, I go there. It's all kind of the same. I do enjoy a good hamburger.*

About the woman who walked out of his dressing room with the wrong idea, Berry sounded amused. "She was the daughter of some town official or something and as pretty a thing as you ever saw," he crowed. "She looked a lot younger than 20, like they said in the newspapers. More like 16."[13]

IN THE FINAL DAYS OF THE DECADE, LOUIS JORDAN CAME TO town. The joyful bandleader, who had so powerfully made possible the music in the air, now left a prediction hanging there. Rock 'n' roll, he declared, "It's gotta go. I give it about a year."[14]

With so many bad songs being played by DJs on the take, "it won't be too long now," Jordan said during a December 1959 nightclub stop in St. Louis. Jordan was not the first to issue this prophecy, and more were saying something similar with each day, given the news that Congress would begin hearings on payola.

Louis Jordan had come and gone. The man who laid a sturdy foundation for rock & roll had been let go by the Mercury label; the last single he had put out, more than a year before, was the aptly titled "Wish I Could Make Some Money." The founders were getting pushed aside by the rockers. Even some of the originators were finding the road growing narrower ahead.

In the final days of the decade, Chuck Berry finished his southern trip and completed an exhausting sojourn through the Southwest. There was no rest for him when he came home. Early on the morning of December 23, a St. Louis police officer entered Chuck Berry's Club Bandstand and arrested him. The singer stood talking to one of the few Black officers of the St. Louis Police Department, who had been sent to pick him up, and then was taken in for questioning. The FBI joined the ongoing investigation. A new Mann Act allegation was being made against the singer, and he faced the possibility of prison time.

BERRY HAD A FEEL FOR CIUDAD JUÁREZ, LOCATED IN THE MEXICAN state of Chihuahua. The border town, with its neon schmear of bars, clubs, and sex traffic catering to American tourists, was just a quick drive across the Stanton Street Bridge from El Paso, Texas. Berry had played the El Paso Coliseum in January. Now he was back for a performance on Tuesday, December 1.

He arrived early in the day, after playing Lubbock the night before. The band, with Johnnie Johnson, drummer Jasper Thomas, and tenor saxophonist Leroy Davis, was in Berry's car. "I took my band over to Juarez, Mexico, where we spent some hours stopping at different strip joints, watching the girls, and browsing around," he said.[15]

That afternoon Berry was sitting in a bar called the Savoy while the guys walked to a liquor store. A Black man named Finch recognized Chuck and spoke with him about how Finch might be of assistance. Berry wanted a tour of Juárez, and while Finch didn't have time to give one, somebody he knew just walked in. Perhaps she would be able to show Chuck and the boys the sights before their performance that evening.

She introduced herself to people as "Heba Norine," which she called her "Indian name," though Janice Escalanti was the name on official documents. She was fourteen years old.

Escalanti was compelling, with "an olive complexion, pie face, and stout high cheekbones," said Berry. She kept quiet, which made it harder to tell her age. "Janice was saying little but agreeing to everything by nodding her head."

Chuck carried fan club membership cards in his pocket, and he handed one to her. On the front was that photo of him sitting shirtless on the floor, his legs snaking around his guitar. On the other side it said, "_____ is a member in good faith and standing and is entitled to all the privileges, activities, and functions of the club; never to let it down in any situation." Usually the member signed, but Berry signed for Escalanti.

Now, he explained, she was a member of the club.

Chuck had told the guys not to stray too far from the Savoy; he wanted to set up for the show when they returned. But that was before Escalanti came in. Johnson went into the Savoy to get Chuck, and when they came out she was with the men.

Without a lot of explanation from the boss, the band and Escalanti started driving around, and Escalanti provided a tour of Ciudad Juárez for the next hour or two, directing them to cantinas and landmarks. "She showed us a lot of historical points, a lot of places," Davis said, "like the bullfighting ring, and the restaurants, and we went in to a couple of clubs, to see how beautiful they were built out of these rocks that they, you know, I guess they had gotten them from the mountains."

Berry and she spoke Spanish to one another. Their thing was their thing; band members just kept looking out the window. "There wasn't any mention of her name, her age," said Davis.

Escalanti was three-quarters Mescalero Apache, one-quarter Yuma Quechan. She had lived in Yuma, Arizona, with her grandfather and stepfather, and also in Mescalero, New Mexico, with her mother. In New Mexico she went to the Mescalero Indian school until the eighth grade, when she dropped out in March 1959. From Mescalero she came to Ciudad Juárez to live with a cousin. Later, when she would testify in court, she said that she had been arrested three times by police, once for vagrancy and twice "for prostitution and drunk." Just the day before Berry arrived in El Paso, Escalanti had been released from jail. "I got drunk . . . and got put in jail."

They drove as far as the second-to-last bar in Juárez, and then it was time for the guys to set up for their nine o'clock show. The El Paso Coliseum was a brick livestock exhibition hall that locals called "the Barn"; later that month Vaughn Monroe would sing at the annual Sun Carnival Coronation Ball. This night the band parked by the Coliseum and unloaded equipment from the car. Escalanti waited about fifteen minutes until Berry came out again.

He invited her to the show, and she told him she needed to meet a girlfriend she was staying with in order to get clothes to wear. "She had to go home to dress," said Berry. "Her appearance was not what it should be."

He and Escalanti drove a short distance to a bar she called the Black and Tan. They talked in his car while waiting for her girlfriend. He asked her how old she was, and she said twenty-one. Around this time, she said, he asked her if she had done any prostitution, and she told him she had. Berry said that he'd simply asked her if she had worked before, and she told him about the work.

However he came by the knowledge of her history of prostitution, Berry said it made him want to help. "She also told me she would like to stop, she would like to straighten up, she would like to refrain from her habits, and this is when I first had a sorry feeling for this girl, because I never had any female to ever mention something like this," he later explained.

On the spot the singer offered her a job, asking if she would come to St. Louis and work in his nightclub. "I needed a girl to work in the hatcheck room," he said he told her.

She didn't have money to travel, and Berry suggested she drive back with him and the band. They were playing five shows in as many nights after El Paso and then would break in St. Louis.

He had a stack of signed photos to sell at shows. "Then I asked her would she like to sell pictures, in that way she could get into the dance and see the show as an employee," said Berry. "She said she would like to very much."

The girlfriend she was waiting for at the Black and Tan gave her the key to her place, and Escalanti took Berry to the house, telling him to wait outside. Fifteen minutes later, getting worried she had disappeared, Chuck asked a boy standing by the building where Heba was. The kid said he didn't know anybody by that name. The implication could be drawn that Escalanti wasn't living anyplace and was borrowing clothes from her friend. In a few minutes she came out and climbed into Berry's car.

At the Coliseum, she set up at a table near the front. Pictures of Berry a quarter apiece. Escalanti was thinking of going with the band, or she wouldn't have grabbed a couple of dresses, a pair of shoes, incidentals at her friend's place. But being at the show and watching him perform, she made up her mind. "Before half the dance was over I told him I would come up here and work for him, so he just said okay. He asked me, 'Are you sure this is what you want to do?' I said, 'Yes, this is what I want to do.'"

The band had a late bite in Juárez and then drove all night to Tucson, Arizona. Berry checked them into the Sands Motor Hotel, a motel built around a large swimming pool, with a restaurant and a gift shop. They got the last two rooms—adjoining rooms with Johnson, Thomas, and Davis staying in one, Berry and Escalanti in two double beds in the other, room 257.

While in Tucson, Berry and Escalanti did errands, dropping off laundry at a dry cleaner. The car's turn signal was busted, so Chuck left the vehicle at a garage for repair. He bought her shoes and then walked to Sears and Roebuck, where Berry purchased two sweaters and a white skirt. Picking up the car, they headed to the Black part of Tucson, and Berry had his hair cut at a barbershop. They went next door to a beauty parlor, where she got her hair done. The afternoon was pretty much shot.

The way Escalanti described what happened, next they took a shower together, and then Berry climbed into bed with her.

US attorney: "Now Janice, did he have any relations with you at that time?"

Escalanti: "Yes sir, he did."

"When I speak of sexual intercourse, do you understand what I mean?"

"Yes."

"Did he have an act of sexual intercourse with you?"

"Yes, he did."

It was the first time they had sex, she said.

They slept, and when they woke up they were hungry. Bellhop Robert Kurn took a phone order from Berry: two pork chops, a milkshake, a strawberry shortcake, coffee.

At the door, Kurn was greeted by a shirtless Berry. He saw Escalanti in one of the room's double beds, covers pulled up to her neck.

The bellhop had already noticed the vehicle parked outside and knew who was staying at the Sands. You don't forget something like that: "a '58 Cadillac Fleetwood, painted red, airhorns on the front, and it had, looked like a card, about that long, 'Chuck Berry,' had his picture on it, and his name."

After that night's show at Tucson's Casino Bar, Escalanti and the musicians ate and then returned to the Sands. She described what followed: "Well, then Chuck had taken two girls over to the hotel, with us, and Chuck went in the other room."

The newcomers were Chuck Berry fans whom he had picked up at the Casino Bar, and now they, Berry, and the musicians all went into the adjacent room. Escalanti retreated to hers, clearly agitated. Davis came through the door they shared, sat on her bed, and talked to Escalanti for a while.

She got into bed and was almost asleep when Berry came in some time later. They had sex again. The next morning, Escalanti woke up to see Berry in bed with her, Davis sleeping in the other one.

Berry, she said, took pictures of her in Tucson. A pair of photos in a private collection that documents Berry's rise, his family, and his camera work show a woman with shiny black hair in a cinder-block motel room. There is a TV in the background, and a man in black slacks sitting casually, partly outside the frame. In one she lies on her stomach over a bare mattress. The other shows her sitting up, looking back at the camera, pulling a floral-print silk shirt down to cover her bottom half.

From Tucson, he phoned Fran Gillium and suggested hiring Escalanti to work in the club's hatcheck room. "I told her there was a Spanish-speaking Indian girl that I was interested in working at the club, what did she think about it. She said, 'Good, bring her in, we need her.'"

They drove to Phoenix and the Mirador Ballroom, a venerable dance hall at Central Avenue and Indian School Road. Escalanti again sold photos, for the third night in a row. Berry took the wheel and got them past the town early in the morning of December 4. "After he had drove a few minutes out, a few miles out," recalled Leroy Davis, Chuck "stated that his legs were tired from the job, and he went to the back seat where he could stretch out more. So he asked Jasper and myself to move up to the front, and he and Janice moved to the back."

The group's luggage and instruments were mostly in the trunk. "Everything but Chuck's guitar," Escalanti said. "He keeps it in the back seat." As they drove from Phoenix to Santa Fe, "it was leaning sideways."

Silverstein (Berry's attorney): "Just like a person would be sitting up?"
"Yes."

The car invited attention and blocked it: the sign said there was a celebrity inside, but it also denied a view of what he was doing. When they drove from El Paso to Tucson, Chuck had his arm stretched across Escalanti's stomach in the back seat. Now, as they headed for Denver, Escalanti said they had sex.

At the wheel Johnson would have had a good view, but he made clear he was only looking ahead.

Question: "Did you ever observe anything going on between them in the back seat?"

Johnson: "Nothing, not a thing. I never observed anything." He didn't hear any suggestive sounds between the two, and he never saw him touch her, he said.

The other members of his band said they were asleep, though Davis would remember her talking sometimes as the Cadillac moved through the night. The Mescalero reservation was to their back as they headed north across New Mexico, cutting through Indigenous land and national parks. "She would be showing us, like I said, the different historical points up and down the highways," said Davis. "And if she was sitting near me I would ask her, you know, what question that I thought might would give me some conception of what had went on in the olden days or, you know, like that, when she described the Apache territory, and so forth and so on."

They were on a fatiguing all-night drive from Santa Fe to Denver for a show at the Rainbow Club, arriving at the Drexel Hotel around three in the afternoon. As usual on this trip, Berry went inside and took care of everybody's room, registering one for him and Escalanti, number 334, under the name "Mr. and Mrs. Janet Johnson." When asked why he chose that name, Chuck explained in an offhand fashion, "I used her first name and Johnnie's last name." That is, he used what he thought was her first name.

"I never knew her last name until this case came up," he admitted. "But the first part of her name I thought was Janet, that is why I put 'Janet Johnson.'"

From Denver, Berry called Fran collect, talking some more about the new hire. "Broken Arrow," a recent release, had a bit of a cowboys and Indians theme. The idea came to him that they could "dress her in costume or something, and make a novelty of it" at the Club Bandstand, in order to promote the song.

Later, he would explain, "So we dressed up this Indian girl in some feathers and got her some boxes of cigarettes and we wanted to have her walk around the club selling cigarettes. I wanted to be as far out, for the time, as I could."

Plans were coming into focus. Berry was renting to Gillium the house he and Themetta owned before they bought the Windermere Place home, and he suggested to Gillium that Escalanti stay with her when they reached St. Louis. "I asked Miss Gillium could she stay at her home, as I knew she was—did not have any money, she could not afford a hotel," Berry recalled. "She agreed. She said she would welcome her."

In Denver, Berry gave Escalanti the night off from selling pictures. He might not have put it this way to her, but given the nature of the private event the band was performing at, he thought she would be inappropriate. The job was "sort of an exclusive date, people wore evening gowns to this date in Denver; the club was exclusive, sort of plush-like."

Asked to better explain his meaning, Berry answered, "She just would not fit in at this date, from appearance." Also, he just didn't like her outlook. Escalanti wasn't selling many pictures, and "her attitude at that time had become ridiculous."

She was behaving like a teenager. "I was through with her selling pictures," Berry declared. She didn't care if they sold or not. Not invited to the Denver show, Escalanti stayed in the hotel room and slept. Afterward Berry knocked on the door, and they had sex again, she said.

The next morning they drove to Pueblo, Colorado, for what was the last night of the tour. She went to the dance but didn't sell pictures, and when they were done everyone got in the car and headed toward St. Louis. Early in the afternoon, as they passed through Kansas City, without announcement Chuck double-parked in front of the airport, walked up to the TWA ticket counter, and bought himself a ticket to St. Louis. Standing next to the car he spoke to Johnson, then told Escalanti the pianist would take her to St. Louis. Johnson steered everybody else the rest of the way into town.

THE BOUNDARY JUMPER HAD FOUND A BRIGHT WHITE LINE. HE had launched a business right on it, one challenging St. Louis racism by bringing white and Black patrons under a single roof. Chuck Berry's Club Bandstand stood at the corner of North Grand and Delmar boulevards. Grand ran north–south and was the city's leisure zone, a midtown neighborhood strewn with vaudeville stages, ballrooms, jazz halls, and burlesque houses from the 1920s on. This was entertainment for white folks on a thoroughfare long called "the bright white way."[16]

Meanwhile, Delmar was a division in the making. Just a few blocks south of Club Bandstand, urban renewal was destroying the Mill Creek Valley community, some twenty thousand African American families uprooted via eminent domain laws in the name of freeway construction and "slum clearance." From 1954 on they mostly moved north of Delmar, so much so that at some point the street would have a new handle: the Delmar Divide. By 2014 the blocks north of Delmar would be 99 percent Black; it was 70 percent white just below it.

The corner of Delmar and Grand was a fine place to try to make some money by opening your doors to all because many were on the move.

He saw it coming.

He heard his Cadillac roll up his driveway and stepped out to greet it.

Johnnie Johnson was in from Kansas City, having already dropped off Jasper Thomas and Leroy Davis. With Escalanti in the car, he made it to Chuck's Windermere Place home around nine thirty p.m. on December 7.

No need to dawdle inside the house where the Berry family lived; Chuck told Escalanti he would take her now to where she would stay on her first night in St. Louis. Johnson was a guest at Windermere

Place, so he went in. Berry got behind the wheel and drove to the office he maintained at 4221 W. Easton Avenue, the address of the Chuck Berry Fan Club. In the rear was a bedroom, where Escalanti said they had sex. Berry left her in the room, saying that in the morning he would take her to the Club Bandstand.

Gillium remembered meeting the new hatcheck girl: "I went up to her and introduced myself to her, and she said, 'My name is 'Heba Norine.'" Gillium asked for her social security card and birth certificate, neither of which Escalanti had. Gillium told her to write home to get them so she could be paid for her work.

Escalanti had never seen St. Louis and didn't know anybody but the men who had brought her there. For the next eight days, she was rarely out of Gillium's sight. She slept in a bedroom at her house on Whittier. Escalanti would get up in the late morning and head with Gillium to the club, both setting up for the evening. They ate together, ordering meals from the restaurant on the floor above the Club Bandstand, the Chuck Wagon (not owned by Berry).

Escalanti's work space was a niche with a Dutch door. Inside, the ceiling was low, the walls unfinished, the room barely lit by a seven-watt lightbulb. The new hire was told to stay there and take patrons' coats and hats; she was paid five dollars a night and split the tips with the house.

Patrons came and went, and Escalanti grew restless, wandering out to talk to people. On her second night Berry spotted her sitting at a table and directed her to the booth. "She stalked back into the checkroom," Berry noted.

The next night he caught her watching the floor show. "I again asked her to please obey me and stay in the checkroom," he said.

"What am I supposed to do, just stay in there?" she asked. "He just kept complaining about me not obeying him, and that I should do as he tells me to do and stay in the hatcheck room."

After a third night, "I put her on the admission box," Berry said. That involved charging patrons at the door—those with a fan club card got in for free, all others paid ninety cents.

Limiting distractions, Berry thought, might change her behavior. "First, I was probably the only contact she had there for work and so forth, and by being in a strange place she might try hard, and then, two, she seemed to be willing to change her employment."

But at the front door, it was the same story, she didn't stay in place for long. After she left the money box to get a glass of orange juice one night, Berry complained. He wanted a big personality, a real greeter roping people in, but what he got was a self-conscious and fumbling teenager who refused to follow orders. Whatever he'd seen in Escalanti before looked different to him now. On Sunday the Bandstand was closed, then Monday through Wednesday she sat at the door. By Thursday Berry had made up his mind.

On the morning of December 18, he arrived at Gillium's house and told Escalanti she was going to have to leave. "He said because I was disobeying him."

It was abrupt, Chuck muttering she should put her stuff together because he was taking her to the Greyhound bus station.

"I told her, well, this is the day: I am going to send you back to El Paso."

"I was wondering when you were going to get to that," she said.

Escalanti put the clothes she had with her in a paper bag and climbed into his Cadillac.

At the bus station she told him she wanted to go to Yuma, but he said that would be too expensive. He had made a promise to her when they met that if St. Louis didn't work out, she could always go back to El Paso, and now he was making good on his word.

She was telling him loudly she wanted to go to Yuma, and that made him angry. He took two five-dollar bills and the ticket and gave them to her. The bus was leaving in about thirty or so minutes, and Berry had things he had to do. He left.

"I was disgusted, completely disgusted with her," he said.

There was a new song he was messing with during this time. A version had been cut a few years before, and something more defini-tive a year later, both times at Chess. "Thirteen Question Method" he called his rhumba, and in it he goes fully into salesman mode, selling a procedure, a set of steps for young men to use to ensure they have a successful date. "The thirteen question method is the one for you," he pitches, "when you want to go have some fun." Work the system, score with the girl; it was a lighthearted version of what a later generation of men called the Game. Remove the risk from dating and cut to the reward, with a scientific method. That's the dream.

That's one narrative of what happened in December 1959. He met a pretty girl on the border, made her feel special, and took her away to a place where she knew nobody. She needed him, and she didn't say all that much. He presented himself as her rescuer, dressed her, had her hair done, put her on salary, and, she said, he had sex with her almost every day until he took her to the Greyhound station. Then—poof—she disappeared. That, too, is the dream.

Waiting in a plastic seat at the station, she met a guy. He asked if she wanted to go have a drink. "So I did."

After stuffing her paper bag into a locker at the bus station, they went to a nearby bar and got hammered.

She remembered showing up late that night at Club Bandstand, though she could never figure out what happened to the man she'd met at the bus station. Gillium saw her at the door, inebriated, and told her they didn't allow drunks in.

The next night Escalanti returned to the club and sat talking with one of the Equadors, a vocal group that had backed Berry on a July session. Berry asked her why she hadn't left town. Reaching into her purse, he pulled out the bus ticket and the ten dollars. "When you are ready for this," he said, "I will have it." He handed them to Fran, who put them in the cash register.

With nowhere to go, Escalanti drank until closing time. Leroy Davis drove her to the Deluxe Hotel, a lodging for Black customers. She had sex with Davis there and worked as a prostitute for the next few days, making money to buy a bus ticket to Yuma.

There were things she wanted to say to Berry. On December 19 she called the club repeatedly all day long, asking to speak to him. Fran took the calls, saying he was busy or not there. Two nights later, Escalanti returned to the club. She tried to get in, but her entry was denied, so she went upstairs to the Chuck Wagon, where she sat and drank coffee.

Pulling out paper, Escalanti composed a note to her former employer: "dear Chuck, like I said before, I love you." She was sad and angry at the way she had been treated, barred from the front door of Chuck Berry's Club Bandstand.

From the pay phone at the Chuck Wagon, she called downstairs and asked Gillium why she couldn't enter the club.

Gillium "just said it was Chuck's orders, that I was not supposed to." Escalanti sent her note down to the man who had brought her to St. Louis and now was sending her away, and then she made a long-distance call.

She wanted to go home.

She dialed the Yuma Police Department, telling them that she had met Chuck Berry in Texas and he had brought her to St. Louis but that she now wanted to leave. What, she was later quizzed, did she want to get out of calling an Arizona cop?

"I asked them what I should do to try and get back home again."

The Yuma police officer who took the call told her to stay where she was. He phoned the St. Louis Police Department. Not very much later, St. Louis police officer Roland Norton found her in the phone booth at the Chuck Wagon.

Norton listened to her story, heard her say she was fourteen. His response was to arrest Escalanti, and then with Officer Jim Buford go downstairs and arrest Berry. It was between midnight and two a.m. on December 22. Standing on the sidewalk in front of Club Bandstand, brought together in the bright theater lights of Grand Boulevard, Berry and Escalanti stared at each other. They hadn't seen each other in four days, and soon they were driven to the Lucas Street Police Station a few blocks away. The marquee of the St. Louis Theatre next door announced the film then showing: *Journey to the Center of the Earth.*

11

"THE INDIAN GIRL"

The work and life under examination in the last years of the 1950s present a challenge to the biographer, and possibly to the reader. Chuck Berry was as hungry to travel, as voracious for American culture, as any artist in the moment they shared. Berry was releasing "Johnny B. Goode," "Memphis," "Back in the USA," impressions of a national identity full of honest hope, while putting his life on the line in Mississippi for fun, fighting the city of his birth to create a club open to all in the heart of white St. Louis, and laying the plans for a park that would be open to everyone in rural Missouri. He was recording songs that championed girl power, full of figures who had not existed in music before—"Carol" and "Little Queenie" and "Sweet Little Rock and Roller"—recognizing the autonomy of his female following, all while also peeking into the women's room at Norfolk, cruising for dates with teenage girls across the South. How to make sense of "Sweet Little Sixteen" in the context of fourteen-year-old Escalanti, who Berry claimed looked "twenty-four, twenty-three, twenty-five"? What context is large enough to make sense of these actions all coming from one protean American?

A month after returning from his most recent road trip, in January 1960 he released "Let It Rock," one of his least celebrated great songs.

It starts out in a hurry and finishes in less than two minutes. Nodding to Black folk hero John Henry, the singer is a steel-driving man on a railroad in Mobile, Alabama, working not to show he's the best but to buy himself some shoes. He sets up a teepee on the tracks to shoot some craps in the shade when, wouldn't you know it, a train comes bearing down on him from two miles out. That's it! The tale of a guy trying to own his life through work and play, when an unstoppable force throws everything up in the air. Three verses no chorus. Not once does he sing, "Let it rock." It's rock & roll if anything is, not to mention *A People's History of the United States* with Johnnie Johnson accompaniment. "Can't stop the train, you have to let it roll on," Berry wails at the fade-out.

Here it comes. A grand jury indicted him on December 23, 1959, for "transporting a woman across a state line for immoral purposes." Assistant US Attorney Frederick Mayer made the announcement. Berry posted bail.

Mayer was a former FBI agent who would be prosecuting the case against Berry. He had warned the singer and his attorney after the roadside arrest with Joan Mathis (now Joan Mathis Bates, having recently gotten married) that the federal government would come down on Berry if Mayer caught wind of a future violation. "Basically, with the Indian girl it was age," said Mayer, who died in 2018. He seemed to be saying that Escalanti being fourteen warranted prosecution. "And the girl in St. Louis"—he is speaking of Mathis Bates—

> was either seventeen or eighteen, and I believe that there was some information that Berry had done this on other occasions, which of course I took into consideration but I did not charge him with any of that.
>
> But I felt the fact that he was warned earlier about this and the age of the young girls was sufficient to go ahead and prosecute him.

The arrest at the Club Bandstand triggered a cascade of events. On January 25, Berry was arrested and charged with two violations of the Mann Act with Mathis Bates. Mayer also charged Berry for felony interstate transport of a firearm, tied to the discovery of the handgun in his Cadillac. With five years for each Mann Act charge and five years for the firearm, Berry could see twenty years in prison.

His most recent charge was first up on the calendar. Fearing that Escalanti would leave St. Louis before she testified, Mayer had the court declare her a "delinquent" and requested a court order that she post a $500 bond. Unable to pay bail, she would be under his thumb, behind the walls of the House of the Good Shepherd, a female reformatory run by a cloistered order of nuns.[1]

The massive redbrick institution, built in 1851, rested on eleven acres on Gravois Avenue. "When people just see the outside, they get a grim picture of the place," Sister Gertrude admitted to a *Post-Dispatch* reporter. But inside, iron bars and steel mesh covered the windows and prevented escape, while the wooden stairways were a known fire hazard.

The detention perhaps made legal sense, given the possibility that Escalanti's prosecutions in Texas were ongoing and raised the specter of probation violations. So did the fact that she was a minor whom officials were unwilling to release to the streets of St. Louis. But the effect was that the victim was behind bars while Berry was free.

He would be tried by Federal Judge George H. Moore, whose "portly graying bulldog look," one observer noted, "would have made him perfect casting for Hollywood's version of a senior jurist." At his 1902 graduation, Moore had been handed his law degree by Samuel L. Clemens. He ran and lost as the Democratic Party candidate for governor in 1924, and was appointed to the federal bench in 1935 by Franklin D. Roosevelt.

Moore was eighty-two at the time he was assigned *The United States vs. Charles Edward Anderson Berry*, and by the late 1950s there was courthouse gossip that he was having difficulty, even struggling, in his job. A 1959 newspaper story headlined "Judge Moore Has Busy Day Denying Report He Is Dead" describes him on the phone one afternoon knocking down a courthouse rumor. He died in 1962. In an unusual obituary, the writer noted, "Why he overstayed usefulness was a strange and unhappy facet of his later years. The example of Judge Moore, clinging to his post beyond full capacity, is a strong argument for compulsory retirement of trial Judges."[2]

Moore had handled a number of high-profile cases, and this would be his last. An all-white jury was selected, and on February 29, 1960, testimony began.

On the stand, Escalanti was hesitant and occasionally confused, her voice swallowed up by the courtroom. Along the way, she received pokes and prods from Judge Moore. "Speak louder. Do you hear me?" he admonished.[3]

She was the government's lead witness, and the questions asked of her and others considered whether Berry had had sex with her. But far more questions were asked regarding where Berry and Escalanti were on a given day at a given time when intimacy might have occurred. The case depended on facts establishing that they traveled across state lines on a specific schedule that a group of people, including band members, bellhops, desk clerks, and Berry and Escalanti, all testified to. Proof of that, more than proof of sex between them, would be pivotal. Mann Act prosecutions just needed to convince a jury that "immoral practices and debauchery" had happened, which was a lot vaguer, and easier to prove than, say, that a rape had occurred.

But it also meant evidence like her age and his treatment of her would not be as scrutinized nearly as much as they might have been. As US Attorney Mayer put it, the case was not about "feeling" but about "transportation." The Constitution gave Congress the power to regulate commerce between states, and that gave Congress the foothold it desired to pass the Mann Act in the first place. Being about transportation, not feeling, also indicated how much this was not a case about the assault of a fourteen-year-old.

From the start Moore's opinion of the defendant was part of the public record. When Berry's lawyer quizzed Escalanti about arriving at Berry's Windermere Place home that first night, the judge interrupted with a question that seemed designed to tell the jury he believed Berry didn't belong there.

Silverstein: "This was a home, is that correct?"

Escalanti: "Yes sir."

The Court: "Where it has the big entrance gates, and all that sort of thing?"

Escalanti: "Sir?"

Court: "It had big entrance gates, a fine looking place?"

Escalanti: "I wasn't paying much attention to it."

Throughout, Moore interrupted to inject race into the proceedings.

When the bellhop from the Sands Hotel described getting a phone order "from Mr. Berry," Moore cut in. "By 'Mr. Berry,' do you mean this

Negro, the defendant?" It says "Negro" in the court record, but others in the courtroom reported they heard "nigra," and Silverstein was convinced that Moore on occasion said the N-word. He lined up witnesses who were prepared to state under oath that they had heard it too.

"I certainly do. Mr. Berry, sitting right there," answered the bellhop.

When the desk clerk for the Drexel Hotel in Denver testified, Moore stopped to ask him, "Is that hotel patronized by the white?"

George Dixon, who can't believe the question: "Is it what?"

Moore: "Is it patronized by any white people?"

Dixon: "All white people."

Moore, indicating Berry, Escalanti, and the band members in his courtroom: "Do you call these people white?"

Dixon: "Well, up in Colorado we have a law—"

Moore: "I am not arguing. I am just asking for the facts. Proceed."

The judge even referred to the defendant as "this man Chuck, whatever his name is." His contempt for the defendant was transparent and habitual.

Berry himself registered little interest, as if the events were mundane. From time to time he pulled out a *Life* magazine from his pocket and thumbed through it.

Moved by the story of a stranger, he claimed he brought her to St. Louis to steer her away from sex work. "When she told me that she wanted to refrain from prostitution I had a feeling that I wanted to help her, and I thought I could. I felt sorry for her, and that is why I offered her the job in St. Louis."

Moved by empathy, he also had practical considerations. "My feeling for her was one of sorrow and one of pity. I definitely wanted to help her, and at the same time I could be helped along with my Spanish and the vacancy in the club I could fulfill."

Berry didn't just deny having sex; he acted surprised anybody would think he *would* have sex with her. He testified there was no time or energy for a musician on the road to sleep with someone.

Question: "At the time you made this suggestion that she work in the club in St. Louis, did you have some idea of having any sort of relations with this girl?"

Answer: "No sir."

Question: "Did you have any desire anytime to?"

Answer: "Absolutely not."

Question: "Did you at any time on this trip find yourself in a position of having any desire to have anything to do with this girl in a physical way?"

Answer: "No sir."

The performer's defense was hobbled by his resistance to directly, simply, and believably answering questions. When in cross-examination the US attorney asked him about his arrest for armed robbery, Berry claimed he couldn't remember if a gun had been involved.

Asked how old he thought Escalanti was, he replied, "Twenty-four, I will say."

US Attorney: "You thought she was twenty-four?"

Berry: "Yes sir, which will be twenty-three or twenty-five, in that range."

The hotel rooms they shared, noted by hotel staff, presented a clear problem. They had to share a room in Tucson, he explained, because there were only two rooms available in the motel.

"There was no other place to stay. I could not let her stay in the car."

He even noted fliply that their spending a night together turned out to be a success: "It worked out all right out in Tucson, I mean she did not make any advances, or anything."

Meanwhile, he said, his approach was to show that by not acting on her attraction to him, she would learn she didn't need to be a prostitute anymore. He would teach her self-control.

Take the hotel room in Denver, he explained. He stayed with her only to protect her.

"I wanted to sort of keep an eye on her, sir. I wanted to sort of keep an eye on her."

Mayer: "Did you still feel you would have to keep an eye on a 24 year old woman?"

Meanwhile, the government was able to present Berry as evasive and, worse for his case, uncaring.

Mayer: "Mr. Berry, do you feel a sense of responsibility for her after bringing her up here?"

Berry: "That's why I bought the ticket, sir, for her and took her to the bus station."

The government completed its case by beating up on Escalanti a little bit and on Berry a great deal. In his closing statement, Mayer said, "The Government is not attempting to tell you that she is a sweet, young little girl. She is a little girl. . . . She has led quite a life. We are not attempting to state that she did not work as a prostitute—one of the unfortunate things perhaps in that part of the country that a girl of such tender years can be deployed in such a regrettable occupation at such an age, but that is something that is a fact, and we are not attempting to hide it."

"She is not a saint," said Mayer of the fourteen-year-old victim. "But I will tell you what, I don't think she lied." Berry, he said with mockery, was "a real symbol of virtue, a real chivalrous individual."

The case was given to the jury late in the afternoon on March 4, 1960.

It was snowing hard in St. Louis. The jury foreman came out after deliberating for two hours and twenty minutes and said they had not yet reached a verdict. Moore noted without subtlety that the jury would be expected to stay there all night if they didn't produce a verdict soon. He added he was not excited about the prospect of coming back the next day. "I don't want to have to stay down here myself."

The jury conferred for another fifteen minutes, and the foreman announced they had reached a verdict, and that Berry was guilty of violating the Mann Act.

Moore revoked bond for the defendant, sending Berry straight to jail. Sentencing would take place the following week.

In denying Berry bail, Moore laid bare his feelings. "I would not turn that man loose to go out and prey on a lot of ignorant Indian girls and colored girls, and white girls, if any. I would not have that on my soul. That man would be out committing offenses while his case is on appeal, if this Court is any judge. I have sat here for a quarter of a century. I have never sentenced a more vicious character than that kind I don't believe."

In Moore's opinion, "you are not a very wholesome citizen, and there is nothing about your situation to arouse very much sympathy." He felt compelled to call Berry a liar: "I want you to distinctly understand that now. I think you repeatedly perjured yourself on the witness stand. I don't believe your testimony, or one word of it."

He repeated testimony of Berry's success as an artist and businessman in order to belittle it. Moore delivered a terrible public shaming. "You must be a man of some ability and some intelligence; and you have three daughters yourself, and you were taking this young 14-year old girl, pretending that you were—"

The court record simply reported, "(The defendant is bending over, apparently weeping.)"

Moore commanded him to stand up. Berry's tears drew more rage from the judge. "Don't go through any of that maudlin exhibition in my presence. I am not impressed by it. I have seen your kind before."

The judge continued to attack Berry as the performer sobbed. Saying he wished he could sentence Berry to more time, he delivered the maximum punishment: five years and a $5,000 fine, ordering Berry to the municipal jail without bail until it was decided where he would be sent.

Silverstein crafted an appeal largely based on Moore's frequent racist outbursts, filing it Monday, March 14, 1960. Berry was now able to post bail pending a ruling on the appeal; he was out of jail that day. Escalanti continued to be held behind the walls of the House of the Good Shepherd until May 1960, until a US marshal drove her to the New Mexico Girls Welfare Home in Albuquerque, where she was further detained.

While free pending a ruling on his appeal, Berry went to trial in his other white-slavery case, involving seventeen-year-old Joan Mathis Bates. This prosecution imploded after Mathis Bates explained on the stand that she loved Berry and that none of the sex they had was coerced. Berry also testified that they had been in love.

The charge against him for the French pistol found under his driver's seat was dropped; the search of his car was clearly illegal.

On October 30, the Eighth Circuit Court of Appeals handed down their ruling on Berry's appeal, finding that the "attitude, conduct and remarks" by Moore were troubling. "A trial judge who, in the presence of the jury, makes remarks reflecting upon a defendant's race or from which an implication can be drawn . . . has rendered the trial unfair."

At the same time, the panel of judges felt the evidence against Berry was too strong to acquit him. They vacated his conviction and remanded the case for retrial. Berry's second trial, in March 1961, was a streamlined affair. Escalanti was brought back from Albuquerque by US marshals to testify again. Berry this time did not so fully emphasize his efforts to mentor Escalanti.

In his closing remarks, Berry's lawyer took a different approach from the one he'd adopted during the first trial, attempting to smear Escalanti. "This girl is not so dumb. . . . She is not so dumb or, like they say, 'Dumb like a fox,' maybe. Everything that we have heard about Indians being cunning is true," he said. "She's a smart girl, let there be no mistake about that."

And when it was over, the jury again found Berry guilty.

Before Judge Roy Harper sentenced him on April 14, Harper brought the lawyers into his chamber for a moment of levity. As Berry's attorney recalled later, the judge shared some wisdom, saying, "I learned an old rule when I was young. If you're going to fuck a whore, you've got to pay 'em!" Unlike Moore's remarks, these were not part of the official record.[4]

After all were seated in the courtroom, Harper sentenced Berry to three years and a $5,000 penalty.

An appeal was quickly filed, and while waiting for it Berry felt pulled in several narrowing directions. Chess booked a number of sessions, and pressure was on to stockpile material for the potential hiatus ahead. Berry scheduled a tour of Jamaica and the British West Indies and then a string of fraternity dates in the States. He played a country bar in St. Louis and was booked as the "Bad Man of the Guitar" at a recreation center in Petersburg, Virginia. In Reading, Pennsylvania, he headlined at a banquet honoring the mayor put on by the Berks County Amusement Machine Operators Association. Bookings were dwindling while his fate was being decided.

Berry's business had already taken a big hit. Chuck Berry's Club Bandstand was closed by the end of 1960. Redd Foxx had been scheduled to appear in late December, a breakthrough booking for the club. St. Louis would not hear his routine about the wounded British soldier and the nurse with the Queen and the prince tattooed on her thighs.

And then Berry's appeal was denied, and a date was set for him to report to prison. Years later, when he fielded questions about his prosecution, Berry would maintain that the Mann Act prosecution was an effort to shut down the Club Bandstand, a business run by a flamboyant Black man who was pushing integration into the mainstream.

"I had a nightclub in St. Louis," he said. "Here you've got what they called a mixed racial club that was catered to by the white populace of St. Louis," and the response from local authorities was "now this is going too fast, let's shut the club down." In order to do that, they had to shut the owner down. "They made us paint the walls, fix the pipes . . . made us do all kinds of fire protection. But I knew why. I was never wanted on Grand Avenue. I was the instigator."[5]

His depiction of himself as the only victim fails to address Escalanti's abuse. But evidence gives weight to Berry's assertion that he was targeted. In December 1959, around the time Berry was being arrested on Grand Boulevard, the jazz club called the Holy Barbarian was shut down for hiring a waitress who was a minor. Its owners had created a space where African Americans and whites could be together on the stage and off. Integrationists were targets for harassment, local beatniks and national figures alike.

The motivation for the FBI's involvement is worth probing as well. The bureau had been collecting information on Alan Freed at least since the Boston riot, and they were actively, publicly fueling the investigation of Freed for taking money from record labels to play their music. FBI director J. Edgar Hoover had an obsession with interracial sex, and his field office would likely have been aware that an African American celebrity was trying to run a nightclub where Blacks and whites were welcome. Looking for ways to derail a charismatic proponent of equality would have been in character for the bureau.

Of course they wanted to stop Chuck Berry. From "Maybellene" on, he was a prophet of Black mobility. He was himself in flight, taking Black music to white audiences across the country with a fury. His red Cadillac demanded that you see him and remember his name. He liked fucking in the back seat while Johnnie drove. He was a target, a victim and victimizer.

He was booked, fingerprinted, handcuffed, and placed in the rear seat of a sedan. "Feeling more black but still intact," he declared.

Two men drove him to a federal penitentiary in Terre Haute, Indiana, in February 1962. Along the way, they pulled into a truck stop and offered Berry a chance to get something to eat. With the likelihood of strangers seeing him, he requested a cup of coffee while he waited in the car.

Two months later he would be transferred to Leavenworth Federal Prison in Kansas. Coincidentally, that was where in 1920 Jack Johnson was sent for violating the Mann Act.

12

IS THAT YOU?

THE STOP AT LEAVENWORTH LASTED JUST TWO WEEKS, LONG
enough for Berry to play a show for prisoners, before he was taken to
a facility in Springfield, Missouri, where he would serve out his term.

Springfield surprised Berry when he arrived; he was expecting a
grim facility, but it was nothing like what he had encountered in Leavenworth. The lone federal prison in Missouri was also a medical center
for inmates, and it resembled a large hospital with extra security pre-
cautions. The institution opened in 1933 as the US Federal Hospital
for Defective Delinquents. It had a research component at first, investigating alleged biological roots to a broad variety of behavior deemed
"defective." Both check forgers and "sexual psychopaths," a category
that included homosexuals, were sent to Springfield.

Over time the facility shed those trappings, but it remains startling
that one of rock & roll's motivating forces was sent to an institution
founded to locate a biological root to "antisocial" behavior. Rebranded
as the United States Medical Center for Federal Prisoners, it provided
medical, dental, and mental treatment for federal inmates.[1]

A new inmate's first month was spent largely by himself. Berry
used his time to plan a daily structure and ponder how to keep his
spirits up. "I was determined to live faithfully to my philosophy," he

wrote in his autobiography. "A good mind can never be in bondage nor its body in less than liberty. I would survive."

He learned chess and took classes to receive his high school diploma, including typing, business management, and accounting. There were jobs available at the Springfield hospital, and Berry was critical of inmates who didn't work.

"I thought about the great amount of federal income tax that I'd paid out when I observed over three hundred able-bodied inmates, many of them just walking around, doing nothing but being housed, clothed, and fed. What an expense to the tax-paying citizens. Mother's teaching made me feel that I should be earning my way but, considering my tax bracket, the government wasn't losing any money on me."

The first job he signed up for involved mopping the kitchen floor, then washing pots and pans. He used the work to study social dynamics—noticing how the hard-timers gave him shit for not doing his work very well, and then making sure they noticed him taking their needling. It showed them he wasn't above their hazing, and they warmed to him. Berry worked four hours a day and then went to class.

Promoted to a clerical position in the physical therapy ward, he handled correspondence and wrote progress reports on patients. A guitar came from home, and Berry used it to write new songs, including some that would be among the most important of his career. "Nadine," "No Particular Place to Go," "Promised Land," "Tulane," and "You Never Can Tell" all were written in Springfield. He also played in social settings for fellow inmates, performing not rock & roll, he said, but, knowing his audience, folk and country songs.

Toddy was busy raising their three children. To the girls, his absence just seemed like he was on an extended road trip. "Dad was away from home on tour a lot anyway, so nothing seemed that different when he went away that time. When I got older and could understand, he explained everything to me," said Ingrid. His explanation to her was that he had been set up by the police.

Feeling lonely in prison, he asked his wife to visit, and she did. On a Saturday afternoon when Toddy and his father had driven out, Berry heard his named called out. Berry describes the path he took to see her: he had to undress, take an elevator while "half nude" up to a station, where he was handed a white suit to wear, then he walked out to a public area. When he saw his wife, he wrote, "I was surprised at my not being sexually excited, after not having any for so long. From the anticipation of being near her, I assumed I would have stolen freaky rubs and naughty pinches between kisses. . . . To my surprise, I was a perfect gentleman and regretted it immensely along the time the moon rose that summer night."

At the ceremony where inmates received their high school diploma, Berry was the class valedictorian, and Toddy watched him give his address. She was sobbing, and that moved him, he said, making him stumble over his lines.

His sentence was reduced five months for each year of "good conduct," and he started to see that it wasn't going to be as bad as he feared. "This shouldn't pose too big of a roll for a rocker. No big alligator, just a little old crocodile."

Putting the best face on his time in Springfield, Berry talked about the classes he took. "Life didn't change. When I went away I finished high school number one, number two I took five business courses. When I came back, I knew what a corporation was, I knew what accounting was. Plus, it's easy to count my blessing as well as my misfortunes and I did. And I weighed them. I came back in a better position to handle life. And don't forget I had a little bank account to maintain."[2]

The words make sense on their face, yet the fact is Berry was lacerated by his prosecution and sentencing. His stubborn defensiveness, his shame, his seeming inability to understand his actions, all left him ill-equipped to talk about the behavior that helped bring him to this place. Unseen, those impulses would not be put aside.

He pondered the treatment he had received in the months prior to his incarceration, as his prosecution and word of the fourteen-year-old Escalanti spread to every reporter and disc jockey who requested an interview. Without doubt, he understood he would be asked about his actions for the rest of his career. Turning against the press that white pop stars were learning how to exploit, Berry stewed over their interest in publishing their own "allegations and little of my information." It was "about then that I became averse to giving interviews."

Interviewers acted nice, but they were not nice. They didn't listen to his explanation that he was trying to help "the Indian girl" and that nothing had happened. To Toddy he explained that it was because they got paid better for a story that was controversial and scandalous, for reporting allegations that were "dramatically absurd."

Contemptuously he labeled this practice "the American way"—doing anything for a buck, taking a shortcut to the "American Dream," avoiding all the hard work he had put in. The crowd was full of people who wanted to block his path. "The only thing wrong about that dream is the way it makes you twist and turn in bed from dogging someone else, awakening you and disturbing the peace and plans of other people." He recalled a parable his father told of how you never had to put a lid on a barrel of crabs because the group would always reach up and pull the leader back down. "Consequently, few American crabs will ever climb to the top under the existing system some people dream and seem to follow."[3] He was not like the crowd.

His work ethic, his desire to pull ahead, his intelligence, he felt, all set him apart. The hospital grounds were scattered with hoodlums and slackers. That was one American pot he would never feel a part of. But beyond the prison yard were other crowds he felt increasingly wary of interviewers who meant him harm, cops and federal officials who wanted to take him out. There were music-business colleagues who hid how they would put their own interests ahead of his. Poised to leave the hospital grounds, he thought about community and America, and sought to insulate himself from damage they might do.

His first shot at parole arrived in the fall of 1963, and Berry was given early leave, after one year and 241 days of incarceration. On his birthday, October 18, 1963, he was released. His father, brother Hank, and Toddy were waiting for him. He drove them home—in his Cadillac.

Looking back, he noted that he got something useful out of prison: a diploma and classes in business, achievements he was proud of. "Sorry, great white father, you can't indict me for that."

Publicly he was defiant and at peace, he claimed, in no way "feeling offended at the system for whetting me down for going against the racial barrier of practiced tradition." But in fact his prosecution and sentence had left him with a great deal of bitterness, which grew over time. A gap was inserted between Berry and his audience, and in the years that followed he would control and restrict contact with his public. He was putting out music, on the road constantly over the years ahead, he was doing the work. Yet he became increasingly remote and mistrustful of encounters with others. To the outside world he presented a mask, rigid and unconcerned with how others might view him.

"When people made derogatory remarks about me and the media exploited those remarks at the times of my downfalls, I felt more pitiful toward them than anything else. They affected me little or not at all," he said.[4]

The distance between himself and the world might define his work going forward, but it also made that work possible, because it gave him the stability and focus he needed to write songs. "If I can't be affected on the negative side, it can't affect me to more than a certain extent on the affirmative side, either," he said. Keeping feelings, and the public, in check made many things easier. He kept a tight rein on gratification, because gratification could be a weakness and could put you under the control of others.

"If I hear 10,000 people clapping and cheering, I know how they feel then and there. But the only way I can know that my music in general gives pleasure, other than that specific response, is the revenue it generates." The courses he took in business must have helped him do his books, but their greatest impact was symbolic and grew over the rest of his life. People would be fickle, but numbers did not lie.

A MOTOR CITY DJ CAME DOWN TO CHICAGO IN EARLY 1963, pitching Leonard Chess on bringing Berry to a place outside Detroit where the guy booked shows. Chess had obscured Berry's extended absence the best he could through ads placed in the trades ("Chuck Berry is back!") hyping "new" singles (or stuff never intended for release). So when Chess explained point-blank why Berry wouldn't be available, it was news to the DJ.

Some months later, though, Lee Alan's phone rang in Detroit and it was Chess, saying Berry was now free and available—and they wanted him booked at Alan's Walled Lake Casino *now*, that very weekend. Berry had been out about two weeks, and his probation officer was demanding proof that he held a job. Chess needed a show fast, and it had to be in a place where Chuck could also record live—Chess wanted to show fans and the parole board alike that Berry really was back and playing his way into the future. Alan, who broadcast shows live from the casino, said that would be no problem.

Alan picked up Berry at his Detroit motel, putting his guitar and amp in his Corvette. They were running late, and traffic was unexpectedly bad.

Halfway to Walled Lake with less than an hour to airtime, Alan spotted a highway patrolman driving down the shoulder and waved him to a stop. He asked when the wreck blocking progress would be cleared.

"That's no accident, everybody's lined up to go to Walled Lake and see Chuck Berry," the trooper said.

"Guess what?" said Alan, gesturing to his passenger. "You're the first one to see him."

The patrolman offered to give Berry a ride to the show, but for whatever reason the musician politely declined the offer.

They followed the officer to the casino and made it in time. Alan had hired a profound backup crew, a Motown house band that included bassist James Jamerson, drummer Richard Allen, tenor saxophonist Hank Cosby, and pianist Johnny Griffith. The venue was an old big band dance hall with a polished maple dance floor, about thirty miles from Detroit.

The star was meeting the band offstage when Alan approached to bring Berry out. Instead, Berry told him he wouldn't go on until he got paid. And he wasn't taking checks.

Alan raced to the box office and got $1,000, much of it in singles, packed in a brown paper bag.

All four thousand people in the full house were clapping their hands and stomping to make the wood hall shake.

Berry counted out the money. When he was done, Alan said with a relieved voice, "OK, we're ready."

"No, I want to count it again," said the star. It sure felt good to be having *fun* again.[5]

Berry had a cold that first night, and his voice gave out. He was working to get his guitar skills back in shape; he told Alan they hadn't let him have a guitar in prison and that's why his playing was rough. Announcer Dave Prince heard him wonder out loud if the crowd was going to like him.

Berry was restless after the show; Alan said, "The front desk told me they got a lot of complaints about a guy playing his guitar all night." The second night was better, and by the end Berry must have been relieved. The recorded evidence is that these shows weren't consequential—not rehearsed, not what you want from Chuck's comeback show featuring Motown's Funk Brothers. But he was on his way back.

In a slow moment, Berry showed Alan lyrics to a song he'd written in prison. He didn't play "Nadine" that night, instead sticking to his hits.

His last song on the charts had been "Back in the USA," four years old. But that song and his other hits suddenly were everywhere, while Berry was not.

All around the world for approximately the past four years, people had been absorbing Chuck Berry music, and just as the crowd at Walled Lake was younger and whiter, listeners elsewhere were too. There is no single way to succinctly tell the story of the swathe Berry had cut and now was standing on the far side of, the expanse he was confronting as he stepped out onto the stage after almost two years in the penal system. But one useful way to hear it was by jumping onto the Mississippi River that shot past St. Louis and paddling north and east until it became the Ohio River, then riding on up to where that river hit the border between Indiana and Ohio. Ten miles northwest of the state line is the tiny town of West Harrison, Indiana. A kid named Lonnie McIntosh had traded his bike for a guitar at the age of seven.

McIntosh—eventually he'd go by Mack—grew up listening to bluegrass and gospel. He was a white kid (with some Native American blood), and the radio was his lifeline. The family had a floor-model Zenith radio hooked up to a car battery so they could listen to the Grand Ole Opry. Mack learned how to play his guitar pretty good, and as a youth would hang out along the Indiana train tracks, playing for railroad men while they ate lunch and tossed coins in the kid's guitar. "It was exciting. And I said, daggone, I'm doing what I love to do," Mack recalled.

"I came home and said, 'Someday, Dad, you're gonna hear me on that Grand Ole Opry!'" It was the 1940s, before the world knew the name "Johnny B. Goode," but this, too, is a part of Johnny's story.[6]

He had graduated to the biker bars and frat parties of the Kentucky/Ohio/Indiana region. Mack's band was backing a vocal group's recording session in Cincinnati in March 1963 when the guy in the booth said they had twenty more minutes on their studio rental. Do you have anything to fill out the tape with?

Mack recorded an instrumental version of Berry's "Memphis, Tennessee" that he'd been featuring in the river bars as time expired.

"Memphis" telescoped blues and country picking and rock & roll guitar, the soul-organ jazz and Ray Charles soul and Robert Ward Ohio
blues and, yes, the ton of Chuck that Mack had inhaled; it was the
straight eight flattened out into a smooth ride that featured a twelve-
bar Mack solo that irradiated cornfields. Mack's playing touched on
Merle Travis country picking, and wicked blues notes bent like pen-
nies on the rail. His version went, places Berry's never did, up to four
on the R&B charts, five on the pop.

Mack's mastery set him apart, but he was just one more young
person who had grown up with electric guitars. The domestic market
couldn't contend with the surge in interest, and it was flooded with
cheap foreign knockoffs. According to the American Music Conference, an industry trade group, the rising interest in guitars was nothing short of remarkable. In 1955, some 245,000 guitars were sold in
American retail outlets. Sales rose steadily in the next few years and
jumped from 400,000 in 1962 to 700,000 the following year. And then
came 1964 and the Beatles' first world tour: 1.1 million guitars sold.[7]

Mike Bloomfield was another white kid who learned to play guitar.
He told *Rolling Stone* that the radio introduced him to electric sounds
he had never experienced before. "I thought the spade cats had some
sort of magic device," he confessed, only now the marketplace made
that device available for an affordable price to white kids everywhere.
That magic turned into what Bloomfield called "commercial soul."[8]

Saxophones had been a crucial part of rock & roll, and there was a
lot of sax onstage at the Walled Lake Casino. But the saxophone was
fading fast. "Guitars are easy, they're cheap, everybody plays them. Simple, a few chords. That's why they are buying them," said Bloomfield.

In Southern California new bands were shooting for Beatles fame
and doing it by sounding like Berry. The Beach Boys were not the
first of the surf rock bands, but they became the focus of the sound.
In 1963 *Billboard* declared their "Surfin' USA" the year's best-selling
record. Berry might have heard it while he was typing up a bank robber's medical history at Springfield. "Surfin' USA" was a lively cover
of Berry's "Sweet Little Sixteen" with lyrics written by Brian Wilson
that turned the music into an anthem of a new American craze. ARC
Music, Chess's publishing company, definitely heard it and, unper-
suaded by Wilson's explanation that he meant it as a tribute to Berry,
called it plagiarism and acquired publishing on the song by the time it

was released as a single. Subsequent releases have listed Berry as the song's writer.[9]

For Wayne Kramer, things changed the day he bought *Chuck Berry Twist* in 1962. The album was a greatest-hits collection Chess repackaged while Berry was incarcerated, and there wasn't one twist song on it. Kramer was fourteen, living in Lincoln Park, a downriver suburb of Detroit.

"I took it home and listened to it over and over and I had to call Fred"—his pal Fred Smith, who lived ten blocks away. A few years later, they both would be in the MC5.[10]

"Fred, you gotta hear this record—Chuck Berry, he's just killing it—man you gotta come over and listen to this." To be honest, Lincoln Park was a white racist suburb; it didn't let Black people in. But for kids like us things were going well enough, all those good union jobs that you could get so that the parents could spring for an electric guitar or a drum kit for the kid.

There were bands literally all over my neighborhood; I could ride my bike on a Saturday and hear bands playing block after block. And the measure of a good guitar player was how many Chuck Berry guitar solos do you know note for note? They were hard to get right, at least for me in the beginning. Pretty soon, Fred and I were practicing in the garage and kids were pulling up on their bikes, watching us practice. Those were our first performances.

In blue-collar suburbs and beach towns, teenagers were learning from Chuck Berry and his generation. Berry meanwhile was trying to reassess, and in January 1964 he arrived in Chicago for a three-day recording session, his first in over two years. The goal was to show he was back, though a mere display of life alone wouldn't be nearly enough to return him to the charts. He arrived with two of the best songs he ever wrote.

Essential business had to be done first. His St. Louis probation officer was making it hard for him to leave town for recording or touring. Leonard Chess fixed that, pulling strings and hooking Berry up with a Chicago-based officer and moving him to Chicago for a while.

When he arrived at the Chess studios on January 7, Berry carried his guitar and a tiny overnight bag. According to Marshall Chess, he looked "a little raggedy," so Leonard handed Marshall a couple hundred and told him to take Chuck and buy new suits he could wear on the road.

Chess itself had a new address and a fresh look for the 1960s. Back in 1956 the company had invested the money reaped from "Maybellene" and Muddy Waters's "Mannish Boy" and moved from South Cottage Grove to 2120 South Michigan Avenue, in the heart of Chicago's Record Row.

The very address was magnetic, drawing fans and strivers who wanted to see where Etta James, Little Walter, Baby Cortez, and Billy Stewart all presided.

A first encounter might disappoint visitors. Buddy Guy imagined Chess looking "like a palace." Instead, he encountered a narrow two-story building wedged next to a flophouse. You went inside and there was a desk and receptionist you had to get past to peek into the heart of Chess. The setup reminded visitors of a speakeasy with a false front.

But once you climbed to the recording studio on the second floor, a lot was going on between the spring-mounted acoustic walls. Before moving to Michigan Avenue, Chess had booked most of its sessions at Bill Putnam's Universal Recording. Leonard hired Universal's Jack Wiener to build a studio of his own, and Wiener laid two inches of cork over wood floors and poured concrete over that. There were two echo chambers in the basement carrying a signal from the studio's ribbon mics and then feeding it upstairs onto tape recorders.

The Chess label was building infrastructure, growing past its entrepreneurial roots by hiring songwriters and producers, soul artists, and jazz and comedy acts. Those Motown musicians Berry played with in Walled Lake were among Berry Gordy's secret weapons, ensuring a quality standard on the Motown label. Chess emulated the approach, hiring from the surrounding pool of Chicago talent.

Chess encouraged Berry to update his sound, bringing in electric bassist Reggie Boyd for sessions and adding a second guitar, frequently Matt "Guitar" Murphy. Horns were drafted as accompaniment more than soloing instruments, in the manner of soul songs then appearing on the charts.

Chicago-born guitarist Pete Cosey was playing sessions at Chess when he hooked up with Berry in the mid-1960s. "He had just gotten out of prison," Cosey told an interviewer. "We cut some great things with him—they were really rocking," he recalled. "I remember we did 31 takes of one song, only because he was rusty. They had me play his signature lick for him and it was an honor."[11]

Chess was pushing the artists to respond to the charts, but Berry came back with music showing where the charts were headed.

Among the songs Berry recorded over the next few days in January was "Nadine (Is It You?)." It begins with a pat of hickory guitar, a contented little understatement that launches great consternation. Louis Satterfield's electric bass rationalizes the rhythm, and no longer are the drummer and the bassist mashing threes against fours; this becomes an organized sleazy motion, a fast, twisting hully gully tune—Satterfield hitting on the one and three, Berry scratching eighth notes on the two and four, with horns flickering all kinds of messages like the heavy eyelashes at the Club My-O-My. Musically, "Nadine" was "Wooly Bully" and "96 Tears" and maybe the "Batman Theme" before any of them existed.

Lyrically it's striking from the start, the singer sitting on a bus, looking out the window when he sees his future bride and knows he's got to get off. It's a chase tune told by a guy fully at the mercy of others—the bus driver and cabbies who pick him up, the sidewalk crowd keeping him from breaking into a run. It is wildly subjective: we don't know anything about Nadine, we don't know if she sees him, if he really knows her, though he claims to know her name. Note the subtitle—"Is It You?" There's a lot we can't be sure of.

Berry is like a street photographer swept up by reflections and bodies in motion in a big city—he doesn't know where to look, and everywhere he looks he gets thrilled and anxious. The finding is unresolved, or it resolves not in the way we are used to with pop songs—he wants her and she slips away, and "Nadine" becomes a song about the satisfaction of unresolved desire, of wanting and hunting and being open to the flow around you even when you end up on your own. He's working his way down the sidewalk, caught up in the energy, fully aware he controls nothing. Hanging in on the two and four.

"My portraits of the black subject don't explain or justify anyone or anything; instead, they affirm the presence of the people in them, presuming their right to exist as they are," said the photographer Dawoud Bey, who has often photographed people he sees on the street. "I think about portraiture in terms of how to make interiority visible. That interiority, in its full complexity, is not always ascribed to black or even young people."[12] In a song named for someone else, Berry makes his own inner life visible.

Here in "Nadine" two people caught up in their own emotions are being depicted by a third person, Chuck Berry. *I am hungry*, one says; *you don't own me*, the other says, both speaking past each other and to everyone around them. Chuck Berry wants us to see their inner life. Nadine moves one way, then changes direction and seems about to get into "a coffee-colored Cadillac." "She moves around like a wayward summer breeze / Go, driver, go, go on, catch her for me, please," he sings. She is autonomous. She doesn't represent something: she is someone.

One of the great quotes about "Nadine" comes from Bruce Springsteen about Berry's gifts as a writer. "I've never seen a coffee-colored Cadillac, but I know exactly what one looks like," he said.[13] It surely is a vivid, unusual description, a shade not used very often in the context of a vehicle. But there *is* a context in which *coffee-colored* has been used with frequency, and that is as a descriptor of Black skin.

In the song he calls for Nadine over the crowd, "campaign shouting like a southern diplomat." Berry used the English language like a rhythm instrument, but he also used it like a surgical tool. His words meant things, and he needed to get them all in the right place.

Surely he obscured his true lyric, "southern Democrat," as much as he changed "colored boy" for "country boy" in "Johnny B. Goode." Singing that in public would cause difficulties.

Race, identity are present in this song not as an overt subject, but in the details. They are present as well when the singer compares himself to a "mounted cavalier," a very specific phrase with connections to southern history. ("The cavalier image in the antebellum South represented the pinnacle of white southern manhood," noted one historian.[14]) "Nadine" becomes a song about Black longing hiding in plain sight in the streets.

The moaning saxophones that call out her name were Johnnie Johnson's idea,. Over their keening, Berry's voice cries with a new fullness—he wants what he doesn't have, but there's fulfillment in his shouting, too, a full-throated declaration of being alive. And as if Johnson's horn line isn't enough, his piano playing on "Nadine" has all kinds of glee; it just hums and laughs like a witness with the best seat in the house. *Yep, I was there! I saw it all happen.*

"Nadine" was released in February 1964 and garnered serious attention. The Beatles had arrived in America for the first time on February 8, and after landing in New York they went to radio station WINS, playing records and joking with Murray the K. "Nadine" was played, and the band called it their favorite record of the week. Chess instantly took an ad out in *Billboard* trumpeting the endorsement.[15]

The Beatles had been playing Chuck Berry songs for several years while they made their climb. The week they came to America, to appear on *The Ed Sullivan Show* and tour the country for the first time, a bootleg of their cover of "Roll Over Beethoven" was circulating in Chicago, *Billboard* reported. Perhaps Leonard Chess gave it a spin.

Nadine reached twenty-three on *Billboard*'s Hot 100; it was Berry's first appearance there in four years, since "Let It Rock" had grazed the chart at sixty-four for one week. Chess got their message out: *Cash Box* featured a full-cover shot of Berry, shouting he "is back in action again."[16] The *Cash Box* cover trumpeted Lonnie Mack's hit with "Memphis" and noted that the Beach Boys' "Surfin' USA" "was previously titled 'Sweet Little Sixteen.'" They wanted to tell his story without explaining why he'd been away, which was tricky. "While out of circulation, the star's songs kept his name high on the charts," the *Cash Box* cover said. "It's good to see the swinger front and center again."

Chess sent him out on the road in new clothes and put Leonard's son Marshall out with him. Marshall was twenty-two years old. They fought a lot, and Marshall called him "a real cheap bastard" who would never say he was hungry because he didn't want to pay for food on the road. Marshall recalled Berry packing a hot plate in his suitcase and heating a can of beans so he wouldn't have to dine out.

What money he made, Berry aimed to save. "I was continually being called to do dates," Berry explained. "The fee for the dates constantly rose, for instance when I had my problems with the Indian girl, I was away for almost a couple of years. I went away making $1,200 a night. When I came back, the Beatles had come to America and my salary then was $2,000 a night."[17]

Attention was heating up in Britain. Berry had a small following there in the 1950s, but he had rarely made the UK charts, and Chess ended a distribution deal with Decca's London subsidiary by 1960. In America he reemerged as a fallen star pushing forty. But England was swirling with new bands, and many invoked Berry by name. He was new there, and there was growing interest to book him on a tour.

Don Arden was a feared London gangster and concert promoter who was known to hang rivals out the window until they saw things his way. He was tight with the Everly *and* the Kray brothers, and was bringing American rock & roll acts to England as the mod scene exploded.

He'd had his eye on Berry, and upon Berry's release from prison Arden sent future Led Zeppelin manager Peter Grant, a pro wrestler trying to bull his way into music management, to Chicago to negotiate. Handing the roughneck an envelope of money, Arden told him to close the deal.

Grant arrived at the Chicago airport, surprised to see Berry himself pick him up and drive him to his hotel. Grant offered to take Berry out for a drink, but he wasn't interested. The next day, when Grant arrived at Chess to negotiate with Leonard Chess, he was taken aback by the figure, smoking a cigar and wearing flashy suspenders, who greeted him.

"Oh, you're the limey guy," Leonard said.[18]

Berry's lawyer did most of the talking, though Chuck did insist, "The only thing you have to do for me is get me a real good piano player." Everyone agreed, the envelope crossed Chess's desk, and with that Leonard told Chuck to drive Grant back to the airport. The manager was startled by the power dynamics, but he didn't say anything as Berry walked him behind the building.

"It was like a used car lot full of Cadillacs. Chuck chose one, and we set off," said Grant. But not far from Michigan Avenue, Berry complained about how much gas the Cadillac devoured—it was clear he wasn't interested in driving Grant anywhere. So he dropped him off at the downtown Chicago bus station and returned the Cadillac to the Chess lot.

They had a deal. England beckoned, but it would have to pay for the gas.

13

"HOW MUCH DO THEY OWE CHUCK?"

THE FINSBURY PARK ASTORIA WAS A HUGE CINEMA IN NORTH London, with a diorama of a Moorish village that wrapped around the stage. Stars embedded in the ceiling twinkled when the lights went out.

On the afternoon of May 9, 1964, John Hawken was puttering on that stage, setting up a microphone on his piano.

Hawken was keyboardist for the Nashville Teens, and he was, as well, the superb accompanist Berry had demanded for his first tour of England. As he worked, a tall man carrying a guitar, a long coat draped over his arm, introduced himself. Berry gave his bandleader a few spare instructions for what to expect that night, and then he set up his amp. Hawken: "I just watched as he turned everything up to number ten—that was how he got the Chuck Berry sound."[1]

The Nashville Teens were in fact from Surrey, England. Their first song, "Tobacco Road," had appeared that month and raced up UK charts with a verse straight out of Chess blues songs and a smooth chorus targeting Beatles fans. They were rough and good. Meanwhile, the headliner was advertised as something altogether apart from the likes of the Teens and the Beatles. Chuck Berry was billed as "the real thing," as "the wild man of beat music."

The first show set the tone for the entire tour, which included the Animals, Berry's old driving buddy Carl Perkins, and England's Swinging Blue Jeans. Just before the start, Peter Grant worked with the house emcee on a dramatic entrance for the star. As the announcer gave Berry an extendedly dramatic buildup, Hawken pounded a boogie-woogie fanfare in the dark. Berry's guitar joined in, and then a spotlight hit the man himself, duckwalking onto the stage. The crowd exploded, and the future of British rock & roll exploded too.

Wild dancing erupted around the diorama. "They were absolutely manic," Hawken said of the Finsbury Park fans. "One of the biggest names in rock 'n' roll and an absolute God to some people was playing as well as he ever had. And he was raring to go. After 18 months incarceration there was a lot bubbling up waiting to come out. Those nights launched us and launched the Animals." A young Jimmy Page watched Berry's London debut with a look of surprise. The young Richard Thompson stared at Berry's blond Gibson Switchmaster.[2]

Don Arden had also booked girl group the Other Two; Berry noticed them. "A buxom seventeen-year-old blonde," he wrote in his autobiography, and "a raven-black-haired French [girl] . . . who was questionable but beautiful." The sight of the two of them, he admitted, was why he was riding the tour bus with the rest of the acts.

It might have been the next night, at the Hammersmith Odeon, that Animals singer Eric Burdon observed Berry barricaded in his dressing room, refusing to go on until Arden and Grant paid him another $1,000. Meanwhile, leather-clad rockers were tearing up the hall in anticipation of Berry.

Refusing to budge, Berry had the mobbed-up Arden and the gorilla Grant on their hands and knees, sliding cash under the door and pleading for him to start his set. "Chuck was on the other side counting it, saying 'Nah, it's still another 500 bucks till I come out,'" remembered Burdon.[3]

A casual warmth flourished on the bus. "He would get the chess set out during the day and have a game," said Hawken. "We both knew what we were doing on the chess board—it was surreal playing chess with the great Chuck Berry on a crowded bus loaded with good vibes. 'Fancy playing some chess?' he would say. 'Let's see how the limeys can do.'"

The seats at the back of the bus provided the most opportunity to stretch out horizontally, and Hawken says that Berry and a female guest would regularly lay claim to them. "We were given strict instructions on the bus—you don't look around; no matter *what* was going on in the back seat it was not of your business," said Hawken. "He was a star and the man was having a blast! We might have heard some giggling, but we never looked back."

The tour was extraordinary. "His singing and playing could hardly have been bettered," wrote journalist John Broven. Broven saw a late-tour performance at a basement club off Charing Cross Road. "And the excitement level was just astonishing—to be able to see Chuck live! How *good* he was," said Broven.[4]

The atmosphere was supercharged.

But I can remember going up to him during the break—he was amongst the audience—and I said innocuously, "I've got your records," and told him how much I enjoyed them. And there was just not a reaction at all. Not "thank you," not "pleased you have them," or anything. That apparent coldness, I learned, was a common trait.

But the other thing was, as we left this basement club on a summer evening—I don't think I'd ever been to a club where the sweat of the audience created globules on the ceiling. Talk about a heated atmosphere. It was perfect for his debut in England. Because as you know the English were totally adoring of him—he probably never had that sort of reception in the states since his peak.

ANOTHER SONG RECORDED BY BERRY IN JANUARY 1964 WAS "YOU Never Can Tell." It was as fresh an addition to his body of work as "Nadine." "You Never Can Tell" sketches a teenage marriage (the singer hastens to add in the second line that they really *did* love each other). The old folks watching the kids have their doubts about whether it will last, and a note of generational judgment hangs in the air—but the kids are living their lives. "C'est la vie," the song's grown-ups say—can't say we didn't warn them, they shrug.

But they stick it out, and their marriage is told through the details they gather, the things they buy as they build a life together. The newlyweds fill their apartment with objects from a Sears catalog. They get a Coolerator icebox, and though Coolerator is a word worthy of Berry's invention, like botheration, motorvatin', and the rest, Coolerator was a Wisconsin appliance manufacturer. Then comes a hi-fi set and the couple's seven hundred records—"all rock, rhythm and jazz," he details.

Next they get a cherry-red 1953 car so they can celebrate their anniversary. In the couple's refrigerator are TV dinners and ginger ale. Too busy to cook probably because everybody's working to buy more stuff, own their home, move on up.

In a photo from *Sepia* magazine in the late 1950s, Chuck, Themetta, and the young girls are posed around their own family's hi-fi set, a record in Berry's hand. Everybody is dressed as if for a most proper party in this portrait of middle-class leisure. Like the couple in "You Never Can Tell," they believe in upward mobility, defining it the way other folks on Windermere Place did: the right records, a proper stereo system, and an array of brand names that would make one family as American as any other.

In a 2016 exhibition at London's Saatchi Gallery, curators and artists re-created the flat Keith Richards and Mick Jagger shared in 1962 at the birth of the Rolling Stones. No Coolerator, no ginger ale; there are stains on the walls, beer bottles and plates of beans everywhere, grease holding the room together, and trash covering the floor. The Rolling Stones weren't trying to assimilate with anybody, the installation makes clear they were opting out of respectability. They did it by ingesting Chuck Berry, Bo Diddley, Muddy Waters, and poking holes in middle-class certainties.

Jagger and Richards had bonded in 1961 on a train into London when Keith saw Mick carrying *The Best of Muddy Waters* and Chuck Berry's *Rockin' at the Hops*. When the Rolling Stones released their first single in June 1963, it was a cover of Berry's "Come On." From the start they were full of beans and full of Berry.

Through style and acts the Stones disparaged middle-class aspirations, and through their gestures they found new standing in the world.

The artists who were the foundation of their sound had mixed feelings from the start. A few months after "Come On," the band was on its first tour, billed below Bo Diddley on a Don Arden package program. Roger Fairhurst, a nightclub DJ and rock & roll fanatic, was talking to Diddley before the show in Manchester. "While we talked, Mick Jagger and Keith Richards came along and joined in," he said.

At the time, the Stones' repertoire was pretty much determined by the collection of Chess albums piled on the band's hi-fi. "So Bo Diddley turns around to Mick Jagger and says with emphasis, 'Now, *you're* not the same billing as me, so don't go doing any of my songs.' 'Why not?' Jagger asked. "'Cause I might want to do them myself later on,'" drawled the headliner. That night the Stones did five Berry covers and quickly cleared the stage.[5]

When Berry played at Finsbury Park on his opening night, the Stones knocked on his dressing room door, hoping for an audience with their idol. Berry was not interested. They called through the door, but Chuck only called back, "I'm sorry but I am very busy right now and I don't wish to see anybody." Jagger responded, "Well, we don't want any more of his songs then!"

The band and the man from St. Louis had no relationship, and already their relationship was complicated. He was trying to put his career together. They were taking his sound apart and creating a shambling, international style from it. Berry was looking for a way in and working in a tradition he felt in his bones. The Stones were opting out, creating their own reality.

Money could bring everybody closer. When the Stones made their first US tour in 1964, they swung by the Chess office, recorded in the sacred space, and held a press conference from a safety island on Michigan Avenue. They stopped traffic and made the local papers. While Phil Chess was showing Brian Jones around the office, Leonard looked at his brother and asked, "Who are those freaks?"[6]

The blues were coming to America.

They were brought both by white guitarists with ascetic devotion to "getting it right," and through an arrogant sloppiness that indicated attitude. They arrived with drummers struggling to keep up. Blues and R&B originators booked in remote corners of the world, their voices now carried farther by Yardbirds, Kinks, Beatles, Stones, and Swinging Blue Jeans. The instrument Berry had made the music's leading voice was, as Mike Bloomfield noted, a creative tool and an utterly exploitable fad, a Hula-Hoop on fire. The music and the technology were a cultural and market force, reaping dividends both ways. And even with so many opportunities as close as the traffic island outside the Chess records building, the gap remained vast. And there was no easy way for a noncompliant, thirty-eight-year-old Black man with several felony convictions to make it easily across.

An article appearing on the front page of the *Baltimore Afro-American* newspaper around this time shows the gathering resentment. "How Much Do They Owe Chuck?" asks the headline. Next to a photo of a lean Berry in sunglasses were headshots of John, Paul, George, Ringo looking enthusiastic. The author didn't leave readers in suspense, instantly answering his own question: "We could set down Chuck Henry Berry, guitar man and grandaddy of this thing we call rock and roll, as being the Beatles chief creditor." The article is a quick collection of body punches, none more damaging than this: "The Mersey sound is a weak, pallid imitation of our lusty home-grown rock and roll but it is just that weakness that has made it pay off for the Beatles while the innovators like Berry et al cash in far less on far more talent."[7]

Among those closest to the roots, there was the charge even in 1964 that the new sounds were mere imitations of true mastery, and that the measure of the theft was the money made by the freshly landed stars. Fred Below was a great Chess drummer who played on blues and Chuck Berry sessions. He saw a new presence in the clubs he'd play around Chicago in the early 1960s. "They weren't no Beatles then. They weren't no well-known bands. They were just guys coming around. They heard what we was playing and they couldn't play what we was playing, but, they tried it. And they played it in their English-style way. Next thing that happened a couple of years later, them guys come here and made a million dollars doing some of our same stuff. They just changed the music around."[8]

FROM THE START, "PROMISED LAND" FEELS TOSSED OFF, musically and lyrically, and that's a big part of its power. It arrives like another Chuck Berry road song and rings with artless sincerity, a friendly character eager to tell his story. It could be a superior version of "Route 66," a road trip full of place names and featuring one fresh plot device—a mob in the rearview mirror.

The singer explains he's just left his Norfolk, Virginia, home, telling us from the start with clarity that this isn't Berry's biography; this is a work of fiction. Except of course, it *is* part of Berry's story. He's in a hurry, though he doesn't say why. The song traces a bus journey into the Deep South undertaken to escape Dixie and make it to the promised land of California.

It's a freedom song he had written in the hospital prison, impeded by prison staff. When he requested a road atlas to make sure he had American routes and geography right, at first they turned him down on the grounds that he might use it to plot an escape.[9]

Which in a way he did. He sings as a "poor boy" with "California on my mind," and he gets on a Greyhound bus heading south through Raleigh, then Charlotte, North Carolina, noting that they "bypassed Rock Hill." Where was Rock Hill, and why mention it in a song? Its population in 1960, about thirty thousand, made it hardly the size of the big cities mentioned elsewhere, but Rock Hill is pivotal to this song because Rock Hill and Greyhound travel had a history-making intersection just a few years before Berry wrote "Promised Land." It was a national story in 1961, embodying what the Freedom Rides were all about; "Promised Land" is in essence a ride to freedom.[10]

Activists in the civil rights organization the Congress of Racial Equality saw the integration of interstate commerce, specifically bus travel across state lines, as a way to harness federal pressure to ensure Black movement and access to public life. Local bus lines were a local matter, but once buses crossed state lines they were an issue for the feds, and a recent Supreme Court decision outlawed segregation on interstate highways. The ruling allowed anyone with a ticket—on paper, though hardly in reality—safe passage. When a Greyhound bus rolled into the Rock Hill station on May 9, 1961, an integrated group of activists, calling themselves Freedom Riders, aimed to enter a waiting area marked "Whites Only." They were attacked, and twenty-one-year-old John Lewis and a white protester were left lying in blood.

Those attacked declined to press charges and most returned to the bus, heading for Alabama. Berry's own bus rider bypasses Rock Hill and makes it through Atlanta "by sundown, rolling outta the Georgia state." He is drawing our attention to the "sundown laws," which warned that nonlocals would be subjected to jail or worse if caught after dark.

Then, a verbal dodge. "We had motor trouble, it turned into a struggle halfway across Alabam'," sings Berry on record. Yet live, he did not sing it that way. Live, Berry delivers the line as "We had a little trouble that turned into a struggle." Why he did that was also no accident; he was ushering his song's transit into the American mainstream by coding the message. After that Greyhound bus carrying John Lewis and twelve others left Rock Hill, *it* headed into Alabama. "It was like a damned tomb on that bus," said one of the Riders. "Everybody knew when we crossed the Alabama state line the picnic was over." In Alabama, the Freedom Riders' bus was set on fire and its passengers left by the roadside. That is the literal trouble Berry was referring to in his song.[11]

Musically, "Promised Land" races—three verses, no choruses. The Poor Boy is no Freedom Rider making a point; he just wants out, and the music never rests, though it breaks for two glorious guitar solos. The song is explicitly about transit and speed—another fast Berry number about moving forward. Indeed, Lafayette Leake's piano playing flies off the song like a ticket from a windshield, and somewhere back in Rock Hill there's a snare drum trying to keep up, but this song is all Berry's voice and guitar pushing toward the county line.

On August 28, 1963, while Berry was still in the hospital prison, Martin Luther King Jr. stood at the Lincoln Memorial in Washington, DC, and delivered a speech that was meant to increase pressure for passage of federal civil rights legislation. Before a crowd of 250,000, King said, "We can never be satisfied as long as our bodies, heavy with the fatigue of travel, cannot gain lodging in the motels of the highways and the hotels of the cities. We cannot be satisfied as long as the colored person's basic mobility is from a smaller ghetto to a larger one." His song was Berry's song.

In 1963, novelist and journalist John A. Williams took a magazine assignment to travel across the country while civil rights were being debated in Congress. He started in Detroit, checking into a downtown hotel room carrying "typewriter and bag, rifle and shotgun, a road atlas and *Travelguide*, a listing of places in America where Negroes can stay without being embarrassed, insulted, or worse." He knew who he was: "a long black man in a big car, and vulnerable as hell."[12]

Williams figures the Promised Land for a respite, but right after he arrives in Los Angeles, while shopping with his kid sister on a downtown street, her transistor radio broadcasts that President Kennedy has been shot. The words pour out: a Negro boy saw two fighting on an overpass . . . a Negro man was said to have "fled the scene." At home on TV, a newsman interviewing members of the public is told, "Some n***** did it." That afternoon at his sister's school, a PA announcement said, "A Negro had murdered Kennedy." There was a feeling, wrote Williams, that a race riot was imminent.

Ready to continue his cross-country drive, standing outside his mother's house, "I saw a young woman walking up, her head covered with a veil as if she were just coming from Mass. She was Negro and I wondered if Kennedy's grief for the plight of my people had been as sincere as hers was for him."

The Civil Rights Act was passed in July 1964. "Promised Land" arrived in record stores that December. In the song, after the Birmingham bus fiasco the Poor Boy catches a train to New Orleans. Strangers help him to Houston, where they hand him a new suit and an airplane ticket to Los Angeles. Berry makes events feel jarring and dreamlike, and when Poor Boy wakes up, he's "high over Albuquerque, on a jet to the promised land."

California was out there past the sun, a symbol of racial freedom that had more personal resonance to Berry as well. The Hollywood Berry was steering toward on his disastrous high school road trip; the San Jose he claimed as home in early interviews. His own promised land where great stars belonged.

Flying on a plane, Berry once spotted Bob Hope. Now *that* man was a star, he told newspaper columnist Bob Greene.

"I walked up to his seat and I said, 'Could I have your autograph?' He looked up and said, 'Sure.' He was very polite to me. To my surprise, he was over-polite. He gave his entire attention to me. And he gave me his autograph."

Startled at the imbalance between fame and greatness, Greene asked if Hope knew who Chuck Berry was. Did he tell Hope?

"I would never do that."[13]

In 1964, Chuck Berry had three songs in the Top 40 and released four of his greatest songs ("Nadine," "No Particular Place to Go," "Promised Land," "You Never Can Tell"). It was an achievement surely worth trumpeting, a fine year for a guy reestablishing himself. He was thirty-eight, the same age Michael Jordan was when he returned to the NBA, and having similar success. "I'm back" was all Jordan had to say to drive the basketball world coconuts on his way to winning the Most Valuable Player award.

Berry never acknowledged he'd been away, and the expanding youth culture was looking in other directions for new sounds. Few noticed Berry, given the vast, ongoing story of the British Invasion. Berry was mentioned far more in the context of the rising British acts than regarding anything he had done lately.

It was one of his best years ever in the business, so why did it feel so different? The Beatles and Stones placed his songs with young listeners and then poured out their gratitude in interviews. How did it feel, he would be asked over and over in the years to come, to have the Beatles play your songs? There was an expectation from white interviewers that he would be publicly grateful for the acknowledgment. He had worked for years to distinguish *himself* against all others, and perhaps now it was starting to seem that he had lost his distinction, that he was a barely seen content producer enabling others to express themselves. Rock 'n' roll's Black best friend.

Up close it was hard to deal with the praise. He didn't feel worthy in some basic sense, this man who grew up taking beatings from his dad, who tried to hide his name from his family and church when he started playing music. And now other people were giving him admiration, in ways both self-serving and respectful. Fans, and fan feelings, had to be managed, because they could be kryptonite.

THERE WAS TIME LEFT OVER FROM A CHESS SESSION ONE DAY, and Bo Diddley happened to be hanging around, so he strapped on a guitar and jammed a couple of numbers with Berry. Out of this came a long, wet noodle called "Bo's Beat," and another one, "Chuck's Beat." With very little in the way of additional sauce, Chess slapped together the jams and put them on Chuck's first new album appearance in years, an August 1964 release called *Two Great Guitars*. Featuring little of his or Bo's wit, it did nothing to define Berry in the new age.

Two months later, a better album appeared: *St. Louis to Liverpool*. It holds a batch of recent singles and B sides and gathers older threads to fill an album. The title suggests a dialogue with the English bands, a great idea for somebody chill enough to enter the conversation. It's just a title. What if Berry had covered "A Hard Day's Night" and forced himself into an exchange with this new thing? Or played one of the Animals tunes he'd heard while touring with them in England? At a time when albums were being tasked with speaking to the moment, this one seemed to be a compendium of loose ends.

In a no-way-exhaustive list, among the fresh faces from across the Atlantic, the Beatles covered "Roll Over Beethoven," "Rock and Roll Music," "Too Much Monkey Business," "Carol," "Memphis," "Sweet Little Sixteen," "I Got to Find My Baby," "I'm Talking About You," and "Johnny B. Goode." The Rolling Stones did "Come On," "Carol," "Bye Bye Johnny," and "Little Queenie." Freddie and the Dreamers futzed with "Johnny B. Goode." The Kinks' "Beautiful Delilah" may be better than Berry's, the Animals did a ton of his songs, and Downliners Sect spat out a brutal version of "Our Little Rendezvous," an obscure 1960 B side.

The T.A.M.I. Show was a 1964 star-studded concert filmed in Santa Monica for presentation in movie theaters. In one scene it featured a startling enactment of a process mostly out of view. Berry is on a stage by himself playing "Maybellene" when the camera pans right and reveals England's Gerry and the Pacemakers ready and eager to carry the song home—their home. They finish Berry's song for him, as he looks on.

In America the transition from rhythm and blues to rock & roll was an offshore private transfer of raw goods conducted after everyone had gone to sleep. But in England the handoff was much more matter-of-fact and visible.

British bands giving Berry praise made him feel great, *and* it worked his one good nerve. These bands were paying decent licensing money for the ability to make hit albums with Chuck Berry tunes on them. But when they got too close—when they wanted to vibe with an originator—little good would come from it. Like the time in 1965 when the hotel elevator door opened on the ascending Rolling Stones, and Berry got in, looked carefully around, and turned his back on the adoring faces until he reached his floor. Or the time he was asked his opinion of the Beatles. "I think of them as four Everly Brothers," he said with a laugh.[14]

America and the world wanted Chuck Berry in a different package, and now that they had options in numerous gradations of white, it could make a soul feel unplugged.

Guy Stevens, the president of the Chuck Berry Appreciation Society in Britain, was diligently spreading the word. He put out Berry's music for the English label Pye International and wrote about him for the music press. Stevens was quite a talker, and in 1964 he had talked himself to Chicago, where he watched Berry recording "Promised Land" and interviewed him for a journal.

A question about who his music was for got Berry's back up. "I would like to think of myself as an artiste who can sell to any type of market. In America I am considered a rock 'n' roll artiste, as are most of the artistes that you would call rhythm and blues."[15] He was a rocker, and rockers made music for everybody.

"Rhythm and blues," he understood, might become a cul-de-sac. "The term R&B in America meant what a class of people closer to poverty considered a popular song."[16] He wanted freedom to reach all.

The lucky Stevens stuck close to his hero the next night, following him to a West Side Chicago blues club called the Pride and Joy, where harmonica revolutionary Little Walter was playing. The place was tiny, and Berry sat quietly, but eventually folks noticed who was there. Walter talked him up at length, and then Berry borrowed a guitar and joined the band. "I felt that many of the audience could not actually believe that it was Chuck Berry about to play for them, but the opening bars of 'Guitar Boogie' soon erased any of their doubts," wrote Stevens. "Let It Rock," "Johnny B. Goode," and "Honky Tonk" followed. Nothing to prove, no crowd to win over. Berry requested a song of Walter's, one of his blues that boiled human feelings down to a mathematics of want. "Mean Old World."

"I need you," Walter sings. "And you have left me for another. Have to use somebody else."

There's little more *alone* than hearing Little Walter examine himself from a great distance and evoke his life as a thing. It must have brought Berry some feeling of kinship, that night in 1964, to lose himself in someone else's feelings as he played to a cheering room of grateful listeners from the neighborhood.

14

HERCULES

IN AMERICA HE WAS UNCONNECTED TO THE MACHINERY OF YOUTH culture. In England he was more or less new himself, and the fresh UK bands could be tethered to his headlining appearances in a way that suggested a musical continuum. He could fill a hall. Late in 1964 showman Robert Stigwood had outbid Arden and landed Berry at the top of an upcoming tour. Stigwood was paying him $15,000, Berry said.[1]

The tour stretched from January into early February and featured the Graham Bond Organization, a blues band featuring Jack Bruce and Ginger Baker, Long John Baldry, the Moody Blues, and the Five Dimensions, who would back Berry.

Having seen the style of the British groups, Berry met them on their own turf; photos of the time show him in bespoke suits, brass buttons, leather shoes that reflected the stage lights, ties monogrammed, and lapels as contoured as a Gibson guitar, a towering Black dandy confounding assumptions about the "wild man of beat music." The tour program described the headliner like this:

Chuck is 6'1" and weighs 175 lbs. He has black hair and brown eyes. His favourite foods are chili, strawberry shortcake and orange juice, and his favourite colours are white and blue. His favourite hobby is photography and he has his own dark room for processing his film.

Welcome to Britain Chuck Berry—King of Rhythm and Blues.[2]

On his first time through England, Berry met a group of young fans that included a club DJ named Roger Fairhurst. He made a huge impression on Fairhurst's friends, who told Berry how they had lobbied local promoters to book their hero, and he invited them out for Chinese food after the first show. He shared stories from his life, and told them to call him Charles, not Chuck; he didn't discuss his time in prison and made it clear no such talk would be considered friendly.

As he planned a return trip, Berry invited Fairhurst to join him across England. The twenty-three-year-old curly-haired record hound saw a lot of Berry, more than most people ever did, over the next month. "Up close, oh, he was fine," said Fairhurst. "He was a strange man. He didn't do gratitude and he didn't say sorry or any of that stuff." But it was clear that he liked having Fairhurst and his friends around, and they found him to be thoughtful, slow to answer their questions and full of insights once he did. They didn't at the time understand why he had invited Fairhurst and his pals to travel around the country with him. "I was thinking about this invitation long afterward, and I came to realize this was his way of saying thank you to us for putting his name forward and sharing our interest in his music."[3]

"Where can I find out exactly how many pounds the dollar is worth each day?" Berry asked his new friend. Performing twice a night, Berry insisted on payment between shows. Fairhurst counted his money. "Each morning he asked me to go out and buy the *Financial Times* which had the exchange rates. He was charging $2,000 a night so whatever was the exact British equivalent on that day, that's what he wanted." He became alert to the value of the pound on a given morning. "And he better get it," said Fairhurst.

Cash was stored in a valise, which after three or four nights was bulging, and Berry would deposit it in a local account he had opened for the tour.

He was captivating, demanding of attention, and his followers discovered a complexity they didn't see coming. In his hotel room, he was interviewed by a British writer, talking between simultaneous bites of an enormous steak with strawberry shortcake and cream. The questioner asked him about his songwriting process, and Berry left the question hanging in the air, eating and then moving to a settee while he considered the question.

"I'll answer you this way," he finally responded.

You have to listen to all the words in my songs. They tell a story, or if not a story—well, at least they're descriptive. They're the result of my own impressions and images so I don't see how I can be influenced by anyone or anything outside of people or things actually in the tale I'm telling.

You see . . . no-one else can know the ideas I have in my mind— just as I can't know the ideas in other people's minds. There aren't too many mind-readers about, you know.

He flashed a smile. "In my songs, I try to convey what I have observed, experienced or imagined at one time or another. You'll see that if you listen to the words."[4] It was a cloud of performance—a mystery even to himself.

Manchester . . . Hull . . . Edinburgh . . . Leeds. The shows were exciting, and being around him was something even better to the young men in their twenties. He was a living, creative force, both guarded and outgoing, who thought carefully about how he presented himself in the world.

"He had a great sense of humor then," recalled Fairhurst.

He had the sort of sense of humor as many American Black people do, the endless layers of a put-down issued and one imposed on top of that by the next person and then it goes around in a conversation.

He played with the music sometimes in a way very difficult to describe, but he sort of caricatured himself, if you like—when he did that machine-gun-type delivery of words coming out so fast, deliberately bang bang bang all the time—and it was just, he had his way of saying, "I'm doing this for my own amusement."

Berry was always thinking, always listening. He kept two books close at hand, said Fairhurst, a dictionary and a volume of synonyms and antonyms. "You got the impression he was putting things in the bank all the time—he'd hear something and put it in the back of his brain and maybe you might see it coming out two years later in something he wrote."

Berry smoked Kool menthols, which he said were good for his throat. When a sore throat hit him, he asked what was good for it, and one of the guys said whiskey and hot water. But after trying a sip, he made a face and said it tasted terrible. "He didn't drink at all," said Fairhurst. The guys asked him if he ever tried any drugs. "Naw," he answered. "If you are not in control of what you are doing—somebody else is."

"You hear all these stories about what a miserable bastard he was and everything, but I got along well with him. But if you were not on his wavelength, he didn't have much time for you," said Fairhurst.

Reserving rooms at the Hilton Hotel throughout his stay, Berry held business meetings, including with Don Arden. The Jewish businessman liked to sneak bacon with his breakfast, Fairhurst observed, but on the day they all had breakfast with Arden's mother, Arden was forced to forgo his guilty pleasure. Later Fairhurst said, "Chuck, that's pretty surprising that he brought his mother with him." "Yeah," said Berry, "but it's even more surprising that he had one."

A posh, well-spoken figure not inclined to mask his racism invited Berry to a business lunch and was shocked to be turned down. "We just finished lunch. No one you know," Berry snapped back. "The wicked sparkle in our hero's eye, along with his charming smile, persuaded the suit to retreat as gracefully as he was able," said Fairhurst.

A beautiful, tall, dark-haired woman Fairhurst and his buddies called "Madam" arrived on the scene one day. "She would appear as if by magic when needed, and the dressing room would be declared 'out of bounds' for an hour or so." Then suddenly a different, blond "Madam" appeared. "This second one was less aloof than the first and seemed relieved when we treated her just like everyone else on the tour," recalled Fairhurst. "Each person had their job to do and all were compelled to get along with one another." Most of the time, the party of about thirty floated happily across the island.[5]

At first Fairhurst and his pals were on the bus, but soon Berry asked if they wanted to join him in his car. "He couldn't talk to the girlfriend about music, she didn't know anything. But he could talk about Louis Jordan with us. We had a lot of fun."

In 1965 there was a single motorway running north and south in England. Any band touring would come to know it well. The whole tour, headed toward Birmingham, landed at a service station with a highway café at two in the morning. Another crowd, from another bus going in the other direction, had stopped as well. Everybody got out, and one of the guys in the other band said, "Hey, there's Chuck Berry," and soon a little party was going on.

The bands were at one end of a long channel of thirty or forty deserted tables, and there was another crowd at the far end. "I bet those people would get a shock if you duckwalked down the corridor through all those tables," somebody suggested. "Yeah, let's find out." And so at two a.m. at a transport café, Berry slammed down his Orange Squash and jumped out of his seat. As discarded sandwich wrappers suddenly lifted off the ground, a six-foot-one-inch man, nostrils flared in the roadside lights, came duckwalking into the laps of baffled strangers. "We had fun."

One discordant scene at the end of the tour sticks with Fairhurst, because it stands apart from all the fun. Berry, Madam, Fairhurst, and a friend had enjoyed a meal at a Chinese restaurant, and the waiter brought the check to the table. Quietly, Fairhurst paid for everyone.

But Berry had seen, and he raced down two flights of stairs to grab him on his way to the car. He looked angry.

"*Why did you do that?*" Berry demanded. "*When you are with me, I pay.*"

His friend explained that he just wanted a way to say thank you to his musical hero for taking him on the road with him and showing him the time of his life.

At that the star relaxed a tiny bit, and his expression softened. "Don't ever do that again!"

"I said, 'Okay, sorry about that.'"

"He got me in a bear hug—I thought he was gonna crush me to death. And he said, 'We don't do that anymore, right?'"

"No no!"

MARSHALL CHESS AND LES COCKS, AN EXECUTIVE AT PYE Records, had scheduled a recording session in London. The idea was a riff on international diplomacy, an envoy grooving with a team of locals on a joint training mission. Berry was booked to meet a band Cocks had assembled in the studio and record with them soon upon arriving. The session was booked for noon, and two hours later Berry arrived with Fairhurst and friends, and his sister Lucy Ann, who was visiting from St. Louis.

Berry greeted each of the musicians with a demand that they play a section from one of his songs—the bassist had to know "Let It Rock," say, while the drummer had better have "Maybellene" under control. Around the room he went, testing their aptitude, and when he was satisfied he asked Cocks if there was an office in the studio. They were supposed to finish recording an album and get Berry to the venue by five o'clock for a sound check. "Why do you need an office?" Cocks asked. "Because first I've gotta write the fucking songs," he barked.[6]

At Pye he recorded five songs that day, mostly blues. Fairhurst and friends shouted out, "Olé!" on the best of them, "You Came a Long Way from St. Louis." At the end of the tour another session was booked, but it also amounted to little. Leonard Chess might have wondered why Berry was recording a blues album in London with rock & roll bigger than ever.

Chess had already shown, with the Berry/Diddley collaboration and then *St. Louis to Liverpool*, how unprepared they were for the new market emphasis on albums. At a time when acts like the Beatles and Beach Boys were using the form to launch mission statements, Berry was compiling scraps.

In need of material, Chess added five songs from a recent Chicago session, with Berry backed by a certifiable young, white St. Louis band, Jules Blattner and the Teen Tones. Several good new tunes came of it, a careening cover of Memphis Minnie's "Me and My Chauffeur Blues" and a rewrite of the Teen Tones' "Butterscotch Twist," now "Butterscotch." And, done: *Chuck Berry in London*.

Though he was working with the musician who had made his whole career possible, Blattner was disgusted with the session. Berry was "Impossible! He was always real uncooperative . . . real strange! He would, for instance, arrange a song *all day long*." Then when they recorded it the next day, "he'd do it totally different," complained Blattner. "Not a very nice guy, either."[7]

At home and abroad, Berry was an aloof bandleader. However, Berry the songwriter was getting fresh attention beyond the rock & roll world. In Nashville, producer Billy Sherrill handed a bunch of Chuck's records to bluegrass act Jim & Jesse McReynolds, urging the brothers to make an album of them. Jim & Jesse came from the coal-studded mountains of southwest Virginia; their concerts featured gospel tunes. "Billy had come up with some crazy ideas and that was one of them," said mandolin player Jesse McReynolds. But the brothers were on board, and their *Berry Pickin' in the Country* featured ten rock & roll songs and was a success for the duo. And a controversy: bluegrass warlords Flatt & Scruggs got wind of what Jim & Jesse were doing and decreed *they* would be first out with a bluegrass version of "Memphis," the single the brothers wanted to lead with.

"There was a little conference between me and Earl Scruggs; he got pretty nasty there for a while," Jesse McReynolds chuckled.[8]

Flatt & Scruggs threatened to leave their label, Columbia, unless they released "Memphis" ahead of Jim & Jesse. But the brothers had a whole album of Chuck. Tensions escalated since both acts were regulars on the Grand Ole Opry and both submitted "Memphis" as their featured number for the same week—as did Bob Luman, who had his own rockabilly version. A three-way dustup over Chuck Berry ensued at the Opry.

Berry Pickin' in the Country was controversial for other reasons. Jesse remembers that in the mid-sixties he and his brother Jim were living in Prattville, Alabama, a stronghold of segregation. Stokely Carmichael would be jailed in Prattville in 1967, and workers for the Student Nonviolent Coordinating Committee were trapped inside a building there and shot at by Klan members.

"There was a lot of stuff going on that people didn't talk about much, but the racial thing was very real—they had the big march on Selma in 1965, and it went right by our house," said McReynolds. They had been rehearsing bluegrass rock & roll tunes day and night—"We had Chuck Berry music coming out of the walls," he laughed. "I remember it well. And then we had the record come out and everybody said, well, we were in a racial thing with the Black people of Alabama; Jim & Jesse live here and they are doing Chuck Berry songs! We got a few comments from people. It was pretty aggressive." The response wasn't just from southerners; Jesse says they got criticized in New York when they played the new songs there.

But *Berry Pickin' in the Country* was a best seller for Jim & Jesse; they were still selling it at shows twenty-five years after its release. As Jesse put it, "When you try to do good, you can also do well."

Chuck himself knew what the gesture meant. In his liner notes, the rocker wrote what he felt: "It always enchants me to hear music that comes from the soul, in Jim & Jesse's performances that's just where it comes from. Evidently, these songs that have poured out of my soul in past years have reached theirs. I shall always be grateful that my work has moved them so deeply." He probably never said anything so elaborate about the Beatles.

Nashville had never not been fond of Chuck Berry music; it just preferred to keep a distance from Chuck Berry. In the 1960s, country music was in the middle of a demographic drift: there was a young audience to court, while many older listeners were moving to big cities yet longing to hold on to their roots. Pressure was exerted on fans and musicians to show they were keeping it real in the face of social change.

Buck Owens was fielding criticism—for being successful without the help of Music City mandarins, for playing a raucous version of "Twist and Shout" live, for drums and loud Telecasters and other offenses. Suddenly Owens was getting blowback for being not "real" country.

Who belonged in country music was increasingly a source of anxiety, even for a rising superstar. In early 1965, Owens responded with an ad in the local *Music City News*. It was a drawing of parchment nailed to a wall, like a religious declaration, titled, "A Pledge to Country Music." Owens's conceit was that audiences come and go, but he was swearing an oath of loyalty to the music itself, which never changes.

I Shall Sing No Song That Is Not A Country Song

I Shall Make No Record That Is Not A Country Record

I Refuse To Be Known As Anything But A Country Singer

I am proud to be associated with country music

Country music and country music fans have made me what I am today

And I shall not forget it.

His renouncement of rock & roll came at the beginning of March. Before the month was over, Owens had released a blazing cover of "Memphis." "I didn't say I wasn't gonna do rockabilly," Buck shot back. The only thing that made such songs objectionable, he said, was that "a black man was singin' it, a black man who I was a big fan of. But if you listen to Chuck's words, they are straight country words. You can sing his tunes and please just about any audience."[9]

Berry brought straight country words—and straight country narratives, one could add. There was a reason why Roy Orbison called Chuck "the first singer-songwriter." When he began, many peers, Elvis most notably, were not writing their own material. By the mid-1960s in New York City, the old Tin Pan Alley songwriting process had moved into the Brill Building, where songs were composed for the Beatles, girl groups, garage bands, and folk singers. Now the process was changing once more as recording artists began insisting on performing songs they also wrote.

One man gets much of the credit for altering the course of the music business. "I didn't know it at the time, but all the radio songs were written at Tin Pan Alley, the Brill Building," Bob Dylan once said, looking back on his career beginnings in the early 1960s. "Tin Pan Alley is gone. I put an end to it. People can record their own songs now—they're almost expected to do it."[10]

It's worth noting that Berry's first album, 1957's *After School Session*, had twelve songs, each of them composed by Chuck. He had his own music-publishing company, Isalee. By the time Dylan was going electric, Berry was upgrading his own electrified songwriting with expressions of craft that included "You Never Can Tell," "Nadine," and "Promised Land." There wasn't a category of music for Black artists writing their own songs, and after somebody created "singer-songwriter" as a job title, it remained a tough job to get.

He was constantly asked what he thought of the Beatles recording his music; his answers always settled on money. "Very nice," he said in 1967, before noting that the Beatles money was only then starting to roll in.

He wasn't going to celebrate versions rendered by the most famous musical force on Earth. He wasn't going to parse achievement and celebrity. Money could be discussed. It was quantifiable, and it provided a clean way to convert rough feelings into the commodity of numbers.

"I keep thinking about the positive side," he told Robert Hilburn later on. "I'd say, 'Look how much money I made from writing my songs and singing them, both of which I like to do.'" He recalled the Rolling Stones getting $50,000 in Miami for the *Ed Sullivan Show*, "and I was making $500 a night and they were playing my song."[11]

But, look, he joked, $500 a night added up. Why, "in 100 nights, I'd have $50,000."

Others were cashing in on Chuck Berry, he might have concluded; now it was his turn.

In 1966 he left Chess Records. Mercury, a label owned by the Dutch electronics company Philips, offered him a cash advance of $60,000, Berry explained (others have suggested it was actually $150,000). Chess had been his home, and he had helped build Chess a new one. The brothers had started with gut feelings, cast-off sounds, and garbage money, and had been essential to Berry's fame. But the moment called for a sage reading of market potentials, and Berry seized the moment.

Leonard Chess offhandedly told him he'd see Berry again in three years, when his deal was up with Mercury. "Oh no, there were no bad feelings," said Berry. "We just shook hands and they wished me good luck. The change-over was just a business deal."[12]

He wanted control over the music, and more money, and Mercury offered both.

Then they asked Berry to rerecord versions of most of his biggest hits, fresh takes they could sell. Jerry Lee Lewis and Little Richard had both rerecorded their hits upon signing with new labels, and as with them, Berry's heart was not in the production of these duplicates.

When he came to the label, he quickly released a bracing new single, "Club Nitty Gritty," that pointed forward, a soul groove with horns and Berry unleashing a brand-new shout. Some of that energy held for the next album, *Chuck Berry in Memphis*, released in September 1967. It was a sharp idea to go to Memphis, a new center of soul music, and hook him up with some of the best players in town: drummer Satch Arnold, guitarist Reggie Young, and others. But Berry was known for traveling light, and he didn't take many new songs with him when he went to Memphis. While there's some soul energy on the disc, it keeps getting cut off—the songs frequently demand to unfold over time, and there isn't a cut on *Chuck Berry in Memphis* even three minutes long.

AFTER MUCH WORK, BERRY PARK REOPENED AS A RECREATION park fully available to the public. The first thing Berry had built was a guitar-shaped swimming pool. The region had a history of banning races from swimming together. He charged twenty-five cents for anybody who wanted to jump in.

The grounds featured a dance hall where bands played; the owner booked country and rock bands. He said, "Myself, when I feel like dancing then I play rock music. If I'm in a sentimental mood, then Western music. And of course I do play jazz because that's the only music you can learn something from."[13] On Sunday afternoons, casual sessions brought musicians like Little Walter, Muddy Waters, and Louis Jordan playing for a small crowd. There were badminton and tennis courts, go-karts, a fishing pond, and a lake for boating. "All this plus restaurants and guest houses is Chuck's," enthused an article in England's *New Musical Express*.

"Berry Park was our heart," recalled Themetta. "It was a dream. Something Charles had wanted to do was have an amusement park for his fans, the family or whoever else wanted to come."[14] Berry may have lived in Chicago briefly in 1963, and he came to Windermere Place for dinners, but Wentzville was his St. Louis home.

St. Louis guitarist Steve Scorfina played at Berry Park in the mid-1960s and is friends with the family. "So Chuck was married for fifty years or more," he explained. "His wife stayed at the house in St. Louis, and he stayed out in Wentzville. And Melody stayed with mom and was absolutely like a church lady, beautiful, beautiful soul. They're all beautiful souls but. . . . And then Ingrid was like a wild card. She wanted to live with her father and didn't get along with her mom. Lived out at Berry Park, where her father built her this beautiful cabin on a lake that was the most beautiful thing you saw in your life."[15]

The first time Scorfina's band played Berry Park, he was on a break talking to his bandmates on lawn chairs by the pool. All of a sudden Chuck walked by; Scorfina hadn't talked to him yet and sensed this was the time.

He was starstruck, trying to think of what he should say to someone he had emulated since he was a kid. Finally, he blurted out,

"What was the first guitar you ever had to play on?" And he gets this grin and he says, "It was a Star."

And to this day I don't know if he was pulling my leg. But I'm a guitar hound and I've never heard of a Star guitar. . . . I tend to think he might have been putting me on. Chuck was very much a hard person to get to know. I've seen him hundreds of times after that and he was always that way.

One visitor to Berry Park was the concert promoter Bill Graham. He'd been urging Berry to play the Fillmore, a San Francisco venue where he booked shows. "But he just wouldn't come out to play. It was always, 'The Fillmore, man? I don't know.'" It wasn't until Graham flew out to Wentzville that Berry gave him a listen. "Chuck wouldn't even come to the airport to meet me," Graham recalled. "I had to rent a car and drive out to his farm."[16]

Graham wasn't a dreamer; he was about business, and that probably helped him with Berry. He liked music, which was nice, and he had impatience with the San Francisco mystique in the trail of the Summer of Love. "I'm not a hippie . . . don't sell love. I sell talent and environment," he told *Billboard*.[17]

Berry knew the Fillmore as a Black dance hall in a Black neighborhood from when he played there in years past. But in 1966 Graham was booking San Francisco's fledgling psychedelic bands and packing the Fillmore with white teenagers. Seeing that these acts filled the place on their own, he added opening acts he wanted the kids to hear, putting jazz man Charles Lloyd on before Moby Grape, Big Mama Thornton with Jefferson Airplane, telling the hippies to eat their vegetables.

"In 1966 and '67 the average seventeen-year-old kid did not know who Chuck Berry or B. B. King or Albert King were," Graham explained.[18]

He booked Berry to open for the Grateful Dead.

Graham got Berry three March 1967 dates for $800 a night. But on opening night, Chuck was notably absent. It was nine, and then ten, as the crowd grew restless. Graham was in his office calling the airport to see if the plane had landed when he heard a knock at his door.

"How you doin', Chuck. You're a little late," Graham started. Chuck stayed quiet, just standing in the doorway, not really glaring, more like issuing a deadpan soul suction on the man behind the desk. He put his guitar case down on the floor between them, and his eyes never moved. Message received: Berry desired to be paid before he played. "Do you want cash or a check?" Graham asked, a question which succeeded in triggering an active emotion to appear across Berry's face.

Graham wrote out a check for $800 and pushed it across his desktop. Berry pulled it home, signed the back, and then shoved it half way toward his employer, where it stopped in the demilitarized zone. Graham brought out cash and Berry counted it, and then, when he was satisfied, he pushed the check the rest of the way to Graham. His hand shot out, and they shook on their new arrangement. "Mellow," cooed Chuck.

With zero wasted time Berry shot out onstage, and exactly forty-five minutes later there was not a seventeen-year-old present who did not know who Chuck Berry was.

And with zero wasted moves, Berry duckwalked off the stage, dropping his guitar into its case as the crowd called out his name. Graham screamed it too.

"I don't hear it. I don't hear it," Chuck yelled in his general direction. "They don't want me!"

"Chuck, they *want* you. They *want* you."

A playful look, a complicated hybrid of glee and concern, flooded Berry's face. "They don't want me, boss. They don't want me, boss man." Bill Graham was not stupid, and he knew what was wanted.

"They *want* you. They *want* you" was the best he could do in the moment. The cash was upstairs.

Berry dug deep. "They don't *love* me," he groaned, picking up his guitar case and making ready to leave.

Graham's expression was surely one of respect. "They *want* you, Chuck. You can't leave. They *love* you." Then, with exquisite timing, Berry got deep into Graham's face.

"They *love* me? They *want* me? I'm goin' out there." He stalked out in front of the audience, saying into the microphone, "Yeah, you love me, you want me, yeah, and one, two, one, two, three . . ."

Going forward, Graham knew, more money would be required. Message delivered, on all possible levels. Love had come across the stage, and he pushed it back, until it had been exchanged for cash. That was how he could take it home.

Those three days in the Bay Area opened new doors for Berry. He enjoyed himself playing for the avid young fans, and he treated them to rarities and off-menu items, like a recitation of "Vagabond's House," an evocation of the exotic by twentieth-century poet Don Blanding.

A few months later Graham booked him for a week in late June, and this time Graham also reached out to a young blues fanatic whose band was on the rise. Steve Miller was a confident kid raised in Texas whose dad was a music fanatic and gearhead. T-Bone Walker had played in his living room in 1951; Les Paul was Miller's godfather. Miller told Graham his band was ready to back Berry, but he had some preconditions. "I said Chuck Berry's got to come out here and rehearse. I'm not going to just go onstage with Chuck Berry."[19]

Miller had heard about Berry's habit of playing with any pickup band available, often leading to a less than fulfilling experience; he wanted to make the most of his time with Berry. "We were the blues band in town, everybody else was folk musicians who decided to become rock stars. You didn't really want the Grateful Dead to back Chuck Berry," said Miller. "But *I* was there and he asked me to back him up."

Graham reported back that it was a go: Berry was coming out early to rehearse with Miller. "The first thing he said was, 'Nobody's gonna shave or shower until we are through rehearsing.' And he meant it." They practiced for two days in the Fillmore, taking breaks for barbecue. "He was just as cool as he could be," Miller said. "We were doing 'My Dream,' and 'Rockin' at the Philharmonic,' he worked it on out and he was sounding really, really great." After a fruitful nighttime rehearsal, the label decided to make a live recording.

Mercury's artist and repertoire (A&R) director had seen a rehearsal and gotten the label's backing. He paid Miller's band a dollar to play on the record, said Miller, but it was worth it, if only to stand on a stage with Chuck Berry in his prime, whom Miller compared to "a gazelle," and whom he vividly remembered in profile onstage at the Fillmore.

"God! He was absolutely beautiful—the most beautiful human being, looking as delicate and exquisite as Hercules. Not an ounce of fat on his body, just this amazingly healthy and beautiful man." But there was a problem. The label man had taken Berry aside for a walk around the block just before the show began, Miller recalled.

And whatever he gave the star—Miller believes it was a barbiturate—Hercules returned in a mellow mood.

"From the start of the show all the tempos were in a coma," said Miller. They played almost all casual blues, taken at a lugubrious pace. Whether it was something Chuck ate or a subversion of what everybody expected, Berry was in some other space.

"We were playing these songs and they're going okay, but really slow," said Miller. Yet song by song, Chuck was involved and connected to the crowd, and "the audience song by song is loving him more, and near the end of the show, we felt like we had pulled it off." Berry had just done a version of "Vagabond's House" that he and the band worked up. "He's got everybody right in the palm of his hand and then unbeknownst to us or to anybody—he goes into 'My Ding-A-Ling.'" It was part of Berry's plan, a song he had been exploring over the years. Just not a number he'd shared with the band.

To Miller, to any blues purist whether or not T-Bone Walker had once tuned up in their breakfast nook, this "My Ding-A-Ling" thing was worse than commercial twaddle. It was not the electrified Delta blues; it was a ditty about playing with yourself. It, it, it—well, it was "crude. Embarrassing. Way beneath him," Miller railed. Worse than that, the crowd was into it, responding to his instructions and gleefully singing along.

"He turned into a professional wrestler, baiting the audience," Miller sighed. "And they—they went nuts. It just turned the happy place into a sad place."

Still, Miller loved playing with Berry. Graham booked the Steve Miller Band opening for and backing Chuck Berry on the road along the West Coast. "It was fun, it was—well, not hard work." Chuck got $5,000 in cash up top, and the gigs were enjoyable for all parties, until one night at the Carousel in San Francisco. Miller knew Berry could be hard on the band, but he *liked* Miller's group. And yet.

> He stops in the middle of some number and starts embarrassing my drummer, criticizing him and stuff. Then he did "My Ding-A-Ling" and walked off the stage. I was so angry that he'd done that to us—this was like our tenth gig we'd done with him, we gave him our best, everything was good. And this was a guy who never even said thanks, he'd just come and go.

That's not the kind of relationship I wanted with Chuck Berry. So when we got off the stage I just told him, "Fuck you. Fuck you and don't ever do that again with us." It worked.

"You had to say, 'fuck you' to him," explained Miller. "He had to see you as a man, not a fan, or he would just eat you up."

The work for Chuck wasn't hard, and he enjoyed the Bay Area perks.

"Women just came after him," said Miller. One episode happened before the first night at the Fillmore. "Clear as a bell I remember this very, extremely attractive, good-looking woman, and I remember thinking, 'Wow, who is that?' She went up and put her arms around Chuck and planted one on him for a minute. I was like, 'Chuck Berry, rock & roll.'"

A libertine long before the Summer of Love, he was going to be paid, one way or another. According to his kids, he viewed it as the spoils of stardom.

"It wasn't just Pop. It was every rock & roll star. It came with the territory," said his daughter Melody in a 2020 documentary.

According to Charles Berry Jr., his father didn't bring the pop-star life home with him. "Chuck Berry never came into our house. Charles Edward Anderson Berry came in, our father came in. So, all the stuff that went on outside the door, that was Chuck Berry, but it was dad, husband, inside our house."[20]

Chuck Berry grew up hearing his own father warn him, "If a white woman smiles at you, you never smile back." He smiled back. Reflecting on his year and a half in prison, and on what he had lost in the process, he was set now on enjoying himself.

"The sexual revolution was coming in, and long hair . . . ," Chuck mused. "I tell you what I did—I joined the fiesta. I was wanting to live too. Don't forget I'm thirty-five now and still liking how society is moving into this freedom."[21]

One night he was sitting backstage between sets, talking to a newspaper writer. Berry's Italian shoes were off, hands tightly clenched in his lap, and he was making the journalist work.

He was asked about the revival of interest in 1950s rock & roll. The singer said, "Well man, I didn't expect it, but I don't reject it."

Mostly he was fending off questions with vague answers. Until the writer asked him, "How have people changed since your early rock days?"

"Not much man, you can still give someone five dollars and they'll do anything for you. Money is where it's at, baby, not fame."[22]

How have people changed? He explained with a number. "I paid $180 for a coat and went to San Francisco for a concert. All those kids in sneakers and jeans made me feel like a chump. That's what's changed. The kids have."

15

HAPPY DAYS

In Laurel Canyon they discussed pop music's future. Mama Cass's estate was where Paul McCartney, the Mamas and the Papas, and label head Lou Adler dreamed about taking the music, their music, to the next place. Jazz was considered an American art form, they were adamant, so how could rock & roll, at a moment when so much was going on, receive similar respect? Out of such discussions came the 1967 Monterey International Pop Festival.

They invited Chuck Berry to the music's future, but problems occurred. When John Phillips explained that the vision for the three-day festival was that acts would donate their fees to a cause, Berry himself was adamant. "I told him on the phone, 'Chuck, it's for charity,' and he said to me, 'Chuck Berry has only one charity and that's Chuck Berry. $2,000.' We couldn't make an exception." That's the way Phillips skewed it to journalist Michael Lydon: Chuck Berry was a vibe exterminator.[1]

From outside the canyon, there was criticism of the festival's paltry efforts to book Black acts. Motown's Berry Gordy and Smokey Robinson were listed on the festival's board of directors, but "they never answered the phone," complained Phillips.

Smokey was completely inactive as a director.

I think it might be a Jim Crow thing. A lot of people put Lou Rawls down for appearing. "You're going to a Whitey festival, man," was the line.

Phillips was confident in his read of the problem. "There is tension between the white groups who are getting their own ideas and the Negroes who are just repeating theirs. The tension is lessening all the time, but it did crop up here, I am sure."

In the end, only six out of thirty-two acts for a festival aiming to rebrand pop music as a new global force would be Black. Phillips seemed to think it was somebody else's fault, and somebody else's problem.

The audience for this music was itself becoming whiter. If Berry chose to ponder it, he might have noted how when he was traversing the Jim Crow South in the mid-1950s, playing for venues with ropes dividing one side of the room against the other and sheriffs standing at the exits, the crowds were far more diverse than they were at the Fillmore in 1967.[2]

In the mid-1960s, rock & roll became *rock*, and the change required a full-on makeover. The musical culture—the business, the artists, and the audience—aligned in a view that they were not a craze or a market; they were a movement. Rock viewed itself as a social force marked by self-consciousness as an art form while it carried change to the culture at large, the way film or comedy or the new journalism did.

The 1950s youth culture was pushing thirty, and was no longer the vanguard. The African American pop critic Phyl Garland, writing in 1969, conceived of rock as a white music built from R&B but marketed to white teens. Even Chuck Berry, as far as Garland was concerned, was remote from the current moment. "He is now considered the most influential single black contributor to the evolution of white rock," she wrote.[3]

Berry tried to be receptive to new ideas. Mercury had signed a production deal with Doug Sahm, a long-haired rocker from San Antonio, and put Berry together with Sahm's band the Sir Douglas Quintet in a San Francisco studio. It made sense, given Sahm's ability to bring roadside rock & roll into the counterculture.

The two had met in 1965, and Sahm, anyway, remembered it vividly. Both appeared on the TV show *Hullabaloo*, and behind the scenes
Sahm spotted Berry's guitar in its case. The Holy Grail. He reached in
and held it up, and right then Berry came over and said, "Hey white
boy, get your hands off my guitar!"

In 1967, Berry showed up at the studio ready to play, and when he
arrived he saw his producer with the band, busy breaking up a brick of
weed. "Those Frisco days were high days!" explained Augie Meyers, keyboardist for the Sir Douglas Quintet. "We were smoking weed back in
them days and Chuck didn't like it too much, you know. So he booked."[4]

The eventual album, 1968's *From St. Louie to Frisco*, has some life
to it. Berry used his daughter Ingrid on several songs. Ingrid had a
soulful voice and played a snarling harmonica, and she might also have
brought Berry some calm in the studio when he worked with people he
didn't know. But though the album was all new originals the writing felt
tossed off, like he wasn't sure how much to try, and was surely dimin-
ished by the meltdown with Sahm.

A year later came *Concerto in B. Goode*, four slack new numbers
plus one bonkers, eighteen-and-a-half-minute deep ramble. It was
a good season for rambles. Muddy Waters had released a controversial psychedelic document in 1968 titled *Electric Mud*, and in 1969,
months before Berry's record came out, Howlin' Wolf had been pushed
to cut his own nearly groovy *The Howlin' Wolf Album*. Wolf famously
hated his record and told the guitar player on the session to go cut his
Afro and take that bow-wow pedal and throw it into the lake. Berry at
least sounds like he's having a blast on the side-long title cut, all-in as
he glides his Cadillac down the autobahn, the wind whipping around
his phosphorescent cortex. It is said that Chuck Berry records helped
create the rhythmic underpinnings of rocksteady, reggae's first wave.
Concerto sounds like Berry creating Jamaican dub. He's in a jolly
mood; it was the last record he made with Mercury.

An executive offered a postmortem of Berry's three years with the
label. "I think Chuck came to Mercury with full hope that things could
happen and they never did happen for him," said John Sippel. "We
tried and tried and tried with the man and we couldn't do anything
with him. . . . We gave him every kind of a leeway. Chuck had his own
carte blanche. . . . He wanted to do Spanish things, yet when I heard
the stuff it was downright awful."[5]

In the 1950s, Sippel said, "Chuck Berry had the pulse of the world." But now, "I just feel Chuck kinda ran out of gas."

Berry returned to Chess. A February 1970 issue of *Billboard* quoted Marshall Chess boasting that they had just signed "the first black rock group," Detroit's Black Merda. That was a little redundant, given that the story also announced Chess had re-signed the first Black rock & roll *star*.

The name of the record he began to work on: *Back Home*. But the Chess home was unlike the place it had been even three years before. Leonard and Phil were buying radio stations and spending less time in the studio. Then, while behind the wheel of his car on a Chicago side street, Leonard had a heart attack and died in 1969. At the funeral, Muddy Waters cried, "It's all over, Leonard. It's just all over. There ain't no more record company. No more nothing, Leonard." If Berry had any feelings about Chess's death, he kept them to himself, writing in his autobiography that after he returned to the label, "Leonard was never there anymore."[6]

The returning star had received an education in Chessenomics, and he understood how the label and ARC Music held on to his royalties. He rarely admitted it, but it bothered him. In a 2011 interview, he said simply, "Believe me, I still feel it now." He was returning with a desire to undo past practices, with the assistance of attorney William Krasilovsky, a pioneer in getting artists paid their due. Krasilovsky spoke in fast, short sentences that sounded like non sequiturs—you had to pay attention to decipher his meaning. That might have made him a good match for Berry. "It was almost like his own language—his mind went faster than his mouth could move," said a student and peer of Krasilovsky's, entertainment attorney Robert Meloni. Krasilovsky represented many show business clients, including Aretha Franklin and the estates of composers Sergei Rachmaninoff and Thomas "Fats" Waller.[7]

Unlike many of his generation, Berry had the foresight and income to avoid having to sell his publishing rights. After his initial experiences with Chess and ARC, he and Francine Gillium started his own publishing company, Isalee Music Company. A self-publishing songwriter was a rarity in the 1950s, but Isalee didn't have the wherewithal or staff to ensure that royalties were properly calculated and paid, or to make sure that songs were not being used without a proper license.

Krasilovsky helped with that and more; an authority on international publishing, he found that Germany, France, and Japan had been collecting royalties for Berry but not distributing them. As Berry's publishing administrator, he located these "black box monies" and returned them to the artist for whom they were intended. Crucially, Krasilovsky helped Berry gain control of songs he had assigned to ARC before realizing he could create his own publishing company.

Two Chess icons were playing on a bill at this moment, it might have been in Chicago, said musician Bob Baldori. Bo Diddley and Berry were hanging out together backstage, waiting to go on. "Chess was their family, in spite of whatever business things they may have disagreed about. They were all together in that," said Baldori. They were perusing the latest issue of *Billboard* and reading out loud a report that Chess had just been sold to General Recorded Tape, a manufacturer of tape used in recording music. The family business had been sold to a corporation. Baldori said,

> I remember it clear as day. Chuck I can hear saying, "What you gonna do, Bo?" "I don't know," Bo says. "What are *you* gonna do?"
>   And it just sort of hung there. And after that, it kind of fell apart for both of them.[8]

EAGER TO MOVE PAST MERCURY, BERRY WAS IN CHESS'S STUDIO in November 1969 working on a new album. "He was as focused as any musician I have been around," said Baldori, who played harmonica on the sessions.

Jordan Orleans was a fourteen-year-old kid with an uncle who worked for Chess, and he recalls visiting a recording session around that time. Berry worked for hours on the guitar sound for a small part of a song. "He was impressive—a dedicated, committed, tenacious artist," said Orleans. Bringing all his powers into a tiny Chess studio, "he was a perfectionist you didn't want to mess with. He had a respectful, intense presence that you didn't want to interfere with."[9]

His first recording session for Chess in three and a half years yielded a remarkable single, "Tulane" / "Have Mercy Judge." "Tulane and Johnny opened a novelty shop" is how Chuck begins this song of love put to the test. It might put the listener in mind of a distantly related song, one that begins, "Frankie and Johnny were sweethearts . . ." that bubbled out of the St. Louis streets at the end of the nineteenth century. Could this be another Johnny song from Berry? The answer was, only if Johnny kept his name out of the lights and instead ended up selling pot from below the shop counter.

The law busts in during the first verse. Johnny trips while hopping the counter and gets nabbed, but Tulane leaps clean as Johnny cheers her on. That's the story—a bagged man watching his partner run for daylight. The scenario is more immediate, alive, than Berry had been in years, and the admiration he voices for Tulane is palpable, reaching back to Berry's late-1950s anthems of girl power. "Go head on, Tulane, he can't catch up with you / Go, Tulane, he ain't man enough for you," Johnny shouts, barking his love and alibis.

The other side, "Have Mercy Judge," was a strong new blues that carries the story forward—out on bail Johnny gets popped selling again, and the repeat offender comes before the judge who'd sent him away previously. All he can do, as he pleads to anyone who'll help him, is ask them to tell Tulane to get on with her life and forget him.

The blues meant a variety of things to Berry. He loved it. When he first came to Chicago, one story goes, he asked Leonard Chess if he could use a pseudonym and cut just blues for the label (Leonard told Berry to stick to rock & roll). Blues was something other. It was music that he sometimes brought out when he wanted to play just for himself. But the blues was complicated.

Sometimes he'd say he couldn't play like Muddy Waters because of his own story. The form was an index of experience, not race, he continued, and he didn't have much hardship in his background. "I would have to say that I cannot sing the blues because I've never really felt the cold-hearted blues. I can *try* to put it over and I *may* get it over, but I was born in a brick house and went through every grade in school. I've never even seen a cottonfield. I can put it together and try to get it over but, man, I'd be lying like a dog."[10] It's a smart thing to say, but there's a big trapdoor built into his words. He wants to escape experience by invoking success. But he had more than enough experience to sing the blues, this man who graduated from high school after taking classes in prison. He saw the blues as setting the limits of a Black person's cultural limits, and his success as a pop star marked him as a success in the marketplace, in the news cycle, and in the entertainment world, all of which marginalized those who played the blues.

One other thing the music gave him was a set of ready-made structures—for songs, for lyric postures, ways to bend your voice and guitar tone—that must have provided a welcome escape for someone expected to be always an inventor of the new. The blues was a dialogue with the past. Something he could fit into rather than feel like he had to own. It might have been a relief to know you sounded like other people when you played the music, when the rest of the time you were expected to come out and be the only Chuck Berry the world had ever known.

Johnnie Johnson said what he felt when he talked about the very first single they made: "Maybellene" on one side, "Wee Wee Hours" on the other. "It was 'Wee Wee Hours' we was proud of, that was *our* music," he declared.[11]

Berry didn't quite feel the same way, however. He discovered the blues not in his environment but from jukeboxes and the radio, like everything else that mattered to him.

"'Wee Wee Hours' came from pretty much the black culture I was listening to once I got into high school," he told Peter Guralnick. "And I got to have the blues because of politics again—can't get away from that. America is made of politics."[12] He used *politics* as another way of saying *racism*. Success, he thought, offered a way past the blues. But the blues, it found him, the same way politics found him.

THE BLUES WAS AN INTENSE WAY OF TALKING TO THE PAST, BUT suddenly rock was connecting with its own history. In 1969, one of the big stories of the Woodstock Music and Art Fair was a group of Columbia University grads called Sha Na Na. They came to Woodstock without a recording contract and, dressed up as a bunch of 1950s cartoon characters, offered listeners a fresh take on rock & roll's collective past. They were the next-to-last act at the festival and performed doo-wop, surf, R&B, and Elvis songs, with dancers and costumes, for the Woodstock Nation.

Two months later, Sha Na Na were signed to Buddah Records and landed on a bill with Chuck Berry at New York's Felt Forum. He was in great form—"erotic, sardonic and adult," said *Billboard*—and the

show, advertised as a "1950s Rock & Roll Revival," also featured the
first New York appearance in eight years of Bill Haley & His Comets,
plus the Coasters, the Platters, and others.

Promoter Richard Nader said he made $42,000 from the show and
announced he was putting together a package of vintage acts to take on
the road. For the next few years, Berry would appear often on a Revival
bill assembled by Nader. The star bluntly spelled out his terms to the
revivalist: "You use my name. You take money from the public. I show
up. You pay me."[13]

Dick Clark once dissed Nader, saying that *he* certainly didn't want
to be associated with pieces of antiquity. And when Dick Clark says
you aren't cool, you might as well embrace it. Nader wasn't interested
in being in the moment—he could talk about "the Revolution" with
rock writers, but what he yearned for, because his audience yearned
for it, was a good old sock hop. Born Richard Abi-Nader in western
Pennsylvania, and a former dance DJ, Nader was drafted out of college
in 1960 and became an Armed Forces DJ. Stationed in South Korea,
he created a "hometown sound" format, including a feature where
he read letters from home to soldiers stationed in the demilitarized
zone. Then he returned to the US and joined a talent agency. But that
"hometown sound" stayed with him—a calming approach in a place of
tension, an embodiment of American commonality expressed through
music from the past.

"Today, when so much of our lives is complicated, people want to
be able to relax and enjoy themselves without worrying about their
usual routines," said Nader. "Entertainment should give them that
chance—no pressure but refreshing moments to remember their good
feelings. The music of the '50s—its simplicity, basic themes and easy
melodies—creates that type of atmosphere."[14]

The artists he courted were skeptical; Gary U.S. Bonds didn't
believe that anybody would want to hear his old songs and filled his first
Revival spot singing contemporary hits from Top 40 radio. But Nader's
package tours were a big moneymaker in the 1970s, and Nader was
responsible for the Dion and the Belmonts reunion, Little Richard's
comeback, and more.

According to Gary U.S. Bonds, Nader "proved himself to be adept
at managing the often difficult Chuck Berry." And when Berry and Jerry

Lee Lewis were both on the show in 1973, fighting over who would
headline, Nader "operated with the finesse of Kissinger when it came
to maneuvering the prickly rock and roll legends." Lewis wanted to
do his cheating-and-drinking country numbers, not really how Nader
envisioned the wholesome spirit of the show. But he knew that—as
long as he paid Berry more—putting Lewis on last ensured that Lewis
would play his biggest hits and make the crowd roar.

He created a memorial flow from in which artists were fluidly
moved in and out. "By investing in a vehicle rather than an individual
artist, I wasn't packaging Chuck Berry, I was packaging an event," he
noted. By late 1972, since that first Felt Forum night, Nader claimed
to have put on 125 Revival shows in front of five hundred thousand
spectators.

His plans grew in all directions. "I somehow see myself as setting
a standard for the whole entertainment picture, not just musically. I
have ideas on inland waterways, on how to really use them to their best
advantage, and how to make recreation centers out in the middle of
the desert somewhere that aren't typical of Vegas. You know, just fun
things. I have concepts that span possibly the whole gamut of entertainment per se."

Nostalgia was discharging into the waterways. In a year or so
American Graffiti (with Berry on the soundtrack) would be a huge hit,
and in 1974 *Happy Days*, set in the 1950s, was a TV-dinner classic.
Baby boomers who didn't recognize themselves in Nixon or in those
crucifying him bathed in the music of their first bloom.

Now the Beatles and the Stones were oldies. In February 1972
John Lennon and Yoko Ono cohosted Mike Douglas's daytime TV talk
show for a week. Introducing Chuck to the viewing audience, Lennon
shifted into explainer mode, saying, "If you had to give rock & roll
another name, you might as well call it Chuck Berry." Lennon and his
guest had rehearsed "Memphis," but when Berry launched it, he did so
in a different key—just in case anybody thought he was going to make
it easy that afternoon.

Joining Lennon's regular group was a double-bongo lineup of Yoko
Ono and Jerry Rubin. Halfway into the song Ono reached for the
microphone and emanated pulsing wails that washed all trace of *then*
off "Memphis" and instantly made it a tower of *now*. No, Chuck, this
was how you kept a band on their toes! A producer's voice in the booth

shouted to cut from Ono and get a close-up on Chuck, who looked like he had just seen a ghost dance before him. He had lost his control of the moment, and here was some new, random rock & roll. He looked delighted.

More discomfort on the stage of the Hollywood Palladium, when Chuck was booked between Procol Harum and Black Oak Arkansas. One account suggests that Black Oak front man Jim Dandy Mangrum, knowing the Rolling Stones were in town, had personally invited guitarist Keith Richards to join Chuck. Richards had brought keyboardist Nicky Hopkins with him for kicks. Nobody ran it past Chuck.

The two guests jumped up without announcement to "anonymously" play several songs behind Berry. Things went smoothly until Berry, objecting to how the guitar player had turned up his monitor on the stage, announced that the bassist and drummer in his pickup band could stay, but the other two had to go. Chuck Berry had thrown Keith Richards off the stage. Berry later explained that he didn't recognize him.

By this time the Stones were celebrated as the world's rock & roll dance band. They had found the swinging door between the elite heights and the asphalt crud, and they traveled freely in both directions. *Sticky Fingers* was coming out, and there were two brutal Berry covers as featured B sides: "Let It Rock" and "Little Queenie," perhaps the epitome of the Stones' absorption of his music. The Stones did what they wanted. White rope had traversed the room when Berry first made his way, but the Stones had stretched a red rope across rock & roll.

Berry knew all about them, though it tickled him to pretend otherwise. In 1969 he referred to the singer as "Dick Jagger." Richards was becoming the visible embodiment of the group. A photo from the Palladium shows him in an applejack hat, eyes averted as Berry wags a threatening finger his way.

It was a season of memorable encounters. In March 1972, Elvis Presley was in the middle of a long run at the Showroom Internationale in the Las Vegas Hilton. The hotel wedged in hundreds more than the fire marshal allowed, Elvis sometimes playing to as many as two thousand fans. Meanwhile, Berry was booked for a few nights at the Hilton's secondary Casino Lounge. According to Billy Peek, a St. Louis guitarist in Berry's band, Chuck was on the small stage one night when people started screaming. Peek couldn't figure whether there was a fight or a fire, until he glanced to the back and saw Elvis's profile at the door. He wore a jumpsuit and cape.

Presley was a huge draw, and his shows were ritual consecrations of the King of Rock & Roll that left little to chance. He had horns, backing singers, an orchestra. Extending his arms out at the beginning of the show, Elvis gave the crowd permission to love him. Chuck felt he had to work for his audience's love and that the proof was the applause at the end. An astute writer of the era put the two men in sharp contrast: "Chuck Berry is still performing—a little grizzled around the edges, but still full of the devil. Elvis has eyes that look like holes burnt in dreams, but he still lives."[15]

On the second night Elvis was escorted to a booth down front of the Casino Lounge. Flanked by twenty hotel guards and his own personal bodyguards, he sat with his wife, Priscilla, and Sammy Davis Jr.

The intimate room was jolted alive, everybody murmuring, trying not to stare. Chuck stopped strumming his guitar and looked down at the celebrity at his feet.

"Hello, Elvis. Long time ago," he said. Then he jumped into "Memphis," a song about Presley's hometown, and about a father trying to reach his kid.

Elvis loved Berry's music, but the two were strangers.

"Yeah, I tried to get near him, but it was hard as heck," Berry said. "I've never performed with Elvis Presley, nor have I met Elvis Presley—I can't say this about the Beatles—but Elvis was a little too warm or a little too distant for us to come about together."[16]

In 1957, Presley's music publisher sent an urgent telegram to Berry's house: "NEED STRONG ELVIS PRESLEY MATERIAL FOR SESSIONS COMING SHORTLY. WOULD APPRECIATE YOU CONTACTING ME AS SOON AS POSSIBLE." Presley recorded many songs that Berry made famous but never one that Berry wrote *for* him. Berry was proud to be asked. But Presley's manager, Colonel Tom Parker, insisted on Presley's taking a third of any composer's mechanical royalties. That would have been something Berry—and many other songwriters—would have likely turned down.

Although Presley was billed as the King, he generously named others as the true royalty. Still, the world let him wear the crown. Berry all but never shared in Presley's lifetime his complicated feelings about such matters.

A reporter once quizzed him about Presley, and he kept nonanswering. Finally, point-blank he was asked if race played a part in the man from Memphis's success.

"Now that you mention it, actually, it did occur to me," said Berry. "I mean, I'm saying it like it is. It's obvious that his road was free and mine had to be paved."[17]

The Vegas lounge was as close as their paths ever came.

"The London Rock and Roll Show" was both an English take on an oldies show and an attempt to light it on fire. The secretly creepy Gary Glitter and the publicly creepy Screaming Lord Sutch were on the bill, along with Wizzard and the MC5. Jerry Lee Lewis, Little Richard, and Berry were there to uphold the doctrine of the founding fathers.

In advance press Richard had been livid that Berry was closing the show, and he complained poetically for days.

They may be friends, Richard ranted, oh, but he was going to fix Chuck, calling him "black Berry" before noting that his own mama used to make blackberry wine.

He planned to upset Chuck's nerves. To a television audience, Richard shouted, "I'm the creator, the originator, the emancipator. I am the One. And when you come out, I am going to fix Chuck Berry! His black berry will be mashed."[18] (Chuck the wordsmith did not engage.)

The challenge was appropriate, for the event turned out to be a daylong wrestling extravaganza.

The crowd was as divided as the participants; the hippies were loathed by the Teddy Boys, who were a revival of a 1950s juvenile delinquent subculture now decked out in glam raw leather with sculpted, greased quiffs and hockey-stick sideburns. Their tastes were firmly in place; the Teds had warned Jerry Lee Lewis at a bar the night before that he would be booed if he played any country music.

The MC5 were the modern band most under Berry's spell; their 1970 debut studio album *Back in the USA* opened with a Little Richard number and finished with one from Berry, and their "American Ruse" rewrote Berry and turned his seeming Americanism into punk protest. The way they saw it, playing roaring versions of rock & roll music in the 1970s was so unfashionable it must be radical.

The Detroit band had moved to London and was in their final stages; they took Wembley high and hoped to win over the bloodthirsty traditionalists with a lot of Chuck Berry music. However, "we made a terrible strategic mistake on that day," said guitarist Wayne Kramer. "We were trying to upgrade our look."[19] Kramer came out painted silver and gold and wearing a black suit and sunglasses. Fellow guitarist Fred Smith wore a superhero cape and a silver lamé headgear with a lightning bolt over his forehead. Then there was singer Rob Tyner, wearing a toreador jacket, his massive Jewish afro dusted with glitter. "We looked like rough trade from Venus," said Kramer. "Sixty thousand Teddy boys took a look at us and there was a collective groan."

Beer cans rocketed across the stadium, yet the MC5 were stubborn and sort of winning the crowd over. But then Tyner made the tactical error of throwing a can of lager back, and suddenly hundreds of unopened cans came down from all directions.

In the dressing room afterward, Dr. Feelgood guitarist Wilko Johnson, who had backed up the German rockabilly star Heinz before the MC5 played, tried to cheer the band up. "We blew it," said Kramer. "Hey, you gotta try things," Heinz said.

It had been a long night: Little Richard was booed. The MC5 were lucky to be alive. The Coasters, Platters, and Drifters were all on the bill but didn't play, possibly because each was threatened with lawsuits by other acts claiming rights to their name.

"Only Chuck Berry was as wonderful as ever," said *Creem*. When a set might not come together, when it might not make it to a finish, is when his smirk got real. Writer Charlie Gillett said that Berry had been the whole affair's salvation, the exclamation point at the end of "a pathetic parade of has-beens," the one who "gave it some dignity and spirit."[20] His black berry did not get mashed.

There was a lot of talk, in the age of rock, about the need to respect the music's history, all the roots and shoots. How rock was bigger than any one person. How it was a shared force rippling through the culture. Sometimes, though, it was enough just to be the last guy standing on the field after the last beer can comes to the ground.

16

CHUCK BERRY'S
NUMBER-ONE HIT RECORD

SILVER CITY WAS NAMED FOR THE JUNKYARD IN A NEIGHBORHOOD of Uptown New Orleans. Cars and trucks and old scrap piled by the New Basin Canal, metal shining in the sun. Back then, in the 1930s, Louis Bartholomew ran a barbershop in Silver City.

Operating out of his house at the corner of Galvez and Thalia streets, Bartholomew had men coming in and out all day long. It was guys from the neighborhood sitting and talking, working and fleeing work, the windows wide open keeping a breeze going.

Outside a window stood a kid named Smiley Lewis with his hat on the ground, singing so loud those inside could hear him. Flatbed trucks cruised by carrying local bands advertising upcoming dances. During Mardi Gras, the bands and the costumed Indians passed right out front, and people stood around the house all day long having fun.[1]

Louis Bartholomew played the tuba with clarinetist Willie Humphrey in a Dixieland band, and come the weekend he pushed the chairs aside, swept the floor, and his musician buddies had a jam session. That living room boomed with advice and lies, sweet licks and salty talk, and among those soaking it up was Louis's kid, Dave. He was born in 1918.

Somebody might come in and tell a story about an incident they had seen the night before, and by Friday eight guys knew about it, and a day later it was a lyric shouted over what Louis Bartholomew's band was playing.

The windows were open and the scrap was aglow. Words and music blowing in and out.

IN 1971 AND 1972, CHESS WAS SHIPPING ITS BEST-SELLING ARTISTS to London to record with the young stars of British rock. *The London Chuck Berry Sessions* was made in 1972 and intended as a double album. In Pye Studios Berry met his band: guitarist Ron Wood, keyboardist Ian McLagan, and drummer Kenney Jones, all from the Faces, and Traffic's bassist Ric Grech. Not too bad, but the idea was turning to mud while the clock ticked. Wood waited around for three hours and never got a chance to play. Berry was changing songs from take to take, not telling the band what he planned to do but conducting by jumping in the air when he wanted a bridge or a key change to happen.

"Hey, are we listening to each other?" asked producer Esmond Edwards after a take. "'Cause there sure was some boo-boos in that one."

During a break, a visiting journalist asked Berry what he had been up to lately, but Chuck wasn't playing nice. "I can't answer questions like that, there's so much I do. Ask me something specific."

Right, so: How did he like playing with the hotshots gathered in the studio?

"Fine," Berry said.

Berry explained it as a simple accounting decision to make the album. "The business side of music is more important than the pleasure because I play music to satisfy people and my satisfaction is minimal."[2]

They got five weak cuts at the session, not enough for one whole album let alone two. None of which would ultimately matter, because that same week Chess recorded a show Berry played at the Lanchester Arts Festival in Coventry. That decision gave the label a song that truly deserved to be heard, and spoken of. A new anthem that would make Berry famous to an audience too young to see him play on their own, and a song that Berry called "a defining moment in my career."

In Coventry he shared a bill with Billy Preston and Slade. A comic named Uncle Dirty, who looked like a walrus at a strip club, opened to great delight.

When Slade played, singer Noddy Holder cursed out fans and egged them on from the start: "All you miserable fuckers down there—you look as if you're shitting yourselves! Get off your arses and let it rip!" After Uncle Dirty and Uncle Noddy had stimulated the audience, it was left up to Chuck Berry to teach them what naturally came next.[3]

He appeared, wrote Charles Shaar Murray, "with his clean cherry red Gibson and his psychedelic satin shirt and his immaculate white trousers and his two-tone sharpie shoes. He looked good."

The sideburns were endless; the long hair was processed. And from the first Chuck Berry riff he cranked up for the crowd, he was engaged and in command. Having met his contractual obligation for how long to play, Berry watched a cultural official walk to the microphone and ask him to play just one more number, because a line of two thousand fans were at that moment holding tickets to hear Pink Floyd play, once the house was cleared of Chuck Berry fans.

You asked Chuck Berry to play an encore, and he would demand cash. But ask him to cut a show short because Pink Floyd was waiting, and somebody would be made to pay. The eleven-plus-minute song that followed (that's the recorded version; it likely went on longer than that in Coventry) unfurled like a comic monologue, a monologue in which everybody in the house plays a part.[4]

On the recording, he sings at the high end of his range. He explains the song doesn't rock so he's going to turn the volume down on his guitar, "cuz it's real sweet and groovy, wow is it groovy," he purrs.

The performance was ecstatically infantile, a ridiculous routine that Berry had been working on for years and had orchestrated down to the smallest aside. He called "My Ding-A-Ling" "our alma mater" and told the audience this song was "a fourth-grade ditty and it's very cute. I learned it in the fifth—I was a little behind, but it's a beautiful song of togetherness."

This secret sermon "also happens to be a sexy song," he continues. "And there's nothing wrong with sex! *Not a thing* wrong with sex! Nothing wrong with sex!" Repetition and the persuasive force of his delivery put listeners under his control.

He gives the women their part to sing, "my," and the men theirs, "ding-a-ling." Gets them to rehearse their parts in harmony with his melody.

Establishing that the song is indeed about sex organs, he leads the crowd to a joke about oral sex, and everybody laughs; now it's clear it's okay to have a reaction and feel something about these words. He works to gain the audience's consent. More participation.

He sings with a childish false voice; he comments on what he and everybody in the house is doing. In various ways, he steps outside his standard way of performing and wants listeners to understand that whatever this moment is, it's different, slotted in some other category, something you can discount, laugh at, or join. There are no wrong ways to be. Its success and its risk depend on nobody taking it seriously, and nobody does.

Having established the existence of sexual organs, he puts them at the center of things, his ding-a-ling at school, church. He makes it all one hilarious workout, which you may or might not find in the least amusing, but the point is it's "just" a joke, and by embracing that, various things become possible.

Uncle Dirty was a good comic; Chuck Berry was better. He understood his audience and his material, each pause and repetition and *ooh yeah*—that last a catchphrase popularized by Timmie Rogers, America's first Black stand-up comic and someone Berry probably studied—a means of drawing response from the audience. Their participation was essential.

Preacher, riverboat hustler, hippie salesman: Chuck Berry was playing a lot of roles while acting like he was making it up on the spot. He is playing the song on his guitar, but he's also teaching the song as the song is played, and the teaching becomes the song. He's listening to the music the audience makes and commenting on it; also becoming the song. He's the instigator, the audience, and something like a critic all at once. While teaching the women and men their singing parts, Berry offers an aside. "I hear two girls over here singing in harmony. That's alright, honey. This is a free country. Live like you wanna live, baby. Ain't nobody gonna knock it, darlin'." Those in the ballroom cheer and clap as he spotlights, in the words of scholar Shana Redmond, "female sexual agency and same-sex desire."[5]

"Mm-hmm. Yeah, freedom," Berry enthuses. "Yes, sir. There's one guy over here singin'," and then he indicates a male voice singing the women's line. "That's alright, brother. Yes, sir. You got a right, baby.

Ain't nobody gonna bother you." Insofar as Berry seems to be suggesting the man is gay, or perhaps is a masturbator satisfying himself by singing solo, Redmond notes, "his different engagement with the act of music making is read by Berry as a dissimilarity that must be embraced, rather than dismissed or isolated."

The chorus rolls around, and the room reverberates as women sing in unison. "Got about five hundred girls in there," Berry notes, "you know that's future parliament out there singin', future government of England out there singin', and I'll be glad when you get in office—change a few things."

He was a flawed messenger and a great one, and "My Ding-A-Ling" offers a strong, clear message of free play and inclusion.

In 1878, a Philadelphia songwriter leaned out his office window on the first floor of Handel and Haydn Hall. Joseph Eastburn Winner signaled a bootblack to come inside and sit with him at his piano. He did this all the time. According to a 1910 feature in the New Orleans *Times-Democrat*, Winner, who was a music publisher as well as a songwriter, had a reliable method for determining when one of his bops was likely to connect with the public. It required the help of one of the Black kids regularly passing by on their way to work at the railroad depot a block away from Handel and Haydn Hall.

Winner played his new song repeatedly, "watching the effect on the 'audience,' and if it moved its feet, or seemed to have any special effect, or if the 'shine' would go out whistling it after the recital, Mr. Winner put it down a winner," reported the *Times-Democrat*. (Yes, the writer says *it*.) The tunesmith told the journalist, "No song that a bootblack ever whistled as he went out of his store made a failure."[6] And who knows, maybe Winner was as good a listener as he was a composer.

In the interest of full disclosure, the article also noted, "Mr. Winner does not claim absolute originality in the writing" of the song he demonstrated that day, and which he copyrighted under his preferred pseudonym, R. A. Eastburn. The title of his latest composition: "Little Brown Jug."

Oooh, yeah!

"Little Brown Jug" was a quick success, picked up in minstrel houses and beer halls in Philadelphia and beyond. Its undeniable, reductive melody made it a headbanger well suited for its subject—drinking—and the unison verse leading into a harmonized chorus made it a favorite at sing-alongs. Though the lyrics hinted at a message of temperance, by the 1910s it had become a beloved drinking tune, and when prohibition arrived its ubiquity was assured. School kids ever since have been taught this innocent drinking song.

In 1939, Glenn Miller cut a big band instrumental of the number, a hit worldwide. And then Dave Bartholomew, son of an Uptown New Orleans barber, himself a jazz trumpeter who played the Mississippi riverboats, came farther than usual upriver. Fronting a rhythm and blues band, the kind that was injecting fresh boogie-woogie beats into swing, Bartholomew visited Cincinnati's King Records. He laid a naughty set of words on top of a revision of Miller's blockbuster instrumental, dropped in a winking "Pop Goes the Weasel" hook, and gave the tune a new name: "My Ding-A-Ling." It was 1952.

His lyrics were largely the ones Berry used in his version of the song, the one he sang at Coventry. Bartholomew was fond of the words and arrangement he'd perfected; he rerecorded his number for the Imperial label (as "Little Girl Sing Ting-a-Ling"). Sticking with it, in 1954 he cut it a third time with New York vocal group the Bees—this time he called the lyrical rewrite "Toy Bell." The version with the Bees was the most rocking yet, and the most sexual, thus pointing out how coming on innocent, goofy, was more likely to charm the masses than pounding on the double entendres, which made you sound wanton. In any case, with each of these versions, the song takes a central message from the lyrics that Winner put his name to in 1869—the appeal of supposedly "naughty" acts, whether drinking or talking about one's junk. Chuck Berry's gift was to go all in on the naughty and make the song once more a communal sing-along—one that spoke to his moment.

Early in the song Berry jokes that his father, "a Baptist minister, he taught us, 'Son, there's nothing wrong with sex, it's just the way that you handle it, you see.' Oh yeah!" That crack at his dad's expense gets a laugh from the audience, and a *Rolling Stone* writer later asked him how Henry, a pious man, responded to the dirty joke.

"My libido is very strong. I rise in that direction and I'm sure it's inherited," Berry began. "I never knew his personal matters. But for the last ten years on Tuesday nights he's been going to choir practice, and for the last five Mom's not been going, and now I heard, he's gotten a new riding passenger and she's a female lady. So I don't know. Maybe he's not particularly into it anymore. But I do know one thing, he has had a really successful and large history."[7]

He spotlighted his father's infidelity in a *Rolling Stone* interview! Hypocrisy and guilt did terrible things to people, and Berry was taking it upon himself to expose hypocrisy in a song about exposing himself.

IN THE HISTORY OF MUSIC JOURNALISM, NO WRITER EVER anywhere at any moment has dared say something nice about "My Ding-A-Ling." In a book titled *The Worst Rock n' Roll Records of All Time*, the song is given top honors.[8]

When NASA sent the *Voyager* spacecraft into the heart of the universe in 1977, it was loaded with messages from Earth that included a recording of "Johnny B. Goode." However, if the space agency had chosen instead to send "My Ding-A-Ling," it is quite possible that by the time you read this Earth would have been a radioactive husk stalked by revenge-seeking aliens firing slime cannons who felt much the same way Dave Barry did when he wrote, in *Dave Barry's Book of Bad Songs*, "Chuck gave us a whole lot of great songs, and for that we will be forever grateful. But we already know WAY more than we want to about his ding-a-ling."[9]

The overwhelming critical consensus on "My Ding-A-Ling" is that it was the work of a great songwriter pandering to the masses. Not one of the bands he inspired seems to have ever recorded their version of his greatest hit, and most of Berry's hard-core fans remain appalled.

Maybe writer Robert Christgau said it best, as he sorted his feelings and split the difference between empathy and disappointment. "We've always dreamed of another big single for our hero," he wrote in *Creem*.

But "My Ding-A-Ling" has been embarrassing us at concerts for years, and not because we wouldn't sing along. It was just dumb, inappropriate to the sophistication of his new, collegiate audience. . . .

Obviously, what we meant was that it wasn't sophisticated enough for us—his other stuff was so much better. But popularity has changed the song. I feel sure that it's delighting all the 12 year olds who get to figure out that they've snuck something dirty onto AM radio—a rock and roll tradition that has been neglected since the concept of dirty became so passé.[10]

The song filled eleven and a half minutes of *The London Chuck Berry Sessions* when it was released in April 1972. The whole album might well have faded without comment, lore has it, if a Boston DJ hadn't gotten excited when he gave the album a listen. In 1972 Jim Connors had achieved local glory through incessant play of schlock like Mouth & MacNeal's "How Do You Do" and Wayne Newton's "Daddy Don't You Walk So Fast," so it made sense when he put Berry's track in heavy rotation. The song took off in Boston and soon everywhere else; Connor claimed that Chess gave him a gold record for launching Berry's new hit.

It was edited down to four minutes and released as a single in July, and it became the biggest hit of his career. The fact that the song with Berry's name on it had the same name and melody as a tune with Dave Bartholomew's name on it was noted in the press. It's been reported both that Bartholomew did and did not receive compensation from Berry.

In September "My Ding-A-Ling" reached the number-one slot in the country for two weeks, keeping Elvis Presley's "Burning Love" stuck at two. Win-win, Berry might have thought. The song topped charts in England and Australia.

Some Top 40 stations refused to play it. The tune was banned in Australia. In England, Mary Whitehouse, leader of the Christian advocacy group National Viewers' and Listeners' Association, wrote to the director general of the BBC urging that the song be pulled off the air before the nation became overrun by "small boys with their trousers undone, singing the song and giving it the indecent interpretation which—in spite of all the hullabaloo—is so obvious."[11]

On a quickly scheduled tour of England, Berry was asked for his thoughts on Whitehouse's critique. "That tickled me, you know, real featherish," Berry said. When interviewers mentioned her name, he would carefully say it back, extending the first syllable. "I suppose she's entitled to say what she thinks."[12]

Others who had seen Berry up close drew a connection to his personal appetites. "I think that was maybe a shortcoming," said Tom Maloney, a longtime guitar player on the St. Louis blues scene. "He was a pussy hound and it got him into trouble. . . . Isn't it sad that a great talent like Chuck Berry, the only number one record he had was 'My Ding-A-Ling'? But again, maybe this is God's judgment on him or something—if you think with your dick, then here's your song. It's gonna be huge!"[13]

Besides *smut*, the other pejorative that hung over the song was *novelty*. Of course, novelties are what everything on the charts was when Berry and rock & roll started. What was "Maybellene" but a novelty, like Little Richard's coif or Buddy Holly's glasses? In 1972 disco was on the horizon, and that, too, was to be waved off with comparable, and self-revealing, scorn.

Berry didn't care what people called it. "My Ding-A-Ling" helped him get a new contract with Chess, which was announced the same week the song hit number one. Esmond Edwards, vice president of A&R for Chess/Janus Records, presented him with a gold record onstage at a Madison Square Garden oldies show. And it was announced that he was going to be featured in a film bringing the Nader revue to a movie theater near you.

Novelty? He didn't look at it as a joke. "A lot of people liked that song," Berry crowed. "A lot of people *like* that song. And I LOVED that song because that little, weeny song made my wallet so fat and happy, hahaha."[14]

FOR YEARS, BERRY QUIETLY VISITED A CLASSROOM IN COLUMBIA, Missouri, at the request of high school humanities teacher Linda Harlan. A friend introduced them, and when Berry met Harlan he felt he could trust her, so from time to time, when he had a show booked in Columbia, he would arrive early and speak to her students about poetry or music.

The first time he visited he recited a long poem and then took questions, and that was more or less the pattern his appearances fell into in the 1990s. The kids always had plenty to ask him, questions like *How does it feel to invent rock & roll?* and *What song made the most money?*

They would ask if he could play them a number. "He would always say, 'I don't have a guitar. Come to the concert tonight,'" recalled Harlan. After a while, she knew what to expect, and one time she was ready for him, because a student who had a guitar happened to bring her instrument to school that day. *We have one here, Chuck*, she shouted. What could he say to that?

Harlan had invited members of the school board to the assembly. Berry smiled and said, "I'll play you the song that made me the most money."

The kids got a real kick out of it, she said, and so did Berry. As for Harlan, "I kept my job," she laughed.[15]

"My Ding-A-Ling" remains a tune that divides Berry fans. Guitarist Vernon Reid was backstage at a Rock and Roll Hall of Fame tribute in 2012, hanging with Lemmy Kilmister, Rick Derringer, Merle Haggard, Ronnie Hawkins, M. Ward, and others. Everybody was divvying up Berry tunes to play, and Reid innocently asked,

> Who's gonna do "My Ding-A-Ling"?
> They all looked at me like—ha ha ha. But it was his number-one song! It was crazy, but he was a freak.
> Rock & roll is funny, man. It's supposed to be dangerous and supposed to be *Oh my*. That's what rock & roll *is*. And suddenly rock & roll is under manners! That's what was so great about "My Ding-A-Ling." It could only have existed at one moment—it found a crack. It was a novelty tune and taken as one, but I mean, it's *right there*.[16]

It splits Berry fans at home too. "It was a great show," diehards recall of some legendary night at Blueberry Hill in the 1990s. "And he didn't play 'My Ding-A-Ling.'" Which can't be anything like a surprise, given how it divided the guys who tried to claim it as their own. Leaning over his desk in an office near Manhattan's Columbus Circle, attorney Robert Meloni shakes a yellowed fax in the air, one he pulled out for an interview about his former client.

Dave Bartholomew put up some kind of fight, trying to get money from Berry for signing his name to a song that featured Bartholomew's name three times in the 1950s. "This was Bartholomew's claim," Meloni said, looking at the fax. It says that Bartholomew had made first use of "My Ding-A-Ling."

"But there was nothing in common between their versions, other than the words 'my ding-a-ling,'" Meloni seems to believe. "And Chuck didn't agree to settle with him." Meloni throws his arms in the air, shrugs.

Chuck kept it. He said, "No you didn't invent it." Fact is, he said, "Just pull your pants down, take a look, that's your ding-a-ling! You don't own it 'cause a lot of us got one."

This was Chuck Berry—he doesn't need to steal! He's like a fountain of creativity.[17]

Bartholomew died in 2019. He was celebrated as a bandleader, as a crucial figure in the career of Fats Domino, and, really, as the very spirit of New Orleans's communal creativity. If getting paid is the proper indicator (it is not), he didn't get what he deserved, but he made out pretty good. And if seeing Chuck's name on a version of a song Bartholomew put his name on years before rankled him, he didn't vent his disappointment in public.

Bartholomew had a lot to humblebrag about. "I made a few records on my own that made a little bit of noise," Bartholomew said. "'Country Boy,' 'My Ding-a-Ling' and a few little things like that." Why, he said, after he wrote "My Ding-A-Ling" in the 1940s and nothing happened with it, "I threw it in the trash can. Then along came Chuck Berry in 1972 and he recorded the thing in London. Somebody called me and said, 'You got the number one tune in London.' I said, 'What is it?' 'My Ding-A-Ling.' You got to be kidding. The last time I saw it was in the trash can. But all in all I did all right."[18]

You don't own it: a lot of us got one, Berry told Bartholomew. He called it a "beautiful song of togetherness" at Coventry. This was a song created by the group, by an English audience, but not just them.

From Louis Bartholomew's barbershop to the jam sessions at the Club Cosmopolitan, collective improvisation shaped pop music. The trash can, the scrap heap of Silver City, the Dew Drop Inn, wherever juices spread, new things emerged. The musicians worked in a system that did not honor group creation. They found a place in a system of money and law, and they found their footing. Everything sold is a novelty, the sound of the bootblack bringing it back to his boys under the trestle, whistling in the wind.

17

"THERE ARE A LOT OF ADOLESCENTS ON THE PLANET"

THE SUCCESS OF "MY DING-A-LING" LED TO MORE HEADLINING dates on oldies shows. Then Richard Nader decided to shoot a movie of the tour.

Let the Good Times Roll was codirected by Sid Levin, a veteran of rock concert documentaries. Levin was interested in getting to know Berry before filming began and went to a Salem, Oregon, show to say hello.

The crowd was screaming for Chuck, who Levin tracked down in the promoter's office, where he was handing over a briefcase and telling the guy to put it there. Berry then counted the money—rifling the bills so fast that, to Levin, "He looked like some kind of card shark."

"This is short," Berry declared, though he eventually passed the case to Levin, telling him to hold on to it. "I felt like we were pulling off a heist."

After a pointed spell onstage tuning his guitar, Berry commented that the amplifiers were not what his contract stipulated and stomped off, veering toward the promoter with the cash. More went into the briefcase.

After the show, Berry, his blond girlfriend, and Levin went to a Chinese restaurant Berry liked, and then they drove toward Portland. After a little while the car had a flat tire, which Berry changed, though it wasn't but a minute before another tire went flat. The folks in Salem, everybody in the car realized, had knifed his tires. Levin was definitely getting to know his star.

It was weird and fascinating to watch Berry up close. You might not ever know him—you would not—but you would never forget his actions. Levin came to like him and was struck by how he could seem positively warm one minute and the next threatening to cause a riot if the attaché case was light.[1]

They reconnected in St. Louis; more emotional consternation. Berry gave Levin a tour, showing him the house on Windermere Place where Themetta and the kids lived and the house he grew up in, and then he motored out to Berry Park. Levin was going to film his host reminiscing on camera the next day. It didn't go smoothly. The singer arrived in sunglasses, acting remote, tense, and when Levin said he hoped he could make the star feel comfortable, he got "I feel fine" as a brush-off.

Things mutated moment by moment. A cameraman followed Berry around as he reminisced about his first tour through California, describing the band sleeping on a customized school bus, which was parked on the property. Introspective, alive to the camera, he was some other person than the one Levin had been consoling minutes before.

The situation kept turning over. An assistant cameraman got a redwood splinter stuck in his eye, and a crew member took him to the hospital. When they returned, there was Berry, waving a rifle at the front gate. The cameraman had been in plenty of tense situations, but this one made him feel certain he was "looking at death."

Wentzville stayed weird. In a relaxed moment Berry recounted for Levin and others the long-ago time he had been driving through a southern town and the sheriff pulled him over. Enjoying his display of menace, the officer put a hand on Berry's windshield and promised, "If you ever come back, I'll kill you."

Now Levin and his team were themselves driving out of Berry Park, saying goodbye to their host. Leaning forward into their vehicle, the man they had come to film put his huge palm on their windshield and reenacted the promise of the lawman.

Levin didn't wave it off easy. "What a bizarre, sad, compulsive place he was in," the director recalled of his time with the musician at Berry Park. You laughed with the guy, and suddenly you couldn't breathe. "It's like a pendulum that swings between freedom and compulsion."

EXPLAINING WHERE HE LIVED, BERRY SKETCHED HOME TO AN audience this way: "Wentzville is a city of 3,000 people. Mostly German. It's a farm town," he explained. "How I ever drove stakes there, I don't really know. But I was introduced to some property, and I sunk some extra bread into it and began to build, until that's how I landed there."[2]

By the early 1970s, Berry Park was an estate worth half a million dollars, he said. It was a country club, nightclub, and motel all in one. With a swimming pool shaped like a guitar.

Wentzville was his safe place, in wooded farmland and out of view, a spot where the hippie vibe of the Fillmore scene, not to mention the egalitarian spirit of "My Ding-A-Ling," was lived out by the host and his numerous visitors. It was a rural crash pad hosting both paying and nonpaying guests, their Day-Glo vans scattered around the property.

"Incidentally," Berry told the audience, "it's beginning to be what I might call a 'swing city,' with groovy people, and I hope it grows."

After "My Ding-A-Ling" hit, Berry gave a writer the run of swing city. Perhaps it helped that Patrick William Salvo was interviewing him for *Gallery*, an adult magazine published by attorney F. Lee Bailey. Salvo was guided through the electrified fence and came into view of Berry's rooftop surveillance cameras. He reported on the video room and the discotheque with "trapdoors and secret passageways."[3]

There was a two-hundred-year-old cabin on the grounds as well as a modern twenty-four-room lodge. Francine Gillium—all but Berry Park's ranger—greeted visitors via a hidden PA system and posed searching questions before admitting folks in.

Parking his car by a concession stand, Salvo met Berry's brother Hank, who had been painting the bandstand. Then he met "Rhoda, a well-endowed Canadian lady" (that was Rhoda Pfeffer), and Rhoda's mom, smoking Player's cigarettes and wearing Bermuda shorts.

Pfeffer had met Berry at a show in Toronto in the 1950s, and it was said they had a son together who lived with his mother in an apartment building in Kitchener, Ontario, that Berry had bought.[4]

Also on hand for Salvo's visit was a promoter buddy of the owner named "Oakland," "busily picking ticks off several haggard looking dogs," as well as a foursome of beer-drinking campers who Fran Gillium explained were "supporters of Chuck's music, that's why he lets them stay a night or two, then we send them on their way."

The night Salvo visited, he was served "a non-alcoholic orange-lime concoction" by Candy, a Berry Park waitress. Somebody got a chessboard from Chuck's wood-frame, sixteen-room Swiss chalet home, and once the rocker rolled up in his golf cart, wearing a "frilly white shirt, pegged pants, and red, white, and blue Thom McAn casuals," he invited the *Gallery* writer to play chess. For the rest of the night the rocker and the writer were locked in battle, with Berry repeatedly prevailing. He smoked Kools and ate chocolate cake.

Berry Park could have been a cool business or a sexy retreat for Berry and guests, but his vision was to combine a business with something very private, and for a while it thrived. There was plenty to do, and plenty of people to do things with. A musician related being told by Berry, "There's only one cop in Wentzville and I've got Polaroids of him." The guest thought he was kidding.

The proprietor let visitors do what they wanted, within reason. "I can swallow half a cup of wine or a highball and I can also smoke a joint," Berry said. But he explained that he didn't get high, because he wouldn't want his performance inhibited. "You should see the presents I get. Pshewww! I've got a couple of bottles hidden away of assorted pills that the kids sort of give or leave for me backstage which I keep as souvenirs or mementos. All sorts of colors. Pink ones, big ones, black little ones, little ones shaped like hearts . . ."

He said he didn't touch the stuff. "I get high off other things I do. Other things where, you know, nothing else matters." Got it, Salvo makes clear, asking Chuck to please spell it out for readers.

"Okay, I like companionship. You know, I also like, while we're putting it mildly, meeting people, getting close."

Visitors noted the underfed, frightened-looking women who scurried about the park, doing things for Berry and his guests. He felt good with a number-one hit and a groovy scene in Wentzville. To journalists, for a little while he spoke expansively about how the world worked. By surveying his thoughts on morality in this relaxed moment of sharing, it is possible to create a sense of how he saw if not his place in the world at least his place at Berry Park.

"You've got to look out for yourself," he told another writer. Gather what you need—"money, power, wisdom. Whatever it might be. And you've got to have enough of it and be sure yourself before you can do anything for other people."[5]

There was but one judge. "The religion that I have is 'yourself,'" he explained. "You gotta depend on yourself. In the end it's really up to you. I think people shouldn't have crutches and things to grasp onto toward the fulfillment of their goal. God gave man free will and he's infinite. His possibilities are infinite and the only person who can evolve is you."[6]

This was close to the Reverend Ike idea that God wants you to grab it, mingled with the quasimystical philosophy of street-corner capitalists. It was composed, compelling, an act of storytelling, and of control. People, he explained, needed to know the way everything worked. He could help with that.

> First off, there's two things that a man must know in order to get closer to himself. In order to be a man. There's two main factors: one is mathematics in that everything you do, say, see, touch, or get near is determined by a quota of numbers. Under that is a subtopic and I guess the second thing is the numbers that have to be involved with bread—with money. 'Cause I tell you, money helps out, 'cause if you can't find a crumb, you then can certainly always buy a crumb. Lots of times it helps out 'cause, I tell you, if you're alone and you have money you can make out, especially if you're ALL alone.[7]

His was an epic individualism, a belief that he could control his surroundings and protect himself from the worst of the world with money and mother wit. That the things he could take he was supposed to have, because he had survived the world's worst. The individualist came aboveground in the 1970s, in his time of financial security and stardom.

Intrigued by the rock audience's openness and their rhetoric of acceptance, Berry folded them into his vision of self. That spirit reigned at Berry Park.

"You should LOVE people, man," he told *Crawdaddy*.

There's spiritual love and physical love. But this is a materialistic, physical world. And you can't really KNOW anybody else, man, because you can't even really know yourself. And if you can't know yourself then sure as hell no one else can. Nobody's been with you as long as you and you still don't know yourself real well. That's why I say the only way you can know somebody is physically. You can love them physically. Chicks don't understand this, I can't talk about this with a chick because she always sees something else in it. But the only way you can really love someone in this world is physically.[8]

Looking down on the Berry Park scene, he installed surveillance cameras with lenses that could, he boasted, read an album cover at seven hundred feet in the starlight.

HEY CHUCK, THE WRITER ASKED PROVOCATIVELY, HOW COME while there had been literally hundreds of covers of Chuck Berry songs, only a couple were made by Black artists?

"Well that's wrong," said Berry. "The Bill Black Combo did a whole record of my songs."

(Well played. Despite his name, Bill Black was a white bass player from Memphis who released an album of Chuck Berry instrumentals in 1964.)

But others, too, were asking about his relationship to Black America. As if to reconnect, in June 1973 Berry made an appearance on *Soul Train*. The TV show had been in national syndication since 1971, running in many markets against *American Bandstand*; the artists and the dancers on *Soul Train* were mostly African American, and the show was a rising commercial force. The pairing of Chuck Berry with *Soul Train*'s young Black audience was an epic blind date unfolding almost like a reality show.

Host Don Cornelius worked hard to bridge the years as he introduced the parties to one another, puffing up Berry's reputation to the
youngsters watching—*you simply have to meet the guy*. There he was,
fronting a white rock band with shoulder-length hair and fluffy boots,
cranking out the "Johnny B. Goode" boogie. What was all this about a
country boy?

The suitor certainly gave it his all, but the quick cuts to the dance
floor showed expertly dressed couples uncertainly Waacking to the
beat. What were they supposed to do, the Twist?

After that Berry came down from the stage to rap a while. A woman
of college age asked how he classified his music, and the singer, wearing
a purple shirt, said, "Groo-vay!" An audience member named Ricardo
asked how old he was when he started and how many years he'd been
in the business—"sixteen," Chuck said quickly. "I started out when
I was eight!" An amused Don Cornelius slid in with "so that makes
you . . . ," and Berry killed his smile, looked straight into the host's eyes
and doubled down on the surrealism: "Oh I'm sixteen—I *started* when
I was eight," he said.

Time for one last question from one of the dancers: Has this band
behind him been with him "all sixteen years"?

"No—sixteen minutes!" Berry jokes not-jokes. "I just met them this
evening, but they're a *wonderful* bunch of guys, really."

Right then, at the same time Berry was stating his age to the *Soul
Train* dancers, outside of camera range a tussle broke out. The next
guest on the show, actor Max Julian, had arrived wearing a gold doeskin
suit. When they saw him the audience screamed out, deserting the set
and mobbing the star of the box-office-hit movie *The Mack*. "I've never
seen anything like it before," Cornelius said of Julian's show-stopping
entrance.[9]

Chuck, too, was a wonderful bunch of guys. His eyes saying, "Yes,
we can-can" to a *Soul Train* crowd, then giving the death ray to Don
Cornelius.

SUSAN HAMILTON OWNED A PRODUCTION COMPANY IN NEW YORK
that recorded radio jingles. Dr Pepper and advertising agency Young
and Rubicam had created a radio campaign enlisting diverse music
makers to record genre-specific versions of a song written by Randy

Newman—Grandpa Jones, Eubie Blake, Lynn Anderson, B. B. King, Muddy Waters, all extolling the excellence of Dr Pepper.

Hamilton and a team arranged to go to St. Louis and record Berry's roots-rock version of the jingle. Hamilton wanted to book a hotel, but it was made clear that was not happening—Chuck wanted them to stay at "Berry Mansion."

He didn't refer to it as Berry Park. "He told us, 'No no no, you must stay at Berry Mansion,'" Hamilton recalled.

The flight to St. Louis arrived late to an all-but-shut-down airport. They were told no rental cars were available, and just when the team thought they were on their own, they looked down a hallway and saw Berry, his arm draped around a blond teenager, shy and burying her face into his arm while he sized them up. Dressed in shiny pants, polyester semitransparent short-sleeve shirt, black hat. He seemed ageless.

Taking over the situation, Berry talked to the rental car counter attendant and got them their cars. Follow me out, he told the group.

For a mansion it wasn't too good, Hamilton thought. "There it was, this dilapidated crazy place with scrub everywhere and weeds growing up out of the parking lot. He just disappeared and we were standing there." It was two a.m., their bags sitting on the ground, and a "strange, unwell" white girl with brown hair approached the group. She had her head down, avoided eye contact, and walked with a limp. She looked at the Black member of the team and said, "Ooh la la," before escorting everyone to a building with a row of rooms that had numbers on the doors.

Each room had shag carpet and green bedspreads. "It was really freaky—you didn't want to step barefoot on the carpet to get into bed," recalled Hamilton.

"The weirdest thing was, as we were settling down the girl came back again, rapped on each of our doors and told us, 'Whatever you do, don't open the door or windows, don't stray from your rooms. I just let the dogs out!'"[10]

The next morning they followed Berry to a recording studio he owned downtown, where he was to record an interview and the jingle. As he got out of his pink Cadillac, Berry noticed one of the group filming him and threw his hands up over the lens, pushing the camera away and shouting, "No pictures!"

"In presentation he was emotionally turning on a dime—one second friendly and chatty and the next he was 'I'm not doing this fucking job!'" said Hamilton. She reminded him that he had signed a contract. But Berry told her no, they were going to write up the true contract right then and there.

He wanted $5,000. "All I could do was roll with it, writing the contract on the back of envelopes, and I figured, whatever, let the lawyers work it out. I'll get my performance."

The moods shifted without notice. "The wall comes down, he has a whole different look on his face," said Hamilton. But then the actual performance of the jingle went off perfectly: he sang with gusto, did many takes, and knew the song. He recorded an agreed-upon interview, and that went well too. "He oversold the product with humorously broad grimaces and lots of winks. It was highly amusing."

All in all she felt it was a good experience, and as her team gathered their cables and mics, Hamilton felt a hand on her shoulder.

He wanted his $5,000 right then. "You're not leaving here until I get it," Berry said. "The tape is not leaving here, and your people ain't leaving here, neither."

She thought he was joking. But the group was ushered by Berry into a storage room of what she thought was a former radio station, and she realized he meant exactly what he said.

It was late Friday in St. Louis. Hamilton called her office in New York. Miraculously somebody was still there, and they agreed to wire $5,000 to a downtown St. Louis Western Union office. She pled to her employee on the phone that it was ransom money. Berry pulled out a set of keys with a flourish and locked everybody else in. Hamilton climbed into his pink Cadillac.

As they made their way through the city streets, people spotted the car and the local hero who was driving, and Berry happily high-fived fans. At the Western Union they sat waiting until the money arrived, about a half hour.

Berry wanted it immediately, but she wouldn't give him the cash until the crew and tape were freed. "They were sort of in shock and flabbergasted that they were being held for ransom. I made sure they saw me counting the money into his hands."

They collected their equipment, hoping for a quick getaway to the airport. Chuck had other ideas. What kind of a host would he be if he didn't show them one of his favorite places to eat in town? So Berry drove them all to a soul food restaurant.

"It was about being in total control, and wanting us to experience this restaurant where the food was good and he was being treated like a god."

She chuckled. "And the food was great!" she noted.

"It was just a means to an end for him."

WHO KNEW HIM? NOBODY KNEW HIM.

Dick Alen had worked with Berry since the 1950s. He was a brusque show business agent who traveled with the singer, dined with him, offered him career advice. He worked with Berry for the rest of his life. Alen outlived his client.

What was Berry like to work with?

"Nobody," said Alen.

I was able to stay with him all those years because I understood what he wanted, tried to do it the way he wanted, and didn't try to do more than what he wanted.

I was probably his best business friend. I was not a personal friend. He didn't have personal friends.[11]

That sounds so provocative. Maybe it's the beginning of a larger point, something like "Chuck didn't have *personal* friends, he had. . . ." No. Alen meant what he said.

I traveled all the time with him. We were not socially friendly. We'd have meals together, talk or be in the car after the show. He did his thing and I did mine.

I did not try to crawl into his life. He had his life, and he was happy with it. He'd come over to my house. I have nothing bad to say about him on a personal level; we were just not personally friendly. But he wasn't personally friendly with anybody.

Who knew him? Anybody with a record player.

ON AUGUST 16, 1977, WITH CODEINE, METHAQUALONE, AND valium in his bloodstream, Elvis Presley fell forward. Found by his girlfriend on the floor at his Graceland mansion, he was carried by ambulance to Baptist Memorial Hospital, where he was declared dead at three thirty p.m.

On the night Presley died, Geraldo Rivera hosted a tribute on ABC that included commentary from Bing Crosby and Chuck Berry. Asked by a reporter in St. Louis what he thought Elvis would be remembered for, Berry offered, "Boop-boop-boop," almost as a question. "And, uhh, a shaky leg, and fabulous teen music . . . and his movies in the fifties."[12] He was not going to give them what they wanted.

Chuck's hometown newspaper used its civic voice, in an unsigned editorial, to mourn the King's passing. "The death of Elvis Presley leaves no other rock figure who spans that music's evolution," the *St. Louis Post-Dispatch* eulogized. "A poor Southern country boy, he enriched the nation in ways that few if any of us could foresee."[13]

Later, when people asked him about Presley, Chuck could be thoughtful. "I think he had a wonderful manager," he laughed when asked in 2008. "But one thing Presley had that no other person had was that voice. He had a voice better than Bing Crosby's."[14]

Elvis loved Chuck and covered his songs throughout his career, singing a fine version of "Maybellene" on the *Louisiana Hayride* radio program only a month after the song's 1955 release. As Greil Marcus has stated, Presley's "Johnny B. Goode" (recorded live at the International Hotel in Las Vegas, 1969) and "The Promised Land" (1973) were among the most vibrant music Presley made in his final years.

America's late-night TV king, Johnny Carson, also loved Berry. Years after Presley was gone, when Carson had Berry on *The Tonight Show* for a full hour, Berry felt the burden of Presley's freedom, of the love America had given Presley, and brought it to America's attention.

It was 1987, and Berry was promoting his autobiography. Berry only mentions Presley once in the book, in a list of pop stars (Joplin, Hendrix, McPhatter, and Presley) who, unlike Berry, he says were killed by their habits. Carson asks Chuck, "Were you and Presley friends?"

Berry didn't miss a beat. "Yeah, when he was *living*," he said with an edge that probably shocked then drew a big laugh from the audience. *I'm alive. Playing shows nightly. What more do you need?*

Berry had helped create the job of rock star, and the benefits came to him only with a constant fight and only on a percentage basis. Stardom looked different on him (or on Jimi Hendrix, Sly Stone, Larry

Williams, Arthur Lee . . .) than it did when Elvis, Jagger, or Bowie were inducted into the life. Berry would never share a complete set of feelings about Presley because his answer to the question *What did you think of Elvis?* would have been so far outside what the questioner was expecting.

Maybe it goes back to what that southern sheriff told him long ago: What did he think of Elvis? "If you ever come back, I'll kill you."

FOUR DAYS AFTER ELVIS DIED, *VOYAGER 2* WAS LAUNCHED FROM Cape Canaveral. *Voyager 1* would follow in early September. Both of the interstellar robotic probes carried the same carefully packed record album. The so-called Golden Disk featured many sound recordings but just one rock & roll song: "Johnny B. Goode." It would be this planet's greeting to any life that came *Voyager's* way.

The project's mission was to explore Jupiter and Saturn. *Voyager 2* proceeded to Uranus and Neptune, and both continued onward. In about three hundred years, *Voyager 1* will reach the inner edge of the Oort cloud.

Long before launch, the *Voyager* project manager decided to assemble a collection of sounds and images that would explain who we are to any curious aliens. Carl Sagan was invited to oversee its creation. The gold-plated copper album Sagan's team came up with included Stravinsky's *The Rite of Spring*, Blind Willie Johnson's "Dark Was the Night," Javanese gamelan music, Navajo chants, a Bulgarian shepherdess song, and Chuck's most famous tune.

"Johnny" almost didn't make the countdown. Sagan was no great rock & roll fan, and some on the *Voyager* Interstellar Record Committee favored a number from Bob Dylan. But the more he thought about it, the more Sagan liked the idea; when folk scholar Alan Lomax weighed in that Berry was too "adolescent," the Cornell astronomer responded, "There are a lot of adolescents on the planet."[15]

The news that a Chuck Berry song was being shot into space gave the Jet Propulsion Laboratory and NASA a ton of publicity and kindled a connection between Sagan and Berry. When the musician turned sixty in 1986, Sagan and astronomer Ann Druyan sent him a warm letter noting that his recording would last at least a billion years in space, then adding that he had their admiration "for the music you have given *this* world." Sagan also signed a photo of the galaxy.

In 1989, *Voyager 2* passed close to Neptune's moon Triton, trans-
mitting new information about the planet's active ice volcanoes. A
party was planned at the Jet Propulsion Laboratory in Pasadena. After
playing a show in Branson, Missouri, Berry and his band drove back to
St. Louis and hustled onto a plane to Los Angeles, where Sagan and
Druyan met them in a town car.

"We drove from the airport all the way to Pasadena, listening to Carl
Sagan and Chuck Berry talk about the universe," said drummer Mike
Mesey.

> Sagan was explaining its shape, and then Chuck weighed in, back
> and forth. I remember Chuck saying, "Ohhhh, so it's kind of like dirt."
> We were all exhausted, and I heard Carl Sagan say, "Yeah! Exactly!"
>
>   Chuck was a very intelligent guy. And to get to listen to them talk
> about the cosmos, well, I wish I had had a tape recorder with me.[16]

The appearance by Berry was a surprise for fifteen hundred mission
scientists, engineers, and their families; Sidney Poitier stood at the
microphone and called his name, and the star walked out in front of
the crowd, playing "Johnny B. Goode," of course. This night, to mark
the occasion, Berry changed the words, proclaiming to one and all, "Go
Voyager! Go!"[17]

THE 1978 MOVIE *AMERICAN HOT WAX* WAS A FAST-PACED RIFF ON
the life of Alan Freed, mythologizing the DJ as a showman willing to
go down in flames for the music he believed in. Director Floyd Mutrux
got gallons of comic book pulp energy across, and a great performance
from actor Tim McIntire, not to mention appearances by Screamin'
Jay Hawkins and Berry—even though he put up his usual resistance to
doing what others thought he had already been paid to do.

Berry headlining a Freed package show becomes the emotional
acme of the film—he's playing himself, but he's not sleepwalking
through a movie like Elvis did. How did Mutrux get this committed
performance from his star?

"Chuck was very kind of standoffish," said Mutrux.[18] "I made
friends with him right away, and one of the ways I did it was, um, I said
to him, 'Do you want to do some acting?'" The director pointed out an

extra on the set and asked Berry if he'd like to be in a scene with her and then steered them off the set. Later he saw Berry and the woman leave his trailer together.

That, said Mutrux, bought him more time on camera from the man he saw as crucial to his film.

Then I said to Chuck, "Hey you want to do another acting scene?" "Yeah." "Which girl do you think?" "How about that girl there?" And later I saw him walking from the trailer with *that* girl.

I was hooking him up with pussy, obviously.

Mutrux describes a process of making up scenes on the fly. One actor resented the casual approach and told Mutrux, "Someday I'll get you for this." But Berry worked better when there wasn't a set way forward. He shaped the final scene, where the FBI is trying to shut Freed down by taking his money, and Berry has to decide if he'll play the show anyway. It was Berry's idea, he says, to have the show go on.

"Chuck could have been an actor—I think he could have done anything," said Mutrux. "I don't know what happened later on in life. . . . But the guy I worked with could do almost anything he wanted to."

IN THE EARLY 1970S, THE MUSICIAN WAS BRINGING ROCK FESTIVALS to Berry Park. He could see the inherent profit and risk they afforded and decided to use the park's ample grounds to his advantage. He started small in August 1970, when fewer than one thousand people came to hear local bands and Berry play.

In July 1972 he got bigger and made the risky decision to hire a biker gang to work security at the second festival. It was three years after the Rolling Stones had headlined a blowout at Altamont, California, where Hell's Angels members employed as security had beaten a Black concertgoer to death. At Berry Park a guard fired a shotgun into a crowd of attendees, injuring one. A year later Berry, Themetta, and the guard settled out of court with the injured man, who had filed a $100,000 lawsuit.[19]

On the Fourth of July in 1974, Berry planned his biggest foray into concert promotion and leased Berry Park to a group of local promoters. Events staggered from the start. Employees of a New York production company arrived on the third, then left the same day because nobody had their money. When gates opened on the Fourth, ticket takers began pocketing, then reselling, tickets handed over by paying customers.

Nothing got better. More than a hundred Wells Fargo hires arrived to provide security; when they weren't paid, they left. Motorcyclists were hired to police the crowd; "we did have some bike gangs," said Charles Berry Jr. Then the headliners started bailing: Dave Mason and Peter Frampton canceled. Leon Russell flew in on a helicopter, found out he wouldn't get paid, and flew out again. The Band and REO Speedwagon did play that Independence Day, but news of the cancellations enraged the crowd. "All those bikers that were out there, they went ballistic. They started tearing the property up," said Charles Berry.

When it was over, the *Globe-Democrat* quoted one of the promoters saying he had lost $40,000 and alleging, "Someone stole a bunch of tickets. The crowd doubled and we didn't make any money."[20] Promoters told the newspaper they believed that Berry had the missing money; Berry denied it, saying he made considerably less than they suspected.

The festivals ended, but there were other troubles. In August 1974 four girls—three sisters and a friend—waded into the swimming pool. As Berry biographer Bruce Pegg notes, there were no lifeguards on duty at the park, and "St. Charles County ordinances did not require any at that time—nor were there ordinances requiring depth markers, even though it was a public pool." The girls moved into the deep end—they were not good swimmers and started to scream. Bridgette Walters, fourteen, and Deira Cross, thirteen, drowned. (In 1968, a twenty-one-year-old St. Louis man drowned in the pool.)[21]

Berry Park was a bit outside Wentzville, a sleepy town without a robust police force. But the surrounding St. Charles County had ample resources to marshal, and events at Berry Park had not escaped their attention.

The county sent undercover agents to Berry Park parties in August 1974, around the time of the drownings. Two weeks later, forty officers raided a party on the property, arresting Gillium for allowing alcohol to be served after hours and contributing to the delinquency of a minor.

Berry Park didn't have a liquor license, though county law allowed patrons to bring their own until ten p.m. About twenty adults and nine minors, including at least one twelve-year-old, were arrested on drug and alcohol charges.

In September, St. Charles County ordered Berry Park closed for six months. Assistant prosecutor William Lohmar cited one shooting, three rapes, and other violations in the previous two years. Berry did not contest and pointed out that there were few events planned between Labor Day and spring, anyway.[22]

According to an article in the *Post-Dispatch*, Berry "acknowledged reported liquor and narcotics violations appear accurate and said he plans to hold future events during daytime hours 'where there can't be so much hide-and-go-seeking with smoking and stuff.'"

Kevin Fleming was a young music fan who had returned from Vietnam in "the year of 'Smoke on the Water'"—1972. In Wentzville, Fleming and his girlfriend rented a second-floor apartment on Main Street, in a building where Chuck was said to be the owner and where he had shot porno movies.

Fleming partied at Berry Park.

I remember I walked into the house once—I was dancing with his daughter one night and she had to go to the bathroom. She took me into his house—there were bigger-than-life pictures of him all over the place, including one of him kissing his guitar.

[The atmosphere] was just wide open. It was young people getting drunk, and there were drugs everywhere—speed, weed, people did weird drugs back then like yellows and reds, the prescription drugs of the era. And lots of alcohol and wild rock & roll music.[23]

Fleming never crossed paths with Chuck, though a friend of Fleming's asked Berry to sign a petition to legalize marijuana. He refused.

"I heard that when the place was finally busted, there was a lot of nakedness involved," Fleming said. "It got wilder and wilder until the cops couldn't take it anymore, I guess."

Berry Park, Themetta would say, was her and Chuck's *heart*, their dream. Chuck would continue living there, and there would be plenty of guests, but after the raids in September 1974 it became a private vision.

"He really kind of made it his Fortress of Solitude," said Berry's friend, restaurateur Joe Edwards.[24]

THE CHESS LABEL WAS FLOUNDERING IN THE EARLY 1970S AS THE high hopes of corporate owner GRT collided with the economics of the music industry. GRT closed the Chess pressing plant and moved its executive offices to New York in 1970, greatly diminishing the historic Chicago footprint.

What GRT, a manufacturer of magnetic tape, had been interested in from the start was monetizing the back catalog—the master recordings of Berry and Etta James and Howlin' Wolf and Fontella Bass—by releasing classics in cassette and eight-track formats.

But by 1975 that goal was out of reach, and GRT was forced to sell the Chess master recordings to All Platinum Records, a tiny, Black-owned independent business in Englewood, New Jersey. All Platinum was founded by Sylvia Robinson, a singer and record producer, and husband Joe Robinson, a numbers runner from Harlem.

That same year, Berry released his last album for Chess. *Chuck Berry* featured several good new songs and surges with a fresh sound. He was palpably having more fun than he had on record in years, playing an expertly imprecise, double-jointed music that shambled as much as it charged forward. There are interesting revisions to "Swanee River," the Patsy Cline hit "South of the Border," and "You Are My Sunshine," and there is Chuck playing the blues. The sound is off center and heavy on the roll.

He had an impulse, and a talent, for pushing aside emerging crises in order to focus on manual labor. That was a midwestern thing, and Berry had the qualities of the land-owning farmers he saw around him. He cleared the fallen trees at Berry Park and mowed all the lawns. He did stuff to keep from thinking stuff.

Compartmentalizing would be valuable in the immediate future. Richard Nader had filed for bankruptcy, and his bookkeeping was under scrutiny from the IRS. Nader crafted an agreement with Berry to underreport the cash he was paying him—sometimes Nader logged that he was merely offering union scale of $280, a far cry from the $10,000 Berry reported receiving from other promoters. The glaring differential was now being examined by the government.

The IRS also took notice of a European promoter who had failed to report all the money paid to Berry. They interviewed musicians who had played with Berry and grilled Nader.[25]

The finale of *American Hot Wax* involves a sold-out Brooklyn show that is raided by the feds, who impound the box office money. The G-men want to shut the music down, and Alan Freed has to break it to Berry that the show's over because now there isn't any money to pay the headliner.

But as the crowd climbs the movie theater drapes, clamoring for Chuck to play, he swallows his pride and says to the camera, "You know, rock and roll has been pretty good to me. I think I'll do this one for rock and roll." Freed looks on lovingly.

When Nader recalled that scene, he cackled. "I'll do it for rock and roll," he repeated mockingly to a writer. "I laughed when I heard that line. He fuckin' *raped* rock and roll."[26]

In June 1979 the performer was charged in St. Louis with failure to report and pay a portion of his taxes for 1973. He requested before a St. Louis judge that the trial be moved elsewhere, saying he didn't believe he could get a fair trial at home.

Four days after charges were filed, Berry starred at a party on the White House's south lawn for President Jimmy Carter and assembled guests. The event was in honor of Black Music Month, and André Crouch, Billy Eckstine, and Evelyn "Champagne" King also performed. Berry changed "Oh Carol" to "Oh Amy," in honor of the eleven-year-old daughter of the president. Then he played "Roll Over Beethoven," and Jimmy Carter sang along. When the song was over Berry simply said, with a broad professional grin on his face, "Thank you. I think that was very American."[27]

Berry owned property in Los Angeles, and his trial moved there in July. On July 10, he pled guilty to evading federal taxes of about $200,000.

The feds wanted him to serve three years. Before his sentencing, Berry addressed the court. "I am pretty good at holding my own in front of many, many people," he said, but a courtroom was a different matter, and he began crying on the stand. Telling the judge about the frail parents he hoped would not have to hear about this shameful day. "I'm sorry. . . . It shall not happen again." After that, US district judge Harry Pregerson ordered him to serve 120 days and perform one thousand hours of public service.[28]

Berry said later the sentence was no big deal. He declined to simply pay a fine, pay the back taxes, and stay out of prison. "Fuck them!" he told Marshall Chess. "I deserve the fucking money."[29]

Pregerson gave him thirty days to get his affairs in order before reporting to Lompoc Federal Correctional Institute. As he left the courtroom, Berry told reporters his new album, *Rockit*, had been released that very morning.

Days before arriving at Lompoc, he played four nights at the Roxy in Hollywood. The show the *Billboard* reviewer saw was strong, and there was no indication from the crowd or the stage that, as everybody knew, the star was about to go behind bars. There was also no "My Ding-A-Ling."

Between sets, the writer Lou Cohan noted that Keith Richards had recently gotten a slap on the wrist for possession of heroin in Canada, and asked if Berry felt that Richards had gotten just treatment.

Berry responded with evasive honesty.

"I have a funny answer for you. I don't know because I have never done this before," claimed Berry. That is, never been before a judge until now.

"I'm just glad it wasn't *years*." He didn't criticize the decision. "The money wasn't paid, and we see now where it wasn't paid. I never look at my tax returns, anyway."[30]

The interview moves along. When Berry was off the road at home, what did he do for fun? Not listen to music, Chuck said; he played chess or edited his collection of home movies.

"I have a million videotapes . . . really good stuff that we worked many hours compiling, entertainment for somebody—or many bodies—later on. I'm talking about a hundred years from now or whatever."

There he was, hiding in plain sight. Telling the truth, in his fashion. Not running.

18

CHUCK BERRY
WANTS TO PLAY WITH YOU

BACKSTAGE DETROIT CLUB, CIRCA 1969. THE GUITAR PLAYER FOR the local opening band remembers the experience decades later. He spotted the headliner and commenced gushing.

"It was Chuck Berry! Strumming his guitar. I asked for a guitar pick, and he said no," said the Detroiter, who asked to remain anonymous.

"Could I trade you a guitar pick?" He said no.

"Well, could I *buy* a guitar pick from you?" And he said no!

Slick Stefaniak was the drummer in a house band in an Apache Junction, Arizona, nightclub. Chuck came through town in the early eighties; Stefaniak calls himself "an advocator" on Berry's behalf, in broad sympathy with Berry's problems with the IRS. Now his group had been chosen to support Berry.

"He came in, looked us over, and said, 'Oh, this'll do,'" remembered Stefaniak. As was the norm with Berry, there would be no rehearsal. "We had two shows to do with him."[1]

Stefaniak's group played "cowboy country honky tonk," he said. "Now, I've played behind Charlie Daniels one time. Didn't know half the stuff, but we got a list of songs he was gonna play and we learned them." There would be no learning from Chuck, who preferred to live in the moment. But from the moment they started playing, "He just went off on our bass player and tore him a new one. Didn't like the way he was playing, kept saying, 'You missed this lick, Okay. We don't know him inch-for-inch verbatim. I would think for him going from town to town only using local bands that he would be used to this by now."

Berry raged, "I can't even believe you are in this band."

"He just had an attitude that night," said the drummer. Afterward, Stefaniak asked for a photo together, and Berry cut him off, saying, "I don't pose for pictures." So when Berry was relaxing at the piano, Stefaniak slid over beside him and had a picture taken as Berry continued to ignore him. "I got my picture taken with him, but not *with* him," he said.

For the vast extent of his career, from 1955 until he played his last show in 2014, Chuck Berry played dozens, and sometimes hundreds, of shows each year. Past the millennium, when he was in his eighties, he was playing Finland, Russia, Turkey, Uruguay. The road was where he made his nut, in cash paid before the event began. Onstage he wouldn't be asked questions and was in charge of the Chuck everybody could see.

The Chuck Berry performance, like life on the road, took on an ever-changing sameness. The hits had ceased, years went by without a new album, interviews were rare. If you wanted to connect with Berry, you did it when he played your state fair, the opening of the car dealership, the trade show, Native American casino, biker bar. He only played the hits, maybe some blues, fewer obscurities as the years went on. The older he got, the more *Chuck* the show became: focused on the classics, the music (like the music maker) taken down to essence.

This relentlessly mobile life was far more his own invention than is typical for musicians who play for a living. He decided when and where, booking many shows on his own, leaving the backing band up to the local promoter, crafting a simple, iron-clad contract that made this one-man industry possible. You could see instantly how well it would work, as long as other humans did as they were told.

Selection of the band was contracted out to the show's promoter, who was expected to hire musicians with "professional knowledge of Artist's songs."[2] That facilitated him flying in with his guitar just before the performance and disappearing seconds after he walked off the stage. Also it meant he didn't have to pay a salary or expenses for the musicians he shared a stage with. It was a business decision meant to maximize profit.

Of course it also left to the promoter how much they wanted to spend of *their* profit on his musicians. And if Chuck didn't care, how much should they?

There was a good chance that in every town in the country, dozens of musicians, good ones, had grown up playing Chuck Berry's songs and were thrilled to play with him, even for nothing. That should have made it easier, but there were complications. To play with Chuck meant playing the songs in the simplified fashion in which he performed them—not the way they sounded on the classic Chess recordings. Those were the work of top-notch players who anticipated one another's moves because they had spent years playing together. They rehearsed. Berry was known to order a local bass player to unplug their instrument and sit down if they attempted the classic Willie Dixon lines.

In live situations, he was simultaneously the most laid-back and the strictest of bandleaders. No practicing, no setlists, few instructions other than "watch my foot," which signaled that the end of the song, or some big change, was coming.

Asked by a BBC interviewer if he rehearsed his bands, Berry said, "Yes usually; yes always. Did I say usually always? *Always usually*," he enthused. "I try to instill in them the *mood* that I have onstage. . . . I try to project on them the *how* of Chuck Berry, the frame of mind that I'm in onstage that anything might happen. Be watchful."[3]

Setting up this airtight ritual, and then watching it fracture under the pressure of real life, became the best way to see who he was and what he wanted to be. That was true for both audiences and those watching on the other side of the stage. There are a lot of stories.

Jimmy Marsala was a bass player who eventually became the musical director for many of Berry's live appearances. Marsala remembers the fear in the eyes of strangers.

"We played an amusement park in New Jersey, and the drummer there kept slowing down more and more, until finally he quit in the middle of a song." Marsala shrugged. "Just wound down. It had to be intimidating."[4]

He said, "I've had to fire a lot of people from the stage. It had to be in the hundreds." One night that stands out was a date that the band,

with Marsala and Chuck's son, Charles Berry Jr., on guitar, played in
Bonn, Germany.

In was the home of Beethoven, the promoter had hired a percus-
sionist from a local music school to play the drums. Chuck got on the
house PA system and fired him during the first number. "I felt bad for
the guy, he was a professor, he probably had the whole class there, and
his parents, but he just didn't fit," said Marsala.

The problem wasn't that he played like a professor. It was, in the
words of Charles Berry Jr., that he was "a professor of music who goes
and starts playing like the records."[5] That would never do.

Chuck stomped his foot down and shouted, "Stop! I cannot play
with a drummer who *doesn't* know how to play the drums." He was
ordered off the stage, and Berry asked, "Does someone in the hall
know how to play drums?" According to Berry Jr., somebody who was
even less equipped to please Chuck came up onstage. And for the rest
of the show, Berry Jr. stood over the drummer shouting into his ear
what drum to hit and when.

The policy of staging unrehearsed shows with strangers led to frus-
trating performances. Berry argued he had nothing to do with how well
a show came off. "That's up to the promoter. I'm contracted to play for
a fee, and how he gets that back is up to him," he said.

Fans who were disappointed could always stay away next time. "If
people don't like what they get, then they don't come again," he suggested.
"I regard that not so much as losing a fan, but as not gaining one."[6]

Trust was required to share a stage with others, but trust came only
with great difficulty. "I like to be responsible for me and not for the acts
of others. So I have to go alone," he explained.[7]

Eric Carmen described a night when the band the Raspberries
backed Chuck at the beginning of their career. It was circa 1970, and
Berry was booked into the Agora in Columbus, Ohio. Carmen says he
got a "cold stare" upon introducing himself, and then asked how the
band would know what key a song would be in. Berry fish-eyed the kid,
snarling, "However long it takes you to figure out where I'm at, that's
how long you lay out."[8]

They took the stage, quickly discovering that Berry would start in
one key and then, midway through a chorus, switch to another key and
sometimes to another song, while giving the band a broad grin.

The Johnnie Johnson
Trio debuts, St. Louis
Argus advertisement.

The Trio arrives: Ebbie Hardy, Chuck Berry, Johnnie Johnson.

Harry Davis/Bill Greensmith collection

"Now starring at the
Club Cosmopolitan…"

*Harry Davis/
Bill Greensmith collection*

Johnnie Johnson
and Berry, trading
places circa 1955.

*Harry Davis/Bill
Greensmith collection*

In try-anything-once
East St. Louis, even a tenor
saxophone was fair game.
*Harry Davis/Bill Greensmith
collection*

All the way live from East St. Louis. *Harry Davis/Bill Greensmith collection*

Chuck Berry's groundbreaking Club Bandstand, Francine Gillium
tending bar, 1959. *Harry Davis/Bill Greensmith collection*

The jukebox at Club
Bandstand.

*Harry Davis/
Bill Greensmith
collection*

The family
house at
13 Windermere
Place, bought
by Berry in 1958.
Bill Greensmith

Berry family picnic.

Harry Davis/
Bill Greensmith collection

DON'T MISS

MUDDY WATER and His Band

SENSATIONAL RECORDING ARTIST
WILL BE AT

BERRY PARK WENTZVILLE, MO.
SUNDAY, JULY 12—4 TO 8 P.M.

Directions: Highway 70 to Z—3 miles south to Buckner Road.

1964 advertisement
for Muddy Waters
show at Berry Park.

Bo Diddley and Chuck Berry backstage at London's
Wembley Stadium, September 1972.   *Bill Greensmith*

Johnnie Johnson and Chuck Berry in St. Louis, 1985.

Bill Greensmith

The notorious January 1990
issue of *High Society*.

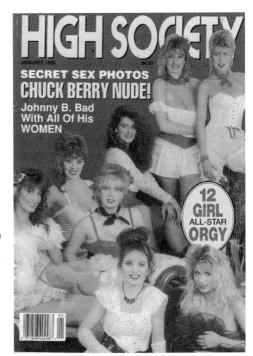

Protesters outside Berry's 2017 memorial service, St. Louis. *Jaime Lees*

Black Lives Matter demonstration outside Blueberry Hill,
St. Louis, June 2020. *Robert Cohen/St Louis Post-Dispatch/Polaris*

The sidemen took to watching his hand on the fretboard and in that way deducing the key he was playing in. But Berry caught on and turned away, out of view. After that happened a few times, they concluded that "he just wanted to make himself look good by making us look bad," Carmen said.

Guitarist Vernon Reid has backed Berry and performed in tributes to him.

> The first time I encountered him, he was kind of a mean guy, not friendly. I didn't even really catch a feeling about it because I kinda knew what he was gonna be like.
>
> He was one of my childhood heroes. [But] I had long ago realized that a lot of these guys had had hard lives, difficult times . . . so I didn't take it personally.

The way Reid views it, it was easy for Berry to look right past all the players he barely met night after night. They stood in for others who had wronged him and became inviting targets for his resentment. "He knew that he started this whole thing, and then seeing these white boys making massive amounts of money with this music. That's part of what's in the mix," said Reid.[9]

In the era of the rock star he had been denied his strokes, but on the stage he controlled, he displayed his place in the world—surrounded by inferiors and fumblers, or so it would seem. Every night he could symbolically kick Keith Richards off his stage.

Like Little Richard, Bo Diddley, and others, he had seen powerful strangers put their names on hit records and learned how bookkeeping worked to their disadvantage. "And then they saw this one dude who was a part of that situation be crowned the King of Rock & Roll," said Reid.

> It was a funny thing about America; we don't have a monarchy but we love having kings of swing and kings of rock & roll.
>
> This kind of thing stuck in their craw. I can't say something is wrong with that—it was a bunch of bullshit they were put through.

Now, he was giving some of it back.

Early in his career, Berry explored the cities and towns where he played, looking around, trying the food, hearing the way people talked. By the 1970s it was harder to fade into the crowd, and anyway, he was less interested in the crowd. Now the shows, their mechanics, the contract, and, yes, the performance, were what kept him going. They were a set of skirmishes enacted before assembled allies, curious strangers, folks who wanted to see what this guy sounded like. His shows became a little like St. Louis at the time of the Civil War: things could go either way, and the crowd was an explosion of feelings surging in various directions. In any audience were folks ready to take you down or chant your name. The uncertainty excited him.

There is a little-seen BBC TV show from 1980 in which the filmmakers follow Berry to a bar in Palo Alto. It's 1979, and he is chewing out a bearded white kid in a T-shirt, a harmonica player who soloed contrary to Chuck's wishes.

Wrapping his arm around the young man's shoulder, putting him at the center of the stage as the music stops, Berry tells him, the crowd, and the universe, "A hundred years ago he was my master. Now he's my son. Come on up here, *son*, and blow your harmonica. *Only* when I'm pointing to you, yeah!"[10]

All Chuck's children were out there, taking their licks. This went beyond payback for Elvis. On any given night between 1955 and around 2000, Chuck Berry shows became a portable Civil War memorial. Somebody had to pay, and Chuck was all about getting paid, right down to extracting reparations from random harmonica players.

AND SOMETIMES, FOR SEEMINGLY NO OTHER REASON THAN because he had somebody vulnerable in view, Berry said things, did things, that did not need to be done.

Writer and musician Ben Sandmel was working for the Kool Jazz Festival in New Orleans in 1983. Berry and Count Basie were on the lineup. Sandmel was troubleshooting backstage for the afternoon concert.

> It was getting close to showtime, and no one had heard anything from him. There weren't a lot of cell phones then. He had a reputation for showing up at the last minute—typically in a rental car, by himself.

So he pulls up in his rental car, he comes backstage, and this woman from an AM station went up to Chuck, and she was just, you know, tingling with excitement. And, starstruck, she says, "Oh! Mr. Berry, I'm so glad to see you, it is such an honor. I'm the emcee, I'm going to bring you on. What would you like me to say to the crowd?"

Giving her a cold, hard stare, Berry told her, "You just say whatever comes into your pathetic little mind."

"It was shitty and aggressively mean for no reason. Just so mean," said Sandmel.[11]

He glided in wanting two things: to be handed his cash and pointed to the stage.

Encores cost extra. In fact he had a routine that made it easy for him to quickly exit the stage and the venue before anybody knew what was going on.

When he determined he had played the contracted amount of time, Berry would invite patrons to dance onstage with him, a fan-friendly big finish. The stage could quickly fill with locals dancing to "Johnny B. Goode" as played by the local band, and while the stage was taken over, Berry would fade away and make his exit. ("My closing number is a disguised encore," he once explained.)[12]

A disastrous 1975 show in Manchester that he cut short garnered so much bad publicity that Berry called a press conference to discuss the fans who had refused to leave the venue and then had circulated a petition after he'd short-changed them.

"Well, people often stay behind after my concerts—in a sense of awe and wonder as to what they'd just seen," he told the gathered British press. "If any people were upset, they could only have numbered about 50 or 60. About 90–95 per cent of the audience went home very happy." (About a hundred spectators had signed a petition demanding reimbursement.)[13]

Shortening his set was an act of crowd control, he explained. "It was getting very rowdy onstage, with a lot of people dancing around me who were very advanced in spirit, and I could sense trouble," he said.

"If you leave them while you're sizzling, you can't do better than that."

Finally, he gave up pretending to make nice. "Yeah, I'll tell you something. The next day a lot of the papers said in a derogative way that I'd left the stage. Well, listen, I've got news for you, because I've been playing for twenty years now, and at the end of every show, I've left the stage."

It was simple, as far as he was concerned. Contracted to play for a certain amount of time, he aimed to honor the commitment. Now, if the agreement was for him to go on at nine p.m. and play forty minutes, and if at nine o'clock the opening act was launching into their big finish, Berry might walk onto the stage and start setting up. *Or* he might simply note that *he* was ready at the agreed-upon time, while the venue was not, and he would play for the remainder of the forty minutes when the stage was cleared.

Booking for an outdoor concert series in San Diego, Kenny Weissberg offered $27,500 for two hour-long shows. It was the late 1980s, and when the William Morris Agency sent Weissberg the contract, it was for two forty-minute shows. The promoter called Berry's agent and was told, "Don't worry, just cross out the '40 minutes' and write in '60 minutes.' I'll make sure Chuck's aware of it. You'll have a hard time getting him to stop."[14]

Arriving ten minutes after the comedian opening the show had finished, Berry demanded a meeting with the promoter in the lobby of the adjoining hotel.

"You and I have a *big* problem," he growled.

Berry pulled out his contract from the inner pocket of his jacket, unfolded it, and tapped a finger on one line.

"What does it say at the very bottom?" he insisted.

Weissberg read it aloud: "Any alterations to this contract shall render it null and void."

And a beaming Berry pointed where "40" was crossed out and "60" penciled in. "This contract is invalid."

Bargaining ensued: Berry wanted $15,000 more and settled for $2,000.

More money was good. But a little torment could also render a contract paid in full. Charlie Pickett was a slide-guitar-playing garage rocker from South Florida, and when Berry came to Fort Lauderdale's Parker Playhouse around 1984, Pickett went backstage to shake his hand. The exchange was warm, but Berry said, "I'd like to be alone now," and it was clear he was steaming about something. Soon it would be obvious to everybody.[15]

The opening band had taken their time, and when Berry was up it was a quarter after midnight.

So he walked onstage, waving his hand in the air as the crowd cheered him, and he smiled, wishing everybody a good evening, and then with great sincerity he asked the audience for their help.

With a confused stutter to his words, Chuck asked the spectators to pull out their ticket, because he had a question. Holding one in his own hand, he said, "I'm looking at this ticket and it says to me that it is for Saturday night. But it's *not* Saturday night—it's Sunday morning."

Abruptly, he "invited" the promoters onto the stage, introducing them by name to the audience. "Give them a hand." He beamed as they inched out, nervously. "They were really sweating," recalled Pickett.

The band commenced playing a little shuffle vamp, and Berry said, "Maybe we'll dance a little bit." Chuck looked on as the show's promoters did what they were told and danced for the man they had hired to entertain.

After a moment, a satisfied Berry declared, "That's right! That's good! Thank you. Give them a round of applause."

Pickett remembers vividly what came next. "I just happened to stand in line of sight to his guitar, and then I happened to hear him say in a completely different tone of voice, 'Okay now get me my guitar.' And the two promoters definitely heard that." They got him his guitar.

And here is the punch line to the story, and to so many Chuck Berry stories: what followed was a house-rocking performance. He was "vivacious and cheerful and innovative, doing everything from the duckwalk to the splits, turning the guitar every which way," said Pickett. The show was good; the star seemed every inch to be enjoying himself.

People would let you down. They misbehaved and wanted to take what was yours. But numbers, laws, provided a way forward. Quint Davis is the producer of the New Orleans Jazz & Heritage Festival, and he road managed for Duke Ellington, B. B. King, Muddy Waters, Fats Domino, and others on tours across Europe and Africa. What struck Davis about working with Berry on tours was that, whatever country he was in, he would look up the current exchange rate and calculate what his fee was going to be on that given day.

"It was more about being right—well, money was important too." Facts were facts. It was Sunday morning, and he'd been hired to play on a Saturday night. "It was part of his smart, tough mechanism for controlling the world."

Another rule: two Fender Dual Showman Reverb amps with factory settings must be available at every appearance. Those amps produced a rich, loud sound and emerged right at the moment when surf guitars were transforming Southern California rock. Berry heard them when he was released from prison in 1963, and they became crucial to his live sound.

Berry exacted a cash penalty from promoters who did not have them. A Fender Showman was vintage by the 1980s and hard to find outside major cities. Onstage they were set at ten, while the volume on his guitar was dialed way down.

Over time, fans and musicians have speculated that Berry's deteriorating hearing, and perhaps a lack of interest, led him to play out of tune. Musicians were known to sneak into his dressing room and tune his guitar before shows. But all of it, the amps, the rough sound he got when he started turning his guitar up while the amps were already on ten, the lack of standard tuning, the shitty off-brand guitars he sometimes played later in life, all of it defined the space he wished to inhabit. He fought for it. He billed for it.

"There's a comfort zone with everybody, even the most brilliant dudes like Chuck Berry," said Jesper Eklow, guitarist with the band Endless Boogie. "It's just, 'I love my sound coming out this way. I don't know why.' Some bands need Marshall stacks. This is what put him at ease and let him know he could walk up and just be the motherfucker he was."[16]

The Showman amps could also lead to complicated moments. As a skinny, long-haired fourteen-year-old, Peter O'Neill went to a Lake Tahoe club in an old Safeway supermarket. When he got there, he saw a calm, lonely-looking Berry sitting down on the edge of the stage. Near him was a massively built fellow who kept Berry in his sight.

"You are my idol," O'Neill shouted to Berry, who shook his hand and gave him an appraising look.[17] O'Neill said it wasn't until later that he understood the backstory: the club hadn't delivered on the Dual Showman Reverbs and perhaps hadn't delivered on the penalty fee Berry demanded. Instead, they put the club security guard, a San Francisco

49er earning summer money, on the star, making sure he didn't leave the stage before he played his set.

"He was holding Chuck Berry hostage at the side of the stage, and I find it an amazing thing," noted O'Neill. "He had a simple contract. And it said if he didn't have the amps he wanted, he didn't have to play."

The rules did not belong to Chuck. Market forces are not natural forces. They were not devised in the world of collective creation. They existed to protect other folks, and Berry spent his early years understanding how that worked. The rest of his life he spent understanding how to turn them against the owners. He would make their power work for him.

The rules were the "letter of the law," laws that had been used against him. He took the rules apart and built a custom speaker of his own—if the law was the American way, space would be found in it for him. Here, too, he would be explaining America to Americans, night after night.

Dick Alen told a story about booking Berry and Jerry Lee Lewis together in Paris on May Day, a holiday steeped in socialist tradition. Lewis and Berry were arguing about who would finish the show, and Berry said that for a little more cash, he'd let Lewis go on last.

But when he got to the stadium and saw hundreds of thousands of French fans who had the day off from work, he realized he had bargained poorly and demanded more money. Now he wanted tens of thousands more or there would be no show. And the French explained to Berry this was a national holiday, saying, "No, Mr. Berry, you do not understand. We are socialists."

"Fuck socialism," responded Berry. "I want my money."

ON THE ROAD THERE WERE PLENTY OF WOMEN AROUND. MARSHALL Chess noticed how it "seemed like he always had a white paramour on the side."

Richard Thompson, singer, songwriter, and guitarist, remembers a festival he played in Ballisodare, Ireland, in 1981, in the rain. Berry arrived at a quite muddy backstage. "He decided not to get his shoes dirty, and basically sat in the car for about five hours. He would occasionally roll down the window to sign an autograph," said Thompson.[18]

"My ex-wife (who wasn't my wife at that point) was mistaken for the blond hooker that was in his contract, and was encouraged to get into the car with Chuck, where they chatted for a while before she realized the error of her ways. The real hooker turned up later, and they arranged to meet after his set, and she asked him which one was his tent! As if Chuck was going to camp in the rain."

A STICKLER FOR RULES, HE FLOATED ABOVE THEM. QUINT DAVIS toured across Europe with Berry in the 1980s, remembering, "He never signed for anything, and he never showed any ID."[19]

Berry had to have the right car waiting for him in whatever European city he was playing in, but part of the deal was that somebody else handled the transfer. He'd make everyone wait while he inspected his room, but he never signed for it.

"Technically he had stolen that car and would drive it to the wonderful hotel suite and order food and call home. But he wasn't technically registered there, because he would not show his driver's license or sign the registration."

They were playing in Athens, 1987, high on a hillside in an ancient village. It held five thousand people, remembered Davis; some twenty thousand were making their way up the hill to see Chuck Berry.

Pretty soon the fans had demolished the fence around the stage, and everybody charged the dais. Special-forces guys stood on the stage and subdued fans who jumped up, throwing them back into the crowd.

A gallery ramped up to the stage, and as the show raged on the platform moved and separated. While Berry put the fans in a frenzy, they began dismantling the stage, carting flat pieces across the sea of people. Piece by piece, until Berry, the bassist, and the keyboardist were all huddled on the drum riser, playing on. "Chuck loves this," recalled Davis. "This is rock & roll, this is chaos or a riot or something." That's when he went into "Let It Rock."

Somehow the players got off what was left of the stage, and then they had to make their way through the crowd because the barricades were long gone. "Chuck went in front, holding his beautiful red guitar in front of him by the neck, like a medieval axe," said Davis. "High above his head—he never hit anybody, but it was kind of clear you should get out of the way. We got through."

The next day at the airport, they saw the Greek press headlines, something about "Chuck Berry" and "riot."

In Madrid, where he had never played before, a press conference was scheduled. That led him to explain one of his baseline rules for those attending: Do not take a picture of him offstage.

Showing up in a crowd of Spanish media waiting to ask him questions, Berry checked out his hotel room and threw everything into disarray by saying they had to find another hotel for him, this would not do at all.

While Berry sat in his car, a paparazzo shot a photo from a foot away. "That broke so many rules," said Davis. "Ever see the movie *The Matrix*? Everything about to happen was in slow motion." The door opened. Chuck came out. He put his two hands on the chest of the heavy-set photographer, who went flying through the air. Chuck got back in his car, and everything returned to normal time.

General Franco had been dead five years, but democracy was sputtering in Spain in the summer of 1981, just months after pro-Franco paramilitary forces had attempted a coup. The photographer filed a complaint against Berry. There were negotiations at the bullfight stadium to let Berry finish playing before being arrested.

Everyone melted away after the show. Police drew pistols on Davis in the hotel lobby as he signed in for the star, demanding he lead them to Berry's room. Davis knocked on his door, explaining that the police could do things gently or otherwise.

They took the Americans in. "You couldn't do anything about the police rules."

In the back seat of the police car, Berry slipped Davis his passport; Davis still had the cash from the sold-out stadium show in his jeans pocket. From police headquarters, "the Guardia Civil with the little Mickey Mouse hats and machine guns picked us up and put us in this antiquated palace with dark walls," said Davis.

It was quiet, and the Americans shared a bench and a Salem cigarette in their cell. They were told they would have to appear before a judge, and that they must wait for a translator. But Davis claimed he could speak Spanish, and he summoned every word he could remember from his lessons when they were taken before a judge. Davis interpreted while Berry pantomimed the flash going off in his face and his punch, and how the photographer fell backward not forward, and when it was over the judge released them at dawn—after he first asked Berry for an autograph.

"I'll never forget walking the dirty streets at five in the morning with Chuck saying, 'We gotta get out of here.'" They headed straight for the airport.

To the judge Berry had explained that he explicitly told everybody not to take his picture.

"He was defining the world by controlling his rules," said Davis. Those rules were few. "They were simple. Unless you broke them."

HITTING THE STAGE MEANT MANY THINGS TO HIM. MONEY, DUH, and a welcome distraction from stuff out of his control. You sit around too long and you might start thinking about what the papers and strangers said about you.

Flying into a town in 1979, a TV reporter in tow, he boarded an airport shuttle bus. Sat next to a white guy with a laconic way of talking. "Do you know Charlie Pride?" the guy asks. "From Sledge, Mississippi?"[20]

It's a charged encounter when a stranger compares you to someone else. Pride was a great Black star of country music, a resolute presence who worked hard his whole life to put strangers at ease.

"Who doesn't know Charlie Pride?" Berry pushed back. He looked away, and a minute later he started to say, "I used to walk around in Mississippi. Every time I got out, I walked around . . ."

The stranger jumps in: "Every time *you got out*?" It sure seemed like a dig at Berry's time behind bars.

Berry cracks up. Staring into the floor, saying, "Love it . . ."

Being Chuck Berry meant the guy beside you on the bus wished for you to squirm. But on the stage, he knew that the guy's kids, his neighbors, even the Charlie Pride stranger himself wanted what he had.

Chuck Berry wanted to be responsible for himself, and that was it. The shows could be shambling, the money games scandalous, the abuse he dispensed worse still. But understand, whenever he felt like it, he might be triumphant.

The Circle Jerks, a punk band, came from Los Angeles. Their 1980 debut included "I Just Want Some Skank" and "World Up My Ass" on an EP titled *Group Sex*. It was pretty great. In 1995 they were schlepping a new album and arrived in St. Louis to play the club Mississippi Nights. It was a roomy, no-frills rock shrine where everybody from Nirvana to Richard Thompson had played.

The club overlooked the Mississippi River, and the Circle Jerks certainly knew they were in Berry's hometown—bass player Zander Schloss is also from St. Louis, and he called the show a huge homecoming moment.

"Chuck Berry is my ultimate hero," he said. "Dude! You'd have to be stupid if you're a guitar player and you don't idolize Chuck Berry."[21]

Mark Goldman was a Mississippi Nights regular. He'd seen Berry drop by any number of times. "Word was he would go out prowling for women and gambling at a casino on the riverfront. So it wasn't that exotic to see him," said Goldman. "The most surprising thing was that it was the night the Circle Jerks were playing. You would think this was way outside his area of interest."

Goldman adds, "But then hey, all rock music is based on Chuck Berry licks, and even these guys were just playing a louder, more distorted version of Chuck Berry."

Arriving with a couple of women, "I want to say two blonds," Berry approached the stage as the band played. It was an all-ages show, but most everybody was well over the drinking age, because by 1995 the Circle Jerks were something of a nostalgia act themselves.

"Here we are in this room with eight hundred people just going apeshit, just going *nuts*, people leaping off of whatever they could leap off of," said singer Keith Morris. Berry walked over to the guy at the soundboard, and he looked *excited*. Club manager Andy Mayberry went to the Jerks manager and said, "Hey, Chuck Berry is here and wants to get up onstage and play." Mayberry wrote a note on printer paper and laid it in front of the band. CHUCK BERRY WANTS TO PLAY WITH YOU.

Morris noticed him waving from the crowd. "Chuck Berry is wearing his little white skipper hat, like he's been commandeering the riverboat. And then he says, 'Pull me up, I want to play.'" What bassist Schloss remembered was "this very weird silence—we stopped the set and somebody wheeled an amp up onstage and I was just *Wwvwaaa . . . Whhhhaaa . . . WHAT?*"

The first time Schloss played guitar before an audience was at summer camp when he rendered "Johnnie B. Goode." Now, here he was.

> I had no idea what was going to happen. I might've asked somebody in the band, and then they said, "Yeah, Chuck Berry is coming up here to play a couple of songs." I was freaking fucking out.
>
> And the funny thing about it is, when I think about it—and my memory is patchy from all the drugs and alcohol I did in my career—what I most remember is the anticipation, the bizarre anticipation that came with the amp wheeling up onto the stage. I'd never gotten that close to him before.

According to Mayberry, those who knew what was going on wondered how the kids in the audience with all the tattoos and mohawks and orange and green hair would handle this old guy playing with their heroes. "Well," said Mayberry, "they were just blown away."

"I was certainly shocked," said Goldman. "He's very hard on people who backed him up. I wondered if he was going to be nice to them or berate them. They seemed just thrilled by the whole process, and Chuck didn't yell at anybody or chastise—it was just, *Back me up and get out of the way.*"

Angela Pezel was standing close to the stage and saw something she would never forget. "I was at the left side of the stage, by these big monitor speakers, and three or four kids who were hearing impaired were standing there, their hands pressed up against the monitor. You could see that they could *feel* the vibrations. They were experiencing the same kind of thing as I did; they could feel it and see it and they were experiencing it themselves. They were signing to one another, and there was some older person minding them who looked really stressed out. But they were having the time of their life."

Berry hit the first notes of "Roll Over Beethoven" and signaled for Morris to sing with him. "I'm listening to the guys play along with him and they're doing a really good job," Morris said. "This is not supposed to be happening. It doesn't happen to a band of our stature."

"I was off and running," Schloss laughed. "I was in the right key and pretty excited about that." There was jumping and screaming—it *was* a Circle Jerks show. "I'm looking over to the other side of the stage and [guitarist] Greg Hetson is leaping into the air, I'm doing my moose kick, and Keith is going nuts. He's dancing with Chuck Berry."

The way Goldman remembered, Berry went into a sampling of some of his other hits. Did he fit with them? It was like a pretty straightforward Chuck Berry set—they didn't up the tempo.

Later, speaking of Morris, Berry would say to Schloss, "Tell that little guy that he's *insane*."

"We didn't even speak!" said Morris. "I guess he'd already spoken to us and all of the punk rockers. The modern geniuses, the future lawyers and brain surgeons and knuckleheads, all of them, he spoke to everybody with 'Roll Over Beethoven.'"

The show of course ended there, and later, with the band drying off and loading up for the next town, the club manager pulled Morris into his office.

"Sit down," he said. "Chuck Berry told me to tell you guys that you are one of the greatest bands he's ever seen." What could possibly be better than that? Not even having a hit record. Schloss said he was "vibrating for weeks."

That's how it would be for any band if Chuck Berry unexpectedly joined them. But Pezel points out how Berry looked: like there wasn't anything remarkable about the night.

He had come to a show, loved the spirit, and wanted to be a part. He sized up his crowd and knew what would happen every step of the way. Chaos ensued.

"It was really kind of old hat to Chuck," she said. "It was just, 'I know who I am. And here I am with my guys.'"

19

PROMISED LAND

IT HAD BEEN A LONG DAY AT MAGIC MOUNTAIN, THE THEME PARK northwest of Los Angeles. Diane, a single mom with blond hair, was with her son, who was in his stroller, and his babysitter. They had been walking around for hours and sat on a bench while they talked about going home.

On a bench beside them was a couple, and as Diane sat down she felt the man slide his hand under her bottom. "I was paralyzed. This was very bizarre, him putting his hand under there. I just froze. I didn't know what to do."[1]

Right then others at the park rushed past her to ask the stranger, "Are you Chuck Berry?"

"Well, I've been called that," he said. They asked for autographs, and he pulled his hand out. "No, no, *after* the show," he said while waving them away.

Diane asked who he was, and he cocked his head up to the sign that said, "50s Revival with Chuck Berry."

The three were invited to the show, and before she had time to discuss it Berry had picked up her son out of the stroller and marched toward the dressing room.

After the performance, the two exchanged phone numbers. She was coming out of an abusive relationship, and Berry was attentive, magnetic, overpowering. A few weeks went by, then he invited her to his show at LA's Roxy Theatre. The woman who had accompanied Berry at Magic Mountain was at the Roxy too, but he told her, "Diane's with me now." The other woman threw her keys at him and stormed off.

Los Angeles meant murky things to Berry. He didn't like celebrity culture, which he defined himself against. Yet he was attracted to the sexual freedom and opportunities the city offered for redefining who one was. From his high school joyride to "Promised Land," LA embodied a liberty he craved.

Appearing on *The Mike Douglas Show* in mid-April 1971, he told the audience that "just last week" he had bought his first piece of Southern California property. "I'm digging in," he declared. "Just trying to get some kind of hold out here because this sunshine is so beautiful!"[2]

By 1982, when Diane met him, he owned several buildings in Los Angeles, including a house at 7600 Fountain Avenue and two more at 2145 and 2151 Hollyridge Drive, in the Hollywood Hills. He showed her his Hollywood Hills property: a two-story, three-bedroom house that he leased out, and the big house, with six bedrooms, five baths, a swimming pool, and tennis courts, all situated on a one-acre lot billed as the only real estate in the Hills set on a perfectly circular plot. Berry lived there up to ten days a month, Diane said; any more and he would have to pay California taxes. Wentzville remained his primary home, but Los Angeles was a getaway he went to many times over the next few decades.

The houses, and the man, made an impression on Diane. "I was coming out of a dysfunctional relationship with the father of my son, who said, 'I'll ruin you if you tell people who the father is,'" she said. "And now I'm with somebody who is taking me out with my kid." She struggled to avoid being swept off her feet, but Chuck Berry made her feel special.

Taking Diane down to the basement of the main house in the Hills, Berry said he had something to show her. "He had all these wires down there, connected to, like, a cable box or something. He said, 'I can listen to anybody's conversation in either house on the loop.' Now, why would he want to do that? Well, he was a voyeur."

After hearing how much rent she paid, Berry offered her one of his houses. "He said, 'I want you to have all this.' 'I'm not sure I'm ready to be a kept woman,' I told him." But not long after, she and her son moved into the smaller house.

"At the beginning, it was kind of unbelievable how well I was treated in the light of him that shined on me."

They drove around Los Angeles, listening to the Everly Brothers on the car radio, going to Baskin-Robbins (Berry liked to let the ice cream melt before he ate it), Winchell's Donuts, Kentucky Fried Chicken, Taco Bell. "He called high-end dining eating at Denny's!" she laughed.

"The best part was he was an amazing lover, there's no doubt about it. It could be very exhilarating."

He told her the estate was hers, calling it his wedding gift to her. Sometimes he would impulsively tell Diane to order a pizza for her son, and then insist that she get in the car because the two were going for a quick drive to Vegas. "He'd never gotten divorced from his wife, but a couple of times he took me to wedding chapels in Las Vegas and talked about getting married. I had to ask, 'What are you doing? You are still married.'"

Diane did errands for him when he wasn't in Hollywood, appearing in his place at award ceremonies, collecting rent, and contracting for work at properties he owned. It was when she was visiting the building at 7600 Fountain Avenue that she met Diane Gardiner, a girlfriend of Berry's from a decade before.

Gardiner was an attractive, outgoing music-industry publicist who in the 1970s worked for the Doors and Jefferson Airplane and was said to have dated Ahmet Ertegun. According to Diane, Berry met Gardiner at a Venice bookstore called Midnight Special and became "really smitten with her."

The pioneering rock writer Ellen Sander was in Massachusetts in 1971 when Gardiner called her from Hollywood. The Sylmar earthquake, a major temblor in California history, had just occurred that February, a national news story at the moment Gardiner phoned. Sander recalls, "I thought she was calling to tell us she was okay. But she was talking excitedly and saying, 'I'm in love.'"

"*What?*"

"I'm in love with Charles Berry," Gardiner repeated. "He's in love with me and we see each other constantly and I am in love with him."[3]

Plenty of people had crushes on Gardiner, including major rock stars, said Sander. Gardiner treated these lightly. "She had her own life. But she was overwhelmed in love with Charles Berry."

A friend of Gardiner's says Berry had bought a house for her in the Hollywood Hills at the beginning of their relationship. A month or so later, he was on *The Mike Douglas Show*, announcing his arrival in LA.

When the two met, Gardiner called her friend Mirandi Babitz, a clothing designer with a shop on Sunset Strip, where she made Jim Morrison's stage leathers. (Babitz is also the sister of the late Los Angeles scene chronicler Eve Babitz.)

Gardiner, calling from a house in the Hollywood Hills, invited Babitz and her family over for a visit with her new boyfriend—who went as Charles in his offstage guise. Babitz's father, Sol, played chess, and noting that Charles was looking for a new chess partner, Gardiner suggested they play a game together. So Mirandi, Sol, his wife Mae, and Mirandi's boyfriend all went to the house on Hollyridge Drive.

The first thing visitors noticed was the statue of a deer perched on the slope that ran up to the big house. Two enormous front doors led them into a lofty living room with tobacco-colored, flocked wallpaper. In the center of the space was a chess table.

Sol was a sixty-five-year-old revered musician, an "Albert Einstein-esque classical violinist/baroque musicologist," according to Mirandi.[4] He and Berry sized each other up. They exchanged expressions of "I admire your playing" and other terse words, then sat down and performed their opening moves.

Diane stood behind her man; the Babitzes hovered behind Sol. One hour, maybe two passed, figured Babitz. Then Charles pulled off the sunglasses he had been wearing, stared at Sol, and gently said, "Draw?" "Draw."

Their hands hovered over the board as they shook. As Sol walked away he said pointedly to his daughter, "He's smarter than he looks."

Silence came easy to Berry. He and Gardiner took a drive from Los Angeles to Mexico City, during which he spoke only once, asking her when she was born. At a 1971 dinner party at Eve Babitz's Fairfax apartment, Charles walked around the room photographing everyone with his brand-new video camera, while saying nothing.[5]

But over time the relationship cooled, and by the 1980s Gardiner was living in the house Berry owned on Fountain Avenue, and Berry was telling Diane that Gardiner's old house "is your house now."

Ultimately, Diane rented the smaller house across the street from him and helped him lease out the main house when he was out of town.

He came and went without letting her know when he might be back. Charles would arrive at her house, make love to her, and then leave a hundred dollars on her dresser, saying he was headed to the airport. "'You know that's kind of diminishing our relationship, treating me like a hooker, right?'" she would say.

> What the heck was that? I do all this work for him and then I get a hundred left on the dresser. That's a mixed message, isn't it?
>
> He wanted me to be this lady in buttoned-up suits, but then the whore in the bedroom. And he opened me up so that I would satisfy him that way.

HE WOULD PHOTOGRAPH HER AND VIDEOTAPE THEIR SEX. DURING sex she says he put a pillow over her face, telling her it would intensify her orgasm—"I could have suffocated," she said. "Another time I found chewing gum in my vagina after I had been with him. I thought, 'What is this gum doing here?'"

Being with him meant doing things he wanted to do and being swept up into his schedule, his drama. "It was clear he was having a lot of sex with other people," she said. "He had body lice the size of tarantulas! I'm looking at the bed thinking, *What the heck? Where did these come from?*" He shared his "discography," as he called it, letting Diane read a running tally he was composing, covering a life's worth of sexual encounters.

They went shopping for his captain's hat at Sears, and he said he liked the nautical-style caps because they looked so good on "Captain" Daryl Dragon of the Captain and Tennille. He called her "my Nancy Reagan" and took her out for Mexican food.

"He liked to share a bowl of albondigas soup," Diane recalled. And when Chuck got a meatball he would lean over and kiss her, passing the meatball from his mouth to hers. "Now that's kind of weird," she said. "I didn't know what to do, so I'd swallow it. But it was weird behavior."

IN 1985, STEPHANIE BENNETT, A BRITISH PRODUCER OF MUSIC documentaries, was assembling an ambitious project: a cable-TV all-star tribute to Chuck on his sixtieth birthday. Keith Richards was the musical director of the show. Over six months or so of negotiating a TV and video deal with Berry, the project expanded into a motion picture in which the concert became one element.

The film was titled *Hail! Hail! Rock 'n' Roll*. If a movie of the making of *Hail!* had been produced, it surely would have turned out as interesting as the feature film. *Hail!* shows sides of the star his fans rarely saw. By the 1980s Berry had constructed a vast array of electrical fences, contractual language, and emotional apparatus to keep the world away. But when a major director and his crew bought his cooperation with large sums of money, along came the largest intrusion into his life in years. Celebrities, cameras, gawky fans, people telling him what to do, pushing in on all sides through 1985 and 1986. How did he do? Chuck did *great*.

Bennett saw the possibilities in a full-on biographical feature, and presentations were made to directors Richard Tuggle, Milos Forman, and Barry Levinson. Bob Rafelson thought he was smart, booking a power lunch with Berry and Bennett's team at the nouveau French Le Dome restaurant, where fabulous industry deals were greased. Berry arrived late. Rafelson signaled for the sommelier and ordered an expensive bottle of wine. Berry countered by putting his briefcase on the table, pulling out a Big Mac, fries, orange juice, and hot apple pie. The director buttered forth, "Chuck, please, you're my guest. Please order anything you want." The guest responded, "Nobody tells Chuck Berry what to eat."[6]

Taylor Hackford, hot off *The Idolmaker*, a drama about 1960s pop stars, understood that a different approach was needed. He suggested they meet at a dive Chinese restaurant in Hollywood that he knew Berry liked, because he had once hit him up for an autograph there. The two connected—Diane said Berry liked Hackford because he looked like Kris Kristofferson—and Hackford made his pitch for a comprehensive film in which Berry would talk about his time in prison. The cable deal was superseded by a movie deal, which meant more money for the star.

The production team wanted assurance Berry was still playing at peak level, so line producer Thomas Adelman went to Chicago, where he was appearing at the halftime of a Bulls basketball game. While Berry watched the first half of the game, Billy Crystal and Gregory Hines tried to engage him in conversation. Berry just ignored them and stared ahead, without comment. "He didn't care," Adelman said with awe. "He wasn't impressed by celebrity." At halftime Berry met the band and they played a set, more than enough to convince Adelman that "this guy, even turning sixty, still had all the charisma and all the sex appeal." He could carry a movie.

Afterward he told Adelman to take him to a McDonald's, where he ate silently, staring at the producer. Then they went to a blues club to see Robert Cray play, and when the doorman said it would cost five dollars, he balked: "Chuck Berry doesn't pay to go into this shithole." Adelman stood there whipping out all the cash he had, but by then Berry had driven off—with Adelman's luggage in his car.

Adelman heard Cray for the first time—he would later play in *Hail! Hail!*—and when the producer bummed a ride to his hotel, he found that his luggage had been dropped off by Berry, who had already departed.

There would be trips to Wentzville to confer, shoot scenes, and rehearse the band for the concert in St. Louis planned as the film's finish. On their first trip to town, Berry picked up Bennett and Adelman at the airport in a thunderstorm and drove them downtown, explaining he had to renew his driver's license. But it was Sunday afternoon, and they watched him pound on the door of city hall for a while as the rain poured down, before he returned to his car saying, "I think they are closed."

Driving toward Wentzville that night, Berry ran out of gas and pulled over on the freeway shoulder. In a fluid set of motions, in cascading rain, he pivoted to retrieve a gas can, skated across many lanes of freeway traffic in both directions, then disappeared up a muddy embankment in the distance.

Adelman idly asked out loud if the cast insurance had kicked in yet.

Bobbing and weaving between eighteen-wheelers, Berry eventually made his return. He poured the contents of the can into his tank as the downpour continued, his rain-soaked monumental profile standing out to Adelman in the silvery moonlight.

Hackford had an agreement with Berry to talk about his prison terms. And Berry did drive out one afternoon to the grounds of the youth reformatory in Algoa, to provide a visual backdrop for a scene concerning his past arrests. But the facility had long been converted to a medium-security prison for adults, and it strained to accommodate the visitors.

Berry seemed to have his own ideas of the scene he would be appearing in. Hackford and crew were in one car. Chuck traveled with Bennett and a girlfriend from Berry Park named Yvonne Cumbie. Along the way, say Hackford and Bennett, Berry stopped and picked up one of Berry's daughters.

The cars were waved onto the prison grounds by guards, and Berry parked in the middle of a yard rapidly filling up with about a thousand inmates. Some gathered around Berry, and he wandered into a building with them. That left Cumbie, wearing a tight miniskirt at Berry's request, Berry's daughter, and Bennett in the yard. They were being videotaped by Hackford, who had borrowed a camera from Berry.

Inmates began circling around the women, moving in closer. A female guard quietly but firmly told them to act calm and follow her into a building. It was too late, though, and a mini riot ensued. The three women were surrounded; one of them was knocked to the ground. Inmates groped Bennett's genitals; underwear and clothing were on the ground. "It was terrifying," Bennett said, "and then the guards came out and were hitting on them with batons."[7]

Once they were safely inside, Hackford caught up with Berry, shouting, "What the hell are you doing?" "Well," the director was told, "I know what it's like for prisoners who've been in jail without seeing a woman, so I figured I'd give them a treat."

The scene was shot on Berry's video camera, but Berry took the camera back that night, and Hackford said that was the last time anyone saw the video.

"Nothing could be as hard mentally and physically as making this film, other than maybe childbirth," said Bennett. "I really thought I couldn't make it."

Hired to assemble a backing band for Berry, Keith Richards dug into the work. Mick Jagger was working on a solo album, which allotted

Richards time to devote to the film. His last encounter with Berry had been backstage in New York City. Keith was waiting in Berry's dressing room, spotted his guitar, and picked it up, and just then Chuck arrived and delivered a punch to his face. Keith admitted later that he'd been in the wrong.

He knew better than most who he was dealing with and why it was worth it. Berry's guitar playing had made the Rolling Stones possible. Richards saw the disrepair his legacy had fallen into. He was eager to do restoration work on a subject who was indifferent to the goal, a figure proud, resentful, and at times ready to let it all slide south.

He had an inspired idea: invite Berry to Richards's Jamaican home, have a little me 'n' you time, shoot a few scenes playing guitar together, then sit down and work on new songs and talk about the process for the camera. It was August 1986. First, Berry objected to staying at Richards's house, insisting on a hotel nearby. Then he refused to jam together, explaining he had left his guitar at the hotel—even though Richards had plenty of instruments on hand. Carrying around a fat biography of Albert Einstein, Berry made a point of his discomfort in the presence of the Rastas who moved through the compound. Passive aggression followed him like a cloud.

Not going to be a Rolling Stone's "houseguest." Not a chance on camera Chuck would become Charles and talk about the craft. No group photo with the roots rockers of Jamaica. He was an individualist, not a member of a crowd.

Onward to Missouri, where he showed them Berry Park. Adelman describes six or seven satellite dishes scattered around and evokes the final moments of *The Last Picture Show*, tumbleweeds blowing by and leaves falling into the guitar-shaped pool. Bennett recalls large-screen TVs alternating between scenes from Auschwitz and the Playboy Channel.

Early on, Berry took them all to a Wentzville club he owned. Richards, Hackford, Bennett, Berry, and others walked in, and the bar band launched into "Jumpin' Jack Flash" and "Honky Tonk Woman." Berry leaned into Richards, saying, "There's your band. That's the band that's backing me up." "No it ain't, mate," Richards responded.

"Chuck was not really prepared for it—his thing was, 'Hey, I don't need a rehearsal, I just want to go out and do it,'" said Adelman.

Richards approached everything with his own stubbornness. A fan who was paying a debt, he had to put that awareness away and on a day-to-day basis fend off counterrevolution and sloppy habits, his fists up and ready to take one for posterity.

"Keith was hell-bent on refamiliarizing Chuck with his own genius," said drummer Steve Jordan, who was essential to the effort. A brilliant house band was drafted and then rehearsed with Berry. Bennett tracked down Johnnie Johnson, who was driving a school bus for a living. He agreed to do the film, and the producer agreed to buy him a set of dentures.

Bass player Joey Spampinato, who had a regular gig in the group NRBQ, remembered Richards and Jordan approaching him at a Greenwich Village show. "They said they were putting a band together and wanted to make it a band Chuck couldn't make fun of, basically. They wanted to surprise him with something great."[8] Willie Dixon's stand-up bass was essential to the sound of many Chess recordings, and Spampinato had a rare ability to convey the feel and sound of the acoustic instrument on his electric one. Upon arrival in Wentzville, Richards and Jordan gave Spampinato a warning that Berry was likely to drag him on the carpet, give him a red-hot music lesson at any moment.

Spampinato had studied those foundational Chess 45s. One day Berry brought a rehearsal to a sudden halt. The bassist, he said, was playing the part wrong. "I said, 'I'll play it any way you want,'" Spampinato recalled, while gently noting he had been listening to a lot of Willie Dixon. The next day, Berry shouted, "Bass player! You were *right*." He'd been reacquainting himself with his own music, and "instead of giving me a lesson, he was kind of saying something nice."

In fact, it was Richards who would receive a lesson of tough love from his sensei. While rehearsing "Carol," Berry watched as a sound tech changed the settings on his amplifier. Richards had signed off on the move. There was a twenty-four-track truck outside the clubhouse recording the rehearsals, and the person in the truck noticed what many ticket holders over the years had observed—that with Chuck's powerful amp turned up to ten for all settings and his Gibson ES-355 dialed down to a whisper, the guitar sounded like a tin can scraping on stucco.

There was logic to the argument that the more musical the sounds, the more musical the soundtrack. And yet there was greater logic to the proposition that you don't fuck with a master's sword. On camera, no less.

"That's my amp and I'm setting it the way I want it. It's to sound the way I want it to sound. Don't touch my amp!" Berry declares.

"It's not recording well, and that's the way it'll sound on the film," Richards responds.

"If it winds up on the film, that's the way Chuck Berry plays it. You understand."

This was a philosophical point as well as fighting words, the essence of what Berry had told thousands of local musicians over the years when they met up just minutes before showtime and asked him, "What are we going to play tonight?" *Chuck Berry music* was his only answer. *It's what the people want if I am playing it. The sound is okay if my hands make it.*

Richards invokes eternity. "I understand, but you've got to live with it afterwards."

"I've been living with it for sixty years."

"This is gonna be here after we're all dead and gone."

"Well, I ain't dyin'. Go ahead and sing your song!"

It starts with a fight over, like, the remote. It's trivial—*Who turned down my amplifier?* And within seconds, it goes to that most basic of things: *Who owns my work?* A sound technician tries to make the mix of instruments blend better, and Richards rushes in to defend him. Berry never loses sight about what this is really about, and he is right. Somebody was going behind his back to mess with him. This is not a new motion picture by a rising director. Not an act of personal redemption from one of the most famous rock stars on the planet. It was a Chuck Berry movie.

Chuck looks ready to pop, Keith biting his tongue, maybe thinking about how much fun it was bickering with Mick. And when the argument shook out, they kept the sound in the room how he liked. An independent feed was routed to the sound truck, and on this day no animals were killed in the making of *Hail! Hail! Rock 'n' Roll.*

They were deep in a snarling version of "Carol." He heard what these guys were capable of, and he knew they knew what he was capable of, and they weren't about to go out like a bar band. The insurance was Johnnie Johnson, steady as an owl parked on the little stage at Berry Park. And not just: they had invited drummer Ebbie Hardy from the early days to hang out and hear the rehearsals. The past was in the room.

Another argument unfolds, where Chuck angrily shows his student exactly how a guitar part is supposed to be played while glaring at Richards, who can't nail it the same way twice. They wanted the musicianship of those classic sessions? It was flooding back to Berry, he showed, and Richards's normal-sized hands struggled to follow his lead. "If you want to get it right? Let's get it right," Berry barks.

Charles Berry Jr., who saw a lot of it happen, believed that the fighting was contrived, a provocation meant to generate a great movie scene. "Bullshit!" declared Hackford. "Completely. I couldn't create that."[9]

A parade of celebrity musicians dropped off in Wentzville to attend rehearsals. Etta James was invited by Richards, and after Berry balked—complaining he didn't want a drug user in his home—Richards insisted she be kept. Julian Lennon and Robert Cray passed through, while Berry sat in a big couch up in front of the stage, then disappeared for hours to clear the gutters, repair a leaking roof.

Many visitors stayed at a small hotel a few miles away. One night Richards, Hackford, and Eric Clapton arrived, and the women behind the counter went nuts. Everybody stayed there for days, partying until the sun came up. Thomas Adelman remembers the quietness of the morning, when Bennett would sit at a little table in the coffee room, talking with him and Clapton.

"You know what my greatest love is?" Clapton asked one morning. "Fishing. I love fishing."

Twenty years earlier, Adelman noted, if you had walked through the Underground of London, you would have seen the graffiti proclaiming CLAPTON IS GOD. The man made "Layla" and "White Room," he made a science of the blues and was a major influence on dozens of guitar players. "It was funny to sit there and hear him talk about his passion in life," said Adelman. "Eric Clapton loves fishing."

THE PATTERNS OF EXCHANGE ASSERTED THEMSELVES AGAIN AND again in dealing with the crew. Bennett estimates Berry made around $800,000 from the production. They wanted him to rehearse? Pay him for a performance. Want to use his sound equipment for your film? That will be $500 cash. Need to pick up Linda Ronstadt from the airport? Another $500 for use of the car. It was aggravating, but Richards, seeing the panorama, found empathy. He viewed Berry's actions as the ingrained defenses of a man adrift in a world he had actually built—falling back on blunt, petty tools because they were the only way he knew to keep the world at bay.

Everything was building up to the shows at the Fox Theatre in St. Louis, the sparkling deco stage a few blocks from where the Club Bandstand once stood. Two sold-out performances were scheduled, and Berry outdid himself—requiring money up front before he would play the first show and demanding $25,000 more, cash, before the second. Bennett recounts scraping bills together from the box office and concessions, stuffing them into a paper bag, barging into Berry's dressing room, and throwing the bag at him. "It hit him in the head," she said.

It was a very long evening. Johnnie Johnson showed the world again what he could do, and Berry drove onto the stage in one of his Cadillacs.

"I remember on the night of the show, an hour or so before and the audience was filtering in, I stood in the wings with Eric Clapton standing next to me," said Adelman. Someone came out and was reading messages from officials and celebrities. "They read a telegram of congratulations to Chuck Berry that President Ronald Reagan had written. I remember Eric Clapton standing there going, 'Oh wow, that's cool!' I'll never forget how impressed he was by Reagan's telegram."

Richards had instituted a dress code for the musicians, forbidding the red pants and 1970s print shirts Berry was fond of. To see the show in person was tedium—there were frequent stops and starts for retakes, reloading of the cameras. Berry's voice was shot from so much rehearsing and a last-minute booking in Columbus, Ohio, that he hadn't mentioned to the filmmaker. Linda Ronstadt appeared in the first show, singing "Back in the USA." She left before the second show, a perfectionist irked by Berry's capricious key changes.

Some in the band found it a tough slog too. "After we did it, I didn't even want to see him again," drummer Steve Jordan said later.[10] But the finished evidence, the engagement of Berry and the band, the smile on his face, his own guitar playing, are evidence of how good a night it was.

After it was over, a friend of Johnnie Johnson's was sitting beside him backstage. Johnson had no way of processing the night, except as some kind of Hollywood goof—he was going back to driving his school bus the next weekday. "Johnnie doesn't know who Eric Clapton is, and he doesn't believe it when Keith Richards says he wants to take him on the road with him," said guitarist Tom Maloney.[11]

He kept kicking me under the table.

He kind of stands in for hundreds of guys more and less talented than him who were driving a bus. Only Chuck and a few others made it all the way.

It didn't even seem real to Chuck. He was having cake after two endless shows. The Cadillac was parked outside; soon the sun would be up. To well-wishers gathered around him, he sounded happy and stunned. "I had no idea I could grow to this, but the fame never reached the inside of me," he said.

"I never looked for recognition. I just wanted to see how far a person could go if he applied himself."[12]

20

SOUTHERN HOSPITABOO

THE SHOWS WERE OVER, BUT THE FILM WAS FAR FROM DONE. Postproduction work was underway in Los Angeles in early 1987, and Berry put up some of the crew at his Hollyridge Drive houses. He was in town too, recording new vocals for the film and dropping in unexpectedly on the guests.

The Hollywood houses were the worse for wear. The statue of the deer still side-eyed the street from on high. Inside was a casual mix of period decors—if it evoked golden-age Hollywood in the 1970s, now the main house was becoming more like Berry Park, mix-and-match artifacts, casual and freaky, people coming and going. Orange shag carpet.

In the living room was an exotic table. Plate glass was spread atop a bronze-sculpted naked woman who was lying on her back, her left arm and knees holding up the table top while her bare breasts pointed to the ceiling. A switch when toggled sent a hot, golden oil flowing down the statue's legs.

Thomas Adelman stayed there and recalled hearing the Cadillac approaching unannounced some midevening. "In walked Chuck and he'd sit at the kitchen table right across from me." "Oh hi, Chuck, how are you doing?" Adelman would ask. Berry wouldn't respond. "He'd just sit there while I continued my paperwork. He wouldn't say anything, just stare at me." Then he would walk to the back of the house and disappear for half an hour, and soon would drive away.

Jim Mervis, Stephanie Bennett's partner, was also at the house. Berry would call him sometimes, reminding him that if Mervis brought any women home, he should "remember where the video button was."

The washing machine broke and the laundry room flooded. Berry had made a big deal to Mervis about never allowing anyone in the house without first letting him know, so Mervis called him up to say they needed a repairman to come by.

"No, you're not. I forbid it," Berry made clear. "I'm going to be there Saturday to collect the rent anyway—I'll bring my tools."

Berry showed up with his briefcase—full of money stuffed in envelopes gathered from his various LA properties—and tools to fix the washing machine. Standing in a flooded room, he ripped the back of the machine off and touched various wires together, trying to jump-start it.

"And sure enough, a giant spark went bang," Mervis groans. "Chuck Berry gets thrown across the whole room and lands in a puddle on his ass, and for a split second we think he's dead. But the washing machine actually started; he got it to start. And then his eyes open, and he says, 'TOLD YA I could get it to start!'"[1]

The vocal lines he dubbed into the recordings of the St. Louis shows were expertly done, perhaps even saved the project, some say. The studio had given him final approval of the film. With all work finished, a viewing on a giant screen was scheduled at Universal Studios.

This, too, was a Chuck Berry production. Upon arrival he pulled a video camera from a bag and began recording the unreleased film. Studios really don't like unauthorized copying of their productions, and the projectionist shut off the film and ran down the stairs to tell the subject of the film that if he didn't stop recording, security would be called.

Unfazed, Berry proceeded with his recording. A small group met outside the theater with the studio's heads of business and legal affairs and a number of security guards. They detained the subject of the film, taking him to the Tower of London set on the studio lot. Somebody finally called the head of Universal and asked if the studio really wanted the headline in the next day's papers to be "Chuck Berry Arrested at Universal Studios." He was released.

The scene would have made a great end piece for a documentary. The real film ended with those triumphant homecoming shows and was released to acclaim in October 1987. It is a vivid testimony; Berry interferes with interviews of his wife and Francine Gillium, and in so doing blocks one kind of truth but shares another. On camera his patron and student Keith Richards says things about him that would be brutal if said about anyone else. The movie has stood ever since as a rare close-range encounter with one of the most complicated great American artists of the century.

"I had a huge admiration for him. I loved him," said Hackford.

> He was throwing me curves not because he was unstable, but because he wanted us to know "I'm in control here."
>
> He invited us into his life, and he ended up pushing us away because it was more than he expected. But he could handle it—he was proud and a bit diabolical. Chuck was a provocateur.

BERRY CLEARLY FELT PRIDE ABOUT THE FILM AS HE HANDED OUT free tickets around Wentzville. And he continued to want to tell his story his way. The same year *Hail!* came out, Berry finished an autobiography, one he had been working on with Gillium for some time.

Michael Pietsch was an editor with Scribner when William Krasilovsky and Chuck came to his office in 1985. Publishers had told Berry that he needed to work with a cowriter; Berry was absolutely clear that he wanted to write his own story. It was Pietsch's vision to let Berry tell it.

"He's a writer," Pietsch said. He found collaborating with Berry thrilling.[2]

> The purity of that voice, his insistence on the things he wanted to insist on, is what made it. He really cared about word choices. He's a poet and a writer, and he cared about the voice and worked on every line. I felt exalted to be involved with this.

Working with him was one of the great editing experiences of my life, an enormous delight and challenge.

Idiosyncratic about how he wanted to work, Berry insisted on Pietsch flying out to Berry Park to read material—he didn't want the manuscript to leave his sight. Pietsch asked if he could take some of the pages back to New York to show others at his publishing house. But Berry felt if that happened, the writing would turn up the next day in Denmark, like a bootleg recording.

The songs that had established him he viewed as distant triumphs, and though the editor drew some strong passages out of Berry regarding specific numbers, in general the music is not the heart of his book. It's more the story of an artist of ungauged energies in a world of work and money. He drifts through early trauma and abuse without a lot of judgment and turns a singular voice on everything he describes.

Far closer to his consideration was "what partner he had, what cars he owned," said Pietsch. These were signal moments. "They were the bright signposts that he remembered as important in his life."

It wasn't "the truth," but while veracity has its value, Berry offered something rarer, something alive and genuine and imbued with weird power. A reader can't fail to notice the strength of his hand, sharing what he insists is important and steering you away from the thing in the corner.

Like Taylor Hackford had done, Pietsch pushed him to talk in the book about what Berry called "the Indian girl story." Did he know her age? Was he guilty of what he had been charged with? Readers would call him evasive if he didn't write about it. And so Berry did talk about it, in his way.

"There was this amazing moment where things just dropped off and then he said, 'Okay,' and started writing," Pietsch recalls. "The first thing he wrote was that poem about their relationship. A poem: a form of obfuscation that is hard to argue with." It's a very odd poem, of regret for letting go of a girl he tried so hard to make disappear. He casts the relationship as a romance undone by her immaturity, a love he was sorry to leave behind.

His conversational voice made all kinds of experiences and wishes feel matter-of-fact when they were anything but. He's a string-puller, delighting in what he can wish into being. At one point late in the autobiography, he confesses to having "had a desire since childhood to be houseboy on a Southern plantation, preferably during the Civil War." He doesn't explain it, and the voice is so magnetic nothing feels off-limits.

Only later does the intensity of life register. The person in *Chuck Berry: The Autobiography* is on a crucifix of sexual and racial impulses he can't organize. An object of desire wherever he traveled, he could have all his fantasies fulfilled, though in exchange he would be hunted by police. That is one clear thread of his story: how to be a sexual being and survive.

A signal voice, making accommodations with a country; reaching an understanding. "He lets me be proud of what is special and distinct about the weird, terrible history of this country," said novelist Rachel Kushner.[3]

He was in a tradition of American voices (George Herriman, Slim Gaillard, Mark Twain, S. J. Perelman, Ed Ruscha) who sought to evade the limits of category by upending the way people spoke and insisting that their words were everyone's. Speaking themselves into the nation.

Chuck Berry: The Autobiography was a success, and the author hinted at other books on the way: one going deeper into the music, another expanding on his sex life and America's hypocrisy. No manuscript has ever turned up.

With a major film and a book out, it was a moment to bask in the acclaim. He tried. At the Hard Rock Cafe in Dallas in 1987, restaurateur Isaac Tigrett introduced him as "the living king of rock & roll" and unveiled a stained-glass portrait. Although Berry blew kisses to *Dallas* star Linda Gray, he declined to speak at the event. While in Dallas he announced he would soon put out a new album, one that might be his finale.

At Blueberry Hill, the St. Louis nightclub, there was a book party. A band played his music, and Berry even came up and jammed. Still, it was hard for him to have a good time.

"Chuck went to a different part of the room and sat and signed books. He was very cold and standoffish in a room full of adulation for him," said Tom Maloney, who played guitar in the band that day. "It was kind of sad that he wasn't receiving the love that was being given to him. I felt sorry for him." He sat by the wall, looking down and writing his name. Over and over.[4]

THAT FALL, THE CHRISTIAN BROTHERS DISTILLERS MOUNTED AN expensive ad campaign in major American magazines. Full-page photographs showed Berry wearing an orange shirt, vest, socks, playing an orange Gibson guitar. "C.B. in orange," the ad declared. "With a little CB brandy and orange juice, Johnny B. very good indeed."

His name appears nowhere on the page, and nationally syndicated newspaper columnist Bob Greene saw in this fact a hopeful sign for the country. Berry had become a given, an established American icon who needed no introduction to the widest audience. The columnist asked readers if they could envision a major brand using Berry even ten years before as their corporate symbol, describing how not long ago, Berry marked a dividing line between cultures, viewed as a dangerous upstart by the World War II generation.

Not to mention between races: Greene noted the rarity of a Black star being used to sell stuff, especially a figure like Berry, whose public persona "bordered on being downright nasty." That was no longer the case, and Greene saw a chance for America to transcend civil strife and intergenerational combat. Baby boomers were a full-fledged market force, he reckoned, and their icons were being embraced by all. "If the Baby Boom generation is finally mainstream America, then Chuck Berry is finally mainstream America, too."[5]

That was in September 1987. In December Berry was in New York and staying at the Gramercy Hotel when he was arrested for assaulting a woman: hitting her in the face, loosening several teeth, and causing five stitches and facial contusions. He failed to appear for two court dates, and in mid-June 1988, while he played two nights at the Ritz, she filed a lawsuit demanding $5 million. Berry pled to a reduced charge of harassment and paid a $250 fine.[6] The victim, who once sang in punk bands in New York, has declined to speak about that night.

In late June that year, Berry headlined a classic-car show in Deer Valley, Utah, as part of the Cherry Coke Fifties Festival.

Baby boomers had handed Berry a role to play, the Black Fonz, and thought they were doing him a favor. He had his own ideas about how to act. Neither role was all that sustainable.

At least in Wentzville the media could be avoided. A wing of
what had been the motel was kept heated and active for visitors.
Big screens in the main room broadcast raw satellite feed from news
channels. Pietsch saw three women living there: Yvonne Cumbie,
Francine Gillium, and an older blond woman. Two big dogs prowled
the grounds.

"He had boiled it down to the minimum effective support for his
life," said Pietsch. "He just seemed like a really tough entrepreneur
taking care of things best as he could with minimum outlay."

You would have had a hard time living in Wentzville in the 1980s
and not seeing Chuck. Kris Anglemyer first experienced the man at
home, a kid listening to the album *Chuck Berry's Golden Decade*. He
liked the rock & roll hits, but the blues of "Deep Feeling" and "Wee
Wee Hours" transported him. "I was four, and the hair on the back of
my neck stood up!" he said.[7] Then his older brother blew his mind by
saying Chuck Berry lived in their little town.

Anglemyer's mother worked in the local bank; she didn't like Chuck.
The bank manager had shared too many tales of parties at Berry Park in
the 1970s, stories she couldn't put aside. As for the town leaders, says
Anglemyer, "I'm sure they despised everything about Chuck Berry—
not just because of the parties but also because he was Black. And
not just Black—he was successful and Black. That was the double
whammy."

From time to time Berry went downtown to a café or diner, quietly
taking a meal. One restaurant where he liked to have coffee or a sandwich was the Southern Air, an important place in the life of Wentzville.
For a long time, Wentzville supported a handful of businesses servicing
the farms of surrounding western St. Charles County. But in 1934 the
Missouri State Highway Commission authorized a new Super Highway 40, which cut through the heart of town and connected Wentzville
to a new bridge pointing south toward St. Louis.

A couple of weeks after the highway and the bridge were dedicated
in the spring of 1937, a sharp Missourian named J. J. Harlan opened
the Southern Air Cafe and Garage at the intersection of highways 40
and 61. It put a jingle in his pocket as travelers from all around the
county parked in the huge lot out front. They came to savor the "wiener schnitzel ala Holstein," the steaks, and the catfish, and they kept
coming back.

The Southern Air was big—ten thousand square feet—and instantly a fixture in the county. It was a boldly southern establishment, with diners sitting in the Dixie Room and a banquet area named the Rebel Room. Missouri pols including Stuart Symington, John Ashcroft, and Christopher Bond all worked the crowds. And on Saturday nights after a University of Missouri football game, there might be twenty-seven hundred people celebrating at the Southern Air, because liquor by the drink was banned in Columbia, the nearest big city.[8]

Guy Fieri surely would find his way to the Southern Air were it still around today. This was roadside Americana, with a long counter in the main room where they featured Chuck's beloved strawberry short-cake on the dessert menu. And Berry, at least, did find his way to the Southern Air, back in 1944, when he and his high school buddies were driving toward Hollywood on their ill-fated road trip. Being Black, they were told to head around to the back door and take their food to go.

The Southern Air was off-limits to African Americans into the 1960s. Perhaps that was also one of the attractions to Berry, who owned a movie theater, a bar, and other properties in town. When the local paper the *Lakeshore Times* in 1988 reported that he had bought the beloved local landmark, they did it by revealing that a "controversial Wentzville resident" had "purchased the once-famous Southern Air restaurant."

A local quoted in the article sensed a defiant gesture in the purchase. "You know, he's always felt like an outsider here. Once on the Johnny Carson show, he said he had dined with royalty across the world, but in Wentzville, he was treated like a second-class citizen. That's why he's been buying up all kinds of properties in Wentzville—to show the world."

The restaurant was closed for remodeling through much of 1988, and when Berry reopened it in September, the Southern Air featured a music room where live bands played. He had attempted to get a liquor license, but previous convictions were an obstacle; Berry then leased the business to Gillium and she applied, but the county turned her down.

Anglemyer, fourteen that fall, jumped on his bike and rode over to the Southern Air. He saw Berry's black Cadillac Eldorado parked in the lot, the St. Louis Cardinals hat in the back window, and waited until the star came out.

He was in a good mood as Anglemyer explained his reason for waiting in the lot: he was looking for an after-school job. Come back tomorrow, Berry told him, and talk to Francine Gillium, who was managing the Southern Air. He gave Anglemyer the password to give Gillium: *Charles Edward Anderson Berry*.

Anglemyer came back the next day, filled out the paperwork, adding two years to his age, and got the job. He cleaned and set tables in the shadow of his boss.

The place had a retro spirit in Berry's renovation, which Anglemyer compared to Mel's Drive-In in *American Graffiti*. There were big screens on the walls playing *Ed Sullivan* episodes and documentaries about the Beatles.

Gillium sat at a table by the door, a greeter and gatekeeper. Patrons would come in and say they wanted to see Chuck.

"You would see him in a booth, puttering, staring or glaring or writing in a pad of paper nonstop," recalled Anglemyer. Gillium would shoot Berry a look, and then tell the patron, "Not now . . . this isn't a good time. Have some lunch and maybe he'll talk to you later."

Anglemyer got an impression of the man distinct from the jovial fellow locals saw pumping gas.

He was such a galvanic personality, you never knew what was going to happen. You never knew what he was going to do. I'd walk in, start sweeping the floor, and he was in a great mood, being his charming self with patrons. "How you doing?"

It could be five minutes later that he could be brooding in the corner. And not just brooding, it was like he was going to explode. It affected everybody around him. Nobody was joking around anymore—it was like you're a kid and your mother or father is gonna blow up.

He never heard Berry curse, but he yelled a lot, about things that didn't make sense. And he would throw things. "I'd say, 'What's going on?' 'Just be quiet now, be quiet,'" Gillium would say. Ten minutes later Berry would smoke a Kool cigarette, "and he would come through and once again be perfectly charming."

Three days after Anglemyer started the job, Berry seemed particularly angry, staring at the floor. He pointed at Anglemyer. The fourteen-year-old ducked into the kitchen.

"You, who hired you?" Berry thundered. "You did," Anglemyer answered.

He was wearing an apron, and the owner said, "Take the apron off." All the patrons were staring, and it got dead quiet in the Southern Air. "Come with me."

Berry paraded him through the restaurant. "Now, now!" Berry shouted when Anglemyer failed to take the apron off quickly enough. Then he yelled at Gillium to pay the kid for the work he'd done.

"It was brutal, and I was literally sobbing. This was the most humiliating moment of my life, and I didn't want to mention it to anyone. People would ask what happened—I would just say I quit."

He went to his bike, and Gillium gave him a big hug. "I don't know why Chuck gets like this sometimes," she said.

YVONNE CUMBIE MOVED INTO BERRY PARK IN THE LATE 1970S, after it had closed to the public. She came from Texas; she and her mother saw Berry play one night, and the two hit it off.

Berry offered Cumbie a job working as Gillium's assistant in Wentzville, and she jumped at the opportunity. "I was free, white, and way over twenty-one," she said. "I had my personal relationship and a business relationship with Chuck."[9]

He set up a home for Cumbie and her three kids. She says he was a "very generous, caring man" who helped her out a lot when her mother was dying of cancer. "My oldest daughter always referred to him as Big Daddy."

For some thirteen years, Cumbie says, she lived there and worked for Berry. When he went on the road she often traveled with him, "essentially being a road manager." "We were invited to Dolly Parton's house, 'Just take your shoes off, relax, and have some fried chicken!'" she laughed. Bo Diddley had a fear of being poisoned and did a lot of his own cooking. Diddley taught Cumbie's mom how to make sweet potato pie.

When the Southern Air opened up, Cumbie helped design the kitchen and bought equipment for Berry. The way she saw it, Berry worked hard and, far from being morose, had a great sense of humor. "He was so comical!" she said. "He was just what I would call a normal person, a husband, father, and grandfather. Just a good individual."

Diane remembers trips to Berry Park in the 1980s, when Cumbie and her mom and daughter were all living in trailers on the property, and Gillium was present and Diane as well. It could get pretty complicated, women vying for Berry's attention.

"I think people were like cars to him," Diane said. "If Yvonne is giving him trouble, he'll find"—and here she mentions the name of another woman in Chuck's inner circle—"to step in and pick up the slack when Yvonne isn't the pleasure she once was. If I start questioning him, he'll back off and find somebody else." Ultimately there was very little communication, Diane said, except in bed.

"Either he was a very complicated man, or there was no *there* there," she said. "I'm still really not sure which."

ONE NIGHT KRIS ANGLEMYER WAS IN BED WITH A GIRLFRIEND from the Wentzville area. He asked her if she wanted to see Chuck Berry perform that night in St. Louis.

"She says, 'No no no,' and she *loved* rock & roll," he said. He wondered, *Why not?*

She explained that she hated the man and told a story from years before. (Anglemyer says this conversation took place in the 1990s.) She and a couple of girlfriends had run into Berry somewhere in St. Charles County, and they ended up having group sex. "She said half this county slept with Chuck Berry, and she said it with such derision and passion," Anglemyer remembered.

The problem wasn't the act itself. It wasn't rape, not an assault. "It was fun, it was consensual. However, she said when it was over, when he was done, his personality changed." Berry went from being present and lighthearted to stony, menacing. They were all naked, and he abruptly ordered them to leave. "He became upset, glassy-eyed, and he said, 'Get out. Get out. Get your clothes and get out.' He wouldn't even talk to them. Just *leave now*." One of the women said, "Chuck, you're an asshole."

"But he threw them out. And then he said to my girlfriend, as she was crying, 'Now you know what it feels like to be treated like a n*****.'"

The women who had sex with Berry in St. Charles County, Anglemyer said, "are simple people. She was not worldly. She wasn't traveling around on the Led Zeppelin airplane." They were working at the market or a hardware store. They went to a party and Chuck Berry was there.

"I think he was comfortable where he lived, and wasn't gonna be comfortable at Hollywood parties," said Anglemyer. "Being a big fish in a small pond, he could get away with it. What's a clerk at a bank gonna say about it? These were regular people who willingly had these inter- actions. I don't know how you measure things like that."

In his autobiography, Berry had a magical term for what he expe- rienced in the South on those early tours in the 1950s, playing before some of the first racially mixed audiences he had seen in his life: *Southern hospitaboo*. A mash-up of *Southern hospitality* with *taboo*. The collision of sexually available white women and the threat to your life that sex with them promised.

In his mind, for the rest of his life, the racism he experienced and the sex he sought intersected. How could they not?" ("She paid her daddy's sins," Kendrick Lamar rapped in 2022. "Ancestors watchin' me fuck was like retaliation.")

Interviewer in 2008: "You ran into a lot of racism in the early years. What stung the most?"

Berry: "Well, I don't get so much of it now, because of the fame. I'm enjoying much of a free life, and people treat me way better than they did when I was young: I go to the casino, and women I don't even know speak to me, n-i-i-i-ce looking women. But I had noses turned up when I was young."[10]

An unusual answer for a question about discrimination. Racism and sexual freedom fused, moving with him wherever he played.

21

ROCK STAR

THE SOUTHERN AIR HAD SEEN NUMEROUS RENOVATIONS OVER its fifty years. A garage and filling station present at the beginning were later taken out, and a two-story addition arrived in 1963. An owner in the late sixties had turned the upstairs meeting rooms into his family living quarters. So it was not surprising that when Berry bought the restaurant, he had ideas of his own.

By the time it reopened in late 1988, the restaurant had a men's restroom in the basement adjoining a locker room for male employees. On the first floor was the women's restroom, connected to an area where female employees dressed. A room upstairs had been converted to Berry's office. Much of the work had been done by Berry's dad and his son.[1]

Over time, Southern Air employees became aware of certain other structural alterations their boss had made. Ron Balducci lived on a farm in Wentzville and played in a band that often performed at the restaurant. One day Balducci and three other employees came to believe that someone was secretly filming women in the restroom, after a lens had been discovered in a wall. Upon further examination, Balducci noticed there was ductwork missing from the women's restroom, and that a viewer in the locked room Berry maintained upstairs would be able to peer down into that restroom.

Balducci found Berry and confronted him with the device. Berry replied that the Southern Air was his restaurant and therefore he could do what he wanted there. The lens, he pointed out, was his property too.[2]

Word was spreading around town. Vincent Huck described himself as a private investigator, a DEA informant, a former black-belt Green Beret, and someone who helped out at Berry Park in 1989. Late that year, Huck said he received an anonymous call suggesting that he peek into a dumpster outside the Southern Air. As it happened, a local police officer simultaneously got a similar call, and the cops showed up too, observing as Huck pulled a cardboard box out of the bin. In the box were a stack of videotapes and photographs. With law enforcement watching as he reached into the trash bin, nobody could later say that Huck was stealing from Berry's residence.

On one of the tapes Vincent saw his wife, Hosana Huck, who was a cook at the Southern Air, being spied upon, he claimed, by Berry. Hosana quit, and on December 26 Vincent filed a lawsuit in St. Charles County.

Thus entered the public record the charge that Berry placed secret cameras around the restaurant. Vincent Huck's lawsuit stated that Berry had invaded Hosana Huck's privacy by recording her and other women. The allegation, it was instantly clear, was hugely damaging to Berry. Similarly detrimental was the lawsuit's claim that the tapes "were created for the improper purpose of the entertainment and gratification" of Berry's "sexual fetishes and sexual predilections." Huck's suit suggested that Berry got sexual pleasure from watching women defecate and urinate.

Berry's version of what happened was somewhat different from Huck's. He believed that while he was on tour in Australia in September 1989, Huck and others removed videos and photographs from his home without permission. In fact he said that a considerable but unknown stash of videos and photos from his private collection had been stolen from Berry Park. Vincent Huck had handed over the tapes in his possession to his lawyer, and in response to his suit Berry sued for the return of his property. These claims and others would be contested for several years to come.

But the damage was immediately done. On the day Huck filed his lawsuit, Berry shut down the Southern Air, and he would never open it again. Late that afternoon, word began to leak out that an explosive set of charges had been filed against Berry.

The lawsuit stirred his urge to fight. A week after it was first reported, Berry was on the *Tonight Show*, talking defiantly to Johnny Carson about the next book he was thinking about writing.

"It's gonna be more personal?" Carson asked.

"Oh yeah. I think it's time to get personal. I think everybody should, like, let it all hang out," Berry declared. He didn't acknowledge the charges, but he didn't exactly dispute them either. Rather, he had a point he wanted to make. "I mean, nothing's good or bad, by the way, I think—I think it's just different. Who's to say what's good? Who's to say what's bad? You know, it's just different."[3]

In January 1990, the new issue of the porn magazine *High Society* hit the stands. The cover promised, "SECRET SEX PHOTOS CHUCK BERRY NUDE! Johnnie B. Bad with All of His WOMEN." An insert boasted, "THE ONLY MAGAZINE WITH THE BALLS TO SHOW CHUCK'S BERRIES!" *High Society* featured four pages of the artist posing naked with various women. If these were among the pictures allegedly stolen from Berry Park, they weren't taken secretly. The relaxed shots with partners were likely meant to document how the two were enjoying each other's company and to ward off lawsuits by women claiming they had been unwilling sexual partners.

The invasion of Berry's privacy wounded him. It wasn't just the pictures; Berry sued the publisher of *High Society*, noting in an affidavit that in their brief biography of him, *High Society* had revealed he'd been incarcerated for a 1959 Mann Act violation. He complained that in the subsequent thirty years he "had earned a respectable place in society, had made many friends, and had established fruitful social contacts and profitable business contacts with many persons in the music industry who were not aware of those events."[4]

The photos exposed him to humiliation, embarrassment, and "racial hatred," he declared, specifically because "the nude women depicted with him in said photographs were all white." The result was negative publicity that made him "a possible target for assassination by white supremacists and similar violent extremists."

His choice of sexual partners, whatever else it displayed, posed a disturbance in the racial narrative, and he fully knew it. The threat noted in his lawsuit was one indication that others were indeed disturbed.

In Wentzville, a circle was tightening. At five a.m. on June 23, 1990, the St. Charles County Multijurisdictional Enforcement Group raided Berry Park. The affidavit requesting the raid claimed that Berry had been a major cocaine trafficker and that he had liquid assets of $36 million, $9 million of which was derived from selling cocaine. An informant told St. Charles officials that Berry had received a large amount of cocaine and would have it for ten days at Berry Park. The affidavit requested a search of Berry's home in order to find drugs, records of drug trafficking, and pornography. No cocaine was found in the raid. Two bags of marijuana and a chunk of hashish were seized, as were fifty-nine videotapes, pornographic slides and films, three weapons, and $130,000 in cash. Berry himself was not charged.

Complications ensued for the Multijurisdictional Enforcement Group. Beyond the problem that the basic premise for the raid—cocaine—had not been established, it was hard to explain how a guy who traveled by himself with just a guitar case was behind an alleged multimillion-dollar illegal enterprise. The affidavit revealed that Berry had been under surveillance since December 1988, and that he had a library of over a thousand pornographic videotapes and two thousand photographs.

Five days later, the St. Charles County prosecutor William J. Hannah gave a press conference where little more was revealed. A decision on charges, he said, would be coming soon. He may have thought he still had a winning hand now that he had Berry's videos and photos, but Berry wasn't about to play defense. He showed up at the press conference, "just to listen" he said, but when Hannah finished, Berry commanded the room, holding his own press conference and rendering the St. Charles County prosecutor as his already-forgotten opening act.

Denying he was engaged in drug trafficking, Berry said neither he nor anybody in his band used cocaine. He had been framed, he said, adding that whatever police took out of his home had been planted. He vehemently denied the prosecutor's claim that he was worth $36 million. "Don't I wish," he said.

Asked who he thought was behind the charges, Berry said, "I don't know. I just hope it's not any of the government officials, because it's hard to fight City Hall." As he walked back to his car, he was asked if the negative publicity hurt him. "All bad news can hurt," he said. But it also might help, given that Americans have a "fetish to look at someone's downfall."

Had he thought about moving to someplace more welcoming? "I was born here and, thank God, I can stay here," he said. Then he got in the car.[5]

The raid was covered in the local press, and the claims of his involvement in drug dealing made national news, and yet weeks later the prosecutor hadn't filed charges based on evidence collected during the June raid.

Finally, in mid-July, Prosecutor Hannah announced federal charges against Berry: one count for possession of more than thirty-five grams of marijuana, and three counts of child abuse. The latter allegation related to the bathroom videos; beyond the many women spied upon there were also children, and photographing nude children was defined as child abuse under Missouri law.

Worse trouble was coming. By mid-July, as many as two hundred women had filed a class action suit against Berry. A lawyer representing the women said they were in possession of videotapes of their clients undressing and using the bathroom on property owned by Berry, and they were suing him for invasion of their privacy and intrusion upon their seclusion. A judge had sealed the list of their names.

Given that tapes were almost certainly stolen from his house, then circulated among law enforcement and skin-magazine publishers, and now shared with defendants in a class action suit, Berry may well have had an idea that a group of people in St. Charles County was working to bring him down. The fact that Berry's attorney, Wayne T. Schoeneberg, had not been notified about the motion to seal the names of Berry's group of accusers and that no lawyer for the musician was present at the court proceeding emphasized the impression. "Has Charles Berry been stripped of all his rights?" Schoeneberg asked. "I'm amazed, it seems to be open season on Charles Berry."[6]

The possession and child abuse charges hung over Berry's head for months. Prosecutor Hannah was up for reelection in early November, and days before the vote Berry sued him for a "maliciously baseless" and political prosecution, demanding $600,000 in damages to his career and reputation. Four days later Hannah was voted out of office, and by the end of the month it was announced that a plea bargain had been achieved. Berry pled guilty to marijuana possession, accepting two years of unsupervised probation and agreeing to pay a $5,000 fine. The child abuse charges were dropped.

Hannah explained that the videotapes of children were problematic in a court proceeding because they hadn't come to him from the raid but from a confidential informant. Furthermore, intent would be hard to prove; Berry claimed he hadn't made the bathroom videos (though he said he edited them), so it could be argued the kids were "accidentally" recorded by "whoever" controlled the cameras.[7]

The feds had already walked away from Wentzville, having returned the more than $122,000 in cash they had removed during the raid three months before. "I expected it long ago," said Berry. "Of course, I wouldn't have expected it to have been taken in the first place."[8]

But while the overreaching prosecutor was in retreat, St. Charles County courthouse records show how the class action suit was proceeding. The secret videotapes made in the restroom and dressing area got the most attention. Berry was acutely aware of the damage done to his reputation—Berry noted that his bookings were down. Though he claimed he had not made the videos, there were now more videos and photographs in the record, and none of them were good for Berry's reputation.

Women who worked for Berry were coming forth and giving depositions regarding their own experiences. Three women who shared a mobile home at Berry Park said in a deposition that they willingly had been videotaped by Berry, and that they also had been secretly videotaped by him on other occasions. He had keys to their mobile home and was seen entering the property when they were not home.

There were secret recordings and consensual ones, in the bathroom and bedroom. Depositions quoted in court documents, for instance, tell the story of a restaurant employee who also lived in a trailer home Berry owned at Berry Park. She identified herself in footage using the restroom at Southern Air, videotaped without permission. Berry would meanwhile say in a deposition later quoted in public records that he had had sex with the same employee at the restaurant, but that in those instances she had given him permission to videotape. The records and interviews suggest abundant sex with women of St. Charles County, Berry then moving on to their mothers, daughters, friends.

Meanwhile, at least one angry person seemed dedicated to getting the word out, or at least to making some money. Allan MacDonell, an editor at *Hustler* magazine, remembered the day he got a call from a fellow introducing himself as Judge Burt Baker. The judge claimed to possess explosive images *Hustler* would want to publish, and for $1 million the magazine could have them. "This material is gonna knock the socks off the world," boasted the judge. A meeting was set up with the judge and two associates, who arrived at *Hustler's* offices in cowboy boots and denim.[9]

They settled in to watch a compilation of moments culled from various videos.

In his 2006 memoir, *Prisoner of X: 20 Years in the Hole at Hustler Magazine*, MacDonell says he figured out who was on the video screen. And in no time at all he was watching a naked woman poop into Berry's mouth. MacDonell couldn't believe it and insisted on rewinding so he and the house lawyer could confirm what they had seen. "Straight from the oven," the judge affirmed. Then the woman turned around and urinated into his mouth. According to MacDonell, "Chuck's Adam's apple bobbed with frantic urgency."

One of the visitors introduced himself as Vince Huck and told MacDonell that this was just a sample. "We come into a ton more of these tapes," Huck said. "We found these tapes out in the trash bin behind Chuck Berry's restaurant." The judge and Huck did most of the talking, and a quiet guy removed the tape and slid it into a backpack. *This is the one who carries the gun*, thought MacDonell.

A few weeks later, *Hustler's* lawyer got wind of Berry's charge that Huck had stolen tapes from his home, and MacDonell called the judge and said they must decline his offer.

In 2013, *Vice* published letters purporting to have been faxed to Bob Guccione Sr., publisher of *Penthouse* magazine, in July 1990. The unnamed writer said they had an exclusive interview with "the informant the DEA used to gather the evidence to raid Berry's estate last week." The writer said the informant had shared with them affidavits, police reports, and some of Berry's secret recordings, including video of Berry urinating into a woman's mouth, Berry eating a woman's feces, and other acts. "It's not possible to sum up what I saw on those tapes and this brief description doesn't do justice to what I actually witnessed. It is something I will remember forever."[10]

An article in *Spy* further spelled out the nature of some of the tapes circulating magazine publishing in 1990. Themetta Berry is quoted by author Mike Sager as saying, "I never read the papers and most of the time I don't know what's going on in Chuck's life. I've heard he's in trouble, and he knows I'll stand by him."[11]

Years later, when she was asked why she stood by him through it all, Themetta explained it simply. "It was love, and the way you were reared. You were brought up to respect your husband, respect your wife for better or worse when you're married. He was a rock star. I just thought that's the way it was designed to be. I accepted that that was his lifestyle."[12]

A defiant Berry seemed eager to fight back. Much about his current crisis was symbolized by his difficult relationship with Wentzville—as a stand-in for white America, for a life of fighting, for a life affirmed *through* fighting. He had been battling Wentzville since he bought property there, his son noted, and in 1991 he filed a brief to move the lawsuits women were filing against him for his secret videotaping to a federal court, because, Berry said, "a court-house inflamed with racial animus" in Missouri had "polluted the pool of potential jurors."

Berry called himself a victim who "has been and will be denied his equal civil rights because of the [county's] racially-motivated criminal prosecution." His treatment by those who ran St. Charles County, he declared, the efforts to besmirch his name, the theft of his property together amounted to "a race oriented economic lynching" targeting his ability to make a living. He was the victim here, and it all came down to money.

A federal judge dismissed the petition, writing that Berry had failed to prove he couldn't get a fair trial in Missouri. Berry then filed an appeal to the US Supreme Court. In 1993, a description of Berry's video archive had largely been kept out of the mainstream media. A case before the Supreme Court would have injected his sexual fetishes into that media. He did not care.

Amazingly, there was a moment when Berry almost seemed to be pleading for a chance to let the world hear more about what he called his "peccadillos"—the very habits that elsewhere he said brought him

humiliation, embarrassment, and hatred. On February 23, 1993, the
US Supreme Court denied his appeal without comment and quite possibly spared him the punishment he seemed to crave.[13]

The class action suit and several others filed by women who
believed they had been videotaped by Berry crawled on for several
years. Berry finally agreed to settle them in 1995. In a queasy spectacle that opened the curtain on the scandal, a screening of all known
toilet videos was staged in a hotel meeting room. A public notice
announced that anyone who wanted to claim they were victimized by
Berry should show up at the hotel on the specified date. If a woman
saw herself on the screen, she could claim a portion of the fixed
settlement.

Mitch Margo, one of the lawyers who represented Berry, called
it "the *worst* moment of my legal career. We rented a hotel ballroom
out in Wentzville, I believe it was a Holiday Inn, and on a loop in
the ballroom a tape played a recording of all the women who were
filmed when they went into the Southern Air restaurant." When a new
woman came onto the screen, a numeral appeared at the bottom of
the videotape.[14]

"And any woman who wanted to could come in and sit down in the
room, and if she saw her video up on the screen, fill out the form, write
down that number, hand it to us, and she got part of the settlement."
Berry had already agreed to a sum. This was a means to close off all
further discussion.

In 1995 the internet was still young, and sex tapes and porn had yet
to enter everyday life the way they soon would. Chuck Berry got lucky
in that regard. It's true that grainy videos of Berry, or someone looking
a lot like him, are available on the internet, but he escaped the level
of public shame that would have been his just a few years later. And
he escaped the potentially greater shame and punishment that a civil
proceeding before a jury might have exposed him to.

"I should tell you, the final settlement was not substantial," said
Martin Green, one of Berry's attorneys, happy years later. "After you
deduct the legal fees the plaintiffs' lawyer was seeking, there wasn't
much left to distribute to the plaintiffs in the class."[15]

A settlement of $830,000 was divided among the largest group of
women who had sued. Though some claimants received as much as
$17,000, most in the end received $5,000. Nonetheless, they were
depicted as money-grubbing women by some in the media. Berry was

reported to have spent $1,225,000 altogether to settle several suits from women related to the bathroom tapes.

After that the full depositions and all the videotapes were put under seal. "I remember thinking, this is a great settlement for Chuck Berry," said Margo.

"He settled it basically because it was costing more money in [lost] bookings and bad publicity," said Schoeneberg. The videos Schoeneberg saw, he says, mostly showed the tops of women's heads, and he thinks the alleged victims were just looking to make money.

"It was a form of legal extortion. And it happens to so many stars."[16]

Berry spent the early 1990s focused on the fight. And when the fight was over, he shut the door on the issue and never spoke of it again.

"After that we pretty much went back to business as usual. It never came up, we never talked about it," Schoeneberg said. "It was in the past, and he moved on."

Few interviewers dared ask Berry about his Mann Act violation; nobody ever brought up the toilet tapes. Both times, Berry abused his power and by many measures did bad things to people who trusted him. And both times, Berry was victimized by racist forces—in this case, the white, clubby powers in St. Charles County who received videotapes that were almost certainly stolen and tried to use them against Berry because they just didn't like his kind.

Silence prevails: presumably the women who settled their suit with Berry signed an agreement to never talk about the matter. But their voices speak through public records in the county courthouse available to anyone who walks in.

Perhaps there is value in considering the words of one woman who discovered she was videotaped and wrote the judge in the matter to protest the settlement. "I know that I am on the tapes taken at his restaurant. This film was made without my knowledge or consent. It is degrading, embarrassing and a violation of my rights. It has caused a great deal of emotional stress and I consider an offer of approximately $2,000 to be utterly ridiculous," she wrote.[17]

"Being filmed has affected my outlook towards all men, including my husband of many years. Because of the tape, I find myself unable to trust any man and feel as if I've been used with no consideration given to me even by my own lawyer. I am tired of being victimized by men and will find no peace of mind until the responsible parties realize their wrongdoing."

GOING "BACK TO BUSINESS AS USUAL" MEANT PLAYING AT THE
grand opening concert for the Rock and Roll Hall of Fame in
Cleveland's Municipal Stadium in September 1995. Dylan, Aretha,
Iggy, Little Richard, and Al Green were there. Berry was asked to start
the show, playing "Johnny B. Goode" with Bruce Springsteen and the
E Street Band. Almost seven hours later Berry came back and finished
off with a "Rock and Roll Music" in which he kept changing the key,
baffling an increasingly frazzled E Street Band, then duckwalking off
the stage and leaving the band playing six different scales.

Back to business also meant mundane tasks like collecting rent on
his Los Angeles properties. In 1993 the main Hollywood Hills house
was rented out to two young women from Orange County, Lee and
Alice.[18] They had worked out a good deal with him on the big house
because it needed so much work. Squatters had been living there in
recent years, glass and garbage scattered all over. The concrete deer on
the front lawn had broken legs with rebar poking through.

"It was definitely spooky," said Lee.

When Berry played Southern California he invited his tenants to
come with him. At a show in a hotel in the City of Orange, "he was
dressed in this 1970s outfit, and the crowd was basically a lot of white
guys busy drinking beer out of plastic cups," said Alice. Then they
went back to Lee's room and he played a cassette of songs he was
working on with his daughter Ingrid. "He really wanted us to listen to
it with him. I can't say I fell in love with it," she said.

"I'd always heard stories about Chuck in his heyday, all the sexual
stuff. I don't know if that was true or if it was spawned by racist stuff, I
just don't know," said Alice. "He was obviously so powerful as an artist
and a sensitive creator," she said slowly. "We all can become . . . so . . .
damaged along the way."

Something damaged was on view. "I didn't feel safe around him, I'll
tell you that much. He was mercurial, but by the same token I liked
him. He was charming."

The landlord was powerful. He once rounded up Lee's boyfriend
to work with him on the cracked, palm-frond-filled swimming pool. "It
meant a lot to my boyfriend to be cleaning out the pool with the father
of rock & roll," she said.

They drove to a hardware store and bought muriatic acid to scrub
and disinfect the pool. After he poured it into a siphon, Berry jumped

down into the pool and sprayed the acid all around. Breathing muriatic acid can make people vomit; it blurs vision and leads to dizziness. Berry, engulfed in a cloud of acid, remained unaffected, the boyfriend said. And smiling!

The boyfriend fell to his knees, breathing through a rag.

"Go on," Berry told his helper. "Get your little young lungs out of here."

"His essence seemed superhuman," said Lee. "He seemed kind of ageless, this strange person who could emerge from the depths."

One time he arrived unannounced, showing up as the tenants were throwing a big party. Wandering in as hundreds of people flipped out. *Is that Chuck Berry?*

"I feel like the house was possessed in negative and positive ways, and the soul of the house would throw a party that had nothing to do with the inhabitants," said Lee. "But he came to the party and asked to spend the night."

She had nightmares.

It was a dream about getting molested. It was very feverish and strange and real.

I think Chuck inspired that dream. It was because he was sleeping in the next room. . . .

That night he asked me if he could borrow a headscarf to keep his hair up, and all I had was, like, a handkerchief or bandanna, and I gave him my bandanna when my boyfriend and I were in bed. The next morning at six he knocks on my bedroom door. My boyfriend's like, "What the hell's going on?" Chuck said it was just to give the bandanna back.

Alice went out to dinner one night with him on Hollywood Boulevard. "I can't remember if he paid, but I remember being in his car, a Cadillac, and he drove wherever he felt like, in the moment." She laughed uninhibitedly. "He was swaying and weaving and I remember how it felt, the weaving and other cars honking, people leaping out of the way. I just thought, 'If we make it to the restaurant it will be a miracle.' Like he owned the whole road—I don't know if it was his magic power or what, but somehow he had that presence and we made it. But it wasn't an entitled thing, it wasn't like haughtiness or something, not at all. It was almost unconscious, if that makes any sense."

"He had the charisma of a star if anybody did," Lee agreed.

A shadow thrower. Visitor to your dreams. John Henry on a down-bound train. It was said he did not wash for weeks and smelled terrible. He exhaled muriatic acid.

And down the stairs of the main house on Hollyridge Drive, into the basement, was a shrine from a former lover. A velvet painting of Berry, candles, photographs.

He was "an energy force," said Alice. "He blasted in, and you had to wonder what boundaries were possible."

"LISTEN," QUINT DAVIS SAID. "THIS IS THE NIGHT CHUCK BERRY died in my arms."[19]

Davis managed Berry on two European tours. "We were playing this theater in Paris, and these crazy, I mean crazy, guys in the front were jumping up and doing bad stuff. Security should have done something, but they were left unchallenged—left to get worse."

Davis doesn't remember what they did to cause tear gas to be fired at them in the venue. "When the clouds went up, *everybody* in the theater was screaming and running for the exits. Chuck fell on the floor and was as stiff as a board. I went to him, put my arms around him."

He was rigid, his face not moving, eyes closed. "Oh man, this is really not good. The band was God knows where. They ran off." Berry got up, bottled water running down his face, his eyes glowing red.

"He plugged in his guitar and started playing the most maniacal rock & roll riff you can imagine," said Davis. He yelled at Davis to soak a towel in water and lay it across the piano; as Berry played guitar he would roll his face on the piano top.

French patrons outside were crashing into one another and brawls broke out, while fans inside were still pouring out of the hall headfirst into a riot. Suddenly bystanders outside are hearing this loud electric guitar throwing Chuck Berry riffs from the far side of the clouds of gas. They are pushing to get back in.

"It wasn't dedication," said Davis of Berry's effort. "It was chaos."

22

THE APOTHEOSIS OF CHUCK

THE KING OF PERSIA WAS RUNNING OUT OF TIME. LIFE WAS SHORT and its purpose elusive. His Eminence looked for meaning, a message from above. Who wouldn't?

Chuck loved that poem. When the sound went out in Memphis, Tennessee, or Cairo, Illinois, when he wanted to impress the crowd, Berry would recite the rhymed lines he had memorized long before. This was not expected.

The poem was the tale of a weary Persian leader who had seen it all, spent it all—the gems from Samarkand, figs and wine and the women who threw themselves at him. The ruler indulged in the spoils of life, yet nearing the end in the poem, he remained grounded as he recalled the maxim engraved on his golden ring: "Even this shall pass away."

The poem has sometimes been mistaken for "Ozymandias," by Percy B. Shelley. Published in 1818, "Ozymandias" was a greatest hit of Romantic poetry, describing a desert-trekker who comes upon a fallen statue honoring a once-great man, a provider, a shaper of history now just a rock pile on the far side of history's tracks.

"Ozymandias" surely influenced the actual poem Berry recited to audiences, which was Theodore Tilton's "The King's Ring," published in 1866. Tilton was Travis Tritt to Shelley's Dolly Parton, a stick who

established an undeniable bond with his audience in his moment.[1]
The king of Tilton's work lives long enough to scrutinize an idol built
in his image:

> Gazing at his sculptured name,
> Asked himself, "And what is Fame?"
> Fame is but a slow decay,
> Even this shall pass away

That last line repeats throughout the poem, and Henry Berry would
recite it to the family in the Ville, drilling into his son a skepticism of
praise and reward. The adult Chuck held on to it like an inflatable vest.

On his 1979 album *Rockit*, Berry recorded Tilton's poem as "Pass
Away," reciting over a slow bump and roll. He went at it again in 1986
for a scene recorded, but not used, in *Hail! Hail! Rock 'n' Roll*. Robbie Robertson had briefly been hired as the film's musical director
and was filmed sitting with Chuck at Berry Park, thumbing through a
scrapbook of memories. The pictures are yellowed and burned, frag-
ments taped to the pages. Looking over his own life, photos from
his first tour, his boyhood library card, the first combo, the singer
mellows. Berry reaches back for Tilton's rhymes, summoning them at
length, even daring fate by revising the poet's final line: "even *I* shall
pass away," he acknowledges, as Robertson gently strums a guitar
behind him. If *Chuck Berry* could pass away, perhaps the universe
really *was* like dirt.

Another powerful figure, however, was very much alive and present in St. Louis: the Veiled Prophet of Khorassan. He was the mystic
persona from the same part of the world that gave us Tilton's king, the
same imaginary orientalist character from so many nineteenth-century
tales. The Veiled Prophet himself was popularized in a nineteenth-
century poem. He was a literary figure from the East, repurposed by
Gilded Age St. Louis boosters to organize civic society and honor the
powerful earthly potentates of the Gateway City. He could live anywhere, but he chose to come to St. Louis every year and bask in the
love he got from the community.

A wealthy civic leader was selected annually by secret ballot to don
the exotic costume of the Veiled Prophet and represent his values. The
prophet was greeted at an invitation-only high-society ball.

Not everybody in St. Louis loved the prophet. In 1972, while Berry was on tour singing "My Ding-A-Ling," St. Louis protesters crashed the Veiled Prophet Ball. Swinging down from the balcony of Kiel Center, two activists objecting to the racism of the event stormed the stage and—*gasp*—tore the mask off the head of the Veiled Prophet, revealing him to be Tom K. Smith, vice president of the Monsanto Company.[2]

A secret protest had become front-page St. Louis news. It would be years after the unmasking of the Veiled Prophet before African Americans would feel welcome at the festivities. In 1979, Black men were allowed to join the organization. A few years later members created a truly public event, the VP Fair, in the shadow of the Gateway Arch. The front page of the *Post-Dispatch* on July 4, 1982, showed the view from the fair's stage: Chuck Berry, guitar held over his head, waving, along with his daughter Ingrid, to a crowd half a million strong.[3]

Berry was singing from Laclede's Landing, the spot by the Mississippi River where a French trader founded St. Louis in 1764. Within a stone's throw in the mid-nineteenth century was the office of the biggest slave trader in the region. Surrounding that building was a neighborhood where freed Blacks had lived. And Berry could have pointed from the stage to the Old Courthouse, the landmark where Dred Scott and his wife, Harriet, sued for their freedom in 1847 and from whose carved steps the enslaved were auctioned off.

The potentate had come a long distance to be with the people of St. Louis. He had seen plenty, and the folks who were closest to him knew his story best. They had been with him since before there was rock & roll; they followed the Mann Act trials and knew when he was freed. They stuck with him through the hits and the slow years, chuckling at "My Ding-A-Ling" and smiling at the triumph of the tribute shows at the Fox Theatre. They knew the gossip about the cameras and creepy home movies. Chuck had made and spent millions, built a country home and amassed a collection of memories and regrets, hit records and videotapes. In Wentzville, the barn was full of Cadillacs.

> *Then, in answer to the King,*
> *Fell a sunbeam on his ring,*
> *Showing by a heavenly ray—*
> *"Even this shall pass away."*

A TRIM POP-CULTURE FANATIC AND SHREWD BUSINESSMAN, JOE Edwards opened his restaurant Blueberry Hill in 1972. Blueberry Hill had a happening jukebox that Edwards took good care of, switching out the records every two weeks, typing the title strips himself. He was building a shrine to the rock & roll era, and Edwards's Pez, comic book, and bobblehead collections all ended up on display in the gentrified Delmar Loop.

Like the guy whose records he packed the jukebox with, Edwards was born in St. Louis and had never left. In 1980 he asked Chuck's permission to sell Chuck Berry Beer, with the star's image on each can. It was years before microbrews were a thing, and Edwards offered good money to make it happen. He didn't earn much on the deal, but it had a huge impact on both men going forward.

Edwards would pick up Berry, and they would go out to hear music together. The plain-speaking fellow in Hawaiian shirts and longish hair was good at keeping strangers away from Berry, giving him his space. "I never in a million years figured I'd be best friends with Chuck Berry," Edwards said. "Outside his family, he was very, very guarded. We led separate lives. He did his thing and I did mine. Our friendship evolved that way."

They would watch a Cardinals game on TV or go for a drive. The latter experience could leave a mark. "Wow—it was white-knuckle times," Edwards chuckled. Once, on a trip to the West Coast, they went the wrong way on a Los Angeles freeway. "Maybe eleven lanes of traffic at seventy miles an hour, and all those cars getting closer and closer, and he says, 'Oh you know what? I want to go *this* way,' and he went across all the lanes, down the gully, and did a seventy-mile-an-hour U-turn with all those cars going *clunk*." The man who wrote all those songs about freedom on wheels was a terror on the road.

"I was really surprised that he lived as long as he did," Edwards said, shaking his head. "But his reflexes were good. Maybe if you play the guitar that good the skill translates to other kinds of things."

Berry trusted Edwards, and over the years those who wanted to do business with Chuck checked in with Edwards about what approach worked best. But to Edwards, the truth was simple: Just be straight with the guy. Keep the proposal succinct, but don't leave anything out. Chuck would say either yes or no, but if he said yes he would honor the agreement.

"He was that easy to deal with and that difficult to deal with," said Edwards. "People aren't used to 'a deal's a deal.'"

One night Berry was at Edwards's house, reminiscing about his early nightclub days. He said something like, "Man, I'd like to play a place the size of the ones I started out in," and right then they both looked at each other and said, "Let's do it!" It was 1996.

At first, Edwards fixed up a dart room in Blueberry Hill, and Berry played there. Soon, though, Edwards bought the building next door and created a room with Berry in mind: he called it the Duck Room, in honor of the duckwalk. Berry's shows became both legendary and nothing special. That was the curiosity of St. Louis, Edwards says: locals took for granted his monthly appearances until outsiders started flying in to see him play a room that only held 340 people. Between 1996 and 2014, he played 209 shows at Blueberry Hill. Berry felt comfortable there with a stable band featuring his son Charles Jr. (who played guitar) and Ingrid singing and playing harmonica.

He liked to eat chicken wings and french fries before a show. On summer nights he'd park behind the club and sit in his car listening to the ball game, then slide through the back door right at nine o'clock.

Before the concerts became a national story, tickets weren't available in advance; you just showed up a few hours early and bought one at the door. There was a dressing room behind the stage, and at showtime the band would vamp while Berry was still backstage, playing one of his classic guitar intros—you'd hear him long before you saw him make a dramatic entrance.

Sometimes Johnnie Johnson dropped in on the group, and on those occasions Berry bore down on his playing. Musicians passing through town sat in, and family and friends watched him up close, the way they had a long time ago. There was nothing ambitious about the shows, and nothing forced. He didn't haze the band. Not since the Cosmopolitan had he had anything like this: a home stage.

BECAUSE OF *HAIL! HAIL! ROCK 'N' ROLL*, PEOPLE FOUND OUT Johnnie Johnson was still alive.

He played before big crowds with Eric Clapton and the Kentucky Headhunters. He made some money and stopped driving a bus. Along the way, Johnson grew to understand that he deserved more recognition for his role on those early recordings than he was getting.

Keith Richards, who continued playing with Johnson, was telling him, "These songs should really say Berry/Johnson." Other people encouraged him to do something about it, and in 2000 Johnson did: he sued Berry for coauthorship credit on more than fifty songs composed during their time working together. Saying he had been denied cowriting credit for "Roll Over Beethoven," "Nadine," "Back in the USA," and many more, Johnson requested unspecified damages. Berry, he said, had taken advantage of his alcoholism and his lack of understanding of how the music industry worked.

For several hours of videotaped depositions given in 2002, Berry and Johnson sat in law offices and explained how they met, where they played in the early days, and the nature of their interaction. Most of all they talked from each of their perspectives about their work process and the way their records were made. Sometimes they demonstrated on a piano and guitars in the room.

"The best day *ever* for me," said attorney Mitch Margo, who in this lawsuit represented Johnson, "was the day when we had a mediation and we all sat around the table to discuss whether we could resolve this case. To be sitting there, listening to Johnnie Johnson and Chuck Berry talk to each other about how they made these songs was the best day of my legal career."

Berry could easily have been expected to be ornery, but instead he was reflective and took pains to give nuanced, circuitous answers. His empathy for Johnson came across to those in the room, as did his desire to avoid parting with his own money or the sole composing credits.

The star was asked by Johnson's lawyer, "Do you believe as you sit here today, that Johnnie Johnson . . . played any part in creating the songs that we've said he did?"

"In a roundabout sense, I suppose he did," Berry responded. "I don't know, but I suppose he did; but in a legal sense, no, because I consider myself having written any songs that is out now with 'Chuck Berry' on it, because that's the way it went; I composed it and I did it."

Johnson referred to Berry's Mann Act incarceration only as the time when "Chuck was away." "Neither one of them were full of hate," said Margo. "I don't think Johnnie Johnson was capable of it."

Berry's attorney Martin Green recalled deposing Johnson. Green was used to questioning people who were not happy to be there and showed their displeasure. But when Johnson was done being quizzed, he stepped over to Green and offered him tickets to an upcoming show. "There's no way to say anything but that he was a wonderful guy."

According to the one person unrelated to the case but with access to the depositions and related documents, attorney Timothy J. McFarlin, what comes across from their full comments is that the music was a product of a collaboration. However it was legally defined, *they* looked at the songs as something they had made together. Green said Berry offered Johnson a sizable settlement. Johnson, though, was fixated on recovering the acknowledgment he hadn't received for decades, and fought on. But shortly before a jury trial was to begin, a judge ruled that the statute of limitations had expired; without ruling on the merits of the case, the judge declared that Johnson had waited too late to file his lawsuit.

Johnnie Johnson managed to get some solid love in the last years of his life. He worked on the book *Father of Rock & Roll: The Story of Johnnie "B. Goode" Johnson*, published in 1999, and recorded a number of times, including a 2005 session with Styx in the Chess studios. Shortly after, he died of pneumonia and a kidney ailment in St. Louis.

In 2019, his hometown of Fairmont, West Virginia, put up road signs to commemorate what the regional chamber of commerce called two "local legends": Johnnie Johnson and pepperoni rolls. In reporting the honor, the *Fairmont News* said the obvious: "While pepperoni rolls are now a household name . . . the same is unfortunately not true about Johnnie Johnson."[4]

AROUND 1996, JOHNSON COULDN'T MAKE THE BLUEBERRY HILL gig, and Edwards called up a local pianist named Robert Lohr to fill in. Lohr and Berry hit it off and would play over two hundred shows together. If a new sideman was alert they might just stick around, and Lohr paid attention—he knew better than to ask about the past.

"Chuck didn't want to talk about the old days, he just didn't," explained Lohr. "He wanted to talk about today and what we were doing tomorrow. He didn't care about the past—he knew what he did, all the tidbits of information. He really couldn't give a shit."[5]

Lohr traveled with Berry to Europe and South America. In 2008 they were booked for four shows in Brazil. Upon arrival, the star noted that the rental cars weren't the contracted Mercedes S-class vehicles, they were Toyotas, and he sent Lohr, who was an attorney when not playing piano, to extract the penalty from the promoter, a blond fellow in Armani named Fabio. Fabio came through, Lohr handed the cash to Berry in the hotel lobby, and the show went on that night.

The next day they were in Chuck's room having lunch when Chuck related a phone call he'd just gotten. "Chuck said, 'Hey, did you guys hear about Fabio? They found him last night shot and stuffed in his trunk.'"

"It was a mob hit," said Lohr. "He had $25,000 on him and they didn't even take the money, they just shot him in his suit." His face was lacerated, and the speculation was he had been shot in the back of the head.

"And the very next thing Chuck tells me, he smiles and goes, 'Well, I'm just glad we got our business disagreement taken care of *beforehand*.' That's the first thing he says! I told him, 'Man, Chuck, you are a cold-blooded dude.'"

Travel overseas inspired creativity. In July 2008 Berry was paid $363,000 ahead of time for twelve dates across Europe. But the promoter claimed in a 2012 federal suit that he had bailed on three of the shows and pocketed money that belonged to the promoter.

Lawyer Martin Green remembered the judge in the case suggesting what he called "an unusual move. She said to me, 'Martin, do you think maybe if I privately met with your client and I wore my black robe and I told him he's gotta settle?'" Green said she could try, but she didn't know his client—he wouldn't budge.[6]

After their meeting the judge came out and announced that the trial would start on Monday. Then, on Sunday, Berry and the promoter settled for a figure, one on Berry's terms.

But it was not done, not yet. In the courtroom Berry claimed he didn't realize he had to pay on the spot and was waiting on some money that wouldn't come through until four days from then.

"The truth is that Chuck kept bank accounts in amounts you would never believe, and could have written a check that day for any amount," said Green. But it was his little fun that he was having. He'd stood up to a judge who thought she was going to order him to settle, and then fucked with the promoter. He was paying them "almost what they wanted," said Green, but they would have to wait four days for their money.

"And four days later he showed up at my office with a bank check for them."

EDWARDS EXPANDED ALONG THE DELMAR LOOP AND HELPED create the St. Louis Walk of Fame, with sidewalk markers commemorating local cultural figures, including Maya Angelou, Curt Flood, Charles Lindbergh, and Phyllis Diller. In 2011 he helped raise over $100,000 for an eight-foot-tall statue of Berry. The effort to celebrate a local figure who changed the world was controversial. Protesters presented the St. Louis City Council with petitions signed by more than a hundred citizens asking the city to reconsider; critics at a council hearing called Berry a felon and an abuser of women. But in the end the statue went forward, and in July 2011 it was unveiled—a towering presence that mixes with the passing crowd, its feet planted right on the street. Sculptor Harry Weber asked Berry which era the statue should depict and was told the mid-1950s, when he had long, curled hair and sometimes performed in a bow tie and tuxedo.[7]

The statue was set up at a parking lot on the day of its unveiling, the afternoon sunlight backlighting the bronze work, the scene resembling a Renaissance painting. Said Weber, "It was like the apotheosis of Chuck." The statue shows him ready to spring, hunched and primed to duckwalk down Delmar Boulevard.

What many noticed, standing thirty feet away at the Blueberry Hill shows, were the man's hands: enormous steel-driving tools. "It was like he was playing with a baseball mitt—he was such a big guy and his hands were just gigantic, those long fingers," said Kris Anglemyer. "Until I watched him at Blueberry Hill, I could never figure out how in hell he was playing on what seemed like five different frets. But that Gibson he played looked like a toy pressed against his body."

The hands are what one notices most about the statue as well. Weber worked long and hard on them. "They are the stars of the piece. Often I and other sculptors exaggerate the size of the hands because they are so expressive." He said he studied Auguste Rodin's sculpture *The Burghers of Calais*, and how the hands of the villagers are markedly longer than they would be in real life. "They are way, way larger just because they work so well that way," Weber said.

"I didn't have to do that with Chuck."

Berry grew up in a family that believed in being "good with your hands"; his father worked into his seventies as a carpenter.

His father believed that physical labor defined work, and work defined life. Chuck grew up hearing all about it too. Showing off his own carpenter's shed to film director Taylor Hackford, as the camera panned across a wall of tools, he said with tangible pride, "I know every one of them. Dad and I, we used to do renovating work and construction work all over the city of St. Louis. I know what I'm doing when it comes to carpentry, repair work, all my life. . . . I like to take care of things, this is really me. But, I don't know, music took its precedence and I learned how to play guitar instead of hitting a nail."

Vijay Iyer is a pianist, composer, and teacher who thinks expansively about how music is made. Others call the music he makes jazz, though he objects to the term and prefers to call it "creative music." When he talks about music, he sometimes reaches back to describe the touch and mechanics of those he has learned from, including pianists Geri Allen and Andrew Hill. He talks about their hands.

"There's nowhere else except the hands—that is the interphase between the instrument and the person," he explained. "But then there's all this stuff *behind* the hands and how the hands work."[8]

Behind them is "the heritage of African American music, part of which is storytelling." Stories are a way of organizing a shared past, but in their telling they carry the mark of individual lives, personal histories, the bodies of the players.

"What needs to be highlighted is that in Black music in particular, of the African diaspora and in the US context that we are all very familiar with . . . is that we hear people through the sounds they foreground." Iyer contrasts what happens in jazz, blues, and other forms with the Western classical music tradition, which sets up a hierarchy emphasizing the experience of the composer far more than that of the player. The soloist becomes a vessel for the composer's vision rather than their own.

To be "more than just bodies," as Iyer puts it, "is to reinsert and reassert this aural component of Black life in the United States which existed under dire, horrific, violent circumstances." To bring the past into the current moment, and to bring it to life through improvisation. That becomes part of what is asserted when Andrew Hill at the piano, or Chuck Berry at the guitar, puts his body on the line. "What is the sound of someone asserting their personhood in the context of their personhood being legally denied or revoked?"

Always present, Iyer says, is "an insurgent quality and a resistance—it becomes more than just 'bodies are present and I hear them moving'; these are defiant human beings." Flesh becomes more than flesh. History is shared in a flash.

Iyer, like others, hears in Berry's guitar playing the tradition of boogie-woogie piano. Johnnie Johnson and the players he learned from used their left hands, the lower notes, to convey locomotion, a groove that carried the essence of walking, dancing. The right hand in boogie-woogie raised the human voice, the melodic frequencies that were the provenance of breath. There was the whole body in motion coming through Chuck's hands.

A boogie-woogie pianist could groove with their left and speak with their right. And he points out that Berry did the same things through the guitar. "With those big [alternating] open fifths to the sixth bass lines that would evoke a certain quality of movement—with his hands he would conjure the feet. But he could also riff and play lines that evoked the voice—a cry, a wail. I think his ability to move between those two poles set his field in a certain way. 'This is *all* of me; this is how I move.'"

Music brought the parts of the body together, and brought bodies together in flux: *this is how everybody moves*. The way Iyer talks about it, to play music for people in a room—to be in communion with your band and audience—is to "create a bond among us; it reminds us we're not alone." Surely there are endorphins involved. "All I can say is I do know I'm doing it—there's a ritual power that we are able to do this together and gather and behave in a very different way, a way we wouldn't if we were just walking down the street, say. We are engaged in a unified experience built around shared synchronous movement. In pulse. It's extraordinary when you think about it—that we can do it."

Extraordinary to think of the voodoo that happened when folks heard an electric guitar with their feet for the first time, flooding their spines, connecting them to every other spine in the barn. Extraordinary, as well, to think about a human strong enough to invoke that state again and again, hundreds of times a year. It was a form of play from the start, your hands opening up spaces that radiated a shocking form of love, of wildness, lawlessness within community. It was better than work, harder than work. Not work.

All around there were geniuses, goofuses, and hacks building their own maquette of the new thing. Lots of people came up with a blueprint: Little Richard, Elvis, Ike Turner, Henry Glover, Devora and Jack Brown. There were countless ways to invent something, and in the 1950s countless people were trying.

"I've been told that I'm very unique. And I just think it's because I've been around so long," Chuck said to Hackford. "I didn't start anything. There's nothing new under the sun. I participated in it strongly perhaps at a particular time, when it was vulnerable to being impregnated, and I may shine out through those perforations. But other than that, it's just a washboard of time passing." It was one of the more amazing things he said.

There is the washboard flow of time, and there is a second for history to spark. Two lines intersecting. A teepee on a railroad track.

Berry's blueprint was the sturdiest and most transferable of all. He arrived with a new instrument and became an early master of it, just as it was taking over the new sound. He created a role that held the wishes of his audience and his own wishes together tightly: the rock star. Dragging country music into the boogie-woogie woods, Berry bridged races and regions. He spoke with fine diction to white teenagers. He had the world on his mind.

The blueprint led to rock & roll. It was Black, and then mostly Black, and then almost entirely white by the late 1960s, and by then the thing was just called rock.

It's the summer of 1970. Jimi Hendrix is playing a sense-impairing version of "Johnny B. Goode" on his Cry of Love tour. He's heading to Baltimore for a date at the Civic Center when, on June 12, the Pittsburgh Pirates baseball team was playing the San Diego Padres. Pitcher Dock Ellis misread the calendar and dropped acid on what he thought was a day off, then realized he had to throw in several hours.

It's a famous moment in baseball history: the day Ellis pitched a rare no-hitter while he was, as he put it, "high as a Georgia pine."[9]

Ellis vividly described it later. He had a vision while on the pitching mound, hallucinating that Jimi Hendrix came to the plate against him, waving his guitar as if it were a bat. Calling the strikes was the home plate umpire, none other than President Richard M. Nixon. That was the praxis of rock in 1970: Jimi Hendrix was batting cleanup, but Richard Nixon called the shots. The fix was in.

The idea was clear by the time of Ellis's no-hitter: you could change the world through the power of rock. But to do it, you had to *live* in the world of rock. (Elvis famously visited Nixon in 1970.)

A letter from an Ohio radio station employee to *Billboard*, 1980: "I've found that banning black product on our station is in no way a racial thing. In fact, my white co-workers personally like a lot of black product we don't play. But we all know our job—rock 'n' roll. We are committed to that sound." His letter was a defense of the then-popular album-oriented rock format. "A lot of young blacks and whites don't realize the great contribution of blacks to the current rock 'n' roll sound. I played an old Chuck Berry tune to a 14-year-old black. He cringed and said, 'We used to sound like that?'"[10]

It was never as simple as "they stole Black music." The Beatles, the Stones, to employ the two most massive examples, used Berry as source material they ultimately extended into different, new directions, folding his influence into a world of their own. And rock was now a product of that world.

Back to the Future, the 1985 film, imagines teenager Marty McFly (Michael J. Fox) traveling back in time to join a band, Marvin Berry and the Starlighters, as they play a high school dance in 1955. McFly teaches them "Johnny B. Goode." You see bandleader Marvin hold a telephone toward the music after placing a call to his cousin: "Chuck! Chuck," he shouts. "You know that new sound you're looking for? Well, listen to this!"

McFly plays Berry's guitar part, then does the duckwalk, offers a little Hendrix, some Eddie Van Halen squall on his back, and then kicks over a monitor. The history of rock guitar, brought by a white man from the future. That was the joke.[11]

In 2021, a panel of conservative thinkers from the Daily Wire website finally proclaimed that rock & roll was officially dead. "There was rock 'n' roll, then there was Barack Obama, now there is no rock 'n' roll," the host of *Daily Wire Backstage* explained. "Rock 'n' roll was about white male angst, white male teenage angst. Barack Obama came along and said, 'Young white men aren't allowed to have angst. They're not allowed to basically express their dissatisfaction because they're so toxic.'"[12]

Chuck Berry had the best blueprint available. And over many years he would use it to wage war on rock & roll. Stage by stage, he would make them pay. Taking his history and America's out on those around him, while finding a way to give the crowd something worth remembering. Remembering *him*.

In his final years he traveled with the Blueberry Hill Band. Seventeen shows in Europe over eighteen days in 2007, from Moscow to the Canary Islands. It was below zero in Russia, and two weeks later over eighty degrees, a grind that would wear on anybody, let alone someone eighty-one years old. That year they toured Europe three times.

On New Year's Day in 2011, he came to Chicago's Congress Theater. He had played two shows the night before in New York and was fatigued from the start. About an hour in, Berry realized how out of tune he was and approached the keyboardist to give him a note. But then he started arguing and tried to tune himself, until he laid his head down on the keyboard. "I'm struggling," he said, as staff led him off.

Fifteen minutes later he wandered back, his Gibson around his neck, until a stagehand came out, took the guitar away—took Chuck Berry's guitar!—and walked him from the stage. He came out one more time, played "Around and Around" three times, and asked the band what he had just played. Apologizing to the crowd, "Ladies and gentlemen, I've been trying to dig myself out of this hole that I'm in. If I'm living next New Year's, I'm gonna walk on this stage and do a whole new show. I want to apologize." Then, according to *Rolling Stone*, he wandered away, playing his guitar as he exited. Offstage, a crew of emergency medical technicians delivered a hasty examination.[13]

The band of St. Louis veterans knew how to roll with things. Bassist Jimmy Marsala joked, "I told him once, 'That's the first time I played a blues song in five different keys.' But he'd keep changing, and we'd keep going with the flow." Still, the audience could tell. "He knew he was going out upstairs. It was sad to watch," said Bob Lohr. "He would get to the place where he couldn't remember anything." At Blueberry Hill everybody would cut him slack. The fans could see his face, and he could see theirs. But when they played big stages overseas, audiences expected the 1950s Chuck, and they let him know when they felt disappointed.

"It was just terrible. He just couldn't do it anymore and he wanted to keep doing it," Lohr said.

Berry, pretty skinny at this point, was hunched over in his chair backstage. At such a moment, anybody might have their doubts about what was possible. "But they say adrenaline was the big wonder drug," said Lohr, "and it really is. Then he would take the stage and he was twice as big somehow." Nobody could tell Chuck Berry what to do, and nobody could tell him to stop.

The Blueberry Hill Band played in South America in 2013. Lohr said it was on the national news there. "My god. It was 'Fraud'—a big, big scandal, everybody saying, 'Oh, how are they letting a legend like this ruin his reputation?' And they were right. We shouldn't have."

Berry would buttonhole Lohr ostensibly for help with his iPhone, which was the way he asked for company, for somebody to talk to. They met in a hotel lobby in Brazil, Berry looking down a long hallway, turning around, and saying, "You know, I feel it coming closer every day."

He knows he's going mentally, Lohr realized. They had a tour of Europe coming later that year.

"Sit down," Berry said to the pianist. "'Bobby, what am I gonna do? I can't even remember 'Johnny B. Goode' anymore."

When that happens, Lohr suggested, he should just keep playing guitar for another song or two.

But that was poignant: "I can't even remember 'Johnny B. Goode' anymore."

I felt so sorry for him, and felt like saying to Chuck, "You should just hang it up." But who the hell was I to tell Chuck to stop?[14]

There came a day, though, when somebody had to tell him—it was time to stop driving. Joe Edwards, who drove around town a lot with Berry, brought it up several times. If they were going to a charity event in the afternoon, Chuck would drive there, but as the sun went down Edwards would suggest, "Hey, Chuck, why don't you let me?"

"I wasn't gonna say, 'I'm not gonna get in the car with you.' And nine out of ten times he would just flip me the keys."[15]

The idea had been to celebrate his ninetieth birthday playing at Blueberry Hill. But the shows early in 2014 were not good, and Edwards worried about Chuck driving back to Wentzville in the dead of winter. Finally, "I said, 'Chuck, why don't we pause here in the wintertime and see how it looks in the spring. Keep it going then.' He could see he was getting on in time. But he *never* would have been the one to stop. He told me he wanted to play once a month, and he would have honored his word at ninety," Edwards said.

"He said, 'Are you sure—I'm not busting any trust we have, am I?' I said, 'No, I'm just thinking of it for the sake of driving.' And then pretty soon it became clear to both of us that that was the last one."

BY 2015, AN ATTORNEY WAS SHOPPING AROUND A NEW ALBUM TO labels. News of the record was tightly controlled; the pitch was, if you could get a new album by an artist who was unable to do interviews or shows but had two and a half million fans on his Facebook page, would you be interested?

Chuck had been working on new music since the late 1970s. A double album was coming, he said then, with Johnnie Johnson playing on it. But in 1989 a fire in the Berry Park studio destroyed everything, thirty to forty twenty-four-track recordings, the lyric sheets, everything down to the foundation. Berry lost scrapbooks, photos, and memorabilia along with years of work.

"All things change; nothing remains the same," he told an Associated Press reporter. "There's no way to put a value on it."

"Deep down he felt it really intensely. But outwardly there was nothing he could do about it," said Edwards. "He was one of those rare people that went on with their lives. 'This is the new ground zero, and what do I do? I start working on it again.' That's what he did."

He rerecorded the music, but time was bending weird. Berry kept revisiting the songs, transferring them to new technology (he was learning Pro Tools). There was an album finished, he declared, in 2000. Then, when journalist Mark Jacobson visited him a year later he seemed to be putting demos together. Many of the songs Berry was testing out back then appeared on his final album, released in 2017.

Why no new music in so long? Jacobson asked. Berry replied,

For many years, there has been a great laziness in my soul. There
were days I could write songs, but I could also take my four
hundred dollars and play the slot machines at the casino. In a way
I feel it might be ill-mannered to try and top myself. You see, I am
not an oldies act. The music I play, it matters to people. People
want to hear it a certain way. How they remember it. I honor that.
I wouldn't want to interfere with that. I don't want to live in the
past, but I am part of it for a lot of people. I have to respect that,
especially now that it is so far into the future.[16]

Lazy was one thing Chuck was never. But, he told Jacobson, "I confess to schizophrenia," meaning there was the public Chuck and the
private Charles Berry. Maybe he was shrugging off the fact that there
was now one more person: the Chuck audiences grew up with and
carried with them. That guy was hard to compete with in the twenty-
first century.

He was nervous and increasingly alone.

The final days were not for the meek. He was spending almost
all his time at home in Wentzville, said Berry family attorney Martin
Green. "Francine was there until the very end."

By the time his final record was being shopped, it was unclear how
involved the creator was. "He was a leader. He was like the chief,"
recalled a family friend. In his prime, "he was in charge of everything,
and was the one that created things." The family friend, musician Steven
Scorfina, recalls once seeing Berry recite the "even this shall pass" poem,
the image of an old man ruminating with contentment on his life.

"It just brings me to tears because the end of his life was so drasti-
cally different," said Scorfina. "I was never so disgusted in my life, to
see what happened when Chuck died. Chuck had lost his mind; he'd
be on the street throwing rocks at cars, and the police would come to
make sure he got back in the house."[17]

Chuck's girlfriend called Themetta from Wentzville and said the
family had better do something. He'd become "completely out of control," said Scorfina.

"So they got doctors and got him declared incompetent. They fired
all the lawyers and took over his business."

"Big Boys," his first single in forty years, was set to come out in late March 2017. Then, three days before its release, Berry died. He was ninety years old. The initial announcement, made by the St. Charles County Police Department on their Facebook page, said emergency workers had been called to his home at about twelve forty p.m. on March 18. He was unresponsive and failed to revive after lifesaving efforts.[18]

Paul Roper, the president of Dualtone Records, the label releasing Berry's new music, contacted the family to discuss holding the single back. Perhaps it was too soon, in the wake of his death, to launch a full publicity campaign. The call came in the middle of a family meeting in St. Louis where they were discussing the same subject and asking themselves, "What would Dad do?"

Berry's widow, Themetta, pointed out, "Well, he always stuck to the contract. If he had an agreement, that's what he would do. One, because that was him and two because he didn't want to give any money back." So they called Roper, and one of the kids told him, "Paul, Mom says we are on schedule."[19]

The last album, titled *Chuck*, came out in June 2017. It was a satisfying final framing of Berry's sound. The guitar playing is sharp throughout, the vocals full-throated. There were no wild rhythms and no dangerous guitar solos; this was a sustaining Chuck Berry burger-fries-and-shake on a hot Ozark roadside.

The Blueberry Hill Band's style is unambitious, elemental. Berry himself felt forcefully present and focused on making clear several key points. That "I need satisfaction, I didn't get any yesterday"; that he still loved Themetta; that Johnny B. Goode had a son.

Chuck finishes with two unusual spoken-word poems evoking the dinner table recitations with Dad back in the 1930s and '40s. "Dutch-man" is about a tall, old man who pushes into a tavern and tells how he fell down on his luck. "Dutchman" might be modeled on Berry him-self—he plays with the idea of his fame and wealth being behind him, as if now he was just a stranger unburdening himself to an indifferent crowd.

Chuck doesn't make big points, and it doesn't redirect the compass musically. It was a lively late portrait of the artist. But it does offer a faint apology to one woman, among Berry's last words. He dedicates the album to Themetta. "Lady B. Goode" is a tribute to the woman who sacrificed and stood behind Johnny B. Goode. In "Dutchman" he says women were an addiction that all but brought him down.

The last song on the last Chuck Berry album is "Eyes of Man," a distant relative of "The King's Ring." Here, too, is a summing up. Genial more than profound, it gives the listener some grand verses revised from a poem by Hattie Vose Hall, and a potent chorus that recasts lines from Persian proverbs collected by Sir Richard Burton. "Eyes of Man" refers to life's great makers. The temples and nations built by great men eventually fall away, he says. The only building that truly matters is the daily work of women.

At the end of his life, Berry was thinking about rhymes that outlasted the body's weakness, placing his own work alongside that of the great poets he heard growing up. Time was bending weird, and the beginning and the end crisscrossed.

Talking to a journalist in the studio one day, Berry reminisced about his youth. "I like to invent," he said. "My dad was in the manner of trying to invent perpetual motion and I was right there with him trying to get it together." The project was there before he came, and it outlasted him. "But I like to make things, and go places, and that I did with him."[20]

He recited Tennyson's poem "Break, Break, Break," its verses about age and death, as he pondered his time. The work of hands, perpetual motion, the poetry, it was all around him. "So we put it on the music, actually."

23

"MAKE THE ARTS SAFE AGAIN"

Frederick Douglass was on a jaunt to Cincinnati. Invited by the Ladies' Anti-Slavery Sewing Society to speak at their 1852 conference, the African American writer and reformer was traveling from Rochester, New York, by riverboat and railroad. Writing about the trip later, Douglass tellingly focused on an indignity he suffered en route. It happened in the breakfast room of a Cleveland hotel. A "carrot-headed waiter" was to blame.

Approaching Douglass, the waiter reprimanded, "You must leave this table," for it was against the hotel's rules for a Black man to be seated. The young waiter left, in search of support for removing Douglass, when another employee came along. Douglass asked him for a cup of coffee and proceeded to "partake of my morning meal without further annoyance."

The confrontation left the abolitionist wondering why "I am unable to travel in any part of this country without calling forth illustrations of the dark spirit of slavery at every step. . . . My pro-slavery neighbors tell me that the fault is in me; that I am saucy, insolent, and presumptuous, continually assuming rights and privileges which are denied me by the general voice."

Insist on one's rights and one would get blowback. Why subject himself "to such buffetings," he wondered, when he could choose to "travel as other colored men do, walking in the prescribed limits fixed by the wisdom of our enlightened public sentiment." In other words, why not accept the hotel's custom and go where he was welcome? He was in the North and it was 1852, decades from the widespread passage of Jim Crow laws in the South, forty-plus years before the federal government would employ separate-but-equal laws. And Black movement, he diagnosed, was under attack.

Slavery had asserted control over the movement of Black bodies. But as historian Elizabeth Stordeur Pryor and others have shown, free people of color in the antebellum North faced obstacles of established practice, custom, and culture that impaired their movement.

"Such is the hard fate of the colored traveler," wrote Douglass.[1]

To himself he formulated a "rule of my conduct," a refusal to pull away from the full world, or to conceal himself from others. The rule was "that whatever rights or privileges may be enjoyed innocently by white men, may as innocently be enjoyed by men of color. Taking this as incontrovertible, I move about among my fellow-men, thinking no more of them because they are white, and no less of myself, because I am colored; and paying very little regard to what I know to be the existing prejudices about me." Douglass knew that to insist on interaction, to travel across America, to be American, would mean being treated as an aggressor. To succeed in being an American for him would begin as performance, deception, an act that required confidence and misdirection.

A century later, "Maybellene" entered the very world Chuck Berry wished to see. With songs that examined a life that meant one thing to its targeted audience and another to the songwriter, Berry gained rare access to life at large.

From the start he was an anomaly. A wheel of ambition. Over time, others defined him; Berry wrote more songs. More time passed, and he was defined further, and he wrote fewer songs but played on. The shows came into focus when the songs disappeared: as Elvis Mitchell has written, the stage became the place where this "revolutionary black figure" installed "the rage that the crucible of racism created."[2]

Unstoppable in 1955; all the more so decades later, after so many tried to stop him.

Saucy. Insolent. Presumptuous.

THE MEMORIAL TOOK PLACE AT THE PAGEANT, A CONCERT HALL
near Blueberry Hill. On a Sunday morning in April 2017, casually
dressed fans viewed the body, and then family and friends, dressed for
church, arrived for the memorial service.

Enflaming both groups were a few protesters. They looked to be
in their twenties and appeared nervous in photos. A woman covered
her face when a photographer arrived; a man in a hoodie peered from
behind a bandanna and sunglasses.

They carried signs that read

> CHUCK BERRY
> ASSAULTS 60+ WOMEN
> Y'ALL SILENT
> WE PROTEST A RAPIST
> EVERYONE LOSES THEIR MINDS

And

> YOUR IDOL IS SOMEONE ELSE'S ABUSER

Down the street by the statue, people were laying album covers,
flowers, and beads at his feet. There were critical messages left there
too, for all to see.

The sculptor, Harry Weber, took note. "These kids had put up signs
that he was a child molester and whatever. So I walked up, took a sign
down, and threw it in the trash. A thousand people there all gave me a
standing ovation," he said.[3]

The city, which frequently kept its distance during Berry's lifetime,
knew what was expected from a big civic ceremony. Coverage of the
dissent was light.

One other protest sign on the day of Chuck's memorial: "Make the
arts safe again."

That was the most poignant one of all. When have the arts ever been
safe? A stroll down the St. Louis Walk of Fame would mean passing
the sidewalk marker for writer William Burroughs, a gun fanatic who
shot his second wife, a dabbler in stereotypes and conspiracy theories.

Keep walking and you get to poet T. S. Eliot, a profound anti-Semite. Our lives would be worse without them.

Chuck Berry earned his place on the Walk of Fame. Did anyone ever leave the world with so much nourishment and then turn the simple enjoyment it demanded into something so complicated? But this life would be infinitely worse without his music in it.

Dave Chappelle has an extended routine about Berry's sex tape, a long, gross, funny description of a video the comic watched. He places it in the context of forgiving people for actions of the past and the wages of so-called cancel culture. Berry has not exactly been "canceled." He is still a provider: since his death his image and music have appeared in commercials, and a live record from a night at Blueberry Hill came out in 2021. What he received was scrutiny and protest from some in the public.

What we have is more interesting. A choice of threading through the details of his life or working around them completely—your call!—and simply *hearing* him. To pull the joy and poetry out of the music he created and have it take us where *it* wants to go—not where he went. To live our lives with it, and not live his life. That's a lot.

He earned the criticism, and he would have shrugged it off.

"I figure it like this," he said once. "What does it matter what they think of me as a person? I've already had some idea of what they think of me as a product, as a musical inspiration, so what they think of me as a person has nothing to do with my music. The person who would condemn someone for their personality, and infiltrate that condemnation into their product—well, it really doesn't matter."[4]

I had an idea for how to end this book. A literary form has established itself in the last decade: the public apology. A famous person does something terrible, a video shows up in the in-box, a deposition is unsealed. A bouquet of mea culpas must be sent.

The utility is marginal and the degree of difficulty immense, because nobody's public apology has ever convinced *anyone*. It is but a step on the path for someone seeking absolution. A statement is proffered, the aggrieved find it lacking, and mockery prevails. Progress.

The idea was to imagine what such a note signed by Chuck Berry might have looked like. What if he apologized to the fourteen-year-old girl whose name he didn't even know and yet to whom he promised a job just so he could fuck her in the back seat of his Cadillac from Juárez to St. Louis? Would he have called it rape? What if he offered a collective unburdening to all the people he had treated shabbily, asked for forgiveness from the women he videotaped as they used the toilet or put on the uniform of the Southern Air restaurant? What if he apologized to everyone who had bought a Chuck Berry record and then met him on an angry night?

But complications ensued, and the idea was put aside. Complexities like the difficulty in saying anything the way Berry would say it. And then there is something even harder to imagine: Chuck Berry asking for forgiveness.

"HEY, DID YOU KNOW THAT CHUCK BERRY MADE A PORNO MOVIE?" The librarian at the State Historical Society of Missouri called out to me one morning in the library. "I have it at home, come on over and watch it!" Then he shared a newspaper front page from 1982, a photo of Berry playing before a sea of faces at Laclede's Landing. Thousands of fans raving for Berry, and the archivist thumped the black-and-white newsprint dots in the lower corner of the photo to show where he was standing. "I was there!" he said with delight.

That is the nature of researching the life of Chuck Berry: one minute you are basking in the greatness of the man, how he made you feel the first time you heard "You Never Can Tell," and the next moment bodily fluids are seeping into the frame.

I was fourteen in 1973, working that summer in my uncle's ice-cream truck, selling Bomb Pops to kids in the streets of Port Huron, Michigan. There was a unique movie theater within walking distance of my uncle's house: the Jerry Lewis Twin Cinema, a chain founded by the comic and promising a fully automated moviegoing experience.

Let the Good Times Roll had just come to town, and walking to the Jerry Lewis Twin I crossed beneath a railroad trestle, passing a couple of drunks throwing beer bottles at me that exploded off the concrete. That summer, the film itself did far more to disturb. Chuck played an all-in "Sweet Little Sixteen" and jammed with Bo Diddley as the crowd went nuts. Plus, he performed his raunchy version of "Reelin' and Rockin'," which seemed creepy even to a fourteen-year-old. That was my first Chuck Berry picture: a man of great boogie action, a purveyor of fun chaos, wild and corny. I went back and watched the whole film again, my summer of ice cream and broken glass.

In the immediate afterglow of "My Ding-A-Ling," Chuck reigned as a charismatic old dude, leeringly asking all of us to go under the trestle with him. The market and the music press might tell me the artists in the film were also-rans, but my eyes showed something else; these elders drew from a power source unlike what the guys in Kansas and Deep Purple were tapping, a source quite possibly contrary to science. Over time I could see Little Richard and Ike Turner and Johnny Ray and Link Wray, hear how their DNA was planted in the music I liked—it just didn't belong to them anymore. The rightness of rock's progress had asserted itself as science will over the supernatural; product and process moved forward. Rocking was a mission.

I was finding my way into the sound, studying Springsteen and Mott the Hoople and Bob Seger and Bowie, canceling the *Sporting News* subscription and reading *Creem* and *Rolling Stone*. The sidewalk schooner in the captain's hat was both distant from the scene and cited by it regularly—accounted for, just not present. In the years since, I have seen Chuck perform, bought his records, and been raised by the world he designed. I grew up thinking that rock was capable of changing the world, and that all were welcome, no doubt because those who had access to that world were those who looked most like me: white, male, capable of talking our way out of a bad scene with a cop.

Chuck outlived Elvis, Johnnie Johnson, Johnny Winter, and Johnny Ramone. He outlived rock & roll. In 2022 he seems less like a rocker and more than ever simply a representative American artist. He had a vision of a country that did not exist, and he willed it into life. A place where anybody might want to live. His reward was a day pass and a warning that it was best he not hang around after sundown.

Whatever was beyond his control was not worth worrying about. "Race matters, they can lay you low, or you can be savvy about them," he said. "Everything can be beaten, if one is smart and patient, and lucky."[5]

Talking to journalist Mark Jacobson one day, Berry opened up and shared a little secret. He admitted he often drove a Toyota Avalon around St. Louis. The writer said the only thing possible to say: that it was surprising, given all those songs and stories of Cadillac glory.[6]

"In a Toyota, the cops don't stop you as much," Berry explained.

Did the cops actually stop him, even now?

"Shit, yeah. They stop me. They'll let me go after they see it's me, but they stop me. Always have, always will."

AFTERWORD AND
ACKNOWLEDGMENTS

It's June 12, 2020, and a new sign hangs on Chuck's statue. "Black Lives Matter," it reads.

Hundreds of people gathered earlier that day along Lindbergh Boulevard, heading east to Delmar. The protest marked the police murder of George Floyd in Minneapolis two weeks before. Around the country, people were demonstrating in Seattle, Tulsa, Los Angeles, New York.

Black, brown, yellow, and white masked protesters raising their fists as they pass Blueberry Hill, a swirl of limbs activating the air all around the statue, calling for justice for victims of racial violence. Some in the crowd referred back to the shooting of Michael Brown by a white police officer in Ferguson, just a few miles from here, in 2014.

A fourteen-year-old from the Ville named Dee Gipson looked over the heads of the St. Louis protesters. "We got all their attention," said Gipson, noting the blocked traffic.[1]

"We even got the attention of helicopters," he added, gesturing to the eyes overhead.

The bodies moved past the bronze figure, whose head peered across the tops of the crowd surging. He remains in the middle of a ruckus, talking to the people and their voices responding.

At the Rock and Roll Hall of Fame induction ceremony in 2017, a recording of Berry talking to an interviewer was played to a packed house. So many things had been said about him, verdicts and reviews and shouts from the crowd. He was asked, *How did you want to be remembered?* "After I'm gone," he said, "I want you to just speak the truth. Be it pro, con, bad, good. . . . Whatever it be, I just hope it's real."[2]

Thank you, Chuck, for the liberty. This book is unauthorized and beholden to nobody but me. I have interviewed over one hundred people in the course of writing it, and I am grateful for their time and impressions of the man. I began work on *Chuck Berry: An American Life* in 2017, seeking to understand his accomplishments in the context of his time and the time in which I write, to represent the often triumphant, sometimes anguished details of his life.

I spent a lot of time in Missouri, and I'm grateful for the help and insight provided by many from the region. Joe Edwards sat me down at a corner table at Blueberry Hill, where I could see the statue of Chuck while he told me about his memories of the man. Writers Chris Naffziger, Daniel Durchholz, and Jaime Lees have lived around the man and in his St. Louis, and their words have been a help to this project.

Jimmy Marsala, Robert Lohr, and Keith Robinson from the Blueberry Hill Band shared their experiences backing up Chuck at home and traveling with him on tour. Other St. Louis–area musicians, including Bob Kuban, Gus Thornton, Herb Sadler, Mark Peterson, Mike Mesey, Steve Scorfina, and Tom Maloney, told me about the musical scene that Chuck came out of and shaped. Calvin Riley Jr. at the George B. Vashon Museum and Bernie Hayes at the National Blues Museum in St. Louis brought aspects of Black St. Louis and the life of the region into focus.

A research fellowship from the Center for Popular Music Studies at Case Western Reserve University allowed me to work for a week at the Rock and Roll Hall of Fame. Smack in the middle of the pandemic, a grant from the PEN America Writers Emergency Fund made a big difference.

Kenn Thomas helped create the Chuck Berry Project Research Papers in the Manuscript Collection of the State Historical Society of Missouri, and he aided my research in numerous ways. Thanks to Charles E. Brown at the St. Louis Mercantile Library, University of Missouri–St. Louis; the staff at the Olin Library, Washington University; and all who work in the Special Collections Department of the St. Louis Public Library.

The staff at the Missouri State Archives, Jefferson City, and Laura Kromer, government documents and reference librarian at the Missouri State Library, provided access and information about the history of Intermediate Reformatory for Young Men. Bob Beebe, archivist at the National Archives in Kansas City, helped locate records of Berry's federal suit filed against those he believed had violated his privacy. In St. Charles County, the Circuit Court clerk's staff for the Eleventh Circuit Court navigated the closed files archives for me. Jim Rhodes and the staff of the St. Charles City–County Library made the history of the region available and understandable to a visitor.

Respect to the many Berry writers, filmmakers, and thinkers who have come before me, including Bruce Pegg, Duane Marburger, Fred Rothwell, George Lipsitz, Greg Tate, Greil Marcus, Howard A. DeWitt, J. P. Robinson, John Broven, John Collis, John Shaw, Kenn Thomas, Krista Reese, Liz Eck, Mark Jacobson, Mikal Gilmore, Patrick William Salvo, Peter Guralnick, Robert Christgau, Robert Hilburn, Steve Waksman, Taylor Hackford, Ted Clisby, W. T. Lhamon Jr.

I wanted to speak to musicians who had known Berry or played with him, and those who had a special understanding of his music and his position in America's musical life. I am grateful for all who gave me their time, including Augie Meyers, Ben Vaughn, Bob Baldori, Bobby Rush, Che Chen, Deke Dickerson, Jesper Eklow, Jesse McReynolds, Joey Spampinato, Paul Major, Richard Thompson, Steve Miller, Stew Stewart, Swamp Dogg, Taj Mahal, Vernon Reid, Vijay Iyer, Wayne Kramer.

So many people helped me tell this story. Suggesting someone I should talk to; sharing an idea. They aren't responsible for my words, though they made this work possible. Thank you: Aaron Cohen, Adiel Kaplan, Alison Fensterstock, Bob Mehr, Carleton Gholz, David

Cantwell, Jeannette Batz Cooperman, Jeff Salamon, Max Marshall, Mark Schone, Max Marshall, Michael Azerrad, Michael Shelley, Red Kelly, Sonnet Retman, Susan Whitall.

Talking to those who encountered Berry was a complicated experience. There were people who officially saw little and remembered less, and others whose words came with a degree of philosophical detachment that is fairly rare when talking about pop stars. That philosophical detachment could lead to a great deal of context and situational understanding, other times to a kind of brutal clarity about the person they knew. Thank you for telling it real: Abraham Bolden, Andy Mayberry, Angela Pezel, Art Holliday, Barb Kirk, Becca Balducci, Ben Sandmel, Bill Greensmith, Bobby Wood, Carl Sally, Charles Broome, Charlie Pickett, David Himmel, Dean Minderman, Diane, Dick Alen, Duane Marburger, Elizabeth L. Kennedy, Ellen Sander, Rev. F. Delano R. Benson Jr., Floyd Mutrux, Garrett Enloe, Gene Chrisman, Harry Simon, Harry Weber, Jerry Saltz, Jim Mervis, John Broven, John Hawken, John Sinclair, Jordan Orleans, Keith Morris, Kevin Belford, Kevin Fleming, Kevin Strait, Kris Anglemyer, Lee Alan, Linda Harlan, Lynn Bruce, Marianne Riley, Mark Goldman, Martin Green, Melody Burgess, Michael Pietsch, Mike Sager, Miles Grier, Mirandi Babitz, Mitch Margo, Pat Lacey, Percy Green, Pete Johnson, Peter O'Neil, Quint Davis, Reggie Young, Rich Frame, Richard King, Robert Meloni, Roger Fairhurst, Sharon Stokes Williamson, Slick Stefaniak, Stephanie Bennett, Susan Hamilton, Taylor Hackford, Thomas Adelman, Timothy McFarlin, Tom Ray, Tony Cabanellas, Wayne Schoeneberg, Yvonne McCue, Zander Schloss.

At Hachette Books, editor Ben Schafer has masterfully shepherded this project from the very beginning. Shout-outs to Carrie Napolitano (associate editor), Terri Sirma (senior designer), Michael Giarratano (publicity manager), Michael Barrs (senior director, marketing). And respect to Paul Bresnick, agent and book lover.

Respect for confidantes, colleagues, and provocateurs, folks who in the before time and whatever comes next keep it going: Abira Ali, Alisha Lola Jones, Allen Lowe, Amanda Marie Martinez, Ann Powers, Annie Zaleski, Bob Pfeifer, Bobby West, Carl Wilson, Charles Aaron, Charles Hughes, Charlie McGovern, Chuck Cleaver, Craig Marks, Dan Weiss, Danny Feingold, David Cantwell, David Peterkin, David Ulin, Elizabeth Nelson, Ella Taylor, Emily White, Eric Weisbard,

Erin Aubry Kaplan, Evelynn McDonnell, Franklin Bruno, Gayle Wald, Gordon Henderson, Greil Marcus, Hanif Abdurraqib, Holly George-Warren, James Marshall, James Porter, Jason Cohen, Jason King, Jeff Feuerzeig, Jenn Pelly, Jessica Bissett Perea, Jessica Good-heart, Jimmy McDonough, Jody Rosen, Joe Levy, Joe Sehee, Jon Lang-ford, Julien Nitzberg, Karen Amano-Tompkins, Karen Tongson, Karen Trott, Karen Wada, Kathy Fennessy, Ken Katkin, Kimberley Mack, Laurie Stone, Leda Ramos, Lisa Walker Hug, Lucretia Tye Jasmine, Lucy Sante, Mandalit Delbarco, Mario Prietto, Mark Anthony Neal, Marty Lederman, Matt Weingarden, Matthew Duersten, Melissa A. Weber, Michael A. Gonzales, Michelle Habell-Pallán, Mike Davis, Mike McGonigal, Mimi Pond, Nancy Jacobs, Nelson George, Nico-las Winding Refn, Norma Coates, Oliver Wang, Pandora Young, Pat Thomas, Paula Mejía, Peter Guralnick, Peter Herdrich, Peter Stamp-fel, Regina Bradley, Rik DeLisle, Robert Christgau, Robert Ito, Robert Gordon, Roger Guenveur Smith, Sally Timms, Scott Poulson-Bryant, Scott Timberg, Steacy Easton, Steve Erickson, Steven Mikulan, Ste-ven Rosen, Tamara Zwick, Tom Carson, Tommy Tompkins, Tristin Aaron, Wayne White, Will Amato.

Long before I discovered rock & roll, my mom drove me to the library. A lot. That made all the difference in my world. Shout-outs to Margaret and to all the Smiths, Bussells, Burmans, and Mangiones who have brought me up and have lifted me beyond. And love to Jenny Burman and Mady Echo Burman Smith.

NOTES

INTRODUCTION

1. Jim Utz, interview with author, July 2018.

2. Kevin Strait, interviews with author, November 2018.

3. Kevin Strait, "How Chuck Berry's Cadillac and His Guitar, Maybellene, Came to the Smithsonian," *Smithsonian*, March 23, 2017, www.smithsonianmag.com/smithsonian-institution/how-chuck-berrys-cadillac-and-his-guitar-maybelline-came-smithsonian-180962638/; Steve Johnson, "Smithsonian Head Lonnie Bunch on What It Took to Make the National Museum of African American History and Culture a Smash Hit," *Chicago Tribune*, September 24, 2019, www.chicagotribune.com/entertainment/books/ct-books-fools-errand-lonnie-bunch-0929-20190924-iovmeewxs5ejfor2qpiqyy3xz4-story.html.

4. Joe Edwards, interview with author, March 2018.

CHAPTER 1

1. John M. McGuire, "The Opinionated Chuck Berry," *St. Louis Post-Dispatch*, November 15, 1998, https://www.chuckberry.us/CB1998.html.

2. Tom Hibbert, "Who the Hell Does Chuck Berry Think He Is?," *Q*, May 1988.

3. "Johnny Be Good," *The Listener*, February 1980, 138; Luke Dittrich, "Chuck Berry Goddamn!," *Esquire*, January 2012, www.esquire.com/entertainment/a12109/chuck-berry-biography-0112/; Neil Strauss, "Chuck Berry: American Visionary," *Rolling Stone*, September 2, 2010, www.rollingstone.com/music/music-features/chuck-berry-american-visionary-129350/.

4. "The Axis of Intensity" and William Gilpin: Hubert Howe Bancroft, *The History of the Life of William Gilpin* (San Francisco: The History Company, 1889), 53. For Gilpin's map, see John Krygier, "Making Maps: DIY Cartography," makingmaps.net, September 30, 2014, https://makingmaps.net/2014/09/30/gilpins-map-of-the-isothermal -zodiac-and-axis-of-intensity-round-the-world-calcareous-plain-maritime-selvage-etc -etc-maps-1873/. Several overviews have influenced my understanding of St. Louis: James Neal Primm, *Lion of the Valley: St. Louis, Missouri, 1764–1980* (St. Louis: Missouri Historical Society Press, 1998); Walter Johnson, *The Broken Heart of America: St. Louis and the Violent History of the United States* (New York: Basic Books, 2020); Adam Arenson, *The Great Heart of the Republic: St. Louis and the Cultural Civil War* (Columbia: University of Missouri, 2015).

5. Missouri's Constitutional Congress of 1865: Primm, *Lion of the Valley*, 260–266. Tim O'Neil, "The Day That Missouri Finally Freed Its Slaves," *St. Louis Post-Dispatch*, January 11, 2018.

6. Colin Gordon, *Mapping Decline: St. Louis and the Fate of the American City* (Philadelphia: University of Pennsylvania Press, 2008), 16.

7. David R. Roediger, "'Not Only the Ruling Classes to Overcome, but Also the So-Called Mob': Class, Skill and Community in the St. Louis General Strike of 1877," *Journal of Social History* (Winter 1985): 213–239; Elliot J. Kanter, "Class, Ethnicity and Socialist Politics: St. Louis, 1876–1881," *UCLA Historical Journal* 3 (1982): 36–60.

8. On the Veiled Prophet: Thomas M. Spencer, *The St. Louis Veiled Prophet Celebration: Power on Parade, 1877–1995* (Columbia: University of Missouri, 2000); Devin O'Shea, "Decoding the Veiled Prophet," in *St. Louis Anthology*, ed. Ryan Schuessler (Cleveland: Belt Publishing, 2019), 25–30; Lucy Ferriss, *Unveiling the Prophet: The Misadventures of a Reluctant Debutante* (Columbia: University of Missouri Press, 2005); Karen McCoskey Goering, "Pageantry in St. Louis: The History of the Veiled Prophet Organization," *Gateway Heritage* 4 (Spring 1984): 2–16. The Veiled Prophet Collection in the St. Louis Public Library was also useful.

9. Ntozake Shange, "Growing Up in St. Louis," in *"Ain't But a Place": An Anthology of African American Writings About St. Louis*, ed. Gerald Early (St. Louis: Missouri Historical Society, 1998), 183.

10. John A. Wright Sr., *The Ville: St. Louis* (Charleston, SC: Arcadia, 2001), 7, 10; Mark R. Wilson, *The Business of Civil War: Military Mobilization and the State, 1861– 1865* (Baltimore: Johns Hopkins University Press, 2006), 127, 141.

11. Nell Irvin Painter, *Exodusters: Black Migration to Kansas After Reconstruction* (New York: Norton, 1992); Bryan M. Jack, *The St. Louis African American Community and the Exodusters* (Columbia: University of Missouri Press, 2008).

12. Carlos F. Hurd, "Post-Dispatch Man, an Eye-Witness, Describes Massacre of Negroes," *St. Louis Post-Dispatch*, July 3, 1917, 1; Martha Gruening and W. E. Burghardt Du Bois, "The Massacre of East St. Louis," *The Crisis*, September 1917, 219–238; Josephine Baker, "Josephine Baker Remembers St. Louis," *St. Louis Post-Dispatch*, February 7, 1952, 22.

13. Mary Delach Leonard, "Curious Louis: We Take a Monumental Look at the Civil War in St. Louis," St. Louis Public Radio, March 25, 2016, https://news.stlpublic radio.org/arts/2016-03-25/curious-louis-we-take-a-monumental-look-at-the-civil-war -in-st-louis; Roger N. Baldwin, "Negro Segregation by Initiative Election in St. Louis," *American City*, April 1916, 356; "St. Louis," *The Crisis*, November 1915, 19; *The Crisis*, January 1916, 140.

14. For a lucid discussion of *Buchanan v. Warley*, see Richard Rothstein, *The Color of Law: A Forgotten History of How Our Government Segregated America* (New York: Liveright, 2017), 39–58.

15. Rothstein, *Color of Law*, 48–50; Nathan Jackson, "Harland Bartholomew: Destroyer of the Urban Fabric of St. Louis," *NEXTSTL*, April 10, 2021, https://next stl.com/2021/04/harland-bartholomew-destroyer-of-the-urban-fabric-of-st-louis/; Joan Cook, "Harland Bartholomew, 100, Dean of City Planners," *New York Times*, December 7, 1989, D22.

16. Chuck Berry, *Chuck Berry: The Autobiography* (New York: Crown, 1987). Much of what we know of his early years comes from this source, a book of voice packed with provocative details. Many remain impossible to fact-check, yet they reveal layers of meaning. He may not write at length about his music in this autobiography, but Berry does not skimp on what he believes is important for you to know. Throughout my book, many quotes from Berry and details related to growing up come from *The Autobiography*.

17. The history of the Ville and Black life in St. Louis in the twentieth century: Carolyn Hewes Toft, ed., *The Ethnic Heritage of an Urban Neighborhood* (St. Louis: Washington University, 1975); Sandra Schoenberg and Charles Bailey, "The Symbolic Meaning of an Elite Black Community: The Ville in St. Louis," *Bulletin of the Missouri Historical Society* (January 1977): 94–102; The Ville Collection, State Historical Society of Missouri, University of Missouri–St. Louis (hereafter UMSL), Thomas Jefferson Library, St. Louis; Fannie Cook, *Mrs. Palmer's Honey* (Garden City, NY: Doubleday, 1946); Doris A. Wesley, *Lift Every Voice and Sing: St. Louis African Americans in the 20th Century* (Columbia: University of Missouri, 1999); Priscilla A. Dowden-White, *Groping Toward Democracy: African American Social Welfare Reform in St. Louis, 1910–1949* (Columbia: University of Missouri, 2011); Clarence Lang, *Grassroots at the Gateway: Class Politics and Black Freedom Struggle in St. Louis, 1936–75* (Ann Arbor: University of Michigan, 2009); Vida "Sister" Goldman Prince, *That's the Way It Was: Stories of Struggle, Survival and Self-Respect in Twentieth-Century Black St. Louis* (Charleston, SC: History Press, 2013); Vivian Gibson, *The Last Children of Mill Creek* (Cleveland: Belt Publishing, 2020); Chajuana V. Trawick, "Annie Malone and PORO College: Building an Empire of Beauty in St. Louis, Missouri, from 1915 to 1930" (PhD diss., University of Missouri, 2011); Gordon, *Mapping Decline*; Early, ed., *"Ain't But a Place"*; D. H. Peligro, *Dreadnaught: King of Afropunk* (Los Angeles: Barnacle/Rare Bird, 2013); Raymond Arsenault, *Arthur Ashe: A Life* (New York: Simon and Schuster, 2018); Lawrence P. Jackson, *Chester Himes: A Biography* (New York: Norton, 2017); Dick Gregory, *N*****: An Autobiography* (New York: Pocket Books, 1990); Elijah J. Shaw Scrapbook, 1914–1971, State Historical Society of Missouri, UMSL, Thomas Jefferson Library, St. Louis; Lift Every Voice and Sing Oral History Project, State Historical Society of Missouri, UMSL.

18. Mikal Gilmore, "Chuck Berry: Farewell to the Father of Rock," *Rolling Stone*, April 7, 2017, www.rollingstone.com/music/music-features/chuck-berry-farewell-to-the -father-of-rock-118589/.

19. Gregory Freeman, "Retired Columnist Revels in Recalling an 'Interesting Life,'" *St. Louis Post-Dispatch*, February 28, 1999, B6.

20. Arna Bontemps, "The Relevance of Paul Laurence Dunbar," in *A Singer in the Dawn: Reinterpretations of Paul Laurence Dunbar*, ed. Martin Jay (New York: Dodd, Mead, 1975), 45; James Sallis, *Chester Himes: A Life* (London: Walker Books, 2000),

22; John Gennari, "Miles and the Jazz Critics," in *Miles Davis and American Culture*, ed. Gerald Early (St. Louis: Missouri Historical Society Press, 2001), 75.

21. Paul Laurence Dunbar, "The Poet," *The Collected Poetry of Paul Laurence Dunbar*, ed. Joanne M. Braxton (Charlottesville: University of Virginia Press, 1993), 191.

22. Chuck Berry "The Burnt Scrapbook," interview by Robbie Robertson, disc 3, *Hail! Hail! Rock 'n' Roll: The Ultimate Collector's Edition*, dir. Taylor Hackford (Universal /Image, 2006), DVD.

23. Berry, *Autobiography*, 20.

24. Peter Guralnick and Chuck Berry, interview for 2011 *Summit of Rock*, DVD made by the Rock and Roll Hall of Fame.

CHAPTER 2

1. Chuck Berry, *Chuck Berry: The Autobiography* (New York: Crown, 1987), 25–27; Mary Kimbrough and Margaret W. Dagen, *Victory Without Violence: The First Ten Years of the St. Louis Committee of Racial Equality (CORE), 1947–1957* (Columbia: University of Missouri, 2000); Vida "Sister" Goldman Prince, *That's the Way It Was: Stories of Struggle, Survival and Self-Respect in Twentieth-Century Black St. Louis* (Charleston, SC: History Press, 2013), 33; Clarence Lang, *Grassroots at the Gateway: Class Politics and Black Freedom Struggle in St. Louis, 1936–75* (Ann Arbor: University of Michigan, 2009), 82.

2. Carolyn Hewes Toft, ed., *The Ethnic Heritage of an Urban Neighborhood* (St. Louis: Washington University, 1975), 3, 5; John A. Wright, *Discovering African American St. Louis: A Guide to Historic Sites* (St. Louis: Missouri Historical Society Press, 2002), 65, 68; "Tribute Concert for Dr. Kenneth Brown Billups," *St. Louis American*, September 10, 2014, www.stlamerican.com/entertainment/living_it/tribute-concert-for-dr-kenneth -brown-billups/article_56bb193e-3968-11e4-9fc0-9b7c93d11a13.html; Gary R. Kremer, "Kenneth Brown Billups Sr.," in *Dictionary of Missouri Biography*, ed. Lawrence O. Christensen, William E. Foley, Gary R. Kremer, and Kenneth H. Winn (Columbia: University of Missouri Press, 1999), 69–70; Reverend Dr. F. Delano R. Benson Jr., interview with author, July 2018.

3. Jeannette Cooperman, "A Conversation with Chuck Berry, King of Rock 'n' Roll," *St. Louis*, November 24, 2008, www.stlmag.com/A-Conversation-with-Chuck-Berry/.

4. Berry, *Autobiography*, 18–19.

5. Prince, *That's the Way*, 76; Mark Jacobson, *Teenage Hipster in the Modern World* (New York: Grove Press, 2005), 46–47.

6. John A. Wright, *Discovering African American St. Louis: A Guide to Historic Sites* (St. Louis: Missouri Historical Society Press, 2002), 68; "History of the Charles Sumner High School Centennial Edition," 1975, Julia Davis Collection, box 1, series 1, St. Louis Public Library; Toft, *Ethnic Heritage*, 8–9; Prince, *That's the Way*, 190; Chuck Berry, "The Burnt Scrapbook," interview by Robbie Robertson, disc 3, *Hail! Hail! Rock 'n' Roll: The Ultimate Collector's Edition*, dir. Taylor Hackford (Universal/Image, 2006), DVD; Lawrence P. Jackson, *Chester Himes: A Biography* (New York: Norton, 2017), 47.

7. Cynthia Todd, "Pioneer: Educator Julia Davis Is Honored as She Nears 100," *St. Louis Post-Dispatch*, November 17, 1991, clipping in the Julia Davis Collection, St. Louis Public Library.

8. George Lipsitz, "Livin' in the USA: Chuck Berry and St. Louis Rock and Roll, 1945–1960," manuscript, April 16, 1982, Chuck Berry Project, folder 9, Papers and Articles 1982–1983, State Historical Society of Missouri, UMSL.

9. Berry, "Burnt Scrapbook" interview.

10. Bernard Weinraub, "Sweet Tunes, Fast Beats and a Hard Edge," *New York Times*, February 23, 2003, 1.

11. Bruce Pegg, *Brown Eyed Handsome Man: The Life and Hard Times of Chuck Berry* (New York: Routledge, 2002), 22.

12. Tom Junod, "Chuck Berry: What I've Learned," *Esquire*, January 2002, 64.

CHAPTER 3

1. Much of this account of Berry's teenage spree to the promised land of California is rooted in his version of events in *Chuck Berry: The Autobiography* (New York: Crown, 1987). I have also made use of details he revealed in interviews, and court records. I consulted *The State of Missouri v. Charles Berry*, Circuit Court of Boone County, as well as records relating to James Williams and Lawrence Hutchinson, including affidavits and judgments. Later court proceedings also shed light on his first brush with the justice system.

2. Records of the Missouri Department of Penal Institutions, housed in the Missouri State Archives in Jefferson City, hold a variety of material helpful in understanding the institution Berry gave several years to. Particularly useful were annual and biennial reports covering conditions at the Algoa Intermediate Reformatory for Young Men.

3. Peter Silvester, *A Left Hand Like God: A History of the Boogie-Woogie Piano* (New York: Da Capo, 1988), 5 and passim; Burgin Mathews, "'When I Say Get It': A Brief History of the Boogie," *Southern Cultures* 15, no. 3 (Fall 2009): 24–52; Kevin Belford, *Devil at the Confluence: The Pre-War Blues Music of St. Louis, Missouri* (St. Louis: Virginia Publishing, 2009); Joe Nick Patoski, "Jimmy Reed, Emancipator of the South: An Oral History," *Blues Access*, Summer 2000; Harriet Ottenheimer, "The Blues Tradition in St. Louis," *Black Music Research Journal* 9, no. 2 (Autumn 1989): 135–151; Charlie Gillett, "Chuck Berry and Those Who Influenced Him," *Let It Rock*, April 1973 (discusses the influence of boogie-woogie tunesmith Don Raye); Mack McCormick, album notes, *Robert Shaw: Texas Barrelhouse Piano* (Almanac Records, 1963).

4. Andrew E. Kersten, *Race, Jobs, and the War: The FEPC in the Midwest, 1941–46* (Champaign: University of Illinois Press, 2007), 112–118.

5. Joseph Heathcott, "Black Archipelago: Politics and Civic Life in the Jim Crow City," *Journal of Social History* 38, no. 3 (Spring 2005): 726–727.

6. *Chuck Berry: The Original King of Rock 'n' Roll*, dir. Jon Brewer (MVD Entertainment, 2018), DVD.

7. Program, Sylvia Boonshaft Foundation of St. Louis Presents "Harlem in St. Louis," August 27, 1949. A collector of St. Louis music lore came across it and posted on social media about this discovery, without knowing it was Berry's earliest-known public appearance. A writer who saw the notice reached out to me.

8. Dennis Owsley, *City of Gabriels: The History of Jazz in St. Louis, 1895–1973* (St. Louis: Reedy Press, 2006), 62–65, 94; Bruce R. Olson, *That St. Louis Thing*, vol. 2 (self-pub., Lulu Press, 2016), 74, 77–78; "George Hudson Honored," *Pittsburgh Courier*, February 17, 1940, 20; Kevin Belford, "Abdicating Our History," May 25, 2011, *NEXTSTL*, https://nextstl.com/2011/05/abdicating-our-history-saving-the-palladium-and-st-louis-cultural-history/. Belford, author of *Devil at the Confluence*, knows a lot of St. Louis music history. Email correspondence with him deepened my appreciation for this barely recorded big band, and for the interconnectedness of various St. Louis scenes. Chick Finney, "Blue Notes," *St. Louis Argus*, May 3, 1957, 19; Kevin Belford, "Floyd Smith the St. Louis Club Plantation and the First Electric Guitar Solo," *Devil at the Confluence*

(blog), March 20, 2012, http://devilattheconfluence.blogspot.com/2012/03/floyd-smith-st-louis-club-plantation.html; "Floyd's Guitar Blues = Blues for Hawaiians," *Go Head On!* (blog), March 31, 2012, http://goheadon.blogspot.com/2011/12/all-shook-up-floyds-guitar-blues.html; "T-Bone Blues: T-Bone Walker's Story in His Own Words," *Record Changer*, October 1947, 5–6, 13.

9. John Chilton, *Let the Good Times Roll: The Story of Louis Jordan and His Music* (Ann Arbor: University of Michigan Press, 1997), 114, 123; Dave Rubin, *Inside the Blues, 1942–1982* (Milwaukee: Hal Leonard, 2007), 27.

CHAPTER 4

1. Tom Yarbrough, "'Hot Rod' Moore Pleads Guilty; Gets 8 Months and Is Fined $100," *St. Louis Post-Dispatch*, undated clipping, 1; "Wife of 'Hot Rod' Moore Sues for Divorce, Alimony," *St. Louis Post-Dispatch*, December 4, 1953, 3; "Hot Rod Moore Seeks Change of Venue in Two Cases," *St. Louis Post-Dispatch*, June 18, 1954, 3; "'Hot Rod' Moore Arrested Again on Auto Charge," *St. Louis Post-Dispatch*, May 13, 1961, 1; Florence Shinkle, "Hotrod Moore Took St. Louis Police for a Wild Ride," *St. Louis Post-Dispatch*, January 11, 1998, D1.

2. *Juvenile Delinquency (St. Louis, MO) Hearings Before the Subcommittee to Investigate Juvenile Delinquency of the Committee on the Judiciary*, US Senate, July 6 and 7, 1956, 69; "Teen Age Madness," *St. Louis Argus*, June 22, 1956, 14.

3. Travis Fitzpatrick, *Father of Rock & Roll: The Story of Johnnie "B. Goode" Johnson* (The Woodlands, TX: Thomas, Cooke, 1999), 63.

4. "Rock and Roll: Renegades: Interview with Johnnie Johnson (Part 1 of 3)," Open Vault, WGBH, accessed May 7, 2022, http://openvault.wgbh.org/catalog /V_FC1D5C49292D4B1D927D74A4CE93F355.

5. Mark Peterson, interview with author, October 2018.

6. Fitzpatrick, *Father*, 70.

7. Harper Barnes, "Paying Dues Finally Pays for 'Johnny B. Goode,'" *St. Louis Post-Dispatch*, March 5, 1989, C3.

8. Fitzpatrick, *Father*, 76–77.

9. William P. Shannon IV, "Chuck Berry at the Cosmo: East St. Louis and the Birth of Rock 'n' Roll," Illinois State Historical Society, accessed May 7, 2022, www.history illinois.org/Portals/HistoricalSociety/Chuck%20Berry.pdf; "Three Held in Fatal Shooting of Negro," *St. Louis Globe-Democrat*, March 17, 1945, A8; "Two Acquitted in Fatal East Side Shooting," *St. Louis Globe-Democrat*, September 27, 1945, 9; "Politicians E. St. Louis Nightclub Bombed," *Mattoon (Ill.) Journal Gazette*, April 18, 1946, 1; "Club Asks Eastside Mayor to Be Enjoined," *St. Louis Globe-Democrat*, May 4, 1946, A8; "Club Owner Fined $25 for Attack on Inspector," *St. Louis Globe-Democrat*, May 15, 1946; "Inspectors Doubt Free Liquor Flow," *Pittsburgh Courier*, December 6, 1947, 2; "Report Bid for $13,000 Negro Election Aid," *Chicago Daily Tribune*, March 19, 1951, 3.

10. Jeffrey B. Leak, *Visible Man: The Life of Henry Dumas* (Athens: University of Georgia Press, 2014), 122; Harry Webber, "St. Louis Nights," *Pittsburgh Courier*, December 6, 1947, 12; "Daugherty Talks at Crime Probe," *Edwardsville (Ill.) Intelligencer*, August 1, 1950, 1; "Police Ask E. St. Louis Mayor to Close Nightclub," *West Frankfort (Ill.) Daily American*, September 21, 1955, 2.

11. Lynn S. Summers and Bob Scheir, "Little Milton," in *The Voice of the Blues*, ed. Jim O'Neal and Amy van Singel (New York: Routledge, 2000), 394.

12. Fred Stuckey, "Exclusive: Chuck Berry," *Guitar Player*, February 1971.

13. Anthony Wall, "Chuck Berry 40 Years On," 1977 profile, BBC Radio.

14. Bill Greensmith, Mark Camarigg, and Mike Rowe, *Blues Unlimited: Essential Interviews from the Original Blues Magazine* (Champaign: University of Illinois Press, 2015), 107.

15. John Collis, *Chuck Berry: The Biography* (London: Aurum Press, 2002), 44.

16. Duane Marburger, interview with author, January 2018; Tony Cabanellas, interview with author, March 2018; Liz Eck and Duane Marburger, "Pre-Chess Chuck Berry," *Goldmine*, September 1982, 25; Chick Finney, "Calypso Joe," *St. Louis Argus*, March 13, 1953; Chick Finney, "Blue Notes," *St. Louis Argus*, February 14, 1958, 7B.

17. Chuck Berry, *Chuck Berry: The Autobiography* (New York: Crown, 1987), 87. It's important to underscore how much Berry was not a student of the guitar, per se, but of the *electric* guitar. He was in the first generation of players plugging in to learn. See Steve Waksman, *Instruments of Desire: The Electric Guitar and the Shaping of Musical Experience* (Cambridge, MA: Harvard University Press, 2000).

18. Albin Zak, *I Don't Sound Like Nobody: Remaking Music in 1950s America* (Ann Arbor: University of Michigan Press, 2010), 81.

19. Photograph and caption from *St. Louis Globe-Democrat*, November 23, 1947: "A near riot resulted yesterday when teenagers flocked to see Frankie Laine, Cab Calloway, Dinah Washington and Cootie Williams at a free show given at Club Riviera, 4460 Delmar Bl. The club was damaged in the rush, although there was no vandalism," UMSL digital library, accessed May 7, 2022, https://dl.mospace.umsystem.edu/umsl/islandora/object/umsl%3A185784. Lloyd J. Green, "$20,000-a-Year Disc Jockey Is Proof a Negro Can Go Places in Radio Here; Owes It All to Mother," *St. Louis Globe-Democrat*, July 1, 1951, F1–4, Jesse "Spider" Burks Collection, St. Louis Public Library.

20. Patrick William Salvo, "When Chuck Berry Plays, It's Just Second Nature," *Gallery*, March 1973, 136.

21. Ike Turner with Nigel Cawthorne, *Takin' Back My Name* (London: Virgin Books, 1999), 60.

22. Greensmith, Camarigg, and Rowe, *Blues Unlimited*, 217–218.

23. Turner, *Takin' Back*, 66–67; "Ike Turner Says Officer Harasses Him in 'Feud,'" *St. Louis Argus*, February 14, 1958.

24. Patrick William Salvo, "A Conversation with Chuck Berry," *Rolling Stone*, November 23, 1972, 35.

25. Turner, *Takin' Back*, 69–70; Daniel Durchholz, "We Like Ike," *Riverfront Times*, May 16, 2001.

CHAPTER 5

1. "Special Appeal to Children in Veiled Prophet's Floats," *St. Louis Post-Dispatch*, September 26, 1954, 3A; "V.P. Parade Will Honor Municipal Opera This Year," *Naborhood Link News*, September 15, 1954, 19; "550,000 Witness St. Louis Veiled Prophet's Parade," *Moberly (Mo.) Monitor-Index*, October 7, 1954, 4.

2. Thomas M. Spencer, *The St. Louis Veiled Prophet Celebration: Power on Parade, 1877–1995* (Columbia: University of Missouri, 2000), 75.

3. Chuck Berry, *Chuck Berry: The Autobiography* (New York: Crown, 1987), 89–90.

4. Mike Boehm, "Rollicking and Rolling," *Los Angeles Times*, November 12, 1992.

5. Tom Wheeler, "Chuck Berry: The Interview," *Guitar Player*, March 1988, 58.

6. Berry, *Autobiography*, 94.

7. Buddy Guy with David Ritz, *When I Left Home: My Story* (Boston: Da Capo Press, 2012), 19.

8. Travis Fitzpatrick, *Father of Rock & Roll: The Story of Johnnie "B. Goode" Johnson* (The Woodlands, TX: Thomas, Cooke, 1999), 84.

9. "Rock and Roll: Renegades: Interview with Phil Chess and Marshall Chess (Part 3 of 4)," Open Vault, WGBH, accessed May 7, 2022, http://openvault.wgbh.org /catalog/V_310B44AC503443838CBCF6566647B6EF.

10. William Clark and Jim Cogan, *Temples of Sound: Inside the Great Recording Studios* (San Francisco: Chronicle Books, 2003), 118–120; Bram Nigten, "Recorded Reflections: Sonic Space in U.S. Popular Recordings During the Mono Era (1877–1957), and Its Occurrence in Three Recordings of Studio Pioneer Bill Putnam" (PhD diss., University of Groningen, 2014); Peter Doyle, *Echo and Reverb: Fabricating Space in Popular Music Recording, 1900–1960* (Middletown, CT: Wesleyan University Press, 2005).

11. Patrick William Salvo, "A Conversation with Chuck Berry," *Rolling Stone*, November 23, 1972, 36.

12. Salvo, "A Conversation with Chuck Berry," 42.

13. Norman Jopling, "Chuck Berry: Rock Lives!," *Record Mirror*, March 4, 1967.

14. I am grateful for W. T. Lhamon Jr.'s *Deliberate Speed: The Origins of a Cultural Style in the American 1950s* (Washington, DC: Smithsonian Institution Press, 1990) and Joshua Clover's *Roadrunner* (Durham, NC: Duke University Press, 2021), both of which have greatly shaped my thinking about this song.

15. From our staff correspondent, "Meteor Falls amid Children," *Sydney Morning Herald*, July 29, 1955, 3; see also "Meteor Falls amid Children," *Council Bluffs (Iowa) Nonpareil*, July 23, 1955, 6C.

16. "What Is Pop?," *Cash Box*, September 3, 1955, 3.

17. "Rock and Roll: Renegades: Interview with Dave Bartholomew (Part 2 of 2)," Open Vault, WGBH, accessed May 7, 2022, https://openvault.wgbh.org/catalog/V_7 BF6300CAD044620ACCFFE0A8D4E52EA.

CHAPTER 6

1. Jerry Saltz, interview with author, October 2018.

2. Sandra Cisneros, "Dirt," *Grand Street* 57 (Summer 1996): 122–125.

3. Robert Palmer, *Rock & Roll: An Unruly History* (New York: Harmony, 1995), 138.

4. John A. Jackson, *Big Beat Heat: Alan Freed and the Early Years of Rock & Roll* (New York: Schirmer, 1991).

5. Richard Carlin, *Godfather of the Music Business: Morris Levy* (Jackson: University Press of Mississippi, 2016), 42.

6. Teddy Reig with Edward Berger, *Reminiscing in Tempo: The Life and Times of a Jazz Hustler* (Lanham, MD: Scarecrow Press, 1995), xv.

7. Michael Jarrett, *Pressed for All Time* (Chapel Hill: University of North Carolina Press, 2016), 33–34.

8. Christopher Kennedy, *1950s Radio in Color: The Lost Photographs of Deejay Tommy Edwards* (Kent, OH: Kent State University Press, 2011).

9. Palmer, *Rock & Roll*, 134–135.

10. Chuck Berry, *Chuck Berry: The Autobiography* (New York: Crown, 1987), 124.

11. Berry, *Autobiography*, 126.

12. Sharon Stokes Williamson, interview with author, July 2020.

13. Conchita Nakatani, "Mr. 'B' Back in Philly," *Pittsburgh Courier*, November 12, 1955, B22.

14. John Broven, *Record Makers and Breakers: Voices of the Independent Rock 'n' Roll Pioneers* (Champaign: University of Illinois Press, 2009), 255–257.

15. Broven, *Record Makers*, 451.

16. Broven, *Record Makers*, 328–329.

17. Bill Greensmith, Mark Camarigg, and Mike Rowe, *Blues Unlimited: Essential Interviews from the Original Blues Magazine* (Champaign: University of Illinois Press, 2015), 76.

18. Nadine Cohodas, *Spinning Blues into Gold: The Chess Brothers and the Legendary Chess Records* (Winnipeg, MB: Iconoclassic Books, 2012), 96.

19. Dan Fries, "Chuck Berry: An Exclusive Interview," *Goldmine*, November 1979, 7–8.

20. Glenn Ohrlin, *The Hell-Bound Train: A Cowboy Songbook* (Champaign: University of Illinois Press, 1989); J. Hoberman, "A Road Three Hundred Years Long," *New York Times*, May 31, 2015, AR14; Maya Rhodan, "How a Howard Professor Resurrected Lost D.C. Evangelist Film *Hellbound Train*," *Washington Citypaper*, April 11, 2012, https://washingtoncitypaper.com/article/419216/how-a-howard-professor-resurrected -lost-d-c-evangelist-film-hellbound-train/.

21. Berry, *Autobiography*, 135; Elizabeth Lapovsky Kennedy and Madeline D. Davis, *Boots of Leather, Slippers of Gold: The History of a Lesbian Community* (Abingdon, UK: Routledge, 1993); Elizabeth Kennedy, email correspondence with author, March 2021; "When Jazz and the Jitterbug Ruled," *Buffalo News*, December 4, 1994, https:// buffalonews.com/news/when-jazz-and-the-jitterbug-ruled/article_88b20d1c-a82a-5307 -95c1-bffdeefa5da3.html.

CHAPTER 7

1. George White, *Bo Diddley: Living Legend* (Chessington, UK: Castle, 1995).

2. Deke Dickerson, interview with author, October 2020.

3. "Rock and Roll: Respect: Interview with Jerry Wexler (Part 1 of 4)," Open Vault, WGBH, accessed May 7, 2022, https://openvault.wgbh.org/catalog/V_2889FB3D7E 3841F4A844636856821149.

4. Rick Coleman, notes to *Little Richard: The Specialty Sessions*, three-CD box set, Specialty Records, 1989; Joe Levy, "The Wild Heart of Rock & Roll," *Rolling Stone*, May 20, 2020, www.rollingstone.com/music/music-features/little-richard -digital-cover-wild-heart-of-rock-roll-1001378/.

5. Chuck Berry, "The Burnt Scrapbook," interview by Robbie Robertson, disc 3, *Hail! Hail! Rock 'n' Roll: The Ultimate Collector's Edition*, dir. Taylor Hackford (Universal /Image, 2006), DVD.

6. Chuck Berry, "Godfathers of Rock & Roll," interview by Bryant Gumbel, *Today Show*, March 1993, YouTube video, www.youtube.com/watch?v=jqe1WGQP320.

7. Timothy J. McFarlin, "Father(s?) of Rock & Roll: Why the Johnnie Johnson v. Chuck Berry Songwriting Suit Should Change the Way Copyright Law Determines Joint Authorship," *Vanderbilt Journal of Entertainment and Technology Law* 17, no. 3 (2015): 575–672; Byron Kerman, "Rock 'n Roll Has Two Daddies? New Revelations from Johnnie Johnson vs. Chuck Berry Lawsuit," *St. Louis*, March 16, 2015, www.stlmag.com/culture/music /rock-'n-roll-has-two-daddies%3F-new-revelations-from-johnnie-j/; Timothy McFarlin, interview with author, August 2020.

8. Brian Ward, *Just My Soul Responding* (Berkeley: University of California Press, 1998), 95–105; Brian Ward, "Civil Rights and Rock and Roll: Revisiting the Nat King Cole Attack of 1956," *OAH Magazine of History*, April 2010, 21–24; "Rock and Roll Labelled Weapon of Integration," *Atlanta Daily World*, March 30, 1956, 1; "NAACP Infiltrating Dixie's Youth with Rock 'n' Roll, Alabaman Says," *Atlanta Constitution*, March 30, 1956, 6; "NAACP Blamed for 'Rock and Roll' Music in South," *Baltimore Afro-American*, April 7, 1956, 1.

9. "Nat King Cole Comments on Being Assaulted by White Supremacists (Arlington, VA, 4/13/1956)," video, UCLA Film and Television Archive, posted online February 24, 2020, www.youtube.com/watch?v=5pzheB1460Y.

10. Buddy Lonesome, "Sweet Singer Hurt by Critics of 'Passive Action,'" *St. Louis Argus*, April 20, 1956, 1.

11. Stew, interview with author, August 2020.

12. The Beatles, BBC television interview, Manchester, UK, August 28, 1963, Beatles Interviews Database, accessed May 8, 2022, www.beatlesinterviews.org/db1963.0828 .beatles.html.

13. Carl Perkins and David McGee, *Go, Cat, Go!: The Life and Times of Carl Perkins* (New York: Hyperion, 1996), 216.

14. Carl Sally, interview with author, July 2020.

15. Josh Gardner, "Charles Berry Jr. on His Father's Guitars, Music and Legacy," Guitar.com, January 9, 2020, https://guitar.com/features/interviews/charles-berry-jr-chuck -berry-guitars-music-and-legacy/?fbclid=IwAR2p-7JKfzYyCfP6nH_189A8ogyEqt Pm5U_mFo1NCXuXEqT87NE_XjNKDQY.

16. Peter Knobler, "Chuck Berry: Sweet Little 16 Is 32," *Crawdaddy*, April 16, 1972, 25.

17. John Broven, "'See You Later Alligator': Bobby Charles and the Birth of Rock 'n' Roll in South Louisiana," *Now Dig This*, July 2010; Colin Escott, transcript of interview with Bobby Charles, Rock's Back Pages website, August 31, 1994; Alex Rawls, "Hurricane Bobby," *Blurt*, accessed May 8, 2022, https://blurtonline.com/feature/hurricane -bobby-bobby-charles/.

18. Vernon Reid, interview with author, October 2018.

19. Renee C. Romano, *Race Mixing: Black-White Marriage in Postwar America* (Gainesville: University Press of Florida, 2006), 164; "White Council Editor Napped?," *Baltimore Afro-American*, October 27, 1956, 1; "Sex Violation Trips White 'Supremacist,'" *Pittsburgh Courier*, October 27, 1956, 2; Howard Woods, "Portrait of a White Supremacist," *Pittsburgh Courier*, November 24, 1956, 8; Congressional Record Appendix, May 9, 1955, A3082.

CHAPTER 8

1. John Wilcock, "Rock, Rocker, Rockest," *Village Voice*, December 5, 1956; Joshua Buhs, "Milton Subotsky as a Fortean," *From an Oblique Angle* (blog), October 17, 2014, www.joshualbuhs.com/blog/milton-subotsky-as-a-fortean; "Milton Subotsky," Classic Monsters, accessed May 8, 2022, www.classic-monsters.com/milton-subotsky/; Will Hodgkinson, "Blood and Gutsiness," *The Guardian*, February 12, 2009, www.theguardian .com/film/2009/feb/13/british-horror-film-studio-amicus; "Freed's New Movie Adds Up to Triple Threat $'s," *Billboard*, November 17, 1956, 16; Gary Kramer, "Spiced Teen-Age Dish: 'R.R.R.' Jumbo Size Disk Talent Package," *Billboard*, December 8, 1956, 22. Alanfreed.com, a website run by Judith Fisher Freed, contains a wealth of material related to Freed's life, including information on *Rock, Rock, Rock!*

2. Stew, interview with author, August 2020.

3. Philip J. Hickey, quoted in undated newspaper clipping, *St. Louis Globe-Democrat* clipping file, Crime, St L, Juvenile Crime, July, 1956, Mercantile Library, St. Louis.

4. Robert Christgau, "Chuck Berry's Back from the Blues: Johnny B. Grows Up," *Creem*, February 1973, 45.

5. "Hard Working Americans Announce New Live Album, Share Track," JamBands .com, June 22, 2017, https://jambands.com/news/2017/06/22/hard-working-americans -announce-new-live-album-share-track/.

6. Rick Coleman, *Fats Domino and the Lost Dawn of Rock 'N' Roll* (Boston: Da Capo Press, 2006); John Broven, *Record Makers and Breakers: Voices of the Independent Rock 'n' Roll Pioneers* (Champaign: University of Illinois Press, 2009), 452.

7. "Bobby Parker, Part 2," *Beldon's Blues Point* (blog), November 2, 2010, http:// beldonsbluespoint.blogspot.com/2010/11/bobby-parker-part-2.html.

8. Coleman, *Fats Domino*, 154.

9. Buddy Lonesome, "Strolling Along the Avenoo," *St. Louis Argus*, March 1, 1957, 20.

10. Gerald Early, "One Nation Under a Groove," *New Republic*, July 15–22, 1991, 38.

11. Thanks to WFMU DJ Michael Shelly for sharing a recording of this radio interview with Berry.

12. Tom Wheeler, "Chuck Berry: The Interview," *Guitar Player*, March 1988, 56.

13. "Rock and Roll: Renegades: Interview with Johnnie Johnson (Part 1 of 3)," Open Vault, WGBH, accessed May 7, 2022, http://openvault.wgbh.org/catalog/V_FC1D5 C49292D4B1D927D74A4CE93F355.

14. Bruce Pegg, *Brown Eyed Handsome Man: The Life and Hard Times of Chuck Berry* (New York: Routledge 2002), 85; Mark Jacobson, "Interview: Chuck Berry—Mr. Dynamite," *The Independent*, January 27, 2002, 14.

15. Pegg, *Brown Eyed*, 47; Patrick Goldstein, "The Beat Goes On," *Creem*, June 1977, 20.

16. Cabanellas, interview.

17. "Strolling the Avenoo with Buddy Lonesome," *St. Louis Argus*, May 24, 1957, 20. The discussion of "Rock and Roll Music" was greatly shaped by conversations with writer Joe Levy.

18. Karl Gert zur Heide, "Lafayette Leake," *Blues Unlimited*, October 1969, 8; Graeme Flanagan and Keith Macphail, "Lafayette Leake," *Crazy Music*, September 1974, 36–37; David Whiteis, "Lafayette Leake, c. 1920–1990," *Juke Blues*, Winter/ Spring 1991; undated letter from Leake to Jim Delahant, Michael Ochs Collection, box 1, folder 64, Rock and Roll Hall of Fame Library and Archives, Cleveland, OH.

19. Chuck Berry, *Chuck Berry: The Autobiography* (New York: Crown, 1987), 156.

20. Tony Scherman, *Backbeat: Earl Palmer's Story* (Boston: Da Capo Press, 2000), 90–91.

21. Quoted by Tony Scherman in correspondence with author, March 2018.

22. Tom Maloney, interview with author, January 2019.

23. Abraham W. Bolden Sr., interview with author, September 2020.

24. Jim Dickinson, "The Search for Blind Lemon," *Oxford American*, April 20, 2015, https://main.oxfordamerican.org/magazine/item/555-the-search-for-blind-lemon.

25. Ellis Amburn, *Buddy Holly: A Biography* (New York: St. Martin's Press, 1995), 94.

26. Coleman, *Fats Domino*, 169.

27. Paul Anka, *My Way: An Autobiography* (New York: St. Martin's Press, 2013), 31–33.

28. Anka, *My Way*, 56.

29. Bobby Cochran, *Three Steps to Heaven: The Eddie Cochran Story* (Milwaukee: Hal Leonard, 2003), 103–104.

30. LeRoy Ashby, *With Amusement for All* (Lexington: University Press of Kentucky, 2012), 346; Matthew F. Delmont, *The Nicest Kids in Town: American Bandstand, Rock 'n' Roll, and the Struggle for Civil Rights in 1950 Philadelphia* (Berkeley: University of California Press, 2012); Dick Clark and Richard Robinson, *Rock, Roll & Remember* (New York: Thomas Y. Crowell, 1976).

31. Joseph Armstrong, letter to the editor, "American Bandstand," *St. Louis Argus*, January 3, 1958, 2B; Howard B. Woods, "Does 'Bandstand' Have Two Standards?," *St. Louis Argus*, January 10, 1958, 1.

32. Bo Diddley, Little Richard, and Chuck Berry in conversation, disc 3, *Hail! Hail! Rock 'n' Roll: The Ultimate Collector's Edition*, dir. Taylor Hackford (Universal/Image, 2006), DVD.

33. Ann Powers, "Bittersweet Little Rock and Roller," *The Record*, March 21, 2017, www .npr.org/sections/therecord/2017/03/21/520146232/bittersweet-little-rock-and-roller.

34. Matthew F. Delmont, "*American Bandstand* and School Segregation in Postwar Philadelphia" (PhD diss., Brown University, 2008), 7.

35. Clark and Robinson, *Rock, Roll*, 81.

CHAPTER 9

1. Ben Vaughn, interview with author, November 2020.

2. Mark Jacobson, *Teenage Hipster in the Modern World* (New York: Grove Press, 2005), 56.

3. Chuck Berry, *Chuck Berry: The Autobiography* (New York: Crown, 1987), 155–158.

4. Anita Behrman, "What Alan Freed Really Thinks About Rock 'n' Roll," *People Today*, October 1958, 22.

5. Kim Fowley, "Freed in L.A.," *LA Free Press*, March 23, 1978, 23.

6. "Gary James' Interview with Screamin' Jay Hawkins," Classic Bands, accessed May 8, 2022, www.classicbands.com/ScreaminJayHawkinsInterview.html.

7. Randall J. Stephens, *The Devil's Music* (Cambridge, MA: Harvard University Press, 2018), 75.

8. John Sinclair, interview with author, September 2020.

9. Nick Tosches, *Hellfire* (New York: Delacorte Press, 1982), 146, has the most extreme account of the night Lewis set his piano on fire. But everything—where it happened, what Lewis actually said and did—has been disputed, sometimes by Lewis himself. Bruce Pegg, in *Brown Eyed Handsome Man* (New York: Routledge, 2002), has a convincing account from Jack Hooke, who says it did not happen, but that a different confrontation took place in Columbus, Ohio, in which Lewis used the N-word and his dad pulled a knife on Berry. See also the "Speaker to Speaker" column by Greil Marcus, *Artforum*, April 1987, 12.

10. Bernard Weinraub, "Sweet Tunes, Fast Beats and a Hard Edge," *New York Times*, February 23, 2003, 1.

11. Ellis Amburn, *Buddy Holly: A Biography* (New York: St. Martin's Press, 1995), 160.

12. Amburn, *Buddy Holly*, 161.

13. Edgar B. Herwick III, "The Day Boston Banned Rock 'n' Roll," GBH News, May 9, 2014, www.wgbh.org/news/post/day-boston-banned-rock-n-roll; "Defender of Rock 'n' Roll Asks 'What's Been Done About Hoodlums?,'" *Boston Globe*, May 8, 1958, 10; "Boston Police O.K.'d Rock 'n' Roll License," *Boston Globe*, May 9, 1958, 1.

14. Theodore Irwin, "Rock 'n Roll 'n Alan," *Pageant*, July 1957, 56.

15. Bill Greensmith, Mark Camarigg, and Mike Rowe, *Blues Unlimited: Essential Interviews from the Original Blues Magazine* (Champaign: University of Illinois Press, 2015), 220–221.

16. Chuck Berry, "The Burnt Scrapbook," interview by Robbie Robertson, disc 3, *Hail! Hail! Rock 'n' Roll: The Ultimate Collector's Edition*, dir. Taylor Hackford (Universal/Image, 2006), DVD.

17. Chester Himes, *The Quality of Hurt: The Early Years* (St. Paul, MN: Paragon House, 1990), 109–110.

18. George Schuyler, "Traveling Jim Crow," *American Mercury*, August 1930, 432.

19. Paul Gilroy, *Darker than Blue* (Cambridge, MA: Belknap Press, 2011), 84. See also: Paul Gilroy, "Driving While Black," in *Car Cultures*, ed. Daniel Miller (New York: Routledge, 2001), 81–104; Gretchen Sorin, *Driving While Black: African American Travel and the Road to Civil Rights* (New York: Liveright, 2020); Cotton Seiler, *Republic of Drivers: A Cultural History of Automobility in America* (Chicago: University of Chicago Press, 2008); Cotton Seiler, "'So That We as a Race Might Have Something Authentic to Travel By': African American Automobility and Cold-War Liberalism," *American Quarterly*, December 2006, 1091–1117; Kathleen Franz, "The Open Road: Automobility and Racial Uplift in the Interwar Years," in *Technology and the African-American Experience: Needs and the Opportunity for Study*, ed. Bruce Sinclair (Cambridge, MA: MIT Press, 2004), 132–154.

20. "Why Negroes Buy Cadillacs," *Ebony*, September 1949, 34; Margaret Myers and Sharon G. Dean, "Cadillac Flambe: Race and Brand Identity," *Charm* 13 (2007): 157–161; Isabel Wilkerson, *The Warmth of Other Suns: The Epic Story of America's Great Migration* (New York: Random House, 2010), 299–300.

21. Harry S. Sharpe, "Jack Johnson Tells How Owning 4 Autos Help Him Save at Least $8,000 a Year," *St. Louis Post-Dispatch*, March 10, 1912, A8. Also: "Jack Johnson and White Bride Posing for Photograph at Wedding Ceremony" and "Jack Johnson to Tour Illinois in Auto with Bride," *St. Louis Post-Dispatch*, December 4, 1912, 3; Robert Edgren, "Johnson Longs Most to Break Auto Records," *St. Louis Post-Dispatch*, January 6, 1910, 17.

22. "Jack Sits with White Women," *Los Angeles Times*, May 1, 1910, 13.

23. The narrative of Berry's 1958 roadside arrest and details of law enforcement's increasing interest in him are found in documents from US District Court, Eastern District of Missouri, Eastern Division, including *United States of America v. Charles Anderson Edward Berry, February 12, 1960*. The *Globe-Democrat* Collection at the St. Louis Mercantile Library has news clippings covering the event; "Rock 'n' Roll Star Nabbed on Weapons Charge," *St. Louis Post-Dispatch*, June 3, 1958; "Rock 'n Roller Chuck Berry 'All Tore Up,'" *St. Louis Argus*, June 6, 1958.

24. Pegg, *Brown Eyed*, 95.

25. "White Men Fight Blacks Tonight," *Los Angeles Times*, May 16, 1902, 3; "Pink Furies Blaze Away," *Los Angeles Times*, May 17, 1902, 1.

26. Wil Haygood, *Sweet Thunder: The Life and Times of Sugar Ray Robinson* (New York: Knopf, 2009), 132.

27. Daniel A. Nathan, "Sugar Ray Robinson, the Sweet Science, and the Politics of Meaning," *Journal of Sport History* (Spring 1999): 166.

28. *Jazz on a Summer's Day*, dir. Bert Stern (1959; Kino Lorber 2021), DVD; Nadine Cohodas, *Spinning Blues into Gold: The Chess Brothers and the Legendary Chess Records* (Winnipeg, MB: Iconoclassic Books, 2012), 164.

29. David B. Bittan, "Jazz Purists Razz Berry at Newport," *Variety*, July 9, 1958, 53; Nate Chinen, "Remembering Chuck Berry's Scandalous Stand at the 1958 Newport

Jazz Festival," WBGO, March 18, 2017, www.wbgo.org/music/2017-03-18/remembering
-chuck-berrys-scandalous-stand-at-the-1958-newport-jazz-festival; Irving Lichtman, "Inside Track," *Billboard*, October 31, 1987, 102.

30. Jessica R. Pliley, *Policing Sexuality: The Mann Act and the Making of the FBI* (Cambridge, MA: Harvard University Press, 2014); David J. Langum, *Crossing Over the Line:
Legislating Morality and the Mann Act* (Chicago: University of Chicago Press, 1994).

31. Geoffrey C. Ward, *Unforgivable Blackness: The Rise and Fall of Jack Johnson*
(New York: Knopf, 2004); Finis Farr, *Black Champion* (New York: Charles Scribner's
Sons, 1964); Al-Tony Gilmore, *Bad N*****!: The National Impact of Jack Johnson* (Port
Washington, WI: Kennikat Press, 1975); Jessica R. Pliley, "A Pardon Arrives 105 Years
Too Late," *The Atlantic*, May 30, 2018, www.theatlantic.com/ideas/archive/2018/05/a
-pardon-arrives-105-years-too-late/561407/; Rebecca Wanzo, "Black Slaver: Jack John-
son and the Mann Act," in *The Cambridge Companion to Boxing*, ed. Gerald Early (Cambridge, UK: Cambridge University Press, 2019), 273–278.

32. "Rock 'n Roll Singer Fined for Peeping," *Roanoke World-News*, August 15, 1958;
Dan Casey, "The Day Chuck Berry Got Arrested in Salem," *Roanoke Times*, March 22,
2017; Tad Dickens, "Chuck Berry Left a Sour Note on Roanoke," *Roanoke Times*, August
14, 2008; Tad Dickens, interview with author, February 2021.

33. Ntozake Shange, *Betsey Brown* (New York: St. Martin's Press, 1985); Jane Henderson, "Betsey Brown Gives Voice to a St. Louis Girl Living Through Pivotal Time," *St. Louis
Post-Dispatch*, May 1, 2005, F1; Chris Naffziger, "For One Resident of the Private Street,
Windermere Place, Inclusion Is King," *St. Louis Magazine*, July 31, 2020, www.stlmag
.com/history/windermere-place-west-end-private-street-inclusion/; Kim Plummer, "Daughter of Legend Wants Own Career in Rock 'n' Roll," *St. Louis Globe-Democrat*, March 22,
1983.

34. Melody Berry and Charles Berry Jr., *In Their Own Words: Chuck Berry*, episode of
PBS documentary series, 2021; Charles Berry Jr., "Chuck Berry's Son Remembers Rock
Pioneer," *Rolling Stone*, March 19, 2017, www.rollingstone.com/music/music-news/chuck
-berrys-son-remembers-rock-pioneer-he-was-inspirational-106800/.

35. Berry, *Autobiography*, 163–166.

36. Berry, *Autobiography*, 170.

37. Berry, *Autobiography*, 193.

38. Sharony Andrews Green, interview with author, February 2021.

39. Berry, *Autobiography*, 175.

40. Norman Jopling, "Chuck Berry: Rock Lives!," *Record Mirror*, March 4, 1967.

41. *Chuck Berry: The Original King of Rock 'n' Roll*, dir. Jon Brewer (MVD Entertainment, 2018), DVD.

42. Charles Berry Jr., speaking at a St. Louis Public Library panel discussion,
November 5, 2017.

CHAPTER 10

1. David Brearley, "Race Record? It's Only Rock 'n' Roll," *Weekend Australian*, March 30,
2002, 21; "Country Music as a Bridge to History," Vanderbilt University News, December
6, 2010, https://news.vanderbilt.edu/2010/12/06/country-music-as-a-bridge-to-history/.

2. Peter Cox, "The Ambonese Connection: Lou Casch, Johnny O'Keefe and the Development of Australian Rock and Roll," *Perfect Beat*, October 2015, 1–17; transcript of a February 1993 interview with Lou Casch conducted by Peter Cox; Brearley, "Race Record?"

3. Brearley, "Race Record?"

4. Theresa Runstedtler, *Jack Johnson: Rebel Sojourner* (Berkeley: University of California Press, 2012), 31–67.

5. Charles Berry Jr., *Vinyl Emergency* (podcast), September 8, 2017, https://vinyl emergency.libsyn.com/size/25/?search=berry.

6. Chuck Berry, interview by Greil Marcus and Q&A with students, University of California, Berkeley, 1969, transcript provided to author by Marcus; edited version appears in *Rolling Stone*, June 14, 1969.

7. Etta James and David Ritz, *Rage to Survive: The Etta James Story* (New York: Villard, 1995), 95.

8. Mark Jacobson, *Teenage Hipster in the Modern World* (New York: Grove Press, 2005), 51.

9. Berry, UC Berkeley Q&A.

10. Jimmy Clanton, interview with author, March 2021.

11. "Chuck Berry," unpublished account of the Meridian incident by Charles Broome; Charles Broome, interview with author, December 2020.

12. UPI, "Negro Record Star Held for Asking Date with White," *Delta Democrat-Times*, Greenville, Mississippi, August 28, 1959, 1; "Negro Rock 'n' Roll Singer Is Freed on Bond," *Laurel Mississippi Leader-Call*, August 29, 1959, 1; UPI, "Authorities Escort Berry to Airport at Meridian" *Bristol Herald Courier*, August 30, 1959, 6A; UPI, "Berry Tells His Side of Meridian Arrest," *Delta Democrat-Times*, August 31, 1959, 1; A. S. "Doc" Young, "The Big Beat: News, Notes and Nutmeg," *Los Angeles Sentinel*, September 2, 1959, 17; Ole Nosey's "Everybody Goes When the Wagon Comes," *Chicago Defender*, September 2, 1959, 17; "They Had Me Wrong," *Norfolk New Journal and Guide*, September 5, 1959, 22; "Don't Even Ask for Date in Dixie!," *Amsterdam News*, September 5, 1959, 13.

13. Tom Mitchell, "Chuck Berry Tells of Arrest in Mississippi," *Baltimore Afro-American*, September 12, 1959, 7.

14. Trezzvant W. Anderson, "Louis Jordan Says: Rock 'n' Roll Has Got to Go!," *Pittsburgh Courier*, December 26, 1959, 23.

15. Details of Berry's drive from Ciudad Juárez to St. Louis are drawn from documents from the US District Court, Eastern District of Missouri, Eastern Division, as well as the US Court of Appeals, Eighth Circuit. See also J. P. Robinson, "The Trial of Chuck Berry," *Medium*, November 12, 2019, https://jprobinson.medium.com/the -trial-of-chuck-berry-d016ec3c0175.

16. "Hail! St Louis' Great White Way: Grand Avenue Blazes Again with Opening of Re-beautified St. Louis and Missouri Theaters," *St. Louis Post-Dispatch*, September 3, 1936, 31.

CHAPTER 11

1. John R. Brophy, "Quiet Island in Bustling City to Vanish When Good Shepherd Convent Moves," *St. Louis Post-Dispatch*, July 11, 1969, 51.

2. Harry B. Wilson, "Between the Lines," *St. Louis Globe-Democrat*, October 25, 1951; "Judge Moore Has Busy Day Denying Report He Is Dead," *St. Louis Globe-Democrat*, May 4, 1959; "George H. Moore, Retired Federal Judge, Dies," *St. Louis Globe-Democrat*, November 6, 1962.

3. This account draws from court records of *United States v. Berry* 59CR322.

4. Bruce Pegg, *Brown Eyed Handsome Man* (New York: Routledge, 2002), 157.

5. Robert Hilburn, "Chuck Berry Sets the Record Straight," *Los Angeles Times*, October 4, 1987.

CHAPTER 12

1. Louis N. Robinson, "Institutions for Defective Delinquents," *Journal of Criminal Law and Criminology* (Summer 1933): 373–374; Michael S. Clarke, "'The Fed Med': 90 Years in Springfield, Missouri," *Missouri Medicine*, November/December 2020, 520–522; Jim Burroway, "The Judge Says 'Send Him to Springfield.' So He Is There. Then What?," Emphasis Mine, April 9, 2019, http://jimburroway.com/history/the-judge-says-send-him-to-springfield-so-he-is-there-then-what/.

2. Chuck Berry, "The Burnt Scrapbook," interview by Robbie Robertson, disc 3, *Hail! Hail! Rock 'n' Roll: The Ultimate Collector's Edition*, dir. Taylor Hackford (Universal/Image, 2006), DVD.

3. Chuck Berry, *Chuck Berry: The Autobiography* (New York: Crown, 1987), 212.

4. David Hinckley, "Sweet Little 61," City Lights, *New York Daily News*, October 11, 1987, 17.

5. Lee Alan, *Turn Your Radio On!* (n.p.: KWP Publishing, 2004), 220–238; Alan, interview with author, September 2020; *Chuck Berry: Rock and Roll Music Any Old Way You Choose It: The Complete Studio Recordings Plus!*, October 25, 1963, show, Walled Lake Casino, CD 13 (Bear Family, 2014).

6. Ben Sandmel, "Lonnie Mack Is Back on the Track," *Guitar World*, May 1984, 54–56; Randy McNutt, *Guitar Towns* (Bloomington: Indiana University Press, 2002), 169–179; Michael Buffalo Smith, "Lonnie Mack, the Guitar Player's Guitar Player," Swampland.com, June 2000, www.swampland.com/articles/view/title:lonnie_mack.

7. "The Switched-On Market: How to Turn Up Your Volume," *Billboard*, July 1, 1967, ws47.

8. Jann Wenner, "The Rolling Stone Interview: Mike Bloomfield, Pt. 1," *Rolling Stone*, April 6, 1968.

9. Randy Lewis, "After Blurred Lines Verdict, Brian Wilson Talks Chuck Berry and Surfin' U.S.A.," *Los Angeles Times*, March 12, 2015. In this interview Brian Wilson states it plainly: "I just took 'Sweet Little Sixteen' and rewrote it into something of our own."

10. Wayne Kramer, interview with author, March 2020.

11. Tzvi Gluckin, "Forgotten Heroes: Pete Cosey," *Premier Guitar*, November 19, 2015, www.premierguitar.com/artists/forgotten-heroes-pete-cosey.

12. "Making Interiority Visible: Dawoud Bey Interviewed by Louis Bury," *Bomb*, April 5, 2019.

13. Springsteen said it while being interviewed in *Hail! Hail! Rock 'n' Roll*.

14. Adam Jeffrey Pratt, "The Cavalier in the Mind of the South, 1876–1916" (PhD diss., Louisiana State University, 2007), v.

15. Chess advertisement, telegram from WINS to Chess Records, *Billboard*, February 22, 1964, 14.

16. *Cash Box*, June 6, 1964.

17. Stephanie Bennett, *Johnny B. Bad: Chuck Berry and the Making of Hail! Hail! Rock 'n' Roll* (Los Angeles: Rare Bird Books, 2019), 31.

18. Chris Welch, *Peter Grant: The Man Who Led Zeppelin* (London: Omnibus Press, 2001), 22–30; Mark Blake, *Bring It on Home: Peter Grant, Led Zeppelin, and Beyond* (New York: Da Capo Press, 2018), 36–37.

CHAPTER 13

1. John Hawken, interview with author, November 2018; June Harris, "Chuck Berry: At Last It's the Real Thing!," *Disc*, July 1963.

2. Mark Blake, *Bring It on Home: Peter Grant, Led Zeppelin, and Beyond* (New York: Da Capo Press, 2018), 39–40; Richard Thompson, interview with author, August 2021.

3. Eric Burdon, *I Used to Be an Animal, but I'm All Right Now* (Boston: Faber and Faber, 1986), 59–63.

4. John Broven, interview with author, May 2021.

5. Roger Fairhurst, interview with author, September 2018; James Craig, "When Chuck Snubbed the Rolling Stones," *Record World*, January 2, 1965, 7.

6. "Rock and Roll: Renegades: Interview with Phil Chess and Marshall Chess (Part 3 of 4)," Open Vault, WGBH, accessed May 7, 2022, http://openvault.wgbh.org /catalog/V_310B44AC503443838CBCF6566647B6EF.

7. Joe Hutchins, "How Much Do They Owe Chuck?," *Baltimore Afro-American*, July 17, 1965, A1.

8. Scott K. Fish, "Fred Below: Magic Maker," *Modern Drummer*, September 1983, 108.

9. Steve Knopper, "Hunting for the 'Promised Land,' Haunted by Chuck Berry," *New York Times*, September 11, 2017, TR1.

10. Raymond Arsenault, *Freedom Riders: 1961 and the Struggle for Racial Justice* (Cary, NC: Oxford University Press, 2006), 121–123.

11. Reginald Stuart, "Freedom Riders Find Pride and Pain on '61 Route," *New York Times*, May 10, 1981, 1.

12. John A. Williams, *This Is My Country Too* (New York: New American Library, 1965).

13. Bob Greene column, *Washington Post*, February 15, 1988.

14. Bill Wyman and Ray Coleman, *Stone Alone: The Story of a Rock 'n' Roll Band* (New York: Viking, 1990), 217; Laurie Henshaw, "Enter the Cool Chuck Berry—with an Eye on the Whole Scene," *Melody Maker*, July 12, 1969, 5.

15. Guy Stevens, "Chuck Berry Tells Guy Stevens About 'How I Write My Songs,'" *Record Mirror*, April 4, 1964.

16. "Andy Gray Covers the Sensational 60s," column, undated *New Musical Express* supplement, 1969.

CHAPTER 14

1. Andrew Loog Oldham, *Stoned: A Memoir of London in the 1960s* (New York: St. Martin's Press, 2001), 266.

2. *Robert Stigwood Associates Ltd. Presents King of Rhythm & Blues Chuck Berry*, undated booklet, Ray Topping Papers, box 1, folder 3, Rock and Roll Hall of Fame Library and Archives, Cleveland, OH.

3. Roger Fairhurst, interview with author, September 2018.

4. Peter Meaden, "Berry Favourites," *Record World*, January 30, 1965, 8.

5. This account comes from my interview with Fairhurst and from *On Tour with Chuck Berry: Roger Fairhurst Looks Back to 1964/65*, a booklet accompanying the *Chuck Berry: Rock and Roll Music* CD box set.

6. Jim Irvin, "The Story of Pye Records," liner notes (Sequel Records, 1998).

7. Deke Dickerson, "Deke Dickerson interviews Jules Blattner the Man . . . the Legend," *Show Me Blowout!* #1, 1986, Jules M. Blattner Papers, news clippings folder, Missouri History Museum Archives, St. Louis.

8. Jesse McReynolds, interview with author, October 2018.

9. Buck Owens, "Pledge to Country Music," *Music City News*, March 1965, 12; advertisement, *Billboard*, August 3, 1974, 18; "Buck Owens a Maverick," *Billboard*, August 3, 1974, 18.

10. Bob Dylan and Cameron Crowe, booklet for *Biograph* (Columbia, 1985).

11. Robert Hilburn, "Chuck Berry Talks Music, Race and His 'Difficult' Reputation," *Los Angeles Times*, October 4, 1987.

12. Norman Jopling, "Chuck Berry: Rock Lives!," *Record Mirror*, March 4, 1967; "Mercury Signs Chuck Berry," *Billboard*, August 6, 1966, 52; "Mercury Strengthens Ranks in R&B," *Pittsburgh Courier*, May 20, 1967, 13.

13. Jopling, "Rock Lives!"; "Chuck Berry Records at Home Now," *New Musical Express*, April 30, 1965, 12; Bruce R. Olson, *That St. Louis Thing*, vol. 2 (self-pub., Lulu Press, 2016), 157.

14. Themetta Berry, *In Their Own Words: Chuck Berry*, episode of PBS documentary series, 2021.

15. Steve Scorfina, interview with author, September 2019.

16. Bill Graham and Robert Greenfield, *Bill Graham Presents: My Life Inside Rock and Out* (New York: Doubleday, 1992), 177–180.

17. "Managers, Bookers: The Gray Flanneled Hipsters," *Billboard*, May 6, 1967, SF28.

18. Graham and Greenfield, *My Life*, 178.

19. Steve Miller, interview with author, February 2019; Steve Miller, "Steve Miller Remembers Chuck Berry: He Was Like a Gazelle," *Rolling Stone*, March 23, 2017, www.rollingstone.com/music/music-news/steve-miller-remembers-chuck-berry-he-was-like-a-gazelle-109964/.

20. Charles Berry Jr., *In Their Own Words*.

21. Chuck Berry, "The Burnt Scrapbook," interview by Robbie Robertson, disc 3, *Hail! Hail! Rock 'n' Roll: The Ultimate Collector's Edition*, dir. Taylor Hackford (Universal/Image, 2006), DVD.

22. Ritchie Yorke, "Ritchie Yorke Gets Backstage Interview Between Sets," *Ottowa Journal*, July 5, 1968, 8.

CHAPTER 15

1. Michael Lydon, "Monterey Pop: The First Rock Festival," Criterion Collection website, September 22, 2009, www.criterion.com/current/posts/231-monterey-pop-the-first-rock-festival.

2. Michael Lydon, "Where's the Money from Monterey Pop?," *Rolling Stone*, November 9, 1967; Robert Christgau, "Anatomy of a Love Festival," *Esquire*, January 1968; Elijah Wald, *How the Beatles Destroyed Rock 'n' Roll* (Cary, NC: Oxford University Press, 2009), 245.

3. Phyl Garland, *The Sound of Soul* (New York: NTC/Contemporary Publishing, 1969), 16.

4. Augie Meyers, interview with author, June 2021.

5. Patrick William Salvo, "When Chuck Berry Plays, It's Just Second Nature," *Gallery*, March 1973, 114.

6. Nadine Cohodas, *Spinning Blues into Gold: The Chess Brothers and the Legendary Chess Records* (Winnipeg, MB: Iconoclassic Books, 2012), 301; Chuck Berry, *Chuck Berry: The Autobiography* (New York: Crown, 1987), 246.

7. Peter Guralnick and Chuck Berry, interview for 2011 *Summit of Rock*, DVD made by the Rock and Roll Hall of Fame; William Krasilovsky and Sidney Shemel, *This Business of Music* (New York: Potter/Ten Speed, 2007); "M. William Krasilovsky, 'This Business of Music' Co-Author, Dies at 92," *Variety*, October 10, 2018; Cohodas, *Spinning Blues*, 309; Robert S. Meloni, interview with author, November 2019.

8. Bob Baldori, interview with author, November 2018.

9. Jordan Orleans, interview with author, October 2018.

10. Lou Cohan, "Reelin' 'n' Rockin' with Chuck Berry," *Thunder Road* #5, 1980.

11. Robert Christgau, "Chuck Berry's Back from the Blues: Johnny B. Grows Up," *Creem*, February 1973.

12. Guralnick and Berry, *Summit of Rock*.

13. Krista Reese, *Chuck Berry: Mr. Rock n' Roll* (New York: Proteus Books, 1982), 88.

14. Richard Harrington, "Rock 'n' Roll Returns," *Washington Star*, October 13, 1972, 32; Gary U.S. Bonds and Stephen Cooper, *By U.S. Bonds: That's My Story* (Palm Beach, FL: Wheatley Press, 2013); Claude Hall, "Concept Concerts and Answer to Stars' $$," *Billboard*, October 26, 1976, 35; "RnR Revival Marks Third Year with Vol. 10," *Billboard*, October 14, 1972, 28; Richard Cromelin, "Rock and Roll Revival: Richard Nader's Lament," *Phonograph Record*, November 1972.

15. "Teen Scene," *Kingston New York Daily Sunday Freeman*, May 26, 1974; Erin Williams, "Musician Billy Peek Shares Memories of the Late Chuck Berry," *St. Louis*, April 20, 2017, www.stlmag.com/culture/music/billy-peek-shares-musical-memories-of -the-late-chuck-berry/; Jem Aswad, "Chuck Berry's Guitarist Billy Peek Looks Back on 50 Years of Music and Friendship," *Billboard*, March 21, 2017; Thomas Melin, "When Elvis Met Chuck Berry in Las Vegas," *Elvis Today Blog*, August 23, 2007, www.elvistodayblog .com/2007/08/when-elvis-met-chuck-berry-in-las-vegas.html; Alan Hanson, "Elvis Presley and Chuck Berry . . . Connections and Disconnects," *Elvis History Blog*, April 2011, www.elvis-history-blog.com/elvis-chuck-berry.html.

16. Chuck Berry, interview by Greil Marcus and Q&A with students, University of California, Berkeley, 1969, transcript provided to author by Marcus; edited version appears in *Rolling Stone*, June 14, 1969.

17. Patrick William Salvo, "A Conversation with Chuck Berry," *Rolling Stone*, November 23, 1972, 42.

18. "Little Richard Amazing Interview," video, belfast jack, posted online May 10, 2020, www.youtube.com/watch?v=4nFWpRD8UlY.

19. Wayne Kramer, interview with author, March 2020.

20. Simon Frith, "Letter from Britain," *Creem*, September 1972, 36; Charlie Gillett, "Chuck Berry: Go Chuck Baby Go," *New Musical Express*, February 17, 1973.

CHAPTER 16

1. Jason Berry, Jonathan Foose, and Tad Jones, *Up from the Cradle of Jazz: New Orleans Rhythm & Blues Since World War II* (Athens: University of Georgia Press, 1986), 144; John Broven, *Rhythm & Blues in New Orleans* (Gretna, LA: Pelican Publishing, 1978), 46.

2. Tony Stewart, "Berry Magic," *New Musical Express*, February 12, 1972.

3. Charles Shaar Murray, "Big Red Cars, Little White Chicks and the Chuck Berry Lick," *Creem*, March 1972.

4. Tony Stewart, "Chuck Berry, Pink Floyd, Billy Preston, Slade: Locarno Ballroom, Coventry," *New Musical Express*, February 12, 1972.

5. Shana Redmond, "The Sounds We Make Together: Chuck Berry's Onomatopoeia," (Sonic Burdens Virtual Panel, IASPM-US Conference, February 20, 2013), http://ias pm-us.net/sonic-borders-virtual-panel-shana-redmond-the-sounds-we-make-togeth-er-chuck-berrys-onomatopoeia/. This chapter has been greatly influenced by Redmond's work.

6. Joseph Carthon Wormer, "Famous Songs and Their History," *New Orleans Times-Democrat*, June 19, 1910, 52.

7. Patrick William Salvo, "A Conversation with Chuck Berry," *Rolling Stone*, November 23, 1972, 36.

8. Jimmy Guterman and Owen O'Donnell, *The Worst Rock n' Roll Records of All Time* (New York: Citadel Press, 1991).

9. Dave Barry, *Dave Barry's Book of Bad Songs* (Kansas City: Andrew McMeel, 1997), 39.

10. Robert Christgau, "Chuck Berry's Back from the Blues: Johnny B. Grows Up," *Creem*, February 1973.

11. Ben Thompson, ed., *Ban This Filth!: Letters from the Mary Whitehouse Archive* (London: Faber and Faber, 2012).

12. Russell Leadbetter, "Those Were the Days," *The Herald* (Scotland), September 11, 2018, www.heraldscotland.com/opinion/16836077.days-1973-chuck-berry-subject-mrs -white-horse/.

13. Tom Maloney, interview with author, January 2019.

14. "Berry Signs New Chess Tie," *Cash Box*, October 21, 1972, 7; "Ding a Berry," *Record World*, October 28, 1972, 52; Tom Hibbert, "Who the Hell Does Chuck Berry Think He Is?," *Q*, May 1988.

15. Linda Harlan, interview with author, September 2018.

16. Vernon Reid, interview with author, October 2018.

17. Robert S. Meloni, interview with author, November 2019.

18. John Swenson, "I Did Every God Damned Thing Myself: The Dave Bartholomew Century," *Offbeat*, November 28, 2018, 16–19.

CHAPTER 17

1. Krista Reese, *Chuck Berry: Mr. Rock n' Roll* (New York: Proteus Books, 1982), 87–88; "Metromedia Film Touted as 'Woodstock of Oldies,'" *Billboard*, April 7, 1973, 14.

2. Chuck Berry, interview by Greil Marcus and Q&A with students, University of California, Berkeley, 1969, transcript provided to author by Marcus; edited version appears in *Rolling Stone*, June 14, 1969.

3. Patrick William Salvo, "When Chuck Berry Plays, It's Just Second Nature," *Gallery*, March 1973.

4. Barb Kirk, interview with author, December 2020, and subsequent correspondence.

5. Peter Knobler, "Chuck Berry: Sweet Little 16 Is 32," *Crawdaddy*, April 16, 1972, 25.

6. From a newspaper clipping shown on-screen during *Chuck Berry: The Original King of Rock 'n' Roll*, dir. Jon Brewer (MVD Entertainment, 2018), DVD.

7. Salvo, "When Chuck Berry Plays," 140.

8. Knobler, "Sweet Little 16."

9. Bill Lane, "People, Places 'n' Situwayshuns," *Los Angeles Sentinel*, June 7, 1973, B2.

10. This account comes from an interview with Susan Hamilton, October 2019, and from her book, *Hit Woman* (New York: Hit Woman Publishing, 2013), 193–200.

11. Dick Alen, interview with author, November 2018.

12. Greil Marcus, *Dead Elvis: A Chronicle of a Cultural Obsession* (New York: Doubleday, 1991), 4.

13. Editorial, *St. Louis Post-Dispatch*, reprinted in Neal and Janice Gregory, *When Elvis Died* (Washington, DC: Communications Press, 1980), 252.

14. Jeannette Cooperman, "A Conversation with Chuck Berry, King of Rock 'n' Roll," *St. Louis*, November 24, 2008, www.stlmag.com/A-Conversation-with-Chuck-Berry/.

15. Megan Gambino, "What Is on *Voyager's* Golden Record?," *Smithsonian*, April 22, 2012, www.smithsonianmag.com/science-nature/what-is-on-voyagers-golden-record-73063839/.

16. Mike Mesey, interview with author, October 2019.

17. AP, "Voyager 2 Finds Triton Volcanoes That Blast Nitrogen Ice 20 Miles High," *Indiana (Penn.) Gazette*, March 2, 1981, 1.

18. Floyd Mutrux, interview with author, April 2019.

19. "Suit Against Singer Settled," *St. Louis Post-Dispatch*, October 2, 1975.

20. Charles Berry Jr. quoted in *The Original King*; Richard K. Weil, "Festival in the Red, Promoters Are Blue," *St. Louis Post-Dispatch*, July 5, 1974, 1; Merrill Brown, "Rock Festival a Disaster in Almost Every Way," *St. Louis Post-Dispatch*, July 5, 1974, 4B; reporting from Al Akerson and Bob Pierce, *St. Louis Globe-Democrat*, July 5, 1974; UPI, "Midwest Rock Concerts Turn Out to Be Busts," *Galesburg (Ill.) Register-Mail*, July 5, 1974, 8.

21. "2 Girls Drown in Park Pool," *St. Louis Post-Dispatch*, August 12, 1974, 9A; Bruce Pegg, *Brown Eyed Handsome Man* (New York: Routledge, 2002), 204.

22. Leo Fitzmaurice, "St. Charles County Seeks to Close Club," *St. Louis Post-Dispatch*, August 27, 1974; "Rock Concert Site Is Ordered Closed," *St. Louis Post-Dispatch*, September 11, 1974.

23. Kevin Fleming, interview with author, June 2019.

24. *The Original King*.

25. John Collis, *Chuck Berry: The Biography* (London: Aurum Press, 2002), 179; Chuck Berry, *Chuck Berry: The Autobiography* (New York: Crown, 1987), 273–275.

26. Reese, *Mr. Rock n' Roll*, 113.

27. "Johnny Be Good," *Omnibus*, BBC One, 1980; Joy Billington, "Music Is the Message at This Carter Party," *Washington Star*, June 8, 1979, 42.

28. "Rock Singer 'Chuck' Berry Charged with Tax Evasion," *St. Louis Post-Dispatch*, May 14, 1979, 3A; Linda Deutsch, "Chuck Berry Gets 120-Day Sentence," *San Bernardino County Sun*, July 11, 1979, 3.

29. Marshall Chess, *In Their Own Words: Chuck Berry*, episode of PBS documentary series, 2021.

30. Lou Cohan, "Reelin' 'n' Rockin' with Chuck Berry," *Thunder Road* #5, 1980.

CHAPTER 18

1. Slick Stefaniak, interview with author, April 2019.

2. William Morris Agency contract, Smoking Gun website, accessed May 11, 2022, www.thesmokinggun.com/file/chuck-berry.

3. Anthony Wall, "Chuck Berry 40 Years On," 1977 profile, BBC Radio.

4. Jimmy Marsala, interview with author, March 2018. His *Memories of Chuck* (self-pub., Friesen Press, 2018) offers numerous tales of life on the road.

5. Charles Berry Jr., speaking at a St. Louis Public Library panel discussion, November 5, 2017.

6. Bob Woffinden, "Chuck Berry: Chuck Has Been Leaving the Stage for 20 Years," *New Musical Express*, March 8, 1975.

7. Wall, "40 Years On."

8. Carmen's story appears on the Steve Hoffman Music Forum website, October 18, 2003, https://forums.stevehoffman.tv/threads/happy-birthday-chuck-berry.23073/#post-395772.

9. Vernon Reid, interview with author, October 2018.

10. Chuck Berry, "Johnny Be Good," *Omnibus*, BBC One, 1980.

11. Ben Sandmel, interview with author, October 2018.

12. "Entertainment," *Jet*, August 16, 1979, 54.

13. Woffinden, "Has Been Leaving."

14. This story is told in Kenny Weissberg, *Off My Rocker* (Boulder, CO: Sandra Jonas Publishing House, 2013), 201–210 Kindle edition.

15. Charlie Pickett, interview with author, June 2018.

16. Jesper Eklow, interview with author, July 2021.

17. Peter O'Neill, interview with author, February 2020.

18. Richard Thompson, interview with author, August 2021.

19. Quint Davis, interview with author, July 2019.

20. "Johnny Be Good."

21. Portions of this account first appeared as an oral history of the night Chuck Berry met the Circle Jerks: RJ Smith, "Circleberry," byNWR.com, accessed May 11, 2022 (originally posted November 2020), www.bynwr.com/articles/circleberry. Among those interviewed in 2020: Mark Goldman, Andy Mayberry, Keith Morris, Zander Schloss, Angela Pezel.

CHAPTER 19

1. Diane sought me out in 2019, making clear she wanted to share her story. The account of her relationship with Berry was related via interviews, emails, and documents in Diane's possession.

2. *The Mike Douglas Show*, season 10, episode 154, originally aired April 15, 1971, https://thetvdb.com/series/the-mike-douglas-show/episodes/5560404.

3. Ellen Sander, interview with author, August 2021.

4. Between 2019 and 2021, Mirandi Babitz and I corresponded through email.

5. Dan Wakefield, "My Favorite Year: In Los Angeles with Eve Babitz in 1971," *Los Angeles Review of Books*, November 28, 2018, https://lareviewofbooks.org/article/my-favorite-year-in-los-angeles-with-eve-babitz-in-1971/.

6. The making of *Hail! Hail! Rock 'n' Roll* is described based on interviews with producer Stephanie Bennett (April 2019), director Taylor Hackford (November 2019), line producer Thomas D. Adelman (May 2019), and others. Bennett's memoir *Johnny B. Bad* (Los Angeles: Vireo/Rare Bird Books, 2019) depicts what it was like to work with Berry. Bonus interviews, outtakes, and the film itself, all available on DVD as *The Ultimate Collector's Edition* (Universal/Image, 2006), also inform this account.

7. This account comes from Bennett, *Johnny B. Bad*, 96–107, and interviews with Bennett and Hackford.

8. Joey Spampinato, interview with author, December 2018.

9. Charles Berry Jr., speaking at a St. Louis Public Library panel discussion, November 5, 2017; Hackford, interview.

10. David Hinckley, "Sweet Little 61," City Lights, *New York Daily News*, October 11, 1987.

11. Tom Maloney, interview with author, January 2019.

12. C. B. Adams, clipping without headline, *St. Louis Globe-Democrat*, October 18–19, 1986, *Globe-Democrat* archive, *Hail! Hail!* folder.

CHAPTER 20

1. Jim Mervis, interview with author, March 2019.

2. Michael Pietsch, interview with author, October 2018.

3. Rachel Kushner, *LARB Radio Hour* (podcast), April 2021, https://lareviewofbooks .libsyn.com/2021/04.

4. Tom Maloney, interview with author, January 2019.

5. Bob Greene, *Chicago Tribune* column, September 1987, syndicated nationally.

6. "In Transition," *Newsweek*, June 1988; UPI, "Rock Pioneer Chuck Berry Fails to Show Up on Warrant," UPI wire story; "Chuck Berry Pays Fine for Harassment," AP wire story, November 1988.

7. Kris Anglemyer, interview with author, May 2019.

8. "Southern Air," *Lost Tables* (blog), accessed May 11, 2022, https://losttables.com /southern/southern.htm; Karen Bode Baxter and Ruth Keenoy, *Reconnaissance Level Survey of Historic Downtown Wentzville*, report submitted to Wentzville Downtown Committee, July 28, 2018, 44, 54, 55; Ralph Dummit, "Wentzville Area Sings the Blues for Landmark Restaurant," *St. Louis Post-Dispatch*, February 4, 1996; "As the Sauce Thickens," *Lakeshore Times*, June 13–19, 1988.

9. Yvonne Cumbie (McCue), interview with author, October 2018.

10. Jeannette Cooperman, "A Conversation with Chuck Berry, King of Rock 'n' Roll," *St. Louis*, November 24, 2008, www.stlmag.com/A-Conversation-with-Chuck-Berry/.

CHAPTER 21

1. I've attempted to understand the layout of the Southern Air by drawing on court records, period accounts, and regional documents.

2. This chapter's account of events at Berry Park and the Southern Air draw on numerous records of the Eleventh Judicial Circuit Court, St. Charles County, MO. Court records include: 1988: *Charles E. Berry v. Stacey Rogers*; 1989: *Hosana A. Huck v. Charles E. Berry et al.*; 1990: *Crawford v. Theresa Y. Schmitt*; *Charles E. Berry v. Hosana Huck et al.*; *Thomas F. Jones et al. v. Charles E. Berry et al.*; *Representative Parties v. Charles E. Berry et al.*; *A. Doe v. Charles E. Berry et al.*; 1991: *J. Doe v. Charles E. Berry et al.*; *Rebecca Price v. Charles E. Berry et al.*; 1995: *Vincent Huck v. Ronald Boggs et al.*

3. Daniel Durchholz, "Sex and Videotape—No Lie," *Riverfront Times*, January 10–16, 32.

4. *Berry v. Drake Publishers, Inc., Circuit Court of City of St. Louis*; Tim Poor, "No Particular Place to Show: Berry Sues over Nude Photos," *St. Louis Post-Dispatch*, October 31, 1990.

5. Steve Whitworth, "Berry Denies Drug Possession," UPI, June 28, 1990; Jo Mannies, "Drug Unit Raids Chuck Berry Estate, Seizes Items," *St. Louis Post-Dispatch*, June 28, 1990; Marianna Riley, "Berry Upstages Accuser," *St. Louis Post-Dispatch*, June 29, 1990.

6. Marianna Riley, "Women Sue Berry, Charge He Took Bathroom Videos," *St. Louis Post-Dispatch*, June 30, 1990.

7. "Child Abuse Charges Dropped Against Chuck Berry," UPI archives, November 22, 1990; Marianna Riley, "Child Abuse Charges Dropped in Chuck Berry Plea Bargain," *St. Louis Post-Dispatch*, November 22, 1990.

8. Marianna Riley, "Berry to Get Cash US Took in Raid," *St. Louis Post-Dispatch*, November 27, 1990.

9. Allan MacDonell, *Prisoner of X: 20 Years in the Hole at Hustler Magazine* (Port Townsend, WA: Feral House, 2006), 224–229.

10. "The Perversions of Chuck Berry," *Vice*, September 11, 2013, www.vice.com/en_uk/article/3b7ayv/the-perversions-of-chuck-berry-876109-v20n9. The issue prints letters faxed to Bob Guccione from a writer whose name has been blacked out. Meanwhile, *Screw* magazine was selling a sex tape purporting to feature Berry. Mike Sager, "Sex and Drugs and Rock 'n' Roll, Especially Sex," *Spy*, February 1993, 58–63; Mike Sager, interview with author, July 2019.

11. Sager, "Sex and Drugs," 63.

12. Themetta Berry, *In Their Own Words: Chuck Berry*, episode of PBS documentary series, 2021.

13. Denial of appeal, signed by US Supreme Court clerk William Suter, February 22, 1993, National Archives, Kansas City, MO.

14. Mitch Margo, interview with author, July 2018.

15. Martin Green, interview with author, September 2018.

16. Wayne Schoeneberg, interview with author, July 2018.

17. Letter to Judge Hart, October 24, 1994, Eleventh Judicial Circuit Court records, file CV190, St. Charles County, MO.

18. Their names have been changed for legal reasons.

19. Quint Davis, interview with author, July 2019.

CHAPTER 22

1. Tilton was an abolitionist and a popular public speaker. For a lively portrait of one of Chuck Berry's favorite poets, see Robert Shaplen, "The Beecher-Tilton Affair," *New Yorker*, June 12, 1954, www.newyorker.com/magazine/1954/06/12/the-beecher-tilton-case-ii. "The King's Ring" is available all over the internet. For a marvelous recent musical setting, track down Robert Plant's 2010 album, *Band of Joy*. Set to music from Plant and Buddy Miller, Tilton's words have yet to fade away.

2. Devin Thomas O'Shea, "The Prophet's Bane: How Percy Green's Activism Changed St. Louis," *Slate*, December 21, 2021, https://slate.com/news-and-politics/2021/12/percy-green-st-louis-activism-veiled-prophet-ball-ellie-kemper.html; Thomas M. Spencer, *The St. Louis Veiled Prophet Celebration: Power on Parade, 1877–1995* (Columbia: University of Missouri, 2000), 114–115; Percy Green, interview with author, August 2018.

3. Dale Singer and Sally Bixby Defty, "Half-Million Jam Fair at Gala Opening," *St. Louis Post-Dispatch*, July 4, 1982, 1.

4. Kelly Moffitt, "Joe Edwards Reflects on His Friend, 'the Best-Known St. Louisan of the Last Century,' Chuck Berry," St. Louis Public Radio, March 20, 2017, https://news.stlpublicradio.org/show/st-louis-on-the-air/2017-03-20/joe-edwards-reflects-on-his-friend-the-best-known-st-louisan-of-the-last-century-chuck-berry; Marjorie Kehe, "Entrepreneur Joe Edwards Helps Make St. Louis Vibrant Again," *Christian Science Monitor*, December 14, 2012; Joe Edwards, interview with author, March 2018.

5. Robert Lohr, interview with author, April 2018.

6. Martin Green, interview with author, September 2018.

7. Margaret Gillerman, "Chuck Berry Statue a Go in University City Despite Petitions," *St. Louis Post-Dispatch*, June 16, 2011; Margaret Gillerman, "University City Won't Stop Installation of Chuck Berry Statue," *St. Louis Post-Dispatch*, June 28, 2011; Harry Weber, interview with author, August 2018.

8. Vijay Iyer, interview with author, July 2021.

9. Bryan Armen Graham, "'I'm High as a Georgia Pine': Dock Ellis's No-Hitter on LSD, 50 Years On," *The Guardian*, June 30, 2020.

10. Mike Eiland, announcer at WLVQ-FM, letter to the editor, *Billboard*, December 6, 1980, 14.

11. In January 2022, Chris Martin of Coldplay appeared on *The Kelly Clarkson Show* and discussed how watching Marty McFly perform "Johnny B. Goode" inspired him. "That's what made me want to be in a band, you know? That scene, yeah."

12. Brian Niemietz, "Barack Obama Killed Rock 'n' Roll by Ending 'White Male Angst,' Conservative Panel Says," *New York Daily News*, September 15, 2021, www.ny dailynews.com/snyde/ny-barack-obama-killed-rock-and-roll-daily-wire-20210916 -seuirdpbongozfzngbhdatvijq-story.html.

13. Patrick Doyle, "Chuck Berry Collapses Onstage in Chicago," *Rolling Stone*, January 3, 2011; Lisa Findley, "The Worst Concert Ever, or, I'm Sorry, Chuck Berry," *Greetings from a Stowaway* (blog), January 4, 2011, https://lisafindley.com/2011/01/04/the -worst-concert-ever-or-im-sorry-chuck-berry/.

14. Lohr, interview.

15. Edwards, interview.

16. Mark Jacobson, *Teenage Hipster in the Modern World* (New York: Grove Press, 2005), 55–56.

17. Steve Scorfina, interview with author, September 2019.

18. John Pareles, "Chuck Berry, Rock 'n' Roll Pioneer, Dies at 90," *New York Times*, March 18, 2017, B6.

19. The story of the family meeting comes from a South by Southwest panel on the marketing of the album *Chuck* in the wake of the star's death, March 15, 2018, https:// schedule.sxsw.com/2018/events/PP76898; "Chuck Berry, 90, Announces First Album in 38 Years," *The Guardian*, October 18, 2016; Patrick Doyle, "Inside Chuck Berry's First New Album in 38 Years," *Rolling Stone*, March 22, 2017; Randy Lewis, "Chuck Berry's New 'Chuck' Album Set for June 16 Posthumous Release," *Los Angeles Times*, March 22, 2017.

20. Chuck Berry, "Johnny Be Good," *Omnibus*, BBC One, 1980.

CHAPTER 23

1. It was Elizabeth Stordeur Pryor's *Colored Travelers: Mobility and the Fight for Citizenship Before the Civil War* (Chapel Hill: University of North Carolina Press, 2016) that introduced me to the story of Douglass's travels to Cincinnati. She pointed the way to Robert K. Wallace's "Finding His Voice on the Road, in the Lecture Hall, and in His Newspaper: Frederick Douglass in Cincinnati in 1852," *New North Star* 1 (2019), published by the Frederick Douglass Papers, Institute for American Thought, Indiana University School of Liberal Arts, Indianapolis.

2. Elvis Mitchell, "Chuck Berry, a Revolutionary Black Figure Who Never Hid His Rage," *Billboard*, March 22, 2017, www.billboard.com/music/features/chuck-berry -revolutionary-black-figure-7735707/.

3. Jaime Lees, "Chuck Berry Gets a Loving Goodbye from the City He Always Called Home," *Riverfront Times*, April 10, 2017, www.riverfronttimes.com/music/st-louis-says-goodbye-to-chuck-berry-at-packed-memorial-service-4519097; Harry Weber, interview with author, August 2018.

4. Tom Wheeler, "Chuck Berry: The Interview," *Guitar Player*, March 1988, 63.

5. Mark Jacobson, *Teenage Hipster in the Modern World* (New York: Grove Press, 2005), 47.

6. Mark Jacobson, "Chuck Berry at Home in 2001: Rock Icon Talks Racism, Royalties and More," *Rolling Stone*, April 10, 2017.

AFTERWORD AND ACKNOWLEDGMENTS

1. Max Kozlov and Anastasia Gorelova, "Protesters Gather in Delmar Loop, Creve Coeur on Friday, to Condemn Racial Injustice," *St. Louis Post-Dispatch*, June 12, 2020.

2. "Rock and Roll HOF Chuck Berry Tribute 4/7/17," video, ninah3339, posted online April 8, 2017, www.youtube.com/watch?v=HO0c-PNnFfs.

INDEX

Ackerman, Paul, 82–84
Adelman, Thomas, 308–309, 314,
    316–317
advertising, using Berry for, 321
After School Session (album),
    130–131, 233
"Ain't That Just Like a Woman
    (They'll Do It Every Time)," 47
Alan, Lee, 203–205
"Alan Freed's First Anniversary Rock
    'n' Roll Party," Berry at, 92–94
Alen, Dick, 101, 275, 295
Alexander, Gary, 171
Alexander, Sam, 37–38, 39–40
Algoa Intermediate Reformatory for
    Young Men, 36–40
Allen, Richard, 204
American Bandstand (television
    program), 141–144, 151, 271
American Federation of Musicians,
    51, 60
American Graffiti (film), 250, 324
American Hot Wax (film), 278–279,
    283

"American Ruse," 253
amps, requiring only Fender Dual
    Showman Reverb amps at every
    appearance, 294–295
Anglemyer, Kris, 322–325, 326–327,
    349
Anka, Paul, 139, 140–141
Antioch Baptist Church (St. Louis),
    Berry and, 23–25
ARC Music, 100–101, 206, 245
Arden, Don, 212, 214, 217, 228
Arnold, Satch, 234
"Around and Around," 354
arrests, Berry's, 155–156, 160, 163,
    177, 190, 321
audiences
    Berry aiming at white teenage, 171
    Berry on changing rock & roll, 241
    Berry's first records and Black-only,
        64–65
    growth of teenage in 1950s, 64–65
    integrated, 22, 105, 112, 127, 129,
        327
    race and rock, 243

audiences (*continued*)
　　for rhythm and blues, 108
　　for rock & roll, 108–109
　　segregated, 95–96, 127–128,
　　　141–142
Australia, tour in, 166–169
autobiography, 318–321

Babitz, Mirandi, Sol, and Eve,
　　305–306
Back Home (album), 245, 246–247
backing bands, Berry's treatment
　　of, 168, 230–231, 285–290,
　　311–313
"Back in the USA," 170–171, 176,
　　189, 205, 314, 346
Baker, Burt, 334
Baker, LaVern, 139, 141
Baldoric, Bob, 246
Balducci, Ron, 328–329
Baldwin, Roger, 11
Banks, Isaac, 12
Banks, Martha Bell, 12
Barry, Dave, 261
Bartholomew, Dave, 83, 255–256,
　　260, 262, 264–265
Bartholomew, Harland, 11–12
Bartholomew, Louis, 255–256, 265
Bates, Joan Mathis, 190, 196
Beach Boys, 206–207
Beatles, 115, 217, 218, 250–251
　　Berry on, 223, 233
　　playing Berry songs, 211, 222, 223
"Beautiful Delilah," 223
"Beer Drinkin' Woman" (poem), 57
Below, Fred, 137, 218
Bennett, Alvin, 55–56
Bennett, Stephanie, 307, 310, 313, 314
Bennett, Tony, 93, 94
Benson, F. Delano R. Jr., 24
Berry, Charles Jr. "Butch," 161
　　as backing musician for father,
　　　xii–xiii, 288, 345
　　on "Back in the USA," 170

　　on father at home, 240
　　Hail! Hail! Rock 'n' Roll and, 313
　　on opposition to building Berry
　　　Park, 164
　　on rock festivals at Berry Park, 280
　　on vibrations on stage from Berry's
　　　guitar playing, 117
Berry, Hank, 49, 202, 268
Berry, Henry William, 12, 16, 20, 25,
　　36, 202, 342
　　Berry accompanying father to
　　　work, 31–32
　　church and, 23, 24
　　"Downbound Train" and, 104
　　"My Ding-A-Ling" and, 260–261
　　perpetual motion machine and, 4,
　　　359
　　punishing son for sexual activity,
　　　32, 33
　　warning son of potential for
　　　violence in the South, 95
Berry, Ingrid, 50, 164, 200, 235, 244,
　　338, 343, 345
Berry, Lucy, 16, 30, 32, 43, 50, 230
Berry, Martha, 16, 19, 23, 24
Berry, Melody, 235, 240
Berry, Paul Lawrence Dunbar, 17
Berry, Thelma, 28, 30, 50
Berry, Themetta Suggs "Toddy," 49,
　　279
　　on Berry Park, 235, 281
　　Berry's final days and death and,
　　　357, 358
　　courtship and wedding to Berry,
　　　41–42
　　influence on Berry's performance,
　　　74
　　"Lady B. Goode" and, 358–359
　　picking Chuck up from prison, 202
　　standing by her husband, 335
　　visiting Berry in prison, 200–201
　　on why Berry initially used
　　　pseudonym, 51
　　Windermere Place house and, 161

Berryn, Charles, Berry's early pseudonym, 51, 60–61
Berry Park, xiv, 268–270, 271
  Berry showing visitors around, 267–268, 310
  Dr. Pepper jingle and, 273–275
  investigation and closure of, 280–281
  opening of, 235–236
  Pietsch at, 319
  plans for, 163–165
  raid on, 331
  rock festivals at, 279–280
Berry Pickin' in the Country (album), 231–232
Betsey Brown (Shange), 161
Bey, Dawoud, 209–210
Big Band Era, Berry on, 45
Big Beat (television program), 148
"Big Beat" tour, 147–151
"Big Boys," 358
Bihari, Joe, 65
biker gang, as security for shows at Berry Park, 279, 280
Bill Black Combo, 271
Billups, Kenneth Brown, 24
Billups, Melvin, 112
birth, 15
bitterness over prosecution and sentence for violating Mann Act, 201–203
Black America, Berry on relationship to, 271–272
Black artists, crossing over, 84
Black artists' songs, white artists' covers of, 82–84
Black audiences, Berry's music and, 96, 112, 271
Black community, St. Louis's, 6–7, 23, 13, 20
  African Veiled Prophet celebration, 8–9
  twentieth-century struggle for mobility in, 9–11

See also the Ville (Elleardsville, Missouri)
blackface minstrel revue, Berry appearing as part of, 43, 44
Black music, crossing into country, 70
Black Oak Arkansas, 251
Black rock & roll, transition to white rock, 243, 352–354
Blackwell, Bumps, 109
Blanding, Don, 238
Blanton, Jimmy, 45
Blattner, Jules, 230
Bloom, Allen, 128
Bloomfield, Mike, 206, 218
Blueberry Hill (club), 320–321, 344
  as home stage for Berry, xi–xiii, 345, 355
Blueberry Hill Band, 354, 358
blues
  Berry and the, 29, 247–248, 282
  British invasion and, 217–218
"Blues for Hawaiians," 46
Bolden, Abraham W. Sr., 138
Bonds, Gary U.S., 249–250
Bontemps, Arna, 18
boogie band, Berry's, 37–38, 39–40
boogie-woogie, 37–39, 47, 351
Bostic, Earl, 60
Boston Arena, racial riot at, 150–151
Boyd, Reggie, 208
"Break, Break, Break" (Tennyson), 359
"Breathless," 149
British Invasion, 222
  blues and, 216–218
  covers of Berry songs and, 211, 222, 223, 251
"Broken Arrow," 183
Broome, Charles, 173, 174, 175
Broonzy, Big Bill, 32
Broven, John, 101, 215
Brown, Charles, 80
Brown, James, 60
Brown, Michael, 12

Brown, Walter, 29
"Brown Eyed Handsome Man,"
    120–121, 130
Brown v. Board of Education, 83, 113
Buchanan, Elwood C., 138
Buchanan v. Warley, 11
Buford, Jim, 188
"Buggy Ride" bit, 57
Bunch, Lonnie G. III, xiii–xiv, xv
Burdon, Eric, 214
Burks, Jesse "Spider," 63–64
Burns, Tommy, 169
Burris, Ralph, 74–75
Busby, Paul, 174
business, Berry and, 161–165, 197
"Butterscotch," 230
"Bye Bye Johnny," 223

Cabanellas, Tony, 132
Cadillacs
    Berry and, xi, 152, 155, 157, 181,
        182, 365
    Blacks and, 153, 156
    negotiating donation of his
        Eldorado to the National
        Museum of African American
        History and Culture, xiii–xvi
    police stopping Berry's pink,
        154–156
California, Berry's aborted trip to
    while a teen, 34–36
Calloway, Cab, 64
Campbell, Jo Ann, 167, 170
Carmen, Eric, 288–289
Carnahan, Mel, 44
"Carol," 156, 189, 223, 311, 312
cars
    Berry and, xi, 53–54, 152
    Black families and
        circumnavigation of segregated
        transportation, 153–154
    See also Cadillacs
Carson, Johnny, 276, 323, 330
"car song," "Maybellene" as, 81

Carter, Asa, 113, 122
Carter, Jimmy, 283
Casch, Lou, 167–168
Cash, Johnny, 121
Catlett, Big Sid, 45
Chappelle, Dave, 363
Charles, Bobby (Bobby Charles
    Guidry), 118–119, 120
Charles, Ray, 157, 206
chess, Berry's love of playing, 215,
    269, 305
Chess, Joe, 87–88
Chess, Leonard, 87–88, 217, 234,
    245, 247
    artist royalties and, 100–102
    on audience for Berry's music, 96
    Berry's recording sessions and,
        78–79, 110
    Berry's relationship with, 75–76,
        99
    Berry's return to music after prison
        time and, 203, 207–208
    Berry's tour in England and, 212
    Bobby Charles and, 118
    Diddley and, 107
    Gale Agency, Berry, and, 92
    "Maybellene" and, 80, 88
Chess, Marshall, 131, 207–208, 211,
    229, 245, 284, 295
Chess, Phil, 75, 78, 88, 217, 245
    on "Maybellene," 79, 80
    payment of royalties and, 100,
        102–103
Chess, Revetta, 100
Chess Records
    Berry leaving, 234
    Berry's first album with, 130–131
    Berry's return to, 245
    demise of, 282
    desire to stockpile Berry materials
        in case of prison sentence, 197
    first recording session for, 76,
        78–80
    infrastructure of, 208

music from *Rock! Rock! Rock!* and, 124

music publishing and, 100–101

"My Ding-A-Ling" and, 263

treatment of musicians, 102

Waters referring Berry to, 75

child abuse charges against Berry, 332–333

childhood in segregated St. Louis (the Ville), 13–17, 19–22, 23–24, 26–33

Chitlin' Circuit, 94–95

Christgau, Robert, 261

Christian, Charlie, 3, 43, 46, 61, 167

Christian Brothers, Berry advertising brandy for, 321

Chuch Berry (album), 282

Chuck (final album), 358–359

"Chuckabilly," 139

Chuck Berry Appreciation Society, 224

Chuck Berry Beer, 344

Chuck Berry in London (album), 230

Chuck Berry in Memphis (album), 234

Chuck Berry Is on Top (album), 46

Chuck Berry Music Incorporated, 162

Chuck Berry's Club Bandstand, 162–163, 185–186, 187–188, 197–198

Chuck Berry's Golden Decade (album), 322

Chuck Berry: The Autobiography, 12, 318–321

Chuck Berry Twist (album), 207

Circle Jerks, Berry jamming with, 298–301

Cisneros, Sandra, 86–87

Ciudad Juárez, Berry's tour of, 177–179

civil rights movement, 23, 127

access to Black movement and public life and, 219–221

Clanton, Jimmy, 172

Clapton, Eric, 313, 314, 315, 345

Clark, Dick, 141–144, 249

Clarke, Kenny, 45

class action suit against Berry for invasion of privacy, 332, 333–337

Clayton, Buck, 157

Club Cosmopolitan "the Cosmo" integrated audience at, 70

Johnson and Berry playing at, 55–58, 80

"Club Nitty Gritty," 234

cocaine, raid to search Berry Park for, 331–332

Cocks, Les, 229, 230

code-switching, 71

Cohan, Lou, 284

Cole, Nat King, 28, 71, 73, 76, 109, 165

attack on in Alabama, 112–114, 115, 122

Coleman, Rick, 129

The Color of Law (Rothstein), 11

Columbus, Chris, 48

"Come On," 216–217, 223

Concerto in B. Goode (album), 244

"Confessin' the Blues," Berry's performance of at his high school, 29, 30

conga, 134–135

Connors, Jim, 262

Conover, Willis, 157

control, Berry's need for, 162, 275

Cook, James E., 24

Cordovox, Gus, 145

Cornelius, Don, 272

Cosby, Hank, 204

Cosey, Pete, 208–209

country songs/music

Berry and, 54–55, 57, 58–59, 70, 166–167, 231–232, 233

defining, 232–233

Cowboy Songs and Other Frontier Ballads (Lomax), 104

Cray, Robert, 121, 308, 313
Crosby, Bing, 61–62, 276
Cross, Deira, 280
Crudup, Arthur, 32
Cumbie, Yvonne, 309, 322, 325–326
Czyz, Yasef, 87. *See also* Chess, Joe

Dannen, Fredric, 89
Darin, Bobby, 167
Davis, Billy, 101–102
Davis, Harry, 30, 31
Davis, Julia, 27–29
Davis, Leroy, 177, 178, 181, 182,
    184, 187
Davis, Miles, xv, 18, 138
Davis, Quint, 293–294, 296–298, 340
Davis, Walter, 38–39
death, Berry's, 358
Dee Jays, 167–168
Dempsey, Thomas, 155
Derelict (band), 146
"Diana," 140, 142
Diane
    beginning relationship with Berry,
        302–304, 306
    as Berry's girlfriend, 306–307
    on trips to Berry Park, 326
*Dick Clark's Saturday Night Beechnut
    Show* (television program), 162
Dickens, Tad, 160
Dickerson, Deke, 108
Dickinson, Jim, 139
diction
    Berry's attention to, 26, 71, 122
    Nat King Cole and, 109
Diddley, Bo, 87, 135, 222, 289, 325
    Berry and, 246, 364
    compared to Berry, 106–108
    on how Clark treated Black artists,
        142–143
    Rolling Stones and, 216, 217
    at Universal Recording Studio, 76,
        78
diddley bow, 48–49

Dixon, George, 193
Dixon, Willie, 78, 121, 135, 311
Doggett, Bill, 127, 129
Domino, Fats, 109, 126–127, 128,
    139, 140, 141, 265
Douglass, Frederick, 360–361
Dowd, Edward L., 125–126
"Downbound Train," 104–105
Downliners Sect, 223
dress/appearance, Berry's, 225–226
Dr. Pepper jingle, Berry and, 272–275
drummers, Berry and, 137–138
drumming, rock & roll, 136–139
Druyan, Ann, 277–278
DuBose, Demosthenes, 14
duckwalk, xii, 149, 229, 338
Dumas, Henry, 57
Dunbar, Paul Laurence, 17–19, 20,
    26, 71
"Dutchman" (poem), 358, 359
Dylan, Bob, 120, 233, 277, 338

Early, Gerald, 129
Eastburn, R. A., 259
East St. Louis (Illinois), 9–10, 57,
    68, 70
echo, use of, 76–77
Eckstine, Billy, 14
education, Berry's high school, 26–29
Edwards, Esmond, 256, 263
Edwards, Joe, 282
    Berry's declining faculties and,
        355–356
    Blueberry Hill performances and,
        347
    facilitating negotiations for
        donations to National Museum
        of African American History and
        Culture, xiii, xiv, xv, xvi
    friendship with Berry, 344–345
    St. Louis Walk of Fame and, 349
eighth-note and pop music, 136–137
Einstein, Albert, 15, 310
Eklow, Jesper, 294

electric guitars
  Berry's, xiii–xvi, 78, 92, 117, 145, 168, 311
  rising interest in through 1950s and 1960s, 48–49, 206
Elleardsville (Missouri). *See* the Ville (Elleardsville, Missouri)
Ellis, Dock, 352–353
England
  Berry touring in, 212, 213–215, 217, 225–229, 256–259
  "My Ding-A-Ling" and Berry in, 256–259
Escalanti, Janice "Heba Norine"
  Berry sending her away, 186–187
  Berry's poem about, 319
  Berry's trials and, 191, 192, 196–197
  held at House of the Good Shepherd, 191, 196
  relationship with Berry on the road, 177–184
  working at Club Bandstand, 185–186, 187–188
Everly Brothers, 139, 212
"Eyes of Man," 359

Fairhurst, Roger, 217, 226, 227–229, 230
family tree, Berry, 12
fan club, Chuck Berry, 162
Father of Rock & Roll (Johnson), 347
FBI, Mann Act and interest in Berry, 158–159, 198
Feld, Irvin, 126–127, 139–141
Fillmore, Berry at the, 236–238
films, Berry and
  American Hot Wax, 278–279
  Go, Johnny, Go, 171–172
  Hail! Hail! Rock 'n' Roll, 307–318
  Mister Rock and Roll, 171
  Rock! Rock! Rock!, 123–124
"Fine Brown Frame," 97
First Nations people, Berry and treatment of, 168–169

Fitzpatrick, Travis, 55
Flatt & Scruggs, 231
Fleming, Kevin, 281
Forrest, Jimmy, 45, 60
Fowley, Kim, 148
fraternity shows in the South, 172–176
Fratto, Russ, credited as cowriter on "Maybellene," 88
Freed, Alan, 93, 94, 142, 283
  Berry's relationship with, 89–91
  "Big Beat" tour, 147–151
  credited as cowriter on "Maybellene," 88, 99, 103
  films and, 123–124, 172
  playing and promoting "Maybellene," 80
  term "rock & roll" and, 108
Freedom Riders, 219, 220
From St. Louie to Frisco (album), 244

Gale, Tim, 89
Gale Agency, 92, 93
Gardiner, Diane, 304–306
Garland, Phyl, 243
General Recorded Tape (GRT), 246, 282
Gibson ES-350T guitar "Maybellene," 78
  negotiating donation to National Museum of African American History and Culture, xiii–xvi
Gibson ES-355, 145, 311
Gillespie, Dizzy, 133
Gillett, Charlie, 254
Gillium, Francine "Fran," 161–164, 245, 322, 357
  Berry Park and, 163–164, 268, 269, 280–281
  Berry's autobiography and, 318
  Escalanti and, 181, 183, 185, 187–188
  Southern Air management and, 324, 325

Gilpin, William, 5
Gilroy, Paul, 153
Gist, James and Eloyce, 104
Go, Johnny, Go (film), 171–172
"Going Down Slow," 29
Golden, Freddie, 60
Golden Disk, Berry's music on, 277–278
Goldman, Mark, 299, 300
Goodman, Andrew, 175
Goodman, Gene and Harry, 100–101
Gordon, Colin, 6
Graham, Bill, Berry and, 236–238, 239
Grand Ole Opry, 167, 205, 231
Grant, Peter, 212, 214
Grateful Dead, 236, 238
"Great Balls of Fire," 149
"The Greatest Show of 1957" tour, 126–129, 139–141
Great Migration, 9, 12, 13, 26, 38
Grech, Ric, 256
Green, Grant, 163
Green, Lil, 32
Green, Martin, 336, 347, 348–349, 357
Green, Sharony Andrews, 163
Greene, Bob, 221, 321
Greensmith, Bill, 66
Gregory, Dick, 28
Griffith, Johnny, 204
Guccione, Bob Sr., 334
guilt, Berry and church as symbol of, 24–25
guitar
    Berry deciding to learn, 29–30
    boogie and, 39
    Hawaiian, 46, 49
    See also electric guitar
"Guitar Boogie," 224
guitar playing, Berry's, 71, 117, 146, 300
guns
    arrest for MAB pistol, 158

Berry carrying, 34–36, 99, 155–156, 190, 196
Guralnick, Peter, 248
Gutillo, Jim, 82

Hackford, Taylor, 350, 352
    Hail! Hail! Rock 'n' Roll and, 307–310, 313, 318
    Hail! Hail! Rock 'n' Roll (film), 307–315, 317–318, 342
    dealing with the crew and Berry, 313–312
    performances for, 314–315
    postproduction of, 316–318
Hall, Hattie Vose, 359
Hamilton, George IV, 166–168
Hamilton, John Wilson, 121–122
Hamilton, Susan, 272–275
Hammond, John, 157
hands, Berry's large, 349–350
Hannah, William J., 331–333
Hardy, Ebbie, 56, 111
    Hail! Hail! Rock 'n' Roll and, 312–313
    playing with Berry, 56, 71, 131, 137–139
    recording sessions, 75, 79
Harlan, J. J., 322
Harlan, Linda, 263–264
"Harlem in St. Louis" (minstrel revue), 43, 44
Harmonicats, 76–77
Harper, Roy, 197
Harris, Ira, 42–43, 61
"Havana Moon," 130–131
"Have Mercy Judge," 246, 247
Hawken, John, 213–215
Hawkins, Screamin' Jay, 147, 148, 278
Heathcott, Joseph, 41
"The Hellbound Train," 104
The Hell-Bound Train (film), 104
Hellfire (Tosches), 149
Hendrix, Jimi, 276, 352–353

Henry, John, 190
Hester, Chank, 135
Hetson, Greg, 301
Hickey, Philip J., 125–126
high school diploma, receiving while in prison, 200, 201
High Society (magazine), stolen naked photos in, 330–331
Hill, Andrew, 350, 351
hillbilly boogie, 70–71
"Hillbilly Boogie," 70
Himes, Chester, 18, 27, 152
Hogan, Carl, 3, 46–48
Holder, Noddy, 257
Holloway, Red, 102
Holly, Buddy, 121, 139, 140, 147, 150
Holy Barbarian, 163, 198
"Honky Tonk," 129, 224
Hooke, Jack, 91, 92, 94, 99, 171
Hooker, John Lee, 39
Hoover, J. Edgar, 198
Hopkins, Nicky, 251
"Hot Rod Race," 70
Huck, Hosana and Vincent, 329–330, 334
Hudson, George, 47
Huggins, Celia, 66
Hullabaloo (television program), 244
Humphrey, Willie, 255
Hutchinson, Lawrence "Skip," 27, 34, 35–36

"Ida Mae," 75, 78. *See also* "Maybellene"
"I Got to Find My Baby," 223
"I Hope These Words Will Find You Well," 60
improvisation, 265, 351
"I'm Talking About You," 223
independent music labels, 62–63, 100
individualism, Berry's, 270–271

Industrial Mutual Association Auditorium, racially segregated audiences at, 148–149
influence on younger musicians, 205–206, 223
invention, Berry's pursuit of, 1–2, 359
IRS, Berry and tax evasion charge, 282–284
Isalee Music Company, 233, 245
Iyer, Vijay, 350–351
Izenhall, Aaron, 48

Jackson, Lawrence P., 27
Jacobson, Mark, 131, 356–357, 365
Jagger, Mick, 216, 217, 309
"Jambalaya," 58
Jamerson, James, 204
James, Etta, 107–108, 171, 208, 282, 313
Jazz on a Summer's Day (film), 157
Jeter, James L., 44
Jeter-Pillar Orchestra, 44–48
Jim Crow South, Berry performing in, 94–97, 117–118, 127–128
Joe Alexander and the Cubans, 59–60, 63
"Johnny B. Goode," 111, 155, 165, 171, 189, 224, 338, 355
covers of, 146–147, 223, 352–353
Hogan's influence on, 47
on *Voyager* spacecraft messages, 261, 277–278
Johnson, Buddy, 94–95, 96–97
Johnson, Ella, 97
Johnson, Everett, 37
Johnson, Jack, 153–154, 156, 157, 159, 165, 169, 198
Johnson, Johnnie, 111, 184–185
alcohol use and, 132–133
at Blueberry Hill performances, 345
boogie-woogie piano and, 351
on crowd reaction to Berry, 131
on first single with Berry, 248

Johnson, Johnnie (*continued*)
  Hail! Hail! Rock 'n' Roll and, 311,
    312, 314, 315
  Hardy and, 137–138
  hiring Berry as part of his combo,
    55–56
  "Nadine" and, 210–211
  playing with Berry, 71, 75, 356
  revival of career, 345–347
  suit against Berry for coauthorship
    credit, 346–347
  tour of Southwest with Berry and,
    177, 182, 184
  on watching Berry onstage, 54
  "Wee Wee Hours" and, 80
Johnson, Lonnie, 15, 32
Johnson, Wilko, 254
Jones, Brian, 217
Jones, Jo, 45, 157
Jones, Kenney, 256
Jones, Moody, 58
Jones, Salimah, 27
Jordan, Jacki, 105
Jordan, Louis, 44, 47–48, 176–177,
    228, 235
Jordan, Steve, 311, 314
"jump bands"/ "jump boogie," 47, 70
juvenile delinquency, public concerns
    over, 41, 53, 125–126

Kahl, Phil, 124
Kay Thin Twin guitar, 92
King, Martin Luther Jr., 127, 220
Kings of Rhythm, 65–68
"The King's Ring" (Tilton), Berry's
    love of, 341–342, 343, 359
Kirk, Andy, 46, 138
KMOX radio, 58–59
Knight, Jesse, 66–67
Kool Jazz Festival, 290–291
Kramer, Wayne, 207, 254
Krasilovsky, William, 245–246,
    318
Ku Klux Klan, 8, 10, 41, 127

Kurn, Robert, 181
Kushner, Rachel, 320
KXLW radio, 63

"Lady B. Goode," 358–359
Lalla Rookh (Moore), 7
Landres, Paul, 171–172
Lang, Clarence, 13
Leake, Lafayette, 135–136, 220
Leavenworth Federal Prison, Berry at,
    198, 199
Lennon, John, 250–251
"Let It Rock," 189–190, 211, 224,
    251, 296
Let the Good Times Roll (film),
    266–268, 364–365
Levin, Sid, 266–268
Levy, Joe, 133–134, 135
Levy, Morris, 89–91, 93, 124
Lewis, Jerry Lee, 121, 147–148, 234,
    253
  competition with Berry, 149–150,
    249–250, 295
Lewis, Joe, 56–57, 73
Lewis, Smiley, 255
Lewis, Tom, 56–57
Library of Congress, US Copyright
    Office, "Maybelline" registered
    at, 80, 88–89
licensing money, from British
    Invasion bands playing Berry
    songs, 223
Lipsitz, George, 28
"Little Brown Jug," 259–260
Little Milton, 57, 67, 68
"Little Queenie," 98, 189, 223, 251
Little Richard, 108, 234, 289, 338,
    352, 365
  compared to Berry, 136–137
  covers of, 253
  Dick Clark and, 142
  oldies' tours and, 249, 254
  "Tutti Frutti," 109, 136
Little Walter, 135, 208, 224, 235

Lohmar, William, 281
Lohr, Bob, 354–355
Lohr, Robert, 347–348
Lompoc Federal Correctional
   Institute, Berry sent to, 284
The London Chuck Berry Sessions
   (album), 256, 262
"The London Rock and Roll Show,"
   253–254
Lonesome, Buddy, 129
Los Angeles, property in, 303,
   338–340
Louisiana Hayride (radio program),
   82, 276
Luman, Bob, 231
Lydon, Michael, 242
Lymon, Frankie, 139, 142, 147

MacDonell, Allan, 334
Mack, Lonnie (Lonnie McIntosh),
   205–206, 211
Magnetophons, 61
Malone, Annie Turnbo, 12–13, 41, 50
Maloney, Tom, 138, 262–263, 315,
   320–321
Mamas and the Papas, 242
management contract for Berry with
   Gale Agency, 92
Mandelcorn, Irving, 105
Mandy's (Buffalo club). integrated
   audience at, 105, 163
Mangrum, Jim Dandy, 251
Mann Act, 158–159
   Berry accused of violating,
      180–184
   Berry arrested for violating, 177,
      188, 190
   Berry's indictment and trials for
      violating, 190–197
Manoloff, Nick, 42
manual labor, Berry and, 282, 350
Marburger, Duane, 59–61
Marcus, Greil, 170, 276
Margo, Mitch, 336, 337, 346

marijuana, charges against Berry for
   possession of, 332–333
Marsala, Jimmy, 287–288, 354
"Mary Jo," 56
Matheus, Ollie, 163
Mathis, Joan, 155–156, 158, 190,
   196
Maxwell Street Market, 85–87
"Maybellene," 2, 223, 248
   cowriters added to, 88–89, 108
   as hit, 80–83
   recording, 78–79, 111
   theme of, 81–82, 361
Mayberry, Andy, 299, 300
Mayer, Frederick, 158, 190–191,
   192–195
MC5, 207, 253–254
McFarlin, Timothy J., 347
Mckinney, Edna, 26
McLagan, Ian, 256
McReynolds, Jim & Jesse, 231–232
Meachum, John Berry, 28
"Me and My Chauffeur Blues," 230
meanness, Berry's unprovoked,
   290–291, 325
"Mean Old World," 224
media, Berry and, 201–202, 322
Meloni, Robert, 245, 264–265
memorial service for Berry, 362
"Memphis, Tennessee," 189,
   205–206, 211, 223, 231, 233,
   250, 252
Mercury Records, Berry and, 75, 234,
   238, 243–245
Mervis, Jim, 317
Mesey, Mike, 278
Meyers, Augie, 244
The Mike Douglas Show (television
   program), 303
Miller, Steve, 238–240
Millinder, Lucky, 148
minstrelsy, 43–44
Mintz, Leo, 89
Mister Rock and Roll (film), 171

Mitchell, Elvis, 361
mobility
    Berry's desire for as Black man in
        America, 2–5, 152, 170, 198
    Douglass on lack of Black, 360–
        361
    need for Black access to, 219–221
money
    Berry trying to keep payment for
        performance for self, 72–73
    made from songwriting, 233–234
    payment before playing and playing
        only as contracted, 173, 226,
        237, 274, 291–295
Monroe, Bill, 116
Monroe, Vaughn, 179
Monterey International Pop Festival,
    242–243
Moore, George H., 191–196
Moore, Robert H. "Hot Rod," 52–53
Moore, Thomas, 7
morality, Berry on own, 270–271
Morris, Keith, 299, 300, 301
"Mountain Dew," 58
movement, Berry's music and,
    350–351
Mullin, Jack, 61
Murad, Jerry, 76, 77
Murphy, Matt "Guitar," 208
Murray, Charles Shaar, 257
music, in Berry's childhood home,
    16, 32
musical influences, Berry's, 21–22
musical styles, Berry's embrace of
    variety of, 73–74, 130–131
Music City News (album),
    232–233
musicians
    Berry's influence on younger,
        205–207
    Black and white on tour, 139–140
    Dick Clark's differential treatment
        of Black and white, 141–143

Mutrux, Floyd, 278–279
"My Ding-A-Ling," 239, 256–259,
    260–261, 343, 365
    Bartholomew and, 260, 262,
        264–265
    criticism of, 261–263, 264
"My Dream," 238

Nader, Richard (Richard Abi-Nader),
    249–250, 266, 282–283
"Nadine (Is It You?)," 200, 205,
    208–211, 221, 233, 346
Nashville, Berry music and, 231–232
Nashville Teens, 213–214
National Museum of African
        American History and Culture,
        negotiating Berry's donations to,
        xiii–xvi
"Negro Southern speech," 17–18
Nelson, Iola, 43
Neumann, Paul, 155
Newman, Randy, 272–273
Newport Jazz Festival, Berry's
        appearance at, 156–158
"Night Train," 60
"No Money Down," 3, 103, 104–105,
    153
"No Particular Place to Go," 200, 221
North Alabama Citizens Council,
    112–113, 122
Northwood Country Club, Berry
        refused at door, 173–174, 176
Norton, Roland, 188
novelty songs, 263

Obama, Barack, xiii, 354
Oden, Jimmy, 29
Ohjo, Robert Ward, 206
"Oh Maria," 60, 63
O'Keefe, Johnny, 167
O'Neill, Peter, 294–295
Ono, Yoko, 250–251
Orbison, Roy, 233

Orleans, Jordan, 246
Orphans' Home Day, 13, 41
"Our Little Rendezvous," 223
Owens, Buck, 232–233
Owens, Queenie (Queen Esther), 96–98

Pallardy, Andrew, 154–155
Palmer, Earl, 136–137
parade, Veiled Prophet of Khorassan, 7–8
Parker, Bobby, 127–128
Parker, Tom, 252
"Pass Away," 342
patriotism, Berry's, 170–171
Paul, Les, 238
payola scandal, 151, 172, 176
Peek, Billy, 251
peeping. See voyeurism
Pegg, Bruce, 280
"Peg o' My Heart," 76–77
performance
    Berry's releasing rage of racism in, 361–362
    playing out of tune in later, 294
    sameness of later, 286, 290
    shortening, 291–292
Perkins, Carl, 115–116, 120, 121, 214
perpetual motion machine, father's, 4, 359
Peterson, Mark, 55
Pezel, Angela, 300, 301
Pfeffer, Rhoda, 268–269
Phillips, Homer G., 28
Phillips, John, 242–243
photographs, Berry's rule against unauthorized, 297–298
photography
    Berry and, 30–31, 306
    Diddley and, 107–108
    stolen naked photos in High Society, 330–331

Pickett, Charlie, 292–293
Pietsch, Michael, 318–320, 322
Pillars, Hayes, 44
Plato, 15
poems, Berry writing and performing, 57, 319, 358
"The Poet" (Dunbar), 19
poetry, Berry and love of, 17, 19, 57, 238, 319, 341–342, 358
pornographic materials, Berry and, 331, 333–335, 364
Poro System, 50–51
Porter, Bob, 99
Powers, Ann, 144
Pregerson, Harry, 283–284
Presley, Elvis, 121, 133, 135, 147, 148, 233, 262, 352, 353
    Berry and, 251–253, 276–277
    death of, 275–276
    performing "Maybellene," 82
Price, Lloyd, 160
Price, Will, 124
Pride, Charlie, 298
Priest, John G., 8
Prince, Dave, 204
Prince, Paisley Park and, 164
prison
    Berry at Algoa Intermediate Reformatory for Young Men, 36–40
    Berry at Leavenworth Federal Prison, 198, 199
    Berry at Lompoc for tax evasion, 284
    Berry at US Medical Center for Federal Prisoners, 199–202
    term for violating Mann Act, 197
Prisoner of X (MacDonell), 334
"Promised Land," 200, 218–220, 221, 224, 233
property owned in Los Angeles, 303, 338–340

protesters, at memorial service,
    362
Pro Tools, Berry and, 356
Pryor, Elizabeth Stordeur, 361
pseudonym, Berry's, 60–61
public apology, Berry's imagined,
    363–364
publishing rights, Berry and, 245–246
Putnam, Bill, 76–77, 208
Pye Records/Pye Studios/Pye
    International, 224, 229–230,
    256

race
    Berry refusing to define self in
        relation to, 131–132, 167, 169
    Berry's trial for violating Mann Act
        and, 192–193
racial integration, rock & roll music
    and, 83, 95–96, 129, 197
racism
    Berry and, 12, 68, 140, 169, 170,
        184, 248, 361–362, 365
    intersection with sex, 25, 327
radio, music on the, 62, 74, 82, 353
    See also Freed, Alan
radio jingle, Berry recording,
    272–275
Rage to Survive (James), 107–108
Raggiani, Albert, 150
Raspberries, 288–289
Rawls, Lou, 243
Ray, Johnnie, 365
recorders, access to affordable, 61
recording sessions
    Back Home, 245, 246–247
    Berry's first, 59–60
    final album, 356–357
    From St. Louie to Frisco,
        243–244
    live at the Fillmore, 238
    The London Chuck Berry Sessions,
        256
    "Nadine," 207, 208–211

    at Pye Records in London, 2
        29–230
recording technology
    advances in, 61–62
    Berry and, 61
    echo and reverb, 76–77
record labels, independent, 62–63,
    100. See also Chess Records;
    Mercury Records
Record Makers and Breakers (Broven),
    101
Redmond, Eugene, 57
Redmond, Shana, 258
"Reelin' and Rockin'," 174, 364
Reid, Vernon, 121, 264, 289
Reig, Teddy, 88, 91–92, 93, 98–99
religion, Berry and, 20, 23–25, 270
reputation, damage done by bathroom
    and sex tapes, 329–332, 334–336
restrictive covenants in St. Louis, 11,
    14, 40–41
reverb effect, 77
rhythm and blues, 108, 224
Richards, Keith, 216, 217, 251, 289,
    346
    Hail! Hail! Rock 'n' Roll and, 307,
        309–313, 314, 315, 318
Riddlespringer, Teddy, 43
robberies and car theft, Berry and
    friends arrested for, 35–36
Robbins, Marty, 84
Roberts, Alton Wayne, 175
Roberts, Raymond, 175
Robertson, Robbie, 19, 342
Robinson, Jackie, 120–121
Robinson, Red, 129–130, 132, 134
Robinson, Smokey, 242–243
Robinson, Sugar Ray, 156, 157
Robinson, Sylvia and Joe, 282
rock
    Berry as most influential Black
        contributor to white, 243
    transition from rock & roll to, 243,
        352–354

Rock and Roll Hall of Fame, 264, 338

"Rock and Roll Music," 133–137, 143, 146, 223, 338

rock festivals at Berry Park, 279–280

Rockin' at the Hops (album), 216

"Rockin' at the Philharmonic," 238

Rockit (album), 284, 342

Rock! Rock! Rock! (film), 123–124

rock & roll
  audience for, 108–109
  Berry and invention of, 1–5, 352
  Berry and war on, 354
  Berry on revival of 1950s, 240–241
  Berry's sense would be lasting, 115
  coining term, 90
  death of, 353–354
  focus on female teenage audience, 143–144
  Levy and growth of, 89
  racist attacks on, 113
  transition to rock, 243, 352–354
  youth culture and, 151–152

rock & roll chaos, Berry's love of, 296–297, 340

rock & roll nostalgia, 248–254, 266–268

rock star, Berry and creation of job of, 276–277, 352

rocksteady, 244

Rodgers, Jimmie, 116

Roediger, David, 7

Rogers, Timmie, 258

Rolling Stones, 234, 250, 279
  covers of Berry songs, 222, 223, 251
  debt to Berry, 216–217
  See also Richards, Keith

"Roll Over Beethoven," 111, 115, 116, 223, 283, 300, 301, 346

Ronstadt, Linda, 314

Roper, Paul, 358

Ross, Fred Jr., 173–175

Ross, Fred A., 173

Rothstein, Richard, 11

royalties
  Berry's, 88–89, 101, 245–246, 252
  Chess Records and payment of, 100–103

Rubin, Jerry, 250

Rupe, Art, 109

Rutherford, Rudy, 157

Sagan, Carl, 277–278

Sager, Mike, 335

Sahm, Doug, 243–244

St. Louis, history of, 5–12, 40–41.
  See also East St. Louis (Illinois)

"St. Louis Cyclone Blues," 15

St. Louis to Liverpool (album), 222–223, 230

St. Louis Walk of Fame, Berry on, 349, 362–363

Sally, Carl, 116–117

Saltz, Jerry, 86, 88

Salvo, Patrick William, 268–269

Sample, Fred, 67

Sander, Ellen, 304–305

Sandmel, Ben, 290–291

San Jose (California), as Berry's fictional birthplace, 129–130

Satterfield, Louis, 209

Scarpelli, Tony, 45

Scherman, Tony, 136

Schloss, Zander, 299–301

Schoeneberg, Wayne T., 332, 337

"School Days," 125–126, 130, 157

Schuyler, George, 153

Schwerner, Michael, 175

scoot (performance move), xii

Scorfina, Steven, 235–236, 357

Scott, Clifford, 129

Scott, Dred and Harriet, 5, 343

sculpture of Berry in St. Louis, 349–350

segregation
    of audiences in the South, 95–96,
        127–128
    Douglass's experience of,
        360–361
    of music industry, 83, 141–142
    in St. Louis, 11, 14, 22–23
"Seven Come Eleven," 167
sex
    Berry's sexual practices revealed by
        seized tapes, 334–336
    intersection with racism for Berry,
        25, 327
    loss of virginity, 32–33
shake dancing, 97
Sha Na Na, 248–249
Shange, Ntozake, 8–9, 14,
    161
Shanks, Pearl, 22
Shaw, Arvell, 13
Shaw, Robert "Fud," 38
Shaw agency, 93
Shelley v. Kraemer, 40–41
Sherman, Joe, 50, 61
Sherrill, Billy, 231
Shibley, Arkie, 70
"Shower of Stars" tour, 166–169
shuffle bet, 136
Silver, Mort S., 43
Silverstein, Merle, 156, 193,
    196
Sinclair, John, 148–149
Sippel, John, 244–245
Sir Charles Trio, 56–58, 72–73
Sir Douglas Quintet, 243–244
slapback sound, 133
Slayback, Charles and Alonzo, 7
Smith, Floyd, 45–46, 49
Smith, Fred, 207, 254
Smith, Gerald L. K., 122
Smith, Tom K., 343
Snider, Todd, 126
songwriter, Berry as popular,
    231–234

songwriting
    Berry and collective process of,
        110–112, 346–347
    Berry on his process, 109–111,
        227
    Johnson suing Berry for
        coauthorship credit, 346–347
    while in prison, 200
Soul Train (television program),
    271–272
Southern Air
    Berry as patron and later owner,
        322–325
    Berry denied service at, 35
    class action suit stemming from
        videotaping women in restroom,
        332, 333–337
    discovery of cameras secretly
        filming women in the restroom,
        328–330
Southern hospitaboo, 327
Spampinato, Joey, 311
Sparks, Aaron "Pinetop" and Marion
    "Lindberg," 38–39
Springsteen, Bruce, 210, 338, 365
standing counter, 22
Stefaniak, Slick, 285–286
Steve Miller Band, 239–240
Stevens, Guy, 224
Stevens, Tommy, 29, 43, 51, 54, 56,
    73
Stewart, Billy, 208
Stewart, Mark (aka Stew), 114–115,
    125, 126
Stigwood, Robert, 225
Strait, Kevin, xiii–xvi
Subotsky, Milton, 123–124
"Subterranean Homesick Blues," 120
Suggs, Themetta. See Berry, Themetta
    Suggs "Toddy"
Sumner High School, Berry at,
    26–29
"Surfin' USA," 206–207, 211
"Sweet Little Rock and Roller," 189

"Sweet Little Sixteen," 143, 144, 157, 189, 211, 223, 364
   "Surfin' USA" and plagiarism of, 206–207
Sweets, Melba, 17
Swinging Blue Jeans, 214, 217
Sykes, Robert, 38–39

T.A.M.I. Show, 223
tax evasion, Berry and, 282–284
Teagarden, Jack, 157
Teddy boys, riot at London performance and, 253–254
teenage audience, growth of in 1950s, 64–65
teen magazines, 143
Terry, Clark, 45, 58
Tharpe, Rosetta, 3, 32
Theta Kappa Omega (TKO), 173
"Thirteen Question Method," 186
"Thirty Days," 98
Thomas, Jasper, 137, 177, 182, 184
Thomas, Jimmy "Popeye," 66–67, 68, 152
Thompson, Charles, 38
Thompson, Richard, 214, 295–296
Tigrett, Isaac, 320
Till, Emmett, xiii, 84, 121
Tilton, Theodore, 341–342, 343
"Tobacco Road," 213
"Together (We'll Always Be)," 131
Tooley, Robert, 69
"Too Much Monkey Business," 119–120, 123, 130, 223
"Top Disc Stars of 1956" tour, 115–119
Tosches, Nick, 149
touring/tours
   after "Maybellene," 94–98
   Berry's fondness for, 160
   Berry using hometown bands while, 132
   "Big Beat" tour, 147–151

deterioration of Berry's faculties and final, 354–356
   of England, 212, 213–215, 217, 225–229, 257
   of Europe and South America, 348
   fraternity shows in the South, 172–176
   "The Greatest Show of 1957," 126–129, 139–141
   "The London Rock and Roll Show," 253–254
   rock & roll nostalgia, 248–249
   "Shower of Stars" tour, 166–169
   of Southwest, 177–184
   "Top Disc Stars of 1956," 115–119
   of West Coast with Steve Miller Band, 239–240
Travelguide, 220
Travis, Merle, 83, 206
Trent, Alphonso, 44
Tubb, Ernest, 98
"Tulane," 200, 246–247
Turner, Ike, 58, 65–68, 138, 152, 352, 365
Turner, Joe, 80
"Tutti Frutti," 109, 136
Two Great Guitars (album), 222
Tyner, Rob, 254

US Medical Center for Federal Prisoners, Berry at, 199–202
The United States v. Charles Edward Anderson Berry, 191–197, 198
Universal Recording Studio, Chess and, 76, 208

"Vagabond's House" (Blanding), 238, 239
Valens, Ritchie, 172
Vaughn, Ben, 145–146
Veiled Prophet of Khorassan, 7–9, 15, 342–343
   protesters at ball, 343
   Veiled Prophet parade, 69–70

the Ville (Elleardsville, Missouri), 14,
      25–26, 40–41
   Berry's childhood in, 9, 13–17,
      19–22, 23–24, 26–33
   Orphans' Home Day in, 12–13
Vincent, Gene, 123
Voyager 2, "Johnny B. Goode"
      recording included on, 261,
      277–278
voyeurism, Berry and, 30–31, 160,
      303, 306, 328–330, 332,
      333–337

WABC radio, 151
"Wake Up Little Susie," Berry's
      admiration for, 139
Walker, Madam C. J., 12
Walker, T-Bone, 238, 239
Walled Lake Casino, Berry's return
      to music after prison time and,
      203–205
Walters, Bridgette, 280
Walton, Charles, 102
The Warmth of Other Suns
      (Wilkerson), 153
Washington, Oscar, 59–60, 63
Waters, Muddy, 57, 73, 74–75, 216,
      244, 245, 247
   on Berry and race, 132, 144
   at Berry Park, 235
   Chess and, 75, 76
   at Maxwell Street Market, 87
   use of effects in recordings, 77–78
Weber, Harry, 349, 362
"Wee Wee Hours," 80, 96, 110, 248
Wein, George, 156–157
Weinstock, Bob, 91–92
Weissberg, Kenny, 292
Wentzville (Missouri), 268
   Berry battling, 335
   Berry living in during 1980s,
      322–325
   Berry's final days and death in,
      357–358, 359

purchase of property in, 160
   See also Berry Park
Wexler, Jerry, 108
white covers of Black artists' songs,
      82–84, 98, 146–147, 222, 223,
      251, 253, 352–353
Whitehouse, Mary, 262
white people, Berry learning to
      negotiate/speak with, 31–32, 74
white supremacy, 112–114, 115, 122
white women
   Berry's involvement with, 16–17,
      39–40, 127, 128, 158, 228,
      295–296, 331
   Berry's relationship with Joan
      Mathis, 155–156, 158, 196
   mob after Berry after incident in
      Meridian, 175–176
   police and Berry's involvement
      with, 49–50
"Who Do You Love?," 107
Wiener, Jack, 208
Wilder, Doris, loss of virginity to,
      32–33
Wilkerson, Isabel, 153
Wilkins, Roy, 114
Williams, John A., 220–221
Williams, Paul "Hucklebuck," 127
Williamson, James, 27, 34, 36
Williamson, Sharon Stokes, 96–97
Wills, Bob, 59, 78
Wilson, Brian, accusations of
      plagiarism regarding "Surfin'
      USA," 206–207
Winchell, Walter, 120, 121
Windermere Place, Berry family at,
      161, 216, 235
Winner, Joseph Eastburn, 259
WINS radio, 89, 90, 151
"Wish I Could Make Some Money,"
      177
women, secretly filmed in restroom at
      Southern Air, 328–330. *See also*
      white women

Wood, Ron, 256
Woods, Howard B., 142
Woodstock Music and Art Fair, 248
"Worried Life Blues," 29
The Worst Rock n' Roll Records of All Time, 261
Wray, Link, 365

"You Came a Long Way from St. Louis," 230

"You Can't Catch Me," 124
"You Never Can Tell," 200, 215–216, 221, 233
Young, A. S. "Doc," 176
Young, Reggie, 234
Young, Shirley and LaVern, 43
youth culture, rock & roll and, 151–152, 222

Zak, Albin, 63